A Seeker's Journey into
Sacred Time and Space

A Seeker's Journey into Sacred Time and Space

DAVID TRIMBLE

RESOURCE *Publications* • Eugene, Oregon

A SEEKER'S JOURNEY INTO SACRED TIME AND SPACE

Copyright © 2025 David Trimble. All rights reserved. Except for brief quotations in critical publications or reviews, no part of this book may be reproduced in any manner without prior written permission from the publisher. Write: Permissions, Wipf and Stock Publishers, 199 W. 8th Ave., Suite 3, Eugene, OR 97401.

Resource Publications
An Imprint of Wipf and Stock Publishers
199 W. 8th Ave., Suite 3
Eugene, OR 97401

www.wipfandstock.com

PAPERBACK ISBN: 979-8-3852-3069-3
HARDCOVER ISBN: 979-8-3852-3070-9
EBOOK ISBN: 979-8-3852-3071-6

01/31/25

Map of the *Sephirot* with permission from *A Guide to the Zohar* by Arthur Green. Copyright © 2004 by the Board of Trustees of the Leland Stanford Jr. University. All rights reserved.

"Imagine." Words and Music by John Lennon. Copyright © 1971 Lenono Music Copyright Renewed. All Rights Administered by Downtown Music Publishing LLC. All Rights Reserved Used by Permission. Reprinted by Permission of Hal Leonard LLC

My transcription of the Valley Beit Midrash Youtube interview of Rabbi Arthur Green by Rabbi Dr. Shmuly Yanklowitz, President and Dean of Valley Beit Midrash, is published with permission from Rabbi Yanklowitz and Rabbi Green.

Extract from *The Odyssey: A Modern Sequel* by Nikos Kazantzakis. Translation with intro by Kimon Friar. Copyright © 1958 by Helen Kazantzakis and Kimon Friar. English language translation 1958 by Simon & Schuster, Inc. Renewed 1986 by Simon & Schuster, Inc. Reprinted with the permission of Touchstone, an imprint of Simon & Schuster LLC. All rights reserved.

Biblical quotes are from JPS Tanach: The Holy Scriptures: The New JPS Translation according to the Traditional Hebrew Text. Philadelphia: Jewish Publication Society, 1985.

To my children, Ransom and Jessica:
May we continue to learn, grow, and rediscover each other.

To Jacob, my son of blessed memory, my soul's companion
and guide from the World to Come for years
after his too-brief sojourn in this world.

To Jodie, my spouse and life partner:
May we continue to go from strength to strength
as we journey together.

If you cast yourself into the sea, without any guidance, this is full of danger, because one mistakes things that arise within oneself for things arising from elsewhere. If, on the other hand, you travel on the sea in a ship, this is perilous, because there is the danger of attachment to the vehicle. In the one case, the end is not known, and there is no guidance. In the other case, the means becomes an end, and there is no arriving.

—Niffari in Shah, *The Way of the Sufi*

Although we cannot improve on the divine that flows into our vessels, we can and must take responsibility for keeping these vessels clean and transparent and not at all as essential as the light they contain.

—Zalman Schachter-Shalomi, *Paradigm Shift*

Contents

Acknowledgments		ix
Introduction		1
	Challenge and Opportunity	1
	The Story of My Spiritual Journey	3
	Voices in the Human Spiritual Conversation	5
	Finding Meaning in Relationship	9
	Common Elements of Human Spiritual Traditions	10
	Finding the Universal in the Particular	12
	A Particular Name for the Universal	14
	Time and Memory	15
1	First Encounter	18
	Ancestors	22
	Making My Way Through Childhood	27
	Transitions	33
	Becoming a Social Activist	39
	Continuing the Spiritual Search	40
	Mississippi	41
2	Returning Home and Starting a Family	48
	Madness	55
	Returning to the World of the Sane	66
	Learning to Become a Network Therapist	72
	Ramón	78
3	Family Changes	86
	Welcoming Jacob	90
	Recognizing ADHD	93
	Exploring Nonmaterial Realities	96
	Learning Chi Gong	100

	A Companion on the Journey	102
	Deciding to Convert to Judaism	103
	Jacob's Struggles	104
4	Making the Commitment to Convert	114
	What I Had Learned Before I Became a Jew	119
	Studying for Conversion	120
	Jacob Makes His Way Home	124
	Reconciliation and Loss	128
	Devastation, Desolation, and Connection	132
	Conversion	142
	A Moment of Convergence	145
	Meeting a Guide and Fellow Seeker	147
	A Glimpse into My Understanding of Kabbalah	149
	Weaving Strands Together	154
	An Immigrant with Fresh Eyes	155
	Theology and Psychology	157
5	Restoration	159
	Exploring Emerging Possibilities	163
	Raymond	166
	Deborah	168
	Developing an Integrated Spiritual and Clinical Practice	176
	Exploring the Path of the Shamanic Healer	179
6	Adversary and Companion	186
	Time, Transition, and Transformation	197
	Accompanying My Sister on Her Journey	201
	Healing Family Wounds	206
	Assembling a Gathering in Sacred Space	222
7	The Tapestry of Wisdom	227
	Dancing with God	228
	Finding God in Text	240
	Patterns in the Tapestry of Life	253
	Learning with Yedidah	255
	Moving On	277
Endnotes		281
Bibliography		285
Index		289

Acknowledgments

I HOPE THAT THIS memoir is itself an acknowledgment of the many people who have influenced and supported me on my journey as spiritual seeker and social justice activist. I hope that you will see yourselves through my eyes in the pages of this book. Here, let me acknowledge some who have been particularly influential on the formation of this book.

Jodie Kliman, my spouse and partner, has read every word of this book, more than once. If what you read makes sense to you, and you find some coherence in what you are reading, please join me in thanking Jodie as my first reader and editor.

As Sheila Babbie, my sister of blessed memory, was dying, she invited me into her Tibetan Buddhist understanding of living and dying. That experience laid the foundation for an ongoing conversation in sacred space with her niece and my daughter Jessica Trimble. Conversations with Jessica continue to deepen my appreciation for the paradox of "the same, and different, and the same."

The revolutionary activism of my parents of blessed memory, Glen Walker Trimble and Eleanor Crary Trimble, veterans of the socialist movements of the 1930s before I was born, was the original inspiration for my youthful activism in the peace and civil rights movements. My mentor of blessed memory, D'Army Bailey, who recruited me for the 1964 Mississippi Freedom Summer, set me on the path of antiracist activism that I continue to pursue. Dr. Kenneth V. Hardy continues to inspire, challenge, and hold me accountable for understanding my whiteness and continuing the antiracist struggle.

Another mentor of blessed memory, Carolyn Attneave, nurtured me as I became a network therapist. She gently challenged me to become a shaman to work with personal communities in distress. My work with networks brought me to *espiritista* (spirit worker) Ramón Jiménez, who opened the door for me to continue my spiritual journey. Brian Collins chose to teach me Chi Gong and gave me skills essential to my embodying the mystical wisdom of Kabbalah.

For more than fifty years, my colleagues at the Center for Multicultural Training in Psychology have shaped me as a psychologist and social justice activist. I am particularly grateful to CMTP's founder, Guy Seymour, to its current director, Shamaila Khan, and to my friend, colleague, and comrade of blessed memory, Shani Dowd.

The Boston Institute for Culturally Affirming Practices began as a team who taught together at CMTP. We of BICAP continue to support, challenge, and inspire each other. Thanks to each and all of you, Gonzalo Bacigalupe, MaryAnna Ham, Hugo Kamya, Jay King, Jodie Kliman, Roxana Llerena-Quinn, Patricia Romney, and to our mentor, Elaine Pinderhughes.

While working on this memoir, I assembled a multicultural group of progressive family therapists to produce *Engaging with Spirituality in Family Therapy: Meeting in Sacred Space*, published by Springer in 2018. As editor, I invited us to imagine challenges to the current global discourse of materialist individualism. In those respectful, curious and open-hearted conversations, each of us firmly grounded in the particulars of our faiths, we came to nameless but achingly familiar shared experiences of sacred space. I drew from Hugo Kamya's use of that biblical term to name our shared spiritual experience, and that term also appears in the title of this memoir. My thanks to my fellow authors of *Engaging with Spirituality*, Khawla Abu-Baker, Kiran Arora, Saliha Bava, Hugo Kamya, Jay King, Linda Longo-Lockspeiser, Rockey Robbins, and to Paulette Hines of blessed memory. Paulette and I connected around the complicated blessings and complications of descending from Protestant ministers, and conversations between Paulette and me helped shape the direction of that book.

I am particularly grateful to Hugo Kamya, a fellow member of BICAP and of the Spiritans. In that small group, which also includes Jay King and Patricia Romney, we Spiritans learn from each other's practice of integrating spirituality with clinical practice. Hugo was often a guest when I was leading the Multicultural Family Therapy Seminar at CMTP. When teaching my students about the phenomenon of spiritual radiance, I referred to their experience of sitting in Hugo's presence. Hugo and I co-authored an article about the roots of the impulse to retaliate when attacked or injured. Sadly, the psychological and spiritual ideas that we developed in that article are as relevant now in the Middle East as they were a year after the 2001 attacks on the United States.[1]

The journal article by Mark Rivett and Eddy Street on instrumental and metaphysical practice in psychotherapy gave me the courage to use my voice about spirituality in psychotherapy Thanks to Eddy Street for his generous correspondence with me as I was assembling *Engaging with Spirituality in Family Therapy*. Eddy helped me to ground my intuitive grasp of the *koan* in that article, "The Same and Different and the Same." My daughter Jessica and I draw on the paradoxical wisdom of that *koan* as we discover convergences between her Tibetan Buddhism and my kabbalistic Judaism.

Ongoing video conversations with Rockey Robbins and Charlesetta (Charlee) Sutton continue to nourish me on my journey. Rockey and I find in our spiritual traditions the same and different and the same idea that explains our experience that the two of us share the same soul. Charlee and I strive to live the spiritual messages that we bring to each other from beyond the material world. Charlee's messages help me to slow down and listen, and I live my practice of acceptance with her words "it's all good" ringing in my mind.

My thanks and my love for the Jews who have welcomed and supported me as I join the Jewish people on my spiritual journey: Rabbi Andy Vogel, Rabbi Art Green, Rabbi Reuven Cohn of blessed memory, my friend Joel Ziff, and my teacher, Yedidah Cohen.

My publisher, Resource Publications, is an imprint of Wipf and Stock Publishers. I am deeply grateful for the guidance and support so generously provided by Wipf and Stock's Matt Wimer, George Callihan, and Jordan Horowitz. Your patience with a neuroatypical old man has sustained me on this journey toward publication of my writing. You "walk the talk" of Wipf and Stock's claim of dedication to "superior publisher-author relations."

---

1. Kamya and Trimble, "Response to Injury," 19–29.

Introduction

CHALLENGE AND OPPORTUNITY

WHAT IS TO BECOME of our world? Humans dominate the planet at an accelerating pace. The effects of human activity accumulate so dramatically that the world of one's old age is unimaginable from the perspective of one's youth. I remember my grandmother's tales of a family's lifestyle transformed by the advent of the automobile. Hearing my grandmother's descriptions of a world before air travel and television, I felt some envy for a life lived in the midst of such transformation.

In my grandmother's lifetime, humanity gained the capacity to manipulate the atom. I was born the year that human beings used their understanding of the energy that binds together the material world to destroy other human beings. I grew up with an existential dread that would have been unimaginable to my parents when they were children: that war could destroy all life on the planet. I was a teenager when a violent thunderstorm woke me in the middle of the night, filling me with terror that the nuclear conflagration had begun. Worse than those few minutes of panic were the days of the Cuban Missile Crisis when, fully awake, I contemplated the imminence of nuclear war between the United States and the Soviet Union.

For all the importance of that terrifying change in the world, I believed until I was older that I would not witness in my lifetime the amount of change that my grandmother had experienced. As I sit at my computer composing these words, I reflect on how profoundly I was mistaken. Cultural and technological changes build on themselves, accelerating the pace of change. The diverse peoples and cultures of our planet are increasingly interconnected by an electronic web of communication. The depth and complexity of accumulating human knowledge is penetrable by increasingly sophisticated search and storage technologies. With our enhanced capacity to manipulate information, we continue to expand our knowledge and, sadly, our capacity to injure each other.

The drive for cultural transformation is intrinsic to our species. For good or ill, that drive to transform culture will always shape our planet. The industrial revolution that generated the transformations in my grandmother's life burned enormous amounts of fossil fuel, releasing into the atmosphere the carbon stored in the remains of prehistoric life. Carbon dioxide and other gases released by human activities capture heat, warm the atmosphere, and are dramatically reconfiguring the global climate, threatening human and other life. Disregard for the environmental consequences of human activities may render our world uninhabitable.

The collapse of the Soviet Union and the end of the Cold War offered brief respite from the threat of nuclear extinction, but the capacity to produce nuclear weapons proliferates among nations. Wars continue to break out, and wars persist throughout the planet. Nationalism, with its attendant risk of war, remains a dominant ideology of human collective aspiration. So, also, is religion, which has generated so much warfare in human history. Religious belief is at the core of violence instigated by fundamentalists claiming exclusive access to the truth and willing to kill to protect themselves from perceived threats to the survival of their religions.[1]

The end of the Cold War effectively ended the ideological tension between capitalist and socialist worldviews. Capitalism established its hegemony as the dominant model of human enterprise. Even as the particularistic ideologies of nationalism and religious fanaticism keep the planet mired in war, national boundaries are transcended by multinational capitalist enterprise. The acceleration of technological progress makes possible a post-nationalist world culture, but the current global culture of capitalism is grounded in an individualistic ideology incapable of imagining the exercise of collective responsibility.

Cultures are always in process of transformation. How can we envision a world culture that respects the planet's ecological vulnerability and rejects war? This memoir is my effort to contribute to such a vision of global cultural transformation. I tell the story of my life as a social justice activist and a spiritual seeker. Born in the year that nuclear weapons destroyed Hiroshima and Nagasaki and the Second World War drew to a close, I have witnessed the accelerating pace of historical change. In the shadow of that history, I yearn for the emergence of a life-affirming global culture and celebrate the changes over recent centuries that support that possibility.

As I tell my own story, I invite you to explore your own. Human culture changes when transformations occur within our innermost beings and in the webs of relationships among us. In those relationships, our inner stirrings can find language and meanings that shape emerging shared understandings. I pray that my words may awaken your own inner stirrings and move you to act for cultural change. Cultural change is the most robust when it incorporates a wide range of voices, whose words "interanimate," or enliven, each other.[2] Our words inspire, illuminate, challenge, contradict each other in a process of vital generativity and growth. My story is only one of the many stories that may generate change. You own story may as well. I share my story to inspire your own.

If humanity is to survive, we will need to understand ourselves as spiritual beings, "not as human beings living spiritual lives, but as spiritual beings living human lives," words often attributed to theologian Teilhard de Chardin.[3] Religion, which contributes to war and to human domination of the natural world, is also a home for human spiritual striving. Within the world's religious traditions, and in spiritual practices outside the boundaries of religion, are ideas about humanity and the world that are continually discovered, forgotten, rediscovered, revealed, and concealed. Embodied in those ideas is hope for a world without war, in which human beings live mindfully and interdependently with all other forms of life.

I am grateful be alive at an historical moment when these ideas are being shared increasingly beyond the boundaries of any one human community. There are generative conversations between adherents of different religions, and knowledge that until recently had been closely held by small groups of esoteric practitioners is becoming more widely accessible.

THE STORY OF MY SPIRITUAL JOURNEY

I wrote most of the words above when I began writing this memoir. I was early in my sixties, nearly twenty years ago. I write to you now toward the end of my seventies. As you read, I invite you to witness the story of my search for spiritual meaning. I tell the story of a child of White parents in the United States, overwhelmed and shattered by a prophetic dream that called me, as it had called my ancestors, to serve God and to take responsibility for the world. You will travel with me as I found my path, fleeing from that call yet drawn to answer it. You will read of my struggles through childhood to make sense of other people, my adolescent discovery of spiritually inspiring texts, my activism for social justice as I made my way into adulthood. You will witness my search for revelation exploring psychedelic drugs and a descent into madness that interrupted my professional training as a psychotherapist. You will see me coming to terms with my British colonial ancestral legacy as a participant in the United States Civil Rights Movement, as a lifelong anti-racism activist, in ongoing conversation with Ransom and Jessica, my son and daughter from my first marriage to Betty Ann, a woman with African and Native American ancestors, and in my ongoing collaboration with a multicultural, multiracial community of professional colleagues. Along the way, the narrative will introduce you to masters, teachers, and fellow seekers who have accompanied and guided me along the way. You will read of experiences that have taken me beyond the limits of space and time in the material world, perhaps taking you momentarily along with me into sacred space and time.

My story will take you through the end of my first marriage into over forty years of my current marriage with Jodie Kliman, a woman whose Jewish ancestral legacy shaped our decision to raise our son Jacob, my third child, as a Jew. You will witness how I found in Judaism a religious life that could incorporate the lessons I learned over decades of search among human spiritual traditions. You will read of my experiences with our youngest son's soul after his tragic early death and of how his soul guided me into healing the wound between my God and me from my shattering childhood dream.

In the last two chapters, writing with a voice shaped by the process of writing and reflecting on the memoir, I share from the harvest of a lifetime of spiritual self-cultivation. Over the last two decades of my life, I have found guides and started reading texts in the Jewish mystical tradition of Kabbalah. As the painful tumult from my divorce subsided, the relationship between generations, Jodie and I with our living children, Ransom and Jessica, strengthened and deepened. A paper that I co-authored, on the generative flow of dialogue in psychotherapy, was published when I was sixty.[4] A book that I edited, published when I was seventy-three, brought forth the voices of a multicultural, multi-faith group of colleagues in a conversation shaped by ideas in that earlier paper on dialogue.[5] I found in the nameless but achingly familiar sensations of sacred space a potential seed for cultural transformation. Jessica and I continue a rich conversation about the resonances, the sameness and the difference, of her Tibetan Buddhism and my kabbalistic Judaism, each of us an immigrant to our chosen religion. In these last two decades, I accompanied my older sister and younger brother through the ends of their lives, becoming the sole elder of my family of origin. I continue to develop a practice that integrates spirituality into the healing processes of psychotherapy.

VOICES IN THE HUMAN SPIRITUAL CONVERSATION

As I write and you read, we live lives shaped in a critical moment of historical change, a time of unparalleled possibilities, full of peril and full of opportunities for redemption. We must be awake to our responsibilities as actors who shape the societies and cultures that shape us, drawing on our imagination and determination to realize the best possibilities within our shared humanity. We are not alone. The human creative spirit is awake to the moment. If we attune our ears, we can hear voices of hope amongst voices of despair in this time of possibilities. Those voices sometimes call to us through the media of popular culture, as when John Lennon sang, "You may say I'm a dreamer, but I'm not the only one. I hope someday you'll join us, and the world will live as one."

As I find my voice in my story, I hope to inspire you to find your own. In the human conversation about the future of life on the planet we share with all other living beings, we need many voices.

A section of the bookshelves in our home holds many of the texts that I encountered on my search before I found my spiritual home in the Jewish religion. I continue to engage with their voices even as I continue to cultivate my voice as a Jew. I am struck by what the Russian literary theorist Mikhail Bakhtin called the "interanimation" of the voices of those texts.[6] Some of the texts reveal knowledge that was until recent generations closely held, restricted to a small group of disciples or closely guarded within a religious community. The accessibility of these texts in modern times affords possibilities for dialogue among their voices, generating new possibilities of meaning in their sameness and difference.

On my shelf are books written in English—and contemporary English translations—which convey esoteric knowledge from a wide range of Eastern and Western traditions.

The Kybalion reveals the secret knowledge of the closed circle of disciples of Hermes Trismegistus, an Egyptian sage said to be contemporary with the Hebrew patriarch Abraham.[7] The secrecy of this circle, who selected their replacements when members died, is credited as the origin of the term "hermetically sealed."

Black Elk Speaks is the transcription by a White American anthropologist of the oral autobiography of a Lakota medicine man, recorded at a time in American history when the dominant White culture nurtured the myth of the imminent disappearance of the Indians and their cultures.[8] Sams' *Earth Medicine*[9] and Duran's *Buddha in Redface*[10] are manifestations of resistance to that myth. The flowering of publications embodying Native American voices in fiction, e.g., Magpie Earling's *The Lost Journals of Sacajawea: A Novel*,[11] and nonfiction, e.g., Kimmerer's *Braiding Sweetgrass*[12] continues to give the lie to the myth of the disappearing Indian. Treuer's *The Heartbeat of Wounded Knee* challenges the dominant culture's emerging myth that threatens to succeed the myth of the disappearing Indian, i.e., the myth of Native Americans as embodying a demoralized, broken-spirited and culturally degraded people, whose pitiable state lives as an indictment of White conquest.[13]

Morgan's *Mutant Message Down Under* is the account of a White American activist recruited by an Aboriginal group, the Ancient Ones, to participate in a walkabout through the Australian continent.[14] They had made the collective decision to end their material existence by remaining childless for the balance of their lives. On the journey, they charged Morgan to give the world access to the knowledge they had attained over the course of their spiritual evolution.

Alan Watts, a student of Zen Buddhism and, briefly, an Episcopal priest, introduced Eastern spiritual philosophy to twentieth-century English-speaking popular culture.[15]

Indian Yogi Paramahansa Yogananda brought to the 1933 Chicago World's Fair the message that all world religions embody the same fundamental truths.[16] Much of his writing conveys yogic wisdom made accessible within a Christian framework.

Idries Shah devoted his life to making the esoteric ideas of Sufism, embodied within Islam but claiming ancient origins predating the Abrahamic religions, available to English-speaking readers.[17]

The *Discourses* of Meher Baba distill esoteric wisdom gained by a twentieth-century student and initiate of the leading Hindu and Muslim sages of the Indian subcontinent.[18]

The sacred texts of Judaism describe a people with a history of exile, return, and diaspora. The ancestors of modern Jews encountered a multitude of cultures over the course of their repeated displacements, finding ways to assimilate aspects of foreign cultures while retaining their coherent collective identity. They drew from their own traditions of revelation, as well as from the esoteric ideas of Greek and, later, Muslim cultures. A rich and robust Jewish esoteric tradition can be traced from the Talmud and the *Merkavah* and *Heichalot* literature of the early centuries of the Common Era through to the early medieval era of Europe. Early in the second millennium, the rich interpenetration of Platonic, Sufi, and Jewish mystical ideas contributed to the classic Jewish esoteric texts *Sefer Yetsirah*, the *Bahir*, and the monumental *Zohar*, which together form the foundation for the Jewish esoteric practice of Kabbalah.

Written early in the thirteenth century, the *Zohar* was presented to the reader as the work of second-century Rabbi Simeon bar Yochai and was written in a uniquely stylized version of Aramaic, the common language of second-century Jews. Although voices from other cultures and historical periods may have contributed to the written text of the *Zohar*, many Jews with deep knowledge of Jewish esoteric lore locate its source in closely held, orally transmitted wisdom from ancient Babylonian academies. When the text was written centuries later than the sages of Babylon lived, its highly allusive style was intentionally inaccessible to the uninitiated reader. Understanding was reserved for only the most learned and pious of Jews.

In the eighteenth century, Rabbi Yisrael ben Eliezer, an Eastern European shamanic healer known as the Baal Shem Tov, inspired the Chasidic movement, an effort to revive a Judaism that the Chasidim saw as emphasizing scholarly study at the expense of religious devotion.[19] Chasidism democratized Jewish esoteric knowledge at the same time that it reclaimed esoteric practice from widespread folk medicine and magic, restoring a place for it in pious Judaism. The Baal Shem Tov and his disciples and followers elevated the virtue of wholehearted, passionate prayer above dry scholarly study, even as their leaders, known as *tzadikim*, were often well-versed in Kabbalah as well as the foundational Jewish religious texts of Torah, Tanach, and Talmud.

Originally a reformist movement challenging the Jewish establishment, the Chasidim and their establishment former adversaries joined ranks to resist the Haskalah, or "Jewish Enlightenment" of the late eighteenth and nineteenth centuries that accompanied the emancipation of Jews through much of Europe. Jews of the Haskalah sought to incorporate into their ideas the humanism and modernism of the European Enlightenment. Some became secular "cultural Jews," some converted to Christianity, and others formed what was to become Reform Judaism, a Jewish religious practice that discarded many of the core practices of religious obligation by which Jews through centuries of diaspora had distinguished themselves from the populations around them. Reform Jews sought to retain Jewish identity while assimilating to gentile culture, discarding Kabbalah, which they saw as inconsistent with modern ideas and as reinforcing European stereotypes of Jews as ignorant and superstitious. Reaction to the emergence of Reform Judaism gave birth to Orthodox Judaism (including both traditional and Chasidic observant practice), the beginning of denominational splitting of what had theretofore been a unitary albeit diverse European Jewish religious community.

Until recent decades, esoteric Judaism has been the province of Orthodox and Chasidic Jews, and its Hebrew and Aramaic texts were not translated into other languages. As in the case of other esoteric ideas previously closely held in many cultures, the secrets of Kabbalah are becoming accessible. Aryeh Kaplan published English translations and commentary on *The Bahir* and *Sefer Yetsirah*.[20] Daniel Matt, who has contributed substantially to the translation and dissemination of kabbalistic writing, led a monumental project to translate the multi-volume *Zohar* into English.[21]

The books of rabbis Lawrence Kushner[22] and Arthur Green[23] make Jewish esoteric knowledge relevant and available to contemporary non-Orthodox readers. Green is a scholar whose translations have made a wealth of texts available in English, texts ranging from the early Common Era to mid-twentieth century neo-Chasidic writer Hillel Zeitlin, who integrated European philosophy with distillations of Chasidic and kabbalistic wisdom. Zalman Schachter-Shalomi, a Chasidic rabbi from the Chabad Lubavich tradition, was transformed by his engagement with American psychedelic New Age culture. His generative integration of spiritual practices from a multitude of world traditions, grounded in his deep knowledge of Judaism, contributed to the emergence of the Jewish Renewal Movement in the latter part of the twentieth century.

This book is a memoir of my spiritual life, and the texts that I have described above have helped me to make sense of my spiritual journey since my encounter with an *espiritista*, or spiritual healer and advisor, Ramón Jiménez, when I was thirty years old. Before meeting Ramón, I struggled to find my path through and beyond the complexities of my ancestral heritage of Protestant Christian ministry, absorbing myself in the writings of Alan Watts, Nikos Kazantzakis (whose texts embody a dialogue between Western and Eastern religious traditions), and the nineteenth-century narrative of an anonymous Orthodox Christian pilgrim, *The Way of a Pilgrim*.[24]

FINDING MEANING IN RELATIONSHIP

As important as texts have been, relationships have more profoundly influenced my spiritual experiences, beliefs, and practices. Guides have included mortal mentors and fellow seekers, and immaterial companions from the spirit world. Family members have witnessed, supported, and joined me on my journey. I would not have found Judaism had my wife, Jodie, not asked that we raise our child as a Jew. Attending services with Jodie, I was pleased and surprised that I did not find myself angry with the liturgy, emotion that had driven me away from my native Christianity. While her own life focuses less intentionally on her spirituality, Jodie has been a companion and sounding board on my Jewish journey for nearly forty years.

The beginning of my older son Ransom's spiritual journey was grounded in the traditions of his indigenous ancestors. As a teenager and young adult, he fasted on Thanksgiving, grieving for those ancestors. Alone on a quest in a New England forest, he awoke from a dream of wrestling with a spirit and decided to change direction in his college studies. An agnostic for decades, he witnessed and supported his wife Kim's exploration of her ancestral polytheistic Norse religion. Fascinated by Japanese culture since a college semester abroad, in recent years he has been exploring Zen tradition. He has drawn on the Japanese idea of *shogunai* (which resonates powerfully with my spiritual practice of acceptance) to live with the early deaths of his mother, his brother, his wife, and his lifelong friend Nolan.

Before her death, my sister Sheila and I found resonances between the Tibetan Buddhism she shared with my daughter Jessica and my Jewish spirituality. That conversation now continues and deepens between Jessica and me. I supported Jacob on his spiritual struggles with substance abuse and mental illness, drawing on our ancestral pastoral legacy to help him find his path as he explored his birth mother's Christianity. After his sudden death when he was nineteen years old and I was sixty-one, his soul became a strong presence and guide on my travels through worlds beyond the limits of materiality.

COMMON ELEMENTS OF HUMAN SPIRITUAL TRADITIONS

Embodied within the many traditions I have explored over the course of my life's journey are recurring ideas, ideas grounded in sacred texts and in living experience, which I believe are integral to the emergence of a world culture that preserves life on our planet. In some of those traditions, the ideas have been hidden from most of their followers and reserved for elites who have cultivated the capacity to experience their wisdom. As the world spiritual conversation unfolds, the seals around those secrets are being broken. Particular traditions emphasize some ideas over others, and some traditions hold ideas that others reject, but I have found more convergence than contradictions among traditions. These ideas are at the core of my own spiritual understanding. Rather than beliefs, the ideas are objects of contemplation and form a framework for my efforts to live a meaningful life. With apologies to the many human voices who have so eloquently expressed these ideas over the ages, I use words such as the One, Unity, the Divine, and God interchangeably to describe and refer to what is ultimately indescribable. Here, in this section, I share those ideas as best as I understand them.

We experience the reality of the material world with our conventional senses. As human culture has evolved, we have crafted powerful scientific methods to extend our understanding beyond the immediately perceptible. We know about phenomena such as electromagnetic energy, molecules, atoms, and subatomic particles, relying on logical theories that ultimately require for their proofs measurement of that which is measurable by our conventional senses. The scientific method has been so powerful and so useful that, in many cultural contexts, whatever cannot be discerned or proven by scientific methods is not considered "real."

Yet, there are worlds beyond the material world that are the domain of scientific understanding. Shamans shed their material forms to travel in worlds of the spirits: the world of the animal spirits, the world of the dead, worlds of spirit beings that in various cultures are called angels, ghosts, or ancestors. These are worlds beyond the material categories of space and time, and in these worlds human souls connect with each other in complex ways. These worlds are as "real" as the material world is real.

Human beings are complex creatures, with souls or spirits embodied within our material beings. A soul's existence extends beyond the limits of birth and death. Before birth and after death, souls inhabit higher planes of being, absorbing themselves in knowledge beyond the comprehension of mortals and preparing to be reborn into the material world, where much of what they have learned between incarnations will not be accessible to their consciousness in their physical bodies. The soul's yearning for that deeper knowledge is what moves us mortals to cultivate our spiritual nature, searching for knowledge through religious or other spiritual practice. The search can be difficult, confusing, even heartrending, as our embodiment in materiality is continually distracting us from discovering our true nature.

Just as the material world can be distracting with its compelling claims of reality, so also can be the other, nonmaterial worlds. Ultimately, the seeker may penetrate the veils of illusion to discern an awesome truth: There is nothing beside the One. All that exists is a Unity so complete and perfect that any attempt to describe it can only fail. The seeker fortunate to contemplate the One is no longer a seeker, no longer a self, as the self is an illusion of distinction that obscures the wholeness and unity of the One. From the perspective of some traditions, the purpose of the soul's reincarnation is, over the course of many lifetimes, to cultivate enough understanding in mortal form for the soul to dissolve into the Unity, freeing the soul forever from the illusion of distinction and from the painful cycle of reincarnation. Whether through the sequence of reincarnation, or through other forms of human seeking, the soul seeks to gaze in wonder at the awesome presence of the Divine, yearning to be absorbed into the One.

How do we understand the existence of the material and nonmaterial worlds, filled as they are with distinctions and qualities, so different from the boundless and eternal One? These worlds are created by the One for a purpose. Creation is the means of Divine self-reflection. Emanating from the One, creation is itself embraced within the Unity of the

One. As the soul ascends to contemplate the One to whom the soul owes its existence, God knows God's self.

The nature of divine self-reflection, embodied as it is in creation, has implications for us mortals. For God to know God's self, God's human creatures, endowed with the capacity to seek the presence of God, need to have the capacity to choose between good and evil, between knowledge and ignorance. In making choices, seeking good and resisting evil, struggling to gain knowledge that hides so stubbornly behind veils in the worlds of illusion, the soul becomes the manifestation of divine self-reflection.

I don't want to give the impression that all of these ideas, ideas that I have found useful on my journey, are universally held by all human religious and spiritual traditions. One may not find exactly this set of ideas at the core of any particular tradition. There are disagreements and contradictions among the traditions. More nearly universal are the specifications for living according to any spiritual tradition. Violence, destructive emotions, and disregard for the natural environment are seen as obstacles to living a spiritually meaningful life. Respect for manifestation of the Divine in all life, particularly human life, informs sensibilities that in turn could be fundamentals for a transformed global human culture.

FINDING THE UNIVERSAL IN THE PARTICULAR

Writing a first-person narrative about spirituality is a challenge for one's spiritual life. In these pages, you will read the narrative of my ongoing search for the presence of the Divine, a search shaped by this moment in world history and by the particular circumstances of my family and individual history. As I yearn for the face of the Divine, I seek liberation from the limitations of self-involvement, in order to discern the eternal that cloaks itself with the illusions of material existence. In these pages I take the risk of self-absorption by writing about myself in order to share as authentically and transparently as I am able the story of one life lived at a historical moment that cries out for fundamental transformation of human culture.

By sharing my story, I hope to call attention to the many lives all over the planet that are going through similar changes and to inspire you, the reader, to find within yourself the questions that all of us need to ask of ourselves if we are to recognize who we truly are and to take the responsibility for life and for the world that come with that knowledge. Inspired by the language of Sufi sages, I have chosen language that I use in this narrative to facilitate for the reader what Jewish philosopher Michael Fishbane calls *caesural events*, shifts out of everyday consciousness into heightened awareness of non-ordinary reality.[25]

I have come to appreciate that the design of my life is fitted within a broad, deep, and complex tapestry, most of which is beyond my capacity to discern or understand. Drawing as it does on experiences beyond material reality, the narrative of my life may not always fit within a linear arrangement of time and space. For example, in the minutes and days following my son Jacob's death, as I accompanied his soul on its journey to reunification with its Source, I drew on metaphysical abilities that emerged from a highly structured meditative practice, which, in material reality, I was not to cultivate until years after those heartbreaking events.

I completed my conversion to Judaism a few months after Jacob's death. Converting as I have relatively late in life, I bring mature sensibilities and "fresh eyes" to a venerable religious tradition. I am grateful to Rabbi Lawrence Hoffman for applying the metaphor of "immigrant" to recent converts.[26] Just as literal immigrants have contributed enormously to the vitality of American society and culture, so also are converts contributing to the revitalization of Judaism. I am frequently reminded of my "immigrant" status as I surprise my coreligionists with my particular take on phenomena familiar to them since childhood and which they may have long since taken for granted, or as I stumble in my heavily accented Hebrew through liturgy that flows so readily for them. My journey through a diversity of spiritual practices before making a commitment to Judaism is a particular manifestation of the global conversation between spiritual traditions, most evident in the way that I bring Eastern energy practices into my Jewish prayer and meditation.

Although this book describes the journey of a Jew, it is not written solely for Jewish readers. Although non-Jewish readers may be learning about unfamiliar Jewish text and prayer, Jewish readers may be learning about Sufism, or the Chinese energy practice of Chi Gong. I am a clinical psychologist, and readers unfamiliar with that professional field may be learning something new about psychology. The only qualification one needs to read this book is curiosity, particular curiosity about human spirituality.

I pray that, as you read, your mind, heart, and spirit may be moved to reflect on your own journey and that your reflections may lead you to commit yourself to global cultural transformation grounded in human spirituality.

A PARTICULAR NAME FOR THE UNIVERSAL

Jews take the question of God's name seriously. Arguably, we were the first monotheists, so all the names we use refer to the same One. Many names, such as Elohim, Shaddai, or El, can be spoken relatively freely, although some devout Jews refrain from doing so, even rendering the written English word as G-d, out of their respect for the Divine. But one name, spelled out in four Hebrew letters whose English equivalents are *YHVH*, is understood both to embody and to manifest the awesome power of the Divine. The true name is so sacred that it has been forbidden to utter for nearly two thousand years. Some Jews refrain from even spelling it other than in sacred texts, e.g., prayer book or Torah.

Long before it was forbidden for anyone to anyone to utter the name, only the high priest of the temple in Jerusalem was permitted to speak it aloud, and he uttered it only once a year, when purifying the temple on Yom Kippur. With fear and trembling, he entered the inner sanctum of the temple, the holy of holies, calling on God by the sacred name as he pleaded on behalf of the children of Israel. No Jew has been allowed to utter the name since the destruction of the temple in the year 70 of the Common Era. We no longer know the vowels that accompanied the consonants when the name was spoken.

Since we can't speak it, we have had to find ways to refer to it, such as calling it "the name," or "the Tetragrammaton" (from the Greek for "four letters," the Hebrew letters of the name: *yud, hey, vav, hey*). When the name appears in Torah or prayer book, we use euphemisms to take its place as we talk about or address our God. The word *Adonai*, the Hebrew for "Lord," is often spoken in the place of the name when it appears in texts. Other euphemisms include Hashem (Hebrew for "the name"), *Ya*, or, in English, the LORD or ETERNAL. In an early cultural misunderstanding, when Christians would read our common texts—Torah and Tanach to us, the Old Testament to them—they would pronounce the name "Jehovah" (J often substitutes for Y in transliteration of Hebrew), applying the vowels of our euphemism Adonai to the four consonants of the name.

The name is a fascinating compound of the present, past, and future tenses of the Hebrew verb *li'hyot*, "to be." So, the name of God is "is, was, will be." When I quote English translations of sacred texts that include the name, I sometimes use the euphemism ETERNAL.

At the core of the Shema, the most fundamental Jewish prayer, we call out, *Shema, Yisrael, Adonai Eloheinu, Adonai Echad*—"Listen, Israel, the ETERNAL is our God; the ETERNAL is one." When first uttered millennia ago, *Adonai Echad* meant that God is number one, superior to all other gods in a mostly polytheistic world. In the Second Temple period, 597 BCE to 70 CE, Jews developed a coherent monotheistic theology. *Adonai Echad* came to mean that there is only one God in the universe. I join many contemporary Jews in constructing *Adonai Echad* to mean that God is all—all that is, was, and will be is embraced within a Unity that is named *YHVH*.

When I meditate on the Shema, I strive to experience the words as calling on all human beings who yearn for the Divine, not only Jews. The Hebrew word *Yisrael* readily affords this interpretation. Often used as the name of the Jewish people, and now as the name of the country that claims to be the state of the Jewish people, it affords more possible meanings. *Yisrael* can be translated as "one who wrestles with God." The name *Yisrael* was given to our patriarch Jacob by an angel, after Jacob and the angel wrestled through the night. *Shema, Yisrael:* Listen, all of you who struggle with and for a relationship with God; *YHVH Eloheinu*—the ETERNAL is our God; *YHVH Echad*—the ETERNAL is One. Concentrating on the unutterable name, I listen for a deep meaning in the Shema: *is, was,* and *will be* are One.

TIME AND MEMORY

As you read, I invite you to join me in opening your experience of time. In the course of my spiritual journey, my soul on occasion lifts into realms beyond material reality. At such moments, I do not experience myself as embedded within the linear sequence of time. Is, was, and will be are simultaneously present. It is as though I have emerged from the river of time that flows from the past through the present toward the future. As I stand on the shore witnessing the flow of the river of time, the river transforms itself into a rich tapestry, in which I can begin to discern the design of the soul journey in which my mortal life is embedded.

As a psychologist, I know that our memories of the past exist only in the present moment. Our experience of remembering does not involve searching through some elaborate storage system for a file that contains a moment from the past, a file that when opened reveals an accurate rendition of the original experience. Each time we remember a particular experience, we activate a network of neurons in our brains that resembles, but is not identical with, the neural network that was activated at the moment then that we are remembering now. Although similar to that of the past moment, the neural network that we activate at the moment when we are remembering is shaped and interpenetrated by other networks that are somehow associated with the experience that we remember. We create a novel experience whenever we remember. Each time that we remember, we shape future experiences of the "same" memory. So it is that now, when I remember a terrifying childhood dream of divine appearance, abandonment, and impossible demand for personal responsibility, the memory of that dream resonates with remembering the story I heard later, of my father's childhood experience at my grandfather's deathbed.

As a therapist, I appreciate the strategies that our minds use to protect us from being overwhelmed by negative emotions. At the core of our brain are structures we share with other sentient creatures. Designed for survival, they direct us toward what we feel we need and away from what we perceive as threats to our existence. Evolution has equipped the human brain with the cerebral cortex and its forebrain: structures that can hold in check the core brain's reflexive impulses of approach and avoidance. Language and memory supported by these "higher" structures enable us to delay responses so that we can assess situations before acting, affording the adaptive advantages of judgment, foresight, and flexibility of response.

When the core brain (the inner brain structure we share with "lower" animals) is dominant, its imperatives to avoid pain hijack our higher mental capacities, using them to deploy defenses that limit our range of possible adaptive responses. We repress or vigilantly over-focus on painful memories, selectively avoid awareness of uncomfortable truths, rationalize self-destructive activity, or withdraw into rumination or self-absorption. When the higher structures of forebrain and cerebral cortex operate optimally, they deploy more adaptive defenses that "downregulate," or calm the alarms going off in the core brain, allowing us to make conscious choices.

In my clinical work, I help people tolerate emotional discomfort as they relinquish their limiting psychological defenses. Looking through clearer lenses at their lives, they rewrite their stories of past, present, and future, creating stories that embody hope and possibility. So it is that now I can understand how my frightening childhood encounter with the Divine served to resolve the conflict between filial loyalty to my father, the Methodist minister who did not want his sons to adopt his profession, and my imperative ancestral call to ministry.

The process of writing a memoir is rich with temporal paradox. As I write, I am acutely aware of living in the moment while remembering the past. I observe the rich reworking of my memories by perspectives gained in the years since the events I am remembering. Drawing on lessons that life has taught me about living with emotional pain, I can suspend the limiting defenses with which, over the years, I protected myself from full awareness of past events. As I lift the curtain of my limiting defenses, tolerating the pain from which those defenses had been protecting me, I gain access to deeper and richer awareness of the complexity of remembered events. Such moments feel very much like discoveries. So it is that, trembling with awe and dread of abandonment, I can as an old man retrieve from a memory of childhood the experience of direct dialogical engagement with my God.

Our everyday experience of time is linear, carrying us from our past through the present into the future. So, the narrative form of this memoir recounts the sequence of events in my life. Yet, all that emerges on the page flows forth from the present moment that I write, a present moment continually replaced by its successors over the years of writing this memoir. As I invite you to accompany me through some formative passages in my life, I may at times open the experience of time, affording a glimpse of the design woven into the tapestry in which is, was, and will be, are all one.

1

First Encounter

Oh, ETERNAL, I seek your face. Do not hide your face from me . . .
Do not forsake me, do not abandon me, Oh God.

Ps 27:8–9

. . . My God, My God, why have you abandoned me?

Ps 22:1; Matt 27:46

I AM NINE YEARS old, asleep in my bed in Duxbury, Massachusetts. I have some idea of God from my Sunday School lessons, and I know that my father is a minister. I haven't had to live as a "preacher's kid" under the gaze of my father's congregation, as he is not a parish minister. I understand his work for a Protestant church bureaucracy in Boston no more than most kids my age understand their daddy's office job. I don't question the idea that God exists, but the idea is not particularly important to me.

As I sleep, God calls me by name: "David." I am seized with feelings of wonder and excitement. I feel God's awesome power and majesty. With utter certainty, I experience God's love for me. I am astonished that such a magnificent being, responsible for the entire universe, is paying such particular attention to me. Nothing that I have ever imagined approaches the joy and love that I feel for the presence of God.

Before my body can absorb the ecstasy of the moment, God breaks my heart. "David," says the voice of God, "I am dying." I am flooded with sorrow and distress. How can the world go on without God? What will become of me, to know God's presence, then to lose such a precious love? As intense as my sorrow and worry are, I don't have time to find a place for them in my heart.

God's next move shatters me into fragments that now, writing this in the eighth decade of my life, I am still gathering and reintegrating into my being. God tells me that God's work must go on beyond God's death and that God expects me, David, to carry out God's work. This, finally, is too much for me. I wake up full of terror and confusion.

Traditional shamanic knowledge understands trauma as causing fragmentation of the soul, parts of the soul breaking away from each other. The shaman heals by restoring the fragments to the whole. A sacred myth of esoteric Judaism recounts the "shattering of the vessels" into which the Divine poured God's essence in the process of creation. In that myth, the task of the righteous is to gather the scattered sparks of the Divine from this shattering and restore them to their Source.

As a child, I was shattered by this experience of encounter, which was more than I could contain. For most of the rest of my childhood, my efforts to come to terms with that encounter gave me scant comfort. Although I could not exactly forget what happened to me, neither could I remember it fully. I was often least aware of the event when I was most driven to respond to it. Fragments of my self coexisted uneasily with each other, and for most of the time, I succeeded in suppressing their conscious awareness of each other. In one fragment, there was no way that I could hold the belief that God was dying, particularly now that I had experienced God's love. Another fragment could not imagine contradicting the divine voice, which had announced God's own demise. Hardest of all to bear was the charge to take over the tasks of the Divine. This was impossible to hold in conscious memory, but the power of that message profoundly shaped my life.

I began to pray all the time, silently and urgently, as I made my way through everyday waking life. The prayers were mostly fragments of Christian liturgy learned in Sunday school and church. I remember in particular that, whenever I would hear someone swear, especially if someone cursed with the name of God or Jesus, I would silently utter the words that I had learned Jesus had uttered from the cross: "Please God, forgive them, for they know not what they do" (Luke 23:42). This mental practice gave me no comfort. It didn't give me an experience of relationship with God; that experience was sequestered in a separate fragment that was usually too terrifying to bring into consciousness. As time went on, this silent muttering took up more and more of my internal life. Looking back with the lens of a psychologist, I recognize that I had developed an obsessional disorder, one of the ways that wounded souls have to protect themselves from direct experience of intolerable anxiety. I now understand that a fragment of my being was struggling to carry out the mandate to carry on God's work to the best of my ability, without awareness that this was what I was trying to do, or why.

I note with irony that I often now find Hebrew prayers flowing just below the surface in the stream of my consciousness, as my brain works to assimilate the language and rituals of the religion through which I now serve a living God. Before I rise from my bed when I awake, I give thanks to *melech chai vekayam* (living and enduring sovereign), addressing a sovereign God who manifests in life and in eternity. Unlike the fruitless prayers of my childhood, the background music of Hebrew prayer is comforting and grounding for me.

Had I been raised in a family in which we shared intimately of our inner lives, I might have told my parents of this dream, which in fact I never disclosed to them. Had I done so, my father might have recognized in my nightmare the awful weight that had been placed on him as a twelve-year-old boy. Intergenerational transmission of trauma can be mysterious when it persists for generations and its Source has been lost to collective conscious memory. Less mysterious are the intensely emotional nonverbal transmissions to children of injuries in the living memories of their parents. Years after my terrifying dream, I learned the following family story: my grandfather, a parish minister, died when my father was twelve years old. At his deathbed, he called his only son, my father, to him and told his son that he would have to carry on as the man of the family for his mother and his two sisters. With no conversation about it between us, my father's childhood experience of awful loss and impossible responsibility somehow resonated with my first direct, shattering encounter with God.

When my father was in his eighties, I heard from him directly what I had learned earlier from my mother: that he believed the Methodist Church had killed his father with overwork. It was only after my father died that my stepmother told me what I had always sensed: that my father never wanted his children to become ministers.

It would be a mistake to reduce my dream exclusively within the framework of intergenerational transmission of trauma. Certainly, my experience of being overwhelmed by loss and helplessness facing an impossible demand resonated with my father's experience as a boy at his father's deathbed. But the dream also embodied both the problem and the solution to obeying a powerful ancestral call to serve the Divine while complying with my father's unspoken wish that I not join the Christian clergy.

Christian clergy serve God and their congregation at the behest of the Divine. Catholic clergy and religious (e.g., nuns, monks) speak of vocation. Protestant ministers speak of the call. My father, his father, and several generations before them had heeded the call to ministry in the Methodist Church. The call is initiated by God, and it is not always welcomed. Many wrestle with and against God's summons, a struggle that resonates with biblical stories of the prophets. "Why choose me?" goes the argument; I don't have the necessary abilities; people won't listen to me; people will attack me; I really don't want to do it, etc. Jonah fled and when he finally accepted God's yoke, he complained bitterly about the results of the prophecy that God had commanded him to speak (Jonah 4:2–3).

I certainly had never been told anything about the call when God summoned me in my childhood dream. As I understand it now, my dream was a particularly troublesome call: a paradoxical call that embodied the relationship between my ancestral legacy and my father's childhood bereavement. In ways that I seldom recognized, it organized the course of my life in service to the Divine, ministering to the spiritual needs of others without taking on the formal mantle of a member of the clergy.

I discover new meanings as I write this memoir, late in a lifetime of spiritual searching. Now, more than sixty years later, as I write about my childhood encounter with God, I see embodied in that experience fundamental elements of human spiritual activity: intense joy and love felt in direct encounter with the Source of all being, fear of its awesome power, sorrow and yearning when the connection is lost, and deep commitment to the task of seeking, loving, and praising God.

Now, as a Jew, through the lens of my adopted religion I recognize in my childhood dream the powerful emotions of love and fear. One attains ecstatic experience of the Divine while trembling with an awe that, by preventing one's self from dissolving into the One, assures that one remains rooted in the material world for which one is responsible. Love and fear are the two "wings" with which one ascends toward God, the right and left sides of the Jewish mystical kabbalistic system of the *sefirot*, which are the qualities through which the God that is beyond all space, time, and human understanding both generates and emanates into the worlds of creation.

As I studied Tanach, the Jewish Bible, I was struck by its narrative of the relationship between God and the Jewish people whom God chose as God's servants. It is a story of intense intimacy alternating with anguished estrangement, the sequence repeating itself over the centuries.

At the time that I was falling in love with Judaism, I was practicing a Taoist approach to Chi Gong, using breath and body movement to sense and move subtle energy within my body. From my Taoist perspective, I could see the alternation of redemption and rejection as breath: inhalation and exhalation, neither better nor worse than the other but complementary, both making up the whole. From years of study across a range of esoteric traditions, I understood the purpose of creation to be Divine self-recognition. In the mirror of human gaze upon the presence, God sees Godself. The divine breath that I discerned in the narrative of Tanach embodies God and humanity turning toward, then turning away, then turning toward each other, in a circular process of divine self-awareness.

ANCESTORS

I grew up in a White Anglo-Saxon Protestant ("WASP") family. My father was born in the Western United States. His English and Scots Irish ancestors had moved around the United States and Canada. "Western WASPs," reflecting their forebears' pioneering spirit, tend not to conserve stories of their ancestors, as they direct themselves toward the present and the future. Partly because of his family ethnic culture, and perhaps partly because of his early paternal bereavement, I heard little from my father about his heritage.

Thanks to my sister Sheila's research, I know that my great-great-grandfather, the Reverend Doctor J. B. Trimble, a Methodist Bishop, introduced his grandson Delmar, my grandfather, to Ethel Walker, my grandmother, where they were studying at Boston University, then a Methodist institution of higher learning. J. B. Trimble's wife Lydia founded a Christian Women's College in Fuzhou, China. I suspect that the Methodist clerical tradition preceded my great-great-grandparents. The tradition skipped a generation with my great-grandfather, who was a Canadian farmer, but I know that two of his children, my grandfather

Delmar (a Methodist minister) and his sister Ruby (who was married to the YMCA Executive Secretary in Donato, China) returned to the family tradition of Protestant Christian leadership.

Throughout his life, my father, the Reverend Doctor Glen Trimble, was ambivalent about having become a Methodist minister. To his dying day, he was bitterly resentful of the Methodist Church. His father, like my father himself, was a talented community organizer. A conference of bishops assigns Methodist ministers to their congregations. Recognizing my grandfather's talents, the bishops would assign him to a congregation whose church needed extensive repair and rebuilding. As soon as Delmar completed his mission of church revitalization, he would be "conferenced out" to another congregation in need of his organizing talents. My father spent his childhood in communities throughout the West and Midwest, as his father was assigned to one congregation after another. Delmar had tuberculosis, and my father's narrative was that the Methodist Church had worked a sick man to his early grave. When my grandmother, a college-educated widow, married my step-grandfather, a working-class man whom Delmar had converted to Methodism, my father's two sisters blamed my father for not having protected the family from this embarrassment. The siblings remained estranged to their deaths.

My father, who was warmly and physically affectionate with me early in childhood, became remote after I passed my twelfth birthday. As Ransom, my firstborn son, approached his own twelfth birthday, stirring in me a yearning for the lost warmth and affection of my father, I came to interpret my father's distance from me, his twelve-year-old son, as reflecting his inability to process the grief and confusion of losing his father at that age.

Despite his pain and anger, my father went on to be ordained as a Methodist minister. According to the family story, he did not want to disappoint his mother. So many generations of ministerial ancestry had the momentum of a long freight train. Dad couldn't stop the train, although he tried. Even as he trained for ordination, he became an active Marxist. He lived and preached a particularly activist social gospel. He renamed the church of his first parish in New Bedford, Massachusetts "The Church of the Carpenter" (according to the Christian gospel, Jesus' occupation before he became an itinerant preacher), and Dad's preaching embodied class consciousness.

After Dad's brief tenure at the Church of the Carpenter, my parents spent nearly a decade in the American socialist movement. Dad was briefly editor of the newspaper of the American Socialist Party then split leftward into the Trotskyite socialist movement as he moved around the country editing a series of labor union newspapers. I wonder if he was conscious at the time that his peripatetic pursuit of the socialist dream echoed his father's journeying with his family around the country for the Methodist Church. He and my mother were childless until they left an increasingly fractionated socialist movement and began to raise a family in California. There, Dad ran government camps for migratory farm labor and quickly became entangled in righteous disputes with the growers. When I was born in 1945, Dad had just been reassigned to a new camp in retaliation for his troublemaking. My mother had had to stay behind in the camp in Visalia, California, as she was too far along in her pregnancy to move.

My mother's people were Yankees, descendants of the seventeenth-century English migration to what would become the Northeastern United States. Unlike Western WASPS, the WASP Yankees of New England cling to ancestral stories. When my parents retired to live in Saint Lucia, my mother gave me a box of ancestral lore that had been passed along to her. Included in the box is a set of lineages in nineteenth-century script tracing patrilineal lines of Spinneys, Pratts, and Withingtons back to the seventeenth century.

Tantalizing morsels of information in the box inspire fanciful myths about family. All I know of the Spinney forefather who immigrated to mid-seventeenth-century Massachusetts was that he "met his brother" a decade after he himself settled in the colonies. As we talk about the experience of immigration in seminars where I teach at the Center for Multicultural Training in Psychology, interns and I speculate together about the meaning of this meager bit of information. When my Spinney ancestor migrated, the conditions of travel and communication meant leaving one's family forever and corresponding unreliably if at all. Did the first Spinney help to arrange his brother's passage? Did he know that his brother was coming? Was the meeting, memorialized in a few words for nearly four centuries, a surprise? Were they happy to see each other? Was the first migration the result of estrangement or cutoff? My students, some of them first- or second-generation immigrants, and I contrast these imagined stories with their own family experiences of immigration, shaped by recent technological advances in transportation and communication. We reflect on the contrasts between my ancestral stories and the ancestral stories of my first wife and second wives. The African ancestors of my first wife, Betty Ann, were stolen, displaced, and enslaved, and her indigenous Native American ancestors witnessed and survived genocide and displacement. Their White colonizers and enslavers made deliberate and diligent efforts to erase both African and Native ancestral legacies. My wife Jodie's Jewish ancestors also survived displacement and genocide. They had more success clinging to their ancestral legacy, which their Christian and Muslim oppressors could not erase without destroying the historical roots of their own religions. I am grateful to have joined both Betty Ann's and Jodie's families, whose collectivist values of family solidarity contrast so strongly with the individualist values of my British ancestors.

My middle name, Withington, was the surname of a maternal ancestor who migrated to Boston around 1650. I am fascinated by the narrative possibilities afforded by the family record of the Withingtons in the American Revolution. Days after the battles of Lexington and Concord, a 60-year-old Withington forefather enlisted in the Revolutionary Army. Within days of his enlistment, all three of his sons enlisted. Their father resigned a few weeks after his sons' enlistment. These few facts tantalize the imagination with the story of a father inspiring and/or shaming his sons into taking action at a critical moment in history.

Before the American Revolutionary War, a Withington ancestor was an officer in an earlier war, known to American history as "The French and Indian War," a proxy war between England and France fought by European colonists. Native American nations were allied with each side. That ancestor died crossing a river on the way to an ill-fated English attack on Montreal.

I can feel the shadow on my childhood family life of a more recent Withington military ancestor. My great-great-grandfather, Corporal James Withington of the Union Army, died on the battlefield in the Civil War. A family legend is that when his comrades buried him, they took the time and effort to line his grave with tin from the containers for their provisions. More powerful than any story about James is the letter that he wrote to his daughter Olive, my great-grandmother. His own fear of death is palpable in words about his horse's fear in battle. Holding the letter in my hand, I feel haunted, not just by the words of a man who fears and foresees his death in war but also by the absence of a generational boundary between father and daughter. My great-great-grandfather's sharing of personal experience with his daughter seems more appropriate for an intimate exchange between husband and wife.

My discomfort reading his letter resonates with my discomfort as my mother's favorite and confidant. Looking back at my childhood experience from my adult perspective as a family therapist, I recognize a pattern of "coalitions across generational boundaries." My sister was my father's favored child; I was my mother's. My younger brother was the favorite of neither. Each parent would find in the relationship with favored child some solace for their disappointments with each other. My parents' management of their conflict with each other set the stage for difficulties that my siblings and I had with each other through much of our lives.

Several times over the course of my childhood, I heard stories about the aftermath of my maternal great-great-grandfather's death. The loss of Corporal James Withington as the family's sole earner thrust his widow and daughter, accustomed to the comfort and security of their pre-war position in the middle class, into a situation of dire need. His daughter Olive, my great-grandmother, had to take a position teaching in a one-room school, where some of the students were older than she. Olive yearned to be soothed and comforted at home after her difficult day with disruptive and disrespectful students. Sadly, her mother, James' widow, was bedridden with pathological grief and could not be emotionally present for her daughter. When my mother or grandmother would tell me her story, I imagined my ancestor Olive's feelings of loneliness and abandonment.

I was a few decades into adulthood when this story of relational loss and painful downward social mobility helped me to make sense of how emotionally intense my mother could be with my brother, my sister, and me about "good manners" as we were growing up. My mother could radiate anxiety about manners, and I as her intimate favorite was particularly vulnerable to her emotional displays. I began to wonder why this former socialist reacted so deeply and intensely to our table manners and our attention to formal courtesies. Why did good manners matter so much to her?

As it happened, Olive Withington had no sons but three daughters. I began to wonder about the messages that Olive gave her daughters about the urgent necessity for them as women to find financial security by marrying a man of the proper social class. One of her daughters, my grandmother Maybelle, met and married a fellow student at business school. The family story is that she had married for material security rather than for love and that her marriage was not a happy one

My mother spent her childhood in two homes, her parents' and her grandparents'. For much of her childhood, she bore the burden of caring for her grandmother Olive, whose loss of eyesight was said to have resulted from an alcoholic physician's malpractice. Olive was known to have had a fearsome presence, and I can imagine the intense messages she gave my mother about the importance of mastering the manners of the middle class, so that she could marry appropriately. Perhaps my mother's selection of a Methodist minister and radical socialist for a husband represented a form of rebellion against this intergenerational injunction.

MAKING MY WAY THROUGH CHILDHOOD

My parents found it complicated to come to agreement on a decision about raising a family. They had devoted the early years of their marriage to the socialist movement, even terminating a first pregnancy that they saw as an obstacle to their political activism. The American socialist movement of the 1930s was riven with ideological splits, the intensity of its internal struggles perhaps increased by its powerlessness to bring about revolution. My parents split leftward. Norman Thomas, perennial American Socialist Party candidate for president of the United States, once declared that he would not run for president if my father, Glen Trimble, were editor of the Socialist Party newspaper. My parents migrated to the Trotskyite Socialist Workers' Party, a mortal enemy of the Stalinist American Communist Party. Sitting at a tiny meeting years after they joined the Socialist Workers Party, listening to a leader droning on about "dielectrics" (a mispronunciation of Marx's foundational idea of dialectical materialism), they decided that the American revolutionary movement had lost its vitality. They left the movement and began to raise a family.

My father's comrade Walter Muelder, a fellow socialist and Methodist minister, visited us in California shortly after I was born and persuaded my parents to move back to the East Coast and to Boston University, where Walter was to become Dean of the School of Theology. At BU, while completing his joint PhD in theology and sociology, Dad supported the family as a parish minister, first in Winchendon, Massachusetts, then in Jamaica Plain, a neighborhood of Boston. When I was three years old, he left parish ministry to become director of research at the Massachusetts Council of Churches in Boston, and my parents, my older sister Sheila, my younger brother Robin, and I moved to Duxbury, a suburb on the South Shore of the metropolitan Boston area. No longer the family of a parish minister, we were not to experience religion as a particularly salient dimension of everyday domestic life.

As a family therapist, I know that parents sometimes try to settle accounts from their own personal histories in the way they manage their relationships with their children. I wonder if my mother's injuries around the intersection of class and gender manifested in her anxious ambivalence about the maleness of her favored child. I wonder if my father avoided any deep conversation about religion or spirituality with me because of his determination that his sons not become ministers for the church that he believed had brought his own father's life to a premature end. I remember his anger and embarrassment when I was in college and a campus minister tried to facilitate a conversation between my father and me about my father's religious life. Only in recent years, after his death, did I learn of my father's immersion in the theologies of the Christian theologian Paul Tillich and the Jewish philosopher Martin Buber, which he had shared richly with my sister when she was in college.

My siblings and I were not raised with revolutionary rhetoric. We were told that we were not being taught to be revolutionaries because children rebel against their parents' values as they become adults, and my parents didn't want their radical teaching to lead us to "become Republicans" as adults. I wonder how much this explanation truly accounted for their relative silence about the family's radical legacy. We were children in the heyday of McCarthyism, a savage exercise of government power to expel the remnants of the American revolutionary movement from legitimate public life. Leftists were driven underground, harassed, isolated, or marginalized. "Red Scare" hysteria made no distinction between communists and Trotskyites.

My parents became public liberals, which was enough for them to be eyed with suspicion in the Republican town in which my siblings and I were raised. When my parents took the wrong side in a dispute over the high school principal, my sister, three years older than me, was ostracized overnight by her schoolmates under their parents' instructions. More literal-minded than my older sister, I did not understand that my mother was joking about our being "communists" in the eyes of the local population. I remember my sister beating me up and fiercely warning me when, in a semi-public space, I uttered the notion that we were communists.

Treating families for decades has given me perspective on my parents' strengths and weaknesses. Despite their limitations, I always knew that I was loved. My mother demonstrated her love for me with verbal and physical affection. I felt my father's love in words, hugs, and kisses, until I reached the age at which he had lost his own father. Although his awkward emotional remoteness after that was painful, I never doubted that he loved me. Having treated people who did not know they were loved, or indeed were not loved, I know how precious are the feelings are of personal worth and security that I got from my family.

I internalized Yankee ideas of civic responsibility and grew up on stories of my maternal Great Grandfather George F. Spinney, Olive Withington's husband, a newspaperman who helped Teddy Roosevelt break up Tammany Hall in New York City. My father's Trimble ancestors were combative Scots-Irish, and I identified with his readiness to stand up to injustice. The few sermons that I heard him deliver as a guest preacher embodied radical Christian activist values.

When my family moved from Boston to suburban Duxbury, I walked two houses down from our new home, knocked on the door, and announced to the mother of the household, "I am David Trimble. I am three years old. Do you have any children here that I can play with?" As it happened, she had a son a year younger than me, William "Fizz" Richards, who became my best friend until we moved from Duxbury when I was twelve years old.

I was a quick study in most school subjects and learned to read early. I found great value in the life of the mind and absorbed myself in the worlds afforded by fiction. I was valued by teachers and most adults as a polite, intelligent, well-spoken and curious child. We spent our summers in a small cabin in the Duxbury woods, complete with an outhouse, a well with a hand pump, and an electric generator. We were free to wander in the woods, and times alone in the woods became for me a template for wordless spiritual experience.

Childhood was nonetheless a difficult passage. My boldness in setting out to discover my friend Fizz was exceptional. Temperamentally, I was shy and vulnerable to anxiety. I had rheumatic fever at age 5, and while the pediatrician's insistence on prolonged bed rest spared me from heart disease, it caused me to miss nearly all of kindergarten, a critical year for social and emotional development.

My family's political marginalization had a role in my childhood social alienation. So did my limited understanding of social situations and my distractibility and impulsivity, manifestations of nonverbal learning disability (NVLD) (now known through the kaleidoscope of psychiatric language as "Autism Spectrum Disorder") and attention deficit hyperactivity disorder (ADHD). Although I was fiercely smart in the classroom, particularly in acquiring verbal skills, I was clueless socially with my peers. I didn't get it that my triumphant performances in the classroom, assuring my position as teacher's pet, also assured that I would be targeted on the playground.

I was also hopelessly uncoordinated physically and could not decipher the spoken and unspoken rules of sport. Invariably chosen last, I dreaded humiliation in the ritual of "choosing up teams." Occasionally, when a captain realized that he was going to have the last choice, he would argue for the right to have an extra player, to make up for being "stuck with Trimble." I was fortunate that Fizz was a year younger than me. For the most part, our peer networks did not overlap. He himself was socially fluent and popular in his peer group. I don't know if our friendship would have lasted if we had both been in the same school grade. I was definitely not "cool" and could have been a liability for him socially.

Although my ADHD and NVLD were sources of social difficulties with my peers, my quick verbal intelligence compensated in the classroom, and no one would have considered me as having had learning difficulties. My brother Robin was not so fortunate. He struggled and failed in school, despite my father's efforts to help him with his studies. I have visceral memories of the sound of my father's angry voice at his younger son, as all my father's efforts to drill him in phonics came to naught. My brother did not graduate high school until he got his GED in his forties. Psychological testing around that time revealed that Robin's phonics skills were in the 99th percentile, and his ADHD was so severe that he could not remember what he had read at the top of a page by the time that he was reading the bottom of the same page. The solution that my father was given by the educational specialists of the time was not appropriate for Robin's problem, for which the professions did not yet have a name.

Years later, when I tried to help Ransom, my firstborn, with his difficulty learning mathematics in third grade, I was horrified to hear my father's impatient voice coming out of my mouth. I made sure to get Ransom the special support services he needed and stepped carefully away from this volatile intergenerational family issue. For the first decade of my clinical practice, I avoided taking on cases involving family problems around learning disabilities, although later, as I matured personally and professionally, working with such family problems became one of my specialties.[27]

I had one frightening episode, lasting a few weeks in fourth grade, in which I lost the mooring provided by my intellectual life. Suddenly, I was not retaining what I read, so that I could not retrieve text that I had already read as I made my way through reading a book. I imagine that my anxieties over religiosity, marginalization by peers, and conflicts in the home amplified my attentional problems, temporarily impairing my capacity to become absorbed in reading a book. I was frightened enough to overcome my reticence over telling my parents about my inner life and tearfully shared my distress. My parents were concerned and compassionate but did not know what they could offer to help. Fortunately, the episode was brief and did not repeat itself.

I remember church services and Sunday school in the Duxbury Congregational Church. My father was director of research at the Massachusetts Council of Churches, a consortium of Protestant and Eastern Orthodox Christian denominations. Although a Methodist minister himself, he was committed to ecumenical dialogue and had no trouble participating in a congregation of a different denomination. My mother sang in the choir, and my father would occasionally be asked to lead services. I cannot remember ever connecting my time in church or Sunday school with my terrifying encounter with a God who abandoned me to an impossible mission, although my internal ruminating religiosity probably pervaded that space, as it did so many other spaces in my life.

My mother had her own ambivalence about religion. A distant maternal ancestor, my namesake David Spinney, became a Baptist minister after retiring from his career as a sea captain in the China trade. My mother had been raised in the Christian Science Church, whose founder Mary Baker Eddy's spiritualist theology was noteworthy for its shunning of treatment by the medical profession. I suspect that my grandmother's conversion to Christian Science had been influenced by my great-grandmother Olive's losing her eyesight because of medical malpractice. My mother carried forward the family tradition of resentment over physical ailments, blaming her mother's Christian Science for a lifetime of back pain that my mother attributed to her not getting medical attention after an injury in adolescence. My mother also appeared to be uncomfortable with Christianity's deification of Jesus. Had she not been a Christian minister's wife, I think that she would have been most comfortable as a Unitarian.

My parents' socialization of their children about race was confusing and somewhat anxiety-arousing. We were taught about the moral evils of segregation and learned that racism was a problem throughout American society, not just the South. Although we learned that the social conditions of people of African ancestry were dramatically different from those of Whites, we were also taught a somewhat mystifying "colorblind" stance: that people are people and are no different from us because of the color of their skin. I remember my mother taking my friend Fizz and me to a cookout in Duxbury where we were the only White people among a score of African Americans. Raised to be colorblind, we could read in each other's faces our discomfort about our unaccustomed racial minority positions but found no words to communicate about our experience of difference.

Without the relatively intuitive, automatic social understanding of a neurologically typical child, I lacked clear appreciation for the interconnected issues involved in treating those who are different as the other. Although we adopted our parents' social justice values, our parents' peculiar racial socialization, and my neurobiological limitations as a child on the autism spectrum contributed to my childhood cluelessness about ethnicity and race. There were a few families of African heritage in Duxbury, mostly descendants of immigrants from Cape Verde, who had lived in town for many generations. I was friendly with my Black schoolmates, although none of them were among my few childhood friends. Alan Shane, who lived with his parents above their shoe store, was one of those friends. His was the only Jewish family in Duxbury, an anti-Semitic town whose restrictive covenants on sales of real estate kept all Jews except for the Shane family from living within its borders. I knew that Alan was Jewish but have no memory of his being targeted, nor do I recall hearing anti-Semitic rhetoric as a child. My mother cultivated a few family friendships with Jewish families in Boston.

Bright children with NVLD can overcome their lack of social fluency by acquiring a repertoire of verbally mediated "scripts" to negotiate social situations that are intuitively obvious for children with standard brains. By sixth grade, I had learned to avoid most painful targeting by my peers and had practiced enough scripts to be relatively confident in many situations. Intellectual strength was more valued as my peers and I got older together, and I began to be more respected because of that strength. I was beginning find more security and enjoyment in the company of my preadolescent age mates.

TRANSITIONS

My father got a new job, as director of research interpretation at the National Council of Churches, at their New York headquarters. For a year, Dad worked five days a week in New York and returned to spend the weekend with his family. We moved to join him when I was in sixth grade.

The transition would have been unsettling enough without the interlude of living in my maternal grandmother's house on Long Island while my parents searched for a house. My mother had a difficult relationship with her mother, and the tension in the house amplified my own anxiety at the prospect of negotiating a whole new set of peer relationships in whatever town my parents found for us to settle. My brother Robin was targeted by youth in my grandmother's neighborhood, who taunted him because he had a "girl's name." For the next several years, he would insist on being called "Rick." My internal ruminative prayer became more obsessive in response to all this stress. On one occasion, my prayer "leaked out," and I was horrified to realize that I had actually uttered some words of prayer aloud as I tried to calm myself in a difficult conversation with my mother. My mother appeared equally startled. I recall a smile of apparent surprise and curiosity on her face, and my gratitude that she did not remark or ask questions about my blurting out words from my private inner experience.

After what felt like an interminable search, my parents decided to buy a home in suburban Harrington Park, New Jersey. It was a picturesque small town, still with a lot of undeveloped woodland, some of it protected around reservoirs for the northern New Jersey water supply. There was an old-fashioned swimming hole, with a rope swing from which to plunge into the Hackensack River. Unlike Duxbury, it had a number of Jewish families, which was particularly important for my mother. Only after we moved in did my parents learn that Harrington Park had been an important center for the anti-Semitic and pro-Nazi German American Bund and that the small-town culture was even more socially and politically conservative than Duxbury's.

I immediately got off on the wrong foot with my peers. Trying to build on the social currency that I had finally earned in Duxbury for my intellectual achievements, I introduced myself as a "bookworm," a tactic which did not work well with my fellow sixth graders and which typecast me for the rest of our mercifully brief stay in town. The seventh-grade musical was *Mississippi Melody*, based on the novels of Mark Twain. I was cast as the marginalized intellectual Pudd'nhead Wilson, singing, "I am an individual, have ideas of my own, but they are from Missouri, and say they must be shown . . ."

Harrington Park did not have restrictive covenants to keep out Jews, but it was well understood that no one would sell or rent to Blacks. I had more Jewish friends, both made on my own and as part of family friendships. I read the *Diary of Anne Frank*, as I became aware of the recent history of genocide in Europe. Somehow, I kept this awareness separate from my friendships with other marginalized peers, including kids who were into what they saw as the swagger and romantic symbolism of the Nazis, drawing swastikas on the covers of our books. I never bought into their anti-Semitic rhetoric, but I didn't challenge my friends about it, either.

There was a lot of hooliganism in my Boy Scout troop. I made a holiday candlestick in arts and crafts at a troop meeting, only to drop and break it when an older boy (who later became an Eagle Scout!) surprised me outside by bruising my thigh with a bullwhip. My mother got no satisfaction when she complained to the troop leader about this assault. I was a hooligan myself, ringing doorbells with my friends after Scout meetings and shouting out catcalls from the bushes when people opened their doors. We would steal Christmas light bulbs from displays outside people's homes and throw them into the air to shatter on the streets. My buddy "Hueggi" and I constructed "rumble chains" and swaggered around with our gangster fantasies. Hueggi and I, both fourteen, spent one afternoon trespassing on the dry grassy bank of a reservoir. We were smoking cigarettes and lighting small fires in the grass. Suddenly, one of the fires started spreading. As Hueggi stomped ineffectively on the flames, I took off my sweater vest, soaked it in the water, and beat out the flames. I was relieved that my parents never asked me to account for the missing sweater. Hueggi and I would light off firecrackers at a sand pit, where we once encountered some younger kids and showed off our rumble chains. I got grounded when one of the younger kids' parents reported me to my parents.

I couldn't get out of my own way. I was a Boy Scout Patrol Leader and led my Scouts on a hike through a New York State Park, on our way to rendezvous with the troop to swim at a lake. As it happened, the parent who drove us to the park took the wrong highway, and we lost about an hour as she corrected her route. We started late on the hike. When we had climbed to a relatively high altitude, one of my Scouts, the son of the school principal, developed altitude sickness. Using map and compass, I led us down the hill to a road, where we hitched a ride to the lake, arriving as the troop was preparing to leave. Asked what had happened to us, instead of starting with a report on my resourceful response to the health crisis, I said, "we got lost," referring to the mother's mistake navigating us to the park. That became the story of the incident, as far as the troop leader and the other scouts were concerned, another illustration of "Trimble's cluelessness." The principal let my mother know how much he appreciated my successful efforts to protect his son, but this was not the story that circulated among my peers.

Around this time, the Congregational Church and the Dutch Reformed Church, denominations with common historical roots, were in the process of merging to form the United Church of Christ. Our family began attending church and Sunday School at the Harrington Park UCC Church, soon finding the experience unpleasant. Theologically and practically, the church proved to be rigid and narrow-minded. The minister happened to call on us one Sunday and did little to hide his disapproval that we were playing cards on the Sabbath. This proved to stretch Dad's ecumenical sensibility beyond its limits.

In the middle of all this, I found my way to a book by Alan Watts, which introduced me to Buddhism.[28] His writing opened for me an entirely different approach to spirituality, offering the practical experience of meditation as an alternative to theology. With almost no conscious memory of my harrowing childhood experience of divine manifestation and abandonment, I was still praying ruminatively in a vain effort to placate a frightening and unpredictable God. Teaching myself to meditate, I liberated myself from my empty and fruitless internal monologue of prayer. I had found my way to direct experience of spirituality, and this was to become a touchstone thenceforth for my spiritual search.

My parents were horrified by the effects on our family of living in Harrington Park. While their older son was becoming coarsened by his peer experiences, their younger son was being mistreated by his schoolteachers. Frustrated with Robin's learning disabilities, his fourth-grade teacher had even recommended to my parents that he be institutionalized. My mother had a job as school librarian in the nearby town of Tenafly, whose community values and school system offered more opportunities for healthy child development. She and my father decided to move to Tenafly. So it was that, toward the end of the eighth grade, I faced yet another family move.

A few years older, and informed by the results of my mistakes entering Harrington Park, I did a somewhat better job of entering my peer group in Tenafly. Because I was relatively tall, I did, unfortunately, have to live through a second round of aggressive recruitment to join the school basketball team. The only way to remove the pressure was to endure the scorn of potential teammates when I demonstrated just how uncoordinated I was physically and how clueless I was about the relational music of team sports. Painfully shy, and wary after years of being targeted, I had come to walk with a bent-over posture, perhaps unconsciously trying to make myself inconspicuous as I grew to be taller than most of my peers. This, of course, had the opposite effect. I remember arriving late to chemistry class in junior high school. As I walked across the front of the classroom, a star athlete called out, "Why do you walk like that, Trimble? To cut down wind resistance?"

The community culture in Tenafly placed more value on intellectual gifts, which I displayed without calling attention to them in the way that I had when we moved to Harrington Park. Our high school had two levels of academic honors, and I was placed in the higher level, in small classes organized as seminars. This afforded me membership in a group that valued me for my strengths and whose members included a number of other bright but quirky kids. I flourished in the demanding academic atmosphere and found my closer friends among students who shared a cynical attitude about the competitive values of a town and school system dedicated to sending its offspring to elite colleges. Our principal had convened a meeting of seminar students for a pep talk, telling us we were the "intellectual varsity" of the school. My friends and I responded by producing the *El Retcho* newsletter, a broad parody of the high school newspaper, *The Echo*. The quarterback for our football team was part of the *El Retcho* gang, and he would be summoned to the principal's office after each issue of our sarcastic, provocative, and scatological newsletter was distributed. Our friend learned that the same group of teachers came to the principal after each issue, demanding our suspension. Partly because we (including the football star) were members of the "intellectual varsity," and partly because the principal (whom we so mercilessly skewered on our pages) defended our freedom of expression, we escaped punishment.

The family joined a Methodist Church in Englewood, just south of Tenafly. It was the first experience that I had in a church of my father's ancestral denomination. I remember a much warmer community, embodied for me in the hymn "Blessed Be the Tie that Binds Our Hearts in

Christian Love." I was captured by the Methodist ritual of communion, in which one went to the front of the church to receive the sacraments, rather than their being distributed in the pews, as they had been in the churches we attended earlier. I learned of the "warming of the heart" that had led John Wesley to start the Methodist movement, which resonated for me with my experience of meditation. My mother taught Sunday school to the high school students. Her skepticism about the teachings of Paul embodied both her feminist sensibilities and her doubts about Christian doctrine. When I could not find in Christianity the spiritual experience that I was finding in meditation I became rebellious about going to church.

I became more conscious and intentional in my search for spiritual experience. I identified with the spiritually tormented narrator in Nikos Kazantzakis's *Zorba the Greek* and was attracted to the intense vitality of the character of Zorba. I found my way to Kazantzakis' *The Odyssey: A Modern Sequel*, a massive work in which Kazantzakis recounted in verse a story of Odysseus, who, soon bored after his return to Penelope from the Trojan Wars, set out for new adventure. Restless Odysseus finds his focus when he encounters in the marketplace an idol of a seven-headed god embodying individual spiritual quest and human spiritual evolution:[29]

> Time shut its wings for a brief moment and stood still
> so that the lone mind could have ample time to climb
> with skillful fingers all the rungs of mortal virtues.
> Below, the most coarse head, a brutal base of flesh,
> Swelled like a bloated beast bristling with large boar-tusks,
> and it was fortified with veins as thick as horns.
> Above it, like a warrior's crest, the second head
> clenched its sharp teeth and frowned with hesitating brows
> like one who scans his danger, quakes before death's door,
> but in his haughty pride still feels ashamed to flee.
> The third head gleamed like honey with voluptuous eyes,
> its pale cheeks hallowed by the flesh's candied kisses,
> and a dark love-bite scarred its he-goat lips with blood.
> The fourth head lightly rose, its mouth a whetted blade,
> its neck grew slender and its brow rose tall as though
> its roots had turned to flower, its meat to purest mind .
> The fifth head's towering brow was crushed with bitter grief,
> deep trenches grooved it, and its flaming cheeks were gripped
> with torturous arms as by a savage octopus;
> it bit its lips hopelessly to keep from howling.
> Above it shone serenely the last head but one,

and steadfastly weighed all things, beyond all joy or grief,
like an all-holy, peaceful, full-fed, buoyant spirit.
It gazed on Tarturus and the sky, a slight smile bloomed
Like the sun's subtle afterglow on faded lips;
it sauntered on the highest creviced peaks of air
where all things seem but passing dream and dappled mist;
and from its balding crown, that shone like a smooth stone
battered by many flooding seas and licked by cares,
there leapt up like unmoving flame the final head,
as if it were a crimson thread that strung the heads
like amber beads in rows and hung them high in air.
The final head shone, crystal-clear, translucent, light,
And had not ears or eyes, no nostrils, mouth, or brow,
For all its flesh had turned to soul, and soul to air!

Reading Kazantzakis gave me language and metaphor with which to understand myself as a spiritual seeker and reinforced my desire to find what I was seeking outside the boundaries of Christianity. At the time unaware that the source of my search for the Divine lay in my childhood nightmare, I see now how that first encounter continued to shape the course of my life. Fashioning myself as a seeker, I yearned for the unremembered, intense and unmistakable experience of the Presence I had felt in that moment before God announced God's death. Seeing myself as a seeker, I set myself on the journey to find that experience.

I was a teenager a few years too early for opportunities to explore marijuana or psychedelic drugs in high school, but I did start to drink alcohol with my friends. I was drawn to the sudden and intense shift in experience that came with intoxication, in some ways similar to altering experience through meditation. I felt powerful and had an exaggerated feeling of the compelling importance of my inner life. With strong vulnerability to addiction inherited from both paternal and maternal ancestors, I was eager for opportunities to drink.

Associated with genetic vulnerability to addiction was a heritage of difficulty with mood regulation. As I matured physically, I struggled with episodes of depression. I had a tendency to fall hard romantically, and to become absorbed in brokenheartedness when things did not go well. On one such occasion of miserable self-contemplation, I renounced my ambition, inspired by my charismatic fifth grade teacher, to become a teacher myself. I decided to pursue a career as a psychotherapist. Like some in my profession, my original motivation to become a therapist was to learn how to master my own unhappiness.

BECOMING A SOCIAL ACTIVIST

Although my siblings and I never got direct instruction in radicalism, I had general awareness of my parents' revolutionary past, which contributed to my decision to become an activist. The first issue that drew me was the nuclear arms race in the Cold War. I started going to peace marches organized by SANE, the National Committee for a Sane Nuclear Policy. When President Kennedy planned a national air raid drill, apparently intended to show the Soviet Union that the United States was prepared to engage in nuclear war, I decided to take action. I knew that some organizations were organizing protests and decided that I would stand in Tenafly's downtown park in silent protest during the drill. Another high school student had made that same decision independently, and the two of us were arrested together. Although mine was an individual act, the news of the event circulated among young activists in northern New Jersey. I was recruited into the Bergen County chapter of Students for a Sane Nuclear Policy and was soon elected co-president. My activities with Student SANE connected me with an entirely new peer group, in Teaneck, several towns south of Tenafly. I developed a social life uncontaminated by a reputation for social awkwardness and found love in the most mature romantic relationship at that time in my young life.

Although Tenafly had a much larger Jewish population than Harrington Park, it also excluded African Americans from living in the town. By my mid-teens, I was taking the bus from Tenafly to Teaneck or to Manhattan, where I would take the subway to cultural events and political meetings. The bus route passed through Englewood, where African American residents were protesting the *de facto* segregation of the Englewood public schools. I remember my discomfort when African American passengers got on the bus in Englewood. I was aware of racial difference and of the social injustices of race that I had first learned about from my parents, who, unfortunately, had also socialized me into naïve "colorblindness." This socialization was contradicted by my discomfort with difference, which I had not yet come to understand as dawning awareness of my internalized White privilege.

National news media brought news of racial violence in struggles over the desegregation of schools and public facilities in the South, and I knew from the struggle in Englewood that racial oppression was not restricted to the South. I was 18, just graduated from high school, when I responded to the 1963 call for the March on Washington for Jobs and

Freedom. I boarded a bus in Englewood, this time not with anonymous African American strangers, but with African American and White fellow activists headed for a demonstration to protest racial injustice. I loved the experience of comradeship across racial differences, differences that were freely acknowledged among us rather than denied. Caught up in the intensity and optimism of a crowd of over a hundred thousand, I made my commitment to the Civil Rights Movement.

I followed through on this decision with some deliberation. I was averse to wearing political buttons, being reticent about drawing attention to myself, partly because of my Yankee cultural tradition, partly because of my still-raw vulnerability to feeling targeted by peers, and perhaps partly from unconscious internalization of my parents' fears from the McCarthy era. Resisting this aversion, I bought a large March on Washington button and vowed to wear it until I joined a civil rights organization. The march was the summer after my senior year in high school. As soon as I arrived as a freshman at Clark University in Worcester, Massachusetts, I became an active member of the Worcester Student Movement and took off the button. WSM was led by D'Army Bailey, an African American student who had come to Clark after being expelled from Southern University in Louisiana for his civil rights activism. WSM picketed the main downtown department store, and also the Wyman Gordon factory, owned by a founder of the John Birch Society who also owned the city newspaper, the *Worcester Telegram and Gazette*.

CONTINUING THE SPIRITUAL SEARCH

Living away from family for the first time in my life, I began to explore the emerging sixties counterculture. I began to smoke marijuana, a practice at the time confined to a small group at our small university. I became an earnest advocate for the counterculture, which cast marijuana as a harmless alternative to alcohol, the preferred intoxicant of our parents' generation. I was a member of two small, marginalized groups on the campus that for the most part did not overlap, political activists and psychedelic "hippies." I took a few trips on LSD, shortcuts to profound experiences of the Unity of the universe. I met Abbie Hoffman at the intersection of political and psychedelic countercultures, before Abbie became a national symbol of "Yippie" rebellion. Abbie and I took a couple of psychedelic trips on morning glory seeds and were both local civil rights activists.

Although the words "God Is Dead" were not to appear on the cover of *Time* magazine until a few years later, the early sixties were already a time of deep questioning among Christian clergy. Challenged and inspired by the African American clergy of the Southern Christian Leadership Conference, a number of Catholic priests and Protestant ministers in Worcester were social justice activists. Some were also trying to engage with youth counterculture. A young Episcopal priest approached one of my hippie friends with an invitation to an evening's play in the sanctuary of his church. I remember smoking marijuana with a group of friends before going to the church, where we had a costume party with vestments for clergy and choir. I stood at the pulpit in priestly robes and conducted a mock sermon, aware that my play was not entirely ironic as I felt myself resonating with my preacher ancestors.

By that time in my life, I knew about the call to ministry and was curious about my clerical ancestry. Reading Joyce's *Portrait of the Artist as a Young Man* in high school had given me the term "epiphany," a word that I applied to occasions that felt like revelations, whether from alcohol or psychedelics, from experiences of intense mood fluctuation, or from rare experiences of the Divine in meditation. From reading Kazantzakis's *Modern Sequel to the Odyssey*, I had come to see my life as a spiritual journey and myself as a seeker.

Although I felt alienated by Christianity, I nonetheless wondered whether, if, and when I might receive the call to the ministry. I did not take into account my 9-year-old experience of divine manifestation, abandonment, and impossible mandate that only in recent years have I come to understand as a particularly paradoxical form of call. I knew that I did not want to become a minister and started to play a game with myself. Although I did not know how many of my paternal ancestors had been ministers, I knew that it was more than a handful. Reframing my epiphanies as calls, I told myself that I was in store for one call for each of my clerical ancestors. If I could successfully resist each call until the tally coincided with the number of my minister ancestors, I would be in the clear.

MISSISSIPPI

In 1960, the Student Nonviolent Coordinating Committee (SNCC) was established in the American South by college students, nearly all of them

African American. Born during dramatic sit-in demonstrations to protest segregated public accommodations, SNCC soon turned its attention to grassroots community organizing. SNCC Field Secretary Bob Moses led a small group into Mississippi to support an indigenous movement of African American activists seeking to end the disenfranchisement of Black Mississippians. SNCC and local activists encountered brutal resistance at every level of Mississippi White society: denial of voting registration at county courthouses, arrests and beatings by sheriffs' offices and local police departments, economic retaliation from the White Citizens' Councils, violent threats, beatings, arson, kidnapping, and murder by the Ku Klux Klan and other terrorists.

To be effective, nonviolent action must arouse the moral sensibilities of a society. Knowing that Mississippi White society would continue to countenance systematic terrorist suppression of African American political rights, and that their struggle was not attracting the attention of a nation that might feel moral outrage, SNCC, CORE (the Congress of Racial Equality), and local civil rights activists formed the Council of Federated Organizations (COFO). COFO organized the Mississippi Summer Project, which came to be known as the 1964 Mississippi Freedom Summer. Their idea was to flood Mississippi with a summer's intensive activism by Northern, mostly White student volunteers, thereby drawing the attention of national news media to the encounter between America's privileged White children and the brutality of segregationist Mississippi society.

I first learned of the Mississippi Summer Project when D'Army recruited me to volunteer. Here was an opportunity to make a difference in a struggle that was important to me, as an activist and as heir to a revolutionary legacy from my parents. As I was not well versed in my parents' Trotskyite ideology, my decision to join the Summer Project was inspired primarily by maternal ancestral traditions of Yankee civic responsibility. My great-great-grandfather James Withington had sacrificed his life in the battle against slavery in the South, and my great-grandfather George Franklin Spinney fought against Tammany Hall corruption as a newspaper reporter in New York City. Despite having challenged institutional racism in Worcester with WSM, I still harbored regional prejudice, seeing Southern apartheid as "other" to American values, as I naively constructed them. I was going to an alien land that was still part of the United States, and our struggle would draw attention of the nation to violation of American values. A descendant of a muckraking newspaperman, I believed that exposure of public evil would inspire reformation.

I was honored that D'Army chose to recruit me, and there was no question that I would accept his challenge. I knew that I would be putting my life at risk. I was 19 years old, an age at which young men (and young women) choose to go to battle in wars, knowing but not fully comprehending the meaning of a decision to risk one's life for a cause. My parents supported me, even as they felt understandable fear of what could happen to me. Like most families of Summer Project volunteers, they organized our local communities in meetings, interviews with media, and letters to editors of local newspapers, bringing home the realities of the political and racial situation in Mississippi.

Battle-hardened SNCC leaders were ambivalent about the Summer Project. They calculated, correctly, that the arrests, beatings, bombings, and violent deaths of Northern White students would mobilize the White middle class in the North against the oppression and subjugation of African Americans in Mississippi. The moral implications of this decision, however, had held Bob Moses back from deciding to proceed, until a close colleague, an indigenous Mississippi African American voting rights activist, was murdered with complete impunity by a White racist opposed to African American voting rights. It was clear that violent suppression would continue to succeed as long as the Mississippi struggle remained local. Yet SNCC leaders were appropriately concerned about the naiveté of volunteer recruits. Inexperienced middle-class Northern students, both African American and White, could put SNCC field staff and community members at risk in dangerous circumstances. White students in particular posed the challenge of unintentional racial injuries, displacing Black Mississippians running community organizations, or committing unwitting racial insults that we now call "microaggressions."[30]

Acting on these concerns, SNCC and COFO established an orientation and training program for Freedom Summer volunteers at Western College for Women in Ohio. It was particularly meaningful for me that the National Council of Churches, where my father worked as director of research interpretation, was one of the sponsors of the training program. The training program was nearly as influential on the course of my life as was my time in Mississippi. In addition to training us in the gritty practice of nonviolence when faced with threats, beatings, and potential murder, the program challenged White students to understand racism not just in the bigoted "other" but also in our own unconscious assumptions of White privilege. I learned to be aware of, and take responsibility for, my internalization of White supremacy. More than fifty years later, after fifteen years of marriage to an African American woman and many more years as father of multiracial children, and as a constant activist for racial justice and multicultural sensitivity, I recognize the persistence of that internalized White supremacy. I know that none of us are free from racial stratification as long as it endures, and that my lifelong resistance is not enough to liberate me from its toxic discourse.

That was not the only lesson that I learned in Ohio. Although I was getting by socially, my social skills were still quite limited by my neurobiological limitations and by the painful history of its effects on my relationships. As I prepared to enter Mississippi, I had to confront and take responsibility for my limited social skills. I would be doing community organizing, engaging African Americans to become activists in their struggle for the vote. With the imperative to take responsibility for my actions with others, I committed myself to endure the feelings of embarrassment and failure involved in cultivating more social fluency.

Like the first lesson, I continued to learn this one throughout the Freedom Summer. Our team of three, including Bob Fullilove, the son of an African American surgeon in New Jersey, and Bob Feinglass, the son of White Jewish labor union organizers, went from house to house in rural DeSoto County, Mississippi, asking African American citizens to sign papers enrolling them in the Mississippi Freedom Democratic Party, an alternative to the Mississippi Democratic Party. As it had become apparent that the Mississippi establishment would continue to thwart our efforts to register African Americans to vote, COFO had shifted its strategy to emphasize organizing the Freedom Democratic Party, which would challenge the regular Mississippi delegation at the 1964 Democratic National Convention in August.

The situation demanded that I develop the capacity and sophistication to negotiate conversations with African American citizens. My teammates and I sought to persuade them to join the Mississippi Freedom Democratic Party, while acknowledging the attendant risks to their families, their homes, their livelihoods, and their very lives. I had to take into account their life-preserving awareness of ever-present racial danger and the powerful socialization that compelled an African American in Mississippi to say "yes" to anything that a White man demanded of them. I had to convey authentic deference and respect in what was often for many of them the first conversation in which a White person treated them respectfully. This was a stance that could not be faked, and I could feel powerful intuitive and nonverbal internal changes as I learned to respond to the moral imperative of the situation.

In Mississippi, I encountered an entirely different and unexpected experience of Christianity. The Black church was central to the civil rights effort, as cruelly attested to by the number of church buildings burned to the ground over the course of the struggle. We held mass meetings in churches. The churches were where the Mississippi Freedom Democratic Party convened county caucuses to select representatives for the state MFDP convention in Jackson. Although a substantial proportion of the White volunteers were Jews, there was no question that all of us were to show up for worship services in church on Sundays.

My prior experience of Christian worship services was nothing like what I encountered in Mississippi. At home, the Protestant religious services I attended were emotionally restrained, intellectual gatherings. The services themselves were painfully boring; whatever drama I experienced was internal, as I wrestled with the demand for beliefs that were harder and harder for me to hold. Worship services in African American Protestant services in Mississippi were passionate and dramatic. Perhaps because of the civil rights workers sitting in the congregation, the Bible readings and the preaching dealt primarily with the story of the liberation of the children of Israel from Egyptian bondage. I didn't have to listen to very much christological theology. The preacher would become increasingly passionate as he spoke, moving from earnest pleading and encouragement into an emotionally intense chanting cadence, breathing heavily as his utterances shifted from speech into song. The preacher and congregation reached out to each other, as the "amens" from the congregation buoyed the preacher's rise to heights of ecstasy. The "amens" were usually spontaneous, but if they were not forthcoming, the preacher would call out for them.

It was not uncommon for a congregant, usually an older woman, to become possessed, sometimes calling out Jesus' name, sometimes utterly silent, standing up and waving her arms around. Fellow congregants would step in to protect her and people around her from accidental injury by her waving arms and gyrations. I have since learned about Hausa and Yoruba religious practices indigenous to the West African homelands from which many African Americans' ancestors were captured and brought to the United States in slave ships. Possession by spirits, integral to their ancestors' religious practice, survived White Christian masters' efforts to rob their slaves of their cultural legacies through conversion to Christianity.

I was unaware at the time I witnessed it that this experience of being possessed by the Holy Spirit was an African cultural remnant. My heart told me that the women were authentically engaging with something that was beyond my experience, but that felt more "real" than the myths and miracle stories of my religious upbringing. Although much was beyond my understanding, my experiences in the Southern churches aroused my spirituality in a way that I could neither deny nor understand. It would be another eleven years before I would become the student of an espiritista from the Dominican Republic, whose own practice of spirit possession enabled him to open me to a direct experience of the Divine.

These spiritual awakenings were private experiences for me. All of us were absorbed in the urgent work of organizing the Freedom Democratic Party, convening caucuses in local churches where FDP members elected representatives for the FDP State Convention. The convention selected the delegates who would challenge the regular Mississippi Democratic Party Delegates at the national Democratic Party Convention in Atlantic City in August 1964.

Like many of my fellow volunteers, I found it more and more difficult to imagine leaving Mississippi at the end of the summer. Although we were all risking our lives, I knew that we were asking native Mississippians to take on huge risks, from which they could not escape as we Northern volunteers could when we returned home. Although COFO planned a time-limited volunteer campaign, many of us sought to stay beyond the summer. In my nineteen-year-old arrogance, I wrote to my parents announcing my intention to remain in Mississippi. I told them that, as they had already had to come to terms with the possibility that I would lose my life, they now would have to come to terms with my not returning to college.

DeSoto County was in the northwest corner of Mississippi, just south of Memphis, Tennessee, where D'Army lived. Bob Fullilove, Bob Feinglass, and I arranged for an overnight visit with D'Army and his family in Memphis. I proudly announced to D'Army that I would be staying in Mississippi. He told me firmly that I would do no such thing, that it was my responsibility to return to college and to the civil rights struggle in the North. D'Army had never given me reason to question him as my leader, so I made arrangements to leave Mississippi for the Democratic

National Convention in Atlantic City at the end of August and thence to return to college in Worcester.

At the Democratic Convention, Abbie Hoffman was one of a number of political activists from Worcester at the convention. He introduced me to Diana, one of the three youngest sisters among thirteen siblings in the Roberson family, an African American Worcester family whose ancestors included indigenous Narragansett and Nipmuc peoples from Rhode Island and Massachusetts.

Many have written the history of that convention: how Fannie Lou Hamer's televised testimony captured the hearts of the Credentials Committee and the American people, how Lyndon Johnson exercised political muscle to force a so-called "compromise" to our demand that the Mississippi Freedom Democratic Party (MFDP) delegates replace the regular Mississippi Democratic Party delegates (who had already committed themselves to vote for Barry Goldwater, the Republican candidate for President!), how the MFDP delegates refused the compromise and made their way using credentials from sympathetic delegates to a demonstration on the convention floor. The cynicism of the Democratic Party's marginalization of the MFDP destroyed the intense optimism of Mississippi volunteers, and progressive activists throughout the country. It demonstrated for many of us the futility of working within the established political process, thereby radicalizing our analysis and our strategies. I lost faith in my own commitment to civic responsibility and came to adopt the revolutionary ideology of my Marxist parents' youth.

2

Returning Home and Starting a Family

IT WAS DIFFICULT TO return to Worcester and college. Months of living under constant mortal threat had taken their toll. My experience was analogous to that of a combat veteran returning to civilian society. I remember an incident a few days after traveling from Atlantic City to rejoin my family at our summer cabin in the Duxbury woods. My parents had gone into town, and I began to nap in a lounge chair outside. As I drifted off to sleep, I was bemused as I reflected on how this simple act would have been an unacceptable security risk in Mississippi. I was awakened from my sleep by my dog's barking. I saw a White man standing near me, and I froze with fear, vigilantly scanning the environment for further signs of threat, and preparing myself to defend my life. After a few seconds, which seemed to last forever, I recognized our neighbor from down the road and slowly returned to the present. Now out of an environment that required constant vigilance for survival, I realized in that incident just how deeply fear had become embedded in my being.

Returning to college was deeply alienating. None of my classmates, with the exception of D'Army and Hank Chaiklin (who had served in a far more dangerous region of Mississippi than had I that summer), could understand the complexity and intensity of my summer's experience. The unconsciousness of the casual White privilege of the sixties among my classmates was both visible and intolerable for me. I struggled with the traumatic residue of my aversion to White people, as I understood that I could not be responsible for my own White privilege if I did not master my visceral fear and anger toward White people unconscious of the advantages of their racial identity. D'Army's playful trick when we reconnected at Clark gave a measure of the intensity of my stress response. When he came up behind me in my dormitory and addressed me as "boy" in his Tennessee accent, I boiled with rage, turning to take on my adversary, now free of the constraints of nonviolence, only to discover my mentor and comrade.

I made some efforts to date women, but found it impossible to become emotionally available, until a party at Abbie Hoffman's house a couple of months into the fall. It was a going-away party for Diana Roberson, who was preparing to leave for the Holly Springs SNCC office where I had served in Mississippi. I had already met her younger sister Marsha, as Worcester Student Movement had expanded beyond our college student base to include members of the local African American community. At the party for Diana was Marsha and Diana's older sister Betty Ann, who had been invited by her younger sisters to come back from Boston to meet the civil rights hero returning from Mississippi. It was love at first sight for both of us.

Betty moved back to Worcester, and the two of us got to know each other as we engaged together in WSM community projects. We worked with the local CORE office, testing landlords for racial discrimination in housing. She would go to rent an apartment and be told that it was not available. I would follow later and be told that it was. The two of us would then make a third visit together, along with a CORE lawyer, to confront the landlord. I was struck by how often landlords would react with indignation, focusing on their feelings about being deceived rather than taking responsibility for their racial discrimination.

Our relationship quickly drew deeper. Outside of my circle of closest friends, the reactions of most Clark students who knew of our relationship ranged from criticism to hostility, not always concealed. Betty's family, particularly her siblings, challenged my emerging social skills as they tested me to see if I was genuinely respectful of their sister and to see if I understood what the two of us were up against as an interracial couple. As a member of the very small African American community in Worcester, Betty had spent most of her life around White students, friends, teachers, and coworkers. She was comfortable with her skills of "biculturation," navigating in White and African American contexts, "code-switching" between the discourses expected in each cultural context. I was eager to learn these skills, as I felt that there was no place for an important part of myself in White settings that maintained ignorance of the painful American reality of race. For all the challenges that I encountered, I felt more whole and grounded among her African American family and friends.

Paradoxically, finding a home in the African American world helped me shed the vestiges of post-Mississippi traumatic alienation from my White racial identity. In the White world, I struggled with the invisibility of racial reality. In the African American world, it was not possible to ignore my whiteness, highlighted as it was by my minority status in that setting. In both worlds, I learned to be comfortable standing at the margins, a position that had been so painful for me in childhood.

Before we married, I did ask Betty for one accommodation. I needed to know that she could be comfortable in the psychedelic culture, which was at the time for me the embodiment of my spiritual search. Once we took an LSD trip together, I was wholeheartedly committed to the relationship. Unfortunately, we also shared a taste for alcohol, both of us with strong genetic vulnerabilities to alcohol dependence, which was to emerge later as one of the factors in the unwinding of our marriage. At the time, however, it was just part of the joy of being in love and savoring the pleasures of youth.

We soon became engaged. Today, as a family therapist, I know that the decision to marry and start a family activates themes, issues, conflicts, and ghosts from each partner's family of origin. Betty and I had both grown up in families in which personal disagreements could evoke loud, painful arguments between spouses, fights that sometimes escalated out of control, resulting in deep relational injuries. Our engagement broke off at least once as a result of our own destructive arguments. We would find our way back to each other, determined to make a life together. Given our childhood experiences of family, we unquestioningly experienced our turbulence as part of normal family life.

Embodied in these arguments were genetic as well as relational intergenerational legacies of substance abuse and mood disorder. My difficulty managing my emotions increased as I entered young adulthood. Amplified by psychedelic drugs and alcohol, my moods alternated between grandiose aspirations to become a visionary and well-known psychologist and episodes of hopeless despair.

Despite my ADHD, melodramatic highs and lows, and the challenges of beginning a family while not yet fully adult, I managed to keep up with my studies enough to develop a reasonably firm grasp on my chosen field of psychology. My spirituality was both embodied and obscured by marijuana and psychedelic use, as I sensed and sought the universal beyond the limits of everyday experience. In expansive moods, I imagined myself developing unified theories of psychological experience.

Betty and I endured increasing hostility and verbal harassment from her family, who were deeply skeptical of our declared intention to marry. The historical legacy of White men sexually exploiting Black women powerfully influenced her family's belief that I was taking advantage of Betty and that we would never marry. Betty's oldest sibling was the offspring of her mother's relationship with a White man, and her pregnancy out of wedlock had estranged Betty's mother from her parents. Her mother warned Betty that I would abandon her after she had supported me through college. My parents showed more muted concerns about our plans, noting our immaturity and the volatility of our conflicts. They were silent about the racial difference, and I don't know if they were fully conscious of the racial element in their discomfort. Although I was financially dependent on them for college, I don't think that it entered my WASP parents' minds to try to control my decision about marriage.

Betty's siblings' hostility to our relationship became more overt during her mother's extended hospitalization for kidney disease. We decided to put a stop to their resistance by following through on our firm intention to marry. Rather than pit our families against each other by having only my family present at the wedding, we chose to elope. In front of two witnesses, my roommates from the apartment where I had been living, Betty and I were married by the Clark University Protestant chaplain in the furnished apartment we had rented that morning.

As we predicted, Betty's siblings' hostility subsided as soon as we married. Although her mother welcomed me into the family, she was hurt and angry that her daughter had not included her in planning a wedding. A little more than a year into our marriage, aware that Betty's mother was slowly dying from kidney failure, we decided to have a baby while she was still alive.

We named our son Ransom, a fairly common name in the American South that connected me with my formative time in Mississippi and which was also a family name with a lot of meaning for Betty's mother. Unfortunately, as an unusual name in the North, it was for him to become a source of taunting from childhood peers. Betty's mother's mother was Nancy Ransom, the daughter of Willard Ransom, understood from family lore to have been a full-blood member of the Narragansett, indigenous people of the New England region. Ransom won his maternal grandmother's heart and healed the rift between his mother and grandmother, who nonetheless remained pessimistic to the end about our future. On occasions when she would care for her grandson Ransom, she would be seen rocking him in her arms, crooning, "Poor Rannie, poor Rannie."

I learned indirectly of mutterings among Clark students of our "selfishness" for having a child. We could make foolish decisions about our own personal lives, went the complaint, but we had no right to bring a mixed-race child into the world. The center of my social world having moved from college to the Roberson clan, I was unmoved by the hateful rumors.

Betty and I managed our racial difference in direct and open conversation. Having begun our relationship in the context of the race-conscious Civil Rights Movement, we were tuned to race as a dimension of our relationship and talked about it freely. When I would commit racial microaggressions, unwitting injuries emerging from my position of racial privilege, Betty would call me out. I would see what I had done and be accountable to her for doing it; we would do the necessary relational repair and move on. My performances of gender privilege were less visible to us; neither of us had developed critical consciousness in this domain. The biggest acculturation challenge for me was learning about class.

Although many of the people I recruited into the Mississippi Freedom Democratic Party were impoverished, and although I had some familiarity with class as a Marxist construct, I was ignorant when it came to joining a working-class family. My own experience of class was somewhat anomalous, as the descendant of many generations of parish ministers. Protestant ministers tend to have quite modest incomes, but their social positions take them beyond the limits of their financial means. They often live in parsonages, substantial homes owned by the church parish. They often are well-educated. With the privilege afforded by their social positions, they spend time with the ruling elite of the community in which they live, cultivating donors to their church from the congregation and from leaders in their community.

This tradition had shaped my father's childhood experience, although he himself left parish ministry when I was three years old. Despite my parents' Marxist history, my birth family fashioned ourselves as struggling to maintain our position in the middle class. Our location near the bottom of the wealth distribution in the suburban communities where my parents chose to raise their children amplified the family's sense of relative material deprivation, as did the legacies of downward mobility from early paternal bereavement in my father's and my maternal great-grandmother's childhoods.

There was a different understanding of wealth in Betty's extended family. When I entered her family, most of the adults who did have jobs lived paycheck to paycheck. Members of the Roberson clan felt blessed by our rich relationships with each other, gathering informally to socialize at each others' homes. Most of Betty's older siblings had their own children; one had a son who was a few years older than his Aunt Betty. Ransom's arrival secured our status as a couple in the clan. Coming from a small family with parents who themselves came from small families, I was enormously grateful to join the extended Roberson clan. I am now Uncle David to more than thirty of Betty's nieces and nephews, their children and grandchildren.

Even before Ransom was born, Betty and I struggled to make ends meet. I did janitorial work and dishwashing at the college and drove a taxi. Betty, a high school graduate who was trained as a secretary, took and left a series of jobs, telling me years later that she had not wanted to fulfill her mother's prediction that I would exploit her to support me through college. Despite our financial struggles and our occasional intense arguments, we were deeply in love with each other, and with Ransom.

I learned a dramatic lesson about class when Betty and I had somehow succeeded at accumulating close to one hundred dollars of surplus above what we needed for food, rent, and bills. I was stunned when I returned home one day to learn that Betty had given the money to her younger sister. She was as surprised by my reaction as I was by her action. Her sister, after all, needed the money! I learned that, in poor families, the good fortune of one household is potentially the good fortune of all. Uncertainty about the economic future, and financial emergencies in the clan, contribute to the value that families are obligated to help each other out. The assumption that any surplus anywhere in the clan can be drawn on in emergency assures survival in circumstances of scarcity. It also creates challenges for the social mobility of individual households in the network.

Experiences at the class boundary and disillusionment with the American liberalism that had sold out the Mississippi Freedom Democratic Party contributed to my increasing interest in the Marxism of my parental legacy. The American coalition of progressive African American and White activists was dissolving with the emergence of Black nationalism, itself partly a reaction to White microaggressions in the old coalition. The Black Panther Party was emerging as a Marxist alternative to nationalism. Although its membership was restricted to African Americans, it was not an Afrocentric nationalist party. Her younger sisters Diana and Marsha joined the party, and Betty and I found meaningful roles as party supporters.

The late sixties and early seventies were a difficult time to be politically progressive. Internal dysfunction and government repression combined to restrict the power of the American Left. Loss of momentum in the struggle for African American liberation generated frustrated anger and deep disappointment. Betty and I were not alone at that time in fearing that White society might try to deal with the challenge of African American resistance to the status quo by drawing on the recent historical example of Germany's brutal efforts to exterminate the Jews. This was not an unreasonable fear, given that the Nazis modeled their policies of racial subjugation on US racial segregation.

We were deeply concerned about the present and future vulnerability of our child. In 1967, the year of Ransom's birth, our interracial marriage was illegal in sixteen states. The racial discourse in the country at that time dictated that Ransom would be identified as Black. Through the lens of the present, our fear nearly fifty years ago that the government could load trains with dispossessed African Americans to carry them to concentration camps may seem absurd. At the time, however, we were well aware that less than thirty years before, the government had shipped Japanese Americans to concentration camps, ethnically cleansing the West Coast of America.

We decided on a plan to protect our family. I would go to graduate school at Harvard University, where I had obtained a comparative international scholarship. We would go to live in the newly independent country of Nigeria, where I would study traditional healing in its village context. In addition to providing safety for our family, the plan offered me a way to expand my understanding of spirituality through studies of tribal shamanism.

After my graduation from Clark University, we moved from Worcester to an African American neighborhood of Boston, a few blocks away from Betty's sister Gwendolyn. Looking out Ransom's bedroom window, we could see the house where the young Malcolm X had lived with his aunt. I took two trains from our home to Cambridge and William James Hall at Harvard, where I studied clinical and comparative international psychology in the Department of Social Relations, an interdisciplinary home for sociology, social and clinical psychology, and anthropology. The integrative spirit of the Department resonated for me with my expansive ambition to construct theory embracing all the complexity of human experience.

Stimulating as the intellectual atmosphere was, I developed strong feelings of alienation in what I had hoped would become my academic home. The racial composition of faculty and student body, and the discourses that organized their endeavors, made my experiences of race and radical political activism at best marginal, for the most part invisible. My feelings of estrangement were amplified by daily travel, as my experience of whiteness transformed from my racial minority status in the community where I lived into acute awareness of the stranger and outsider status of the relatively few people of color I encountered in Cambridge's Harvard Square. I did not at the time recognize the echo of my racial discomfort as a teenager on the bus traveling through multiracial Englewood, New Jersey.

Ransom was less than a year old when we moved to Boston. The blessings and challenges of building a new family, the demands of academic study, and the complexities of race felt all-absorbing. With no reflective understanding of my ADHD, it was hard for me to make sense of why I felt so overwhelmed by the rigorous demands of graduate study. I had little awareness of my life in the present as embodying a spiritual journey, except in speculation about a vague future in Africa, where I would learn from spiritual healers in tribal village settings. It felt impossible to experience myself as the activist who had risked his life in Mississippi or to pick up the thread of my spiritual search. History intervened powerfully in the spring of my first year in graduate school, confronting me with these neglected dimensions of my life.

MADNESS

It is the spring of 1968. I am sitting in the dark, in the living room of our home in an African American neighborhood of Boston. I have gone without sleep for several days now, as I work on the urgent project of healing a world torn asunder by the murder of Reverend Doctor Martin Luther King. The architecture of my consciousness, somehow holding the contradictions of my life together enough to allow me to go on, has been ruptured by the recording of Dr. King's voice, speaking the day before his death, a recording that has played over and over again in the news. I hear in his voice not just passion but foreknowledge and acceptance of what is to happen, grounded in his living relationship with God:

> Like anybody, I would like to live a long life. Longevity has its place. But I'm not concerned about that now. I just want to do God's will. And He's allowed me to go up to the mountain. And I've looked over. And I've seen the Promised Land. I may not get there with you. But I want you to know tonight, that we, as a people, will get to the Promised Land! And so, I'm happy, tonight. I'm not worried about anything. I'm not fearing any man! And so, I'm happy, tonight. Mine eyes have seen the glory of the coming of the Lord![1]

Hearing those words in that voice, over and over again on radio and television, and resonating in my heart, I cannot go on as before. I had left Mississippi reluctantly at the end of the Freedom Summer to continue my studies in the North. My African American wife Betty and I, dreading the murderous potential of the White power structure in the United States, planned for me to start my career in Africa, to escape what we feared would be a genocidal turn in American racial politics.

It has been a difficult year for us. The gulf between our family life, absorbed in the rich, intimate, often tumultuous web of relationships with Betty's twelve siblings and their households—and the White world of graduate school at Harvard—has been difficult to traverse. It has been difficult and painful to navigate differences of race, class, and education between family and school.

The loss of Dr. King feels intolerable, as does the contrast between the raw anguish in my home community, disrupted by disorganized collective expressions of rage and pain, and the relatively undisturbed atmosphere of the community where I pursue my studies. I also have to come to terms with what for me demonstrates Dr. King's awesome power of access to the Divine, foreseeing and coming to terms with his own death through his relationship with God. I can no longer assure myself that my decision to refuse the call to ministry is final.

As I sit with my mind racing, the room slowly darkening at sunset and filling with light at sunrise, the picture on the wall shifts. It is a poster of Malcolm X preaching, his finger raised, before a microphone. As the

---

1. Carson and Shepard, 222–23.

room darkens, the glasses on Malcolm's face evoke the glasses on my father's face, and the face becomes the likeness of my father. The resolution of all the contradictions with which I struggle emerges. I will organize the Boston Center for the Liberation of Revolutionary Consciousness, which will prepare a new cohort of activists for justice and civil rights. I am conscious that I am in an altered state of mind. I am not yet aware that I am going mad.

Having fashioned myself as too radical to take what I saw as Dr. King's gradualism seriously, I was completely unprepared for the enormous disruption that his murder would precipitate in my life. Confronted by what appeared to me to be prophetic knowledge of his future murder, I had to reengage with my suppressed ambivalence about my occasional experiences of the call to ministry, which I understood as echoes of the calls that had come to so many paternal ancestors. All the confusion and pain in my efforts to make it in the White academic world became unendurable. I was consumed with determination to make everything somehow fit into a coherent whole. I would finish the academic semester while organizing a program analogous to the training that the National Council of Churches had sponsored for the Mississippi Freedom Summer volunteers. The Boston Center for the Liberation of Revolutionary Consciousness would prepare a multiracial cohort of progressive activists to support Black community liberation and confront a repressive government, thwarting its hidden intention to incarcerate the Black population in concentration camps. I would also take preliminary steps toward moving our young family to Nigeria.

My own turmoil resonated with the turbulence in the world around me. In reaction to the King assassination, insurrectionary riots were emerging in cities throughout the country. In the Black community of Boston where I lived with my family, angry mobs were burning and looting local businesses. I stayed off the street whenever not commuting to school. I was challenged only once, by a group of youths, one of whom called out, "Do you live here?" I said that I did. His peers dissolved in laughter as another called out, "You're moving tomorrow, right?"

Local efforts to organize the community heightened the atmosphere of crisis. Here were some of the alarms raised in a broadsheet handed out on the streets by the Black United Front:

> It's unsafe for White people to move and do business within and throughout the Black community ... *can you survive? Next time They* will turn off all utilities, gas, water lights, phone *and plan*

> to murder *All Black People* . . . When the riot starts, you can expect Martial Law, which will confine you to your home for as long as a month or more. Start your survival plans *Now!* . . . *non-violence is dead—April 4, 1968—the Black community faces disaster* . . . *We must unite now for the attacks on our communities from the police, armed forces, and the White communities. Survival is no plaything.*

Most of the responses in the White community to the King assassination struck me as helpless hand-wringing. At a gathering of concerned professionals at a Boston teaching hospital, I learned of a Black psychiatrist, Dr. Alvin Poussaint, practicing in a public mental health agency in the Black community. I arranged to meet with him and begin brainstorming about a multiracial training program for activists to address the national racial crisis.

Increasing feelings of urgency slipped insidiously into mania. I was in the grip of another call to ministry, which I decided I would address by somehow becoming a "lay minister." I started recruiting a White caucus to organize efforts to establish the Boston Center for the Liberation of Revolutionary Consciousness. I approached Wesley Profit of Phillips Brooks House, a student nonprofit service agency at Harvard that was getting engaged with social justice activism, and he agreed to start organizing a Black Caucus, with the intention that we would bring the two caucuses together to build the center. There was a contemporaneous surge in Boston of hippie culture, and I visited a couple of "be-ins" on the Boston Common, acquiring an Ankh, an Egyptian symbol of life, which I started wearing on a loop around my neck. My fellow graduate students and I having spent the year observing an undergraduate self-analytic training group from behind a one-way mirror, I engaged a couple of junior faculty members in my department to work with the caucus to bring the small-group training model to the center.

I wrote a detailed proposal for the center, which I sent to the local office of the Southern Christian Leadership Conference. The proposal itself tried to bring everything together. Funded by Christian and Jewish religious organizations, the Boston Center for Liberation of Revolutionary Consciousness would be "an orientation center fulfilling the functions of Freedom School, a religious retreat, a national Movement strategy center (Local, if not enough interest in national), a center for the communication and dissemination of information, and a collective corrective emotional experience." It would recruit countercultural hippies and White and Black social activists into training for social activism. Small-group training experiences would address the issue of racism as both a target and as an obstacle to progressive activism. At the end of the summer training, the staff of the center would occupy one of the empty detention camps that were being maintained by the federal government to detain "subversives" under the McCarran Act, the Emergency Detention Act, Title II of the Internal Security Act of 1950. (Paranoid though I was, the law was on the books at the time, and the detention camps existed.) I wrote, "If the polarizations in American society rigidify and create a sufficient threat of civil war, it will not be enough to imprison black leaders. White radical members of the Movement and nonviolent revolutionaries will bring the society to a standstill if such an attempt is made, and the camps will not be able to hold their numbers."

I convened a couple of White Caucus meetings, one of them attended by my professor, Regina Sunny Yando. I met with Canon James Breeden, executive director of the Massachusetts Council of Churches, where my father had served years before as research director, to enlist support for the center. As the scope of my manic activities expanded, I met at the Harvard School of Public Health with Alexander Leighton, author with Thomas Lambo of an epidemiological study of schizophrenia in Nigeria, to talk of my plans for a future career in Nigeria, embedded, of course, in my expansive design to solve every social problem simultaneously.

I had two major papers to write by the end of the semester, each of which became part of my grand effort to address everything at once. I invented a method of "self-confrontation," through which I gave myself permission to make my own internal experience the domain to explore in the papers. Reading one of those papers more than fifty years later, I see a mind in the grip of psychosis that is also seeking to articulate its experience of the Divine:

> I have lost track of the number of days since the paper was started, partially because I have traced its origin to my senior year in high school, and partially because in the process of writing the paper I have gone from sunrise to sunset without sleep. I have been able to suspend time experientially both in order to deal with my crisis and in order to abstract the notion of development from the context of existential time . . . I have come to the self-analytic conclusion that God is within me, and that God's growth is my own growth . . . What I wish to contribute . . . is the notion of threat as it operates through the timeless confrontation with God

> ... These anxieties come to achieve the magnitude of the archaic threats of merging and annihilation, which are received in a new conception of God in the call to vocation. From this crisis, for me emerges the notion of an internal God which determines my self as my self determines it ... The temporal order of life events can be taken as independent of the developmental organization of religious life. Further, the individual personality system at any moment in time contains its entire developmental history. Thus, it is possible for me to "predict the future" and organize my life and work accordingly ...

I began to encounter the helplessness, prejudice, and objectification with which professionals who are entrusted with their care regard the mentally ill. As their student descended publicly into madness, my clinical psychology professors were for the most part uncomfortably silent. The faculty who were not specialists in clinical psychology were more direct. My research mentor, David McClelland, criticized what he saw as my unrealistic plans. Don McNamee, a sociologist and my comparative international studies professor, told me of his telephone conversation with Alexander Leighton, who had called Don after meeting with me at the School of Public Health and had expressed concern about my mental stability. Unlike most of my psychology professors, Don was transparent and respectful. He told me what Dr. Leighton had said, without taking a position himself, respecting me to make my own sense of the feedback.

Sunny Yando was, fortunately, the exception among the clinical faculty. She had attended a meeting of the White Caucus and had observed how I was becoming increasingly grandiose and unrealistic. She was well aware that I was not keeping up with my academic responsibilities. Gently but firmly, she helped me to take an objective look at my situation, and at how my actions were increasingly erratic, irrational, and inappropriate. I had been unable to keep up with my studies, the papers that I wrote being useless for the purpose of academic credit. My course grades at the end of the semester were two incompletes, an absent, and a B-. The Committee on Higher Degrees instructed me to withdraw and get treatment. I was permitted to return in the future, provided that I secured a recommendation from a clinical professional.

Sunny Yando and Milton Kotelchuck, a classmate whom I trusted because of his politics, helped me find my way to treatment. I had an intake interview at Massachusetts Mental Health Center, the premier state mental hospital and a Harvard teaching hospital, but did not follow through after the interview. They had offered to admit me to their day hospital program, where I had already scheduled an appointment later that week to gather data for the research that I was doing for David McClelland. The prospect was too humiliating, particularly as I knew that McClelland, who had in our correspondence been blunt in his criticism of my grandiose plans for the summer, would soon return from traveling.

By the time that Sunny and Milt were helping me to seek treatment, I was fully aware that I was going crazy. That awareness, and the enormity of my enforced departure from Harvard, led me deeper into psychosis, which offered a refuge from the painful reality of the wreck that I had made of my life. As delusional as I was becoming, and as cryptic and incoherent my verbal utterances, I never lost a certain clarity of mind in observing what was going on within me. Having failed at standard academic research, I embarked on a project of "researching" the phenomenology of my own psychosis. Although I did have a somewhat shapeless dread of violent retribution by "the establishment" for my political activism, my delusions for the most part created a world in which everyone was particularly kind and well-disposed toward me, a sort of benign paranoia. This stance was particularly helpful in my encounters with strangers, as my dramatic intensity and assumption of abundant good will were usually met with kindness and appreciation. My speech often had a semi-poetic quality, as I sought to convey the overflowing intensity and deep meaning that I was experiencing. A lifetime of ambivalent searching and years of exploring altered states with psychedelic drugs had prepared me to recognize in my psychosis the intense, almost incandescent spiritual quality of each passing moment.

At that time, the Massachusetts Department of Mental Health divided the geography of the state into "catchment areas." The catchment area of my neighborhood was served by Boston State Hospital in the Mattapan section of Boston. In local slang, being admitted to Boston State was called "going up to Mattapan." I was interviewed at a staff intake meeting on the May Unit of that hospital and left for home having promised that I would return for admission, explaining that my decision was based on my belief that "May Unit" means "thou has permission." An earnest young nursing student pursued me into the hall to tell me "that's not what it means!" I assured her that I knew that. Playing with language, and with people's heads, was a way of feeling some mastery in a situation that was in so many ways beyond my control.

I included three books in the bag that I packed for the hospital: Nikos Kazantzakis's memoir, *Report to Greco*; an anonymous Eastern Orthodox Christian's testament of his spiritual search, *The Way of a Pilgrim*; and Erving Goffman's classic ethnomethodological text, *The Presentation of Self in Everyday Life*—two texts for my spiritual search and one for my "research" on the interpersonal dynamics of the mental hospital. Reading Kazantzakis's *Modern Sequel to the Odyssey* had been an important milestone on my spiritual search in high school; his memoir's account of his evolving understanding of God as a human spiritual creation can be seen in the language of the expansive paper that I had written for graduate school. My imagination had been captured by the practice of "ceaseless prayer" described in *The Way of a Pilgrim*, and I was struggling to master it, not recognizing at the time its resonation with my compulsive childhood efforts to pray.

I had already studied Goffman's work and was fascinated by his metaphor of interpersonal behavior as performance. Even as I was experiencing intense internal disorganization, and knew that I was crazy, I was equally aware that I was performing the craziness that I was experiencing—and, as a performer, had some control in a situation that otherwise filled me with helplessness and confusion. Once I was "in the zone" of intense spiritual awareness and mindful presentation of self, I was able somehow to go on. I got on a regular municipal bus to make my way "up to Mattapan," a bearded, unkempt young White man wearing an ankh and a plastic bear's tooth on lanyards around my neck, expecting and receiving benign and loving reception from Black fellow passengers as a harmless Holy Fool. Later, deeper into my psychosis, I was to say, "Nobody drove me crazy. I took a bus." Puzzled by my experience of mental clarity even while fully aware that I was psychotic, I would say, "I did not lose my mind—I lost my self."

I was both desperate and wary with the psychiatric resident in the intake interview. I wanted not to be objectified and was determined to engage in authentic conversation as an equal. I needed to meet criteria for admission, even as I did not want to render invisible my intense spiritual crisis. I took out my copy of *Report to Greco* and read the lines at the beginning of Kazantzakis's memoir: "Three kinds of souls, three prayers: '1) I am a bow in your hands, Lord. Draw me, lest I rot. 2) Do not overdraw me, Lord. I shall break. 3) Overdraw me, Lord, and who cares if I break!'" I made it clear that I considered myself to have the third kind of soul.[31]

I don't know what the resident made of me as a person, but I succeeded in getting myself admitted, diagnosed with an "acute schizophrenic episode" (schizophrenia at that time being the favored diagnosis for anyone showing delusional thinking). I was prescribed a large dose of the antipsychotic drug Thorazine, to which I had a "paradoxical reaction"—that is, my psychotic symptoms became more florid in response to the medication. Plunging deeper into madness intensified my feelings of the presence of the Divine. I experienced the Divine in every person I encountered, which evoked reciprocal experiences of awe and love in response. I stood out as a White middle-class graduate student in a state hospital ward whose catchment area included Black neighborhoods of Roxbury and the White neighborhood of South Boston and whose patients were predominantly poor and working class.

Writing more than fifty years later, I am struck by the visceral quality of my memories of the hospital. It was a hot summer. We lived in close quarters with dormitories for men and for women, and those of us who had not yet earned "privileges" spent the day together in a common day room, except when we were herded to the hot dining room, where we sweltered while we waited to be fed. I remember the powerful, regressive feeling of dependence on the staff as all the decisions about where to be and what to do were made for my fellow patients and me. I remember chanting and singing and holding my urine during an overnight stay in an isolation room, to which I had been confined after my intense flow of speech was deemed to be too disruptive. I soon learned to play the game to avoid involuntary confinement and to get freedom of movement on the hospital grounds.

I did have a couple of realistic grounds for my sense of a benign universe looking out for me. One of the nursing assistants on the ward was a distant relative by marriage. This kinship relationship allowed me fairly free access to the nursing station, and I was able to read about Thorazine in the Physician's Desk Reference (PDR). Although no one registered that I was having a paradoxical reaction to my medication, I was able to figure out from the PDR that Thorazine was suppressing my anxiety. I correctly identified access to my anxiety as necessary for me to restore my grip on reality and persuaded my psychiatrist to lower my dosage substantially. I had gone to the same college at the same time as Larry Allman, the psychologist for the ward who had some influence over decisions. Larry was perhaps influenced by the countercultural psychiatrist R. D. Laing. He embraced a perspective on young patients in their first psychotic break as going through a developmental crisis rather than as embarking on a career of chronic mental illness. Thanks to Larry's influence, I did not have to wrestle as much with disqualifying messages from the staff as I soared on flights of grandiose delusion.

After a couple of weeks on a reduced dose of medication, the fire in my soul began to burn out. I had been wrestling with the text of *The Way of a Pilgrim*, and I could not see how to master the practice of praying without ceasing. Sitting on the screened-in porch on the third floor of the May Unit, I resolved instead to make my life itself a ceaseless prayer.

Like the awesome command to make God's work my responsibility when I was nine years old, the decision to make my life a ceaseless prayer was profoundly formative for the course of my life. Just as with the first experience, it was sequestered far from immediate consciousness, even as it shaped who and how I was to become as a spiritual being. The first memory was lost in the traumatic shattering of my spirit; the second was buried under the painful depression that I would experience shortly after I reentered the world of sanity.

I recovered enough to leave the regressive environment of the hospital and return home to Betty and Ransom. I did not yet feel secure enough to do without the hospital's support, particularly the daily community meeting in the day room, so I made my way from home to the hospital for community meetings for the next couple of weeks. The social worker on the ward noted in my discharge summary:

> During his stay the patient pretty much made his own rules as to how he should be treated . . . After he began to become more lucid in conversation, he took it upon himself to go home evenings and yet managed pretty well. His wife and friends indicated that they were very much pleased with the patient's recovery, and the wife was glad to have the patient stay at home evenings. The patient also agreed at this time that it was very important for him, although he was going home, to come back for ward meetings.

I was finally discharged with a prescription for Mellaril, a different antipsychotic medicine, and an appointment for a staff conference at which I would be assigned a psychiatric resident for outpatient psychotherapy.

So, how do I now, as a clinical psychologist with over fifty years' experience in my profession, make sense of the psychosis as a clinical phenomenon? After this episode, I never had another psychosis. That, and several other factors, rule out the diagnosis of schizophrenia, a diagnosis that at the time was generously (and dangerously) handed out for many young adults with delusional symptoms. The struggles with moods that plagued me before and after the psychosis until I was to master the Chinese energy practice of Chi Gong years later, offer suggestive evidence that I was in an acute manic psychosis. Mood disorders run strongly through my genetic line; my late aunt and my late brother were both diagnosed with bipolar disorder.

Weeks before I began decompensating, I had smoked marijuana treated with diethyl tryptamine (DET), chemically related to dimethyl tryptamine (DMT). DET was not as widely used as was its psychedelic cousin DMT, probably because of DET's neurotoxic properties. Perhaps that was a precipitant of the psychosis, as were the stresses of my complex identity crisis. For myself, I have settled on the vague diagnosis of "atypical psychosis," a term that has been superceded in psychiatric manuals by the equally vague "unspecified psychosis." As a family therapist, I am not invested in the diagnostic nomenclature of the psychiatry profession, which I find both reductionist and objectifying. Certainly, no clinical diagnosis could capture the intense developmental spiritual crisis, nor explain how my decision to make my life a ceaseless prayer helped me to restore my sanity.

One outcome of my experience was intense anger at the mental health professions. I was now saddled with a profoundly stigmatizing diagnosis. With the exception of Sunny, most faculty members at the graduate school that sent me into exile had not engaged with me authentically as a human being struggling with a confusing and frightening personal crisis. Today, we have the "Open Dialogue" approach of my Finnish colleague Jaakko Seikkula, which effectively prevents or interrupts incipient psychosis through authentic and respectful engagement.[32] Then, as now, most mental health professionals avoid authentic engagement, inadvertently contributing to rather than preventing the emergence of psychosis. Although I did not have this language to explain it, I knew intuitively that the clinicians who were training me had abandoned me.

The physical deprivations and personal indignities of life in a state mental hospital sent a profound message about how little society valued my fellow mental patients and me. The teaching conference following my discharge, at which I was assigned an outpatient therapist, was profoundly humiliating. The enormity of my life situation, with no assurance that I could ever return to graduate school and faced with emotional and financial responsibility for my young family, precipitated a profound depression, without a vestige of delusional escape or spiritual sensibility.

When psychotic, I had often spoken of my doing "research," playing with the word as meaning "to search again and again." Now no longer psychotic, and in enormous emotional pain, I encountered the consequences of a hospital discharge summary's allegation that I had come from home to community meetings because I felt them "quite profitable and also quite important to carry on his research that he was doing in psychology department at school." That was nonsense; by the time that I was coming to community meetings from home I was no longer delusional and certainly not claiming to be carrying on the failed task of serving as David McClelland's research assistant. Smiling, in the presence of the psychiatry residents and staff, the attending psychiatrist opened his interview with me by saying, "I understand that you have been conducting research."

I was humiliated and enraged, both by his patronizing tone and by the profound misattunement. From his first words, he showed that he had no idea of my experience. Having sat as a student on the other side in such teaching conferences, I knew that I was being offered as an "interesting case," a young man with a bemusing delusion that his psychosis was a kind of research project. Coldly, I replied that I had no such idea, knew why I had been hospitalized, and that my purpose for participating in the conference was to get a therapist. While I felt that I had preserved my self-respect when I was admitted to the hospital, I felt that my petitioning to be assigned a therapist was at the cost of being stripped of my dignity.

RETURNING TO THE WORLD OF THE SANE

Fortunately, Robert Tufo, the psychiatry resident assigned to my treatment, was respectful and supportive. I needed all the help I could get. I took the bus to meet him at the hospital, at first several times a week. To support my family, I drove a taxi six days a week. I reconnected with my young son Ransom and with the adults and children of the Roberson clan. Betty showed a new reserve, which I attributed to her fear that I might again be caught in the grip of psychosis, a fear that I understood and shared.

Years later, when we acknowledged that our marriage was over, I learned that the social worker at Boston State Hospital had told Betty that I had a serious, chronic mental illness—that I would always be profoundly disabled and would probably have multiple episodes of psychosis. She acknowledged that the conversation with the social worker had irreversibly removed her confidence that we could share a future as partners. Although we continued to love each other, her unspoken and unacknowledged loss of confidence was one of the factors that eroded our marriage over time, and, in the year after my hospitalization, contributed to my profound feelings of loneliness and depression.

Broken, and afraid of a recurrence of psychosis, I sought to reduce risk by constricting my life and my aspirations. We discarded the plan to leave for Africa, settling for the modest goal of my finishing graduate school and getting established as a clinical psychologist. I avoided exploration of spirituality, for fear of again becoming captured by grandiosity. I never again took psychedelic drugs, although I continued to smoke marijuana. Drinking alcohol and smoking weed became means to get through life, rather than instruments for spiritual search. Raising Ransom remained a source of joy and helped Betty and me to connect with community. We struggled to restore closeness and trust in our marriage that had been ruptured by my personal and vocational crisis.

Although psychotherapy supported me in my struggle to go on, I was deeply depressed. Decades later, I vividly remember my standing in the subway station on my way home from a long day driving a taxi, comforting myself with the promise that, when I could find my way out of the depths of my mood, I would throw myself in front of a train. I had already learned enough therapist lore to know that suicidal risk can increase when patients emerge from the immobilizing depths of depression. Reflecting now on that memory, I do not consider my promise as representing truly dangerous suicidal intention. I think that I was telling myself a story for future recollection about the depth and intensity of my pain at that moment in my life. I was too grounded in my relationships with son, wife, and extended family to seriously consider such a brutal abandonment. Remembering the story does indeed help me recall my pain at that moment. With that recall, and with reflection from a very different perspective, I can see how the promise that I was giving myself offered brief respite from the pain, by allowing me to imagine its cessation.

A year later, when it was time to apply for return to graduate school, I proved to be ready. We had moved out of the Black neighborhood of Boston, partly because of concern over potential danger to a crazy White man in a Black community inflamed by loss and injustice. We found a place in Somerville a short walk away from classes in Cambridge. I went through the ritual of assessment by a psychologist associated with my department, who declared me both psychologically prepared and also a potential contributor to the academic program.

By the time I returned to school, I was still vulnerable to moods but within safe limits. My career aspirations remained limited, but my outspoken and energetic personal style was restored. I was still pissed off at the profession that I was getting trained to join and was not reticent about my outrage. Coincident with my return to graduate school was the emergence of *The Radical Therapist*, a journal whose radical critique of the psychotherapy profession resonated with my own. My teachers and peers were challenged to deal with me as I was, angry and transparent about my recent encounter with psychiatric hospitalization.

I found it hard to swallow what I had to learn to become a clinical psychologist. Research on psychotherapy was in its early stages and not at all encouraging. Psychotherapy outcome research had stagnated since the review published by Eysenck in the early 1950s, which concluded that the only solid evidence of the effects of psychotherapy suggested that it could be harmful![33] At training sites, senior clinicians appeared less concerned with whether or not their interventions actually worked than with the fidelity of their interventions to their theoretical models. It appeared that, in the face of helplessness about effectively treating suffering patients, there were two "religions" at the time, psychoanalysis and behaviorism, which served to reassure practitioners that they were doing the right thing.

Psychoanalysis was the more mystifying of the two religions; one was discouraged from testing its claims unless one was thoroughly inducted into its practice through undergoing its procedures. Once analyzed, of course, one had a vested interest believing in a practice into which one had invested so much money, time, and energy. Psychoanalysis had in its favor enough theoretical depth to take on the complexity of human experience but claimed that its very complexity was too much for it to be fairly tested by existing models of empirical research.

Behaviorism, in contrast, was theoretically sparse and mechanistic, with no room for exploring mental or emotional experience. Although behaviorists did do research on their work (which always showed that it worked!), there was little attention to the theoretical biases of the researchers, themselves behaviorists. Moreover, the strict control of variables in their experimental conditions produced studies depicting unrealistic life scenarios. They did not account for the messy complexities of life and multiple overlapping psychological difficulties experienced by people suffering mental illness.

I was excited to learn about the emerging upstart practice of family therapy. Having had studied von Bertalanffy's general systems theory as an undergraduate, I was thrilled to discover that family therapy was grounded in systems theory, which offered a far less mystifying way to understand complex phenomena than was offered by psychoanalysis.[34]

Working with families was more consistent with my socialist sensibilities than working with individuals. What really sold me was that family therapists matter-of-factly either videotaped their work and distributed it for training purposes to professional audiences, or met with families and did their work live in front of professional audiences. Rather than relying on claims based on reports by practitioners about their work, I could see the work for myself.

Moments when classroom discussion turned from family therapy to "network therapy," however, dampened my enthusiasm. Network therapy, or social network intervention, expands family therapy's systemic perspective to include family networks, personal communities beyond the boundaries of the family household, including everyone who cares about a family problem: kin, friends, neighbors, clergy and other professional helpers, workmates, fellow members of religious congregations, etc.[35] At the moment I first encountered the idea, it resonated too much for me with two paths that I had renounced. The idea of engaging with families' networks felt to me like the pastoral care of parish ministry, while full-scale assemblies of family networks evoked the African tribal village healing practices that I had once dreamed of studying.

Returning to graduate school after sharing the status of mental patient with so many African Americans at the May Unit, and after driving a taxi in the African American neighborhoods where I had been living, I found myself even more uncomfortable with the hegemony of the unconscious discourse of whiteness at Harvard. Fearing a resurgence of grandiosity, I had deliberately constricted my aspiration to make unique, expansive, and comprehensive contributions to the discourse of my chosen profession. I felt deep spiritual despair about the course of my future professional life. When Afro-Caribbean Guy Seymour showed up at a seminar, recruiting for an innovative training at Boston City Hospital, I leapt at this possible opportunity for redemption.

Guy, the scion of a powerful family from the former British colony of Guyana, while still a graduate student in clinical psychology at Boston University, was already challenging the racial insensitivity of the White male psychoanalytic establishment in Boston. In a meeting at Boston City Hospital, Guy had publicly criticized the psychology service for its racial blindness. The director, A. Michael Rossi, the socialist son of an impoverished Italian immigrant family, responded with the challenge, "Put your money where your mouth is. Come work for me!" Over the indignant objections of many in Boston's White psychiatric establishment, who believed the standard psychoanalytic model to be suited to all classes and races, Guy began to design a training model specifically for service to poor and working-class populations of color.

I was blessed to be in the right place at the right time when he began recruiting students to train in a prototype for his training program. I was able to start my clinical training in a practicum at Boston City Hospital under Guy's supervision, staying on for a second year in a part-time unpaid internship. As I negotiated treatment alliances with African American patients, I learned to draw on skills developed as a White man in Mississippi recruiting African Americans for the Freedom Democratic Party. Training at Boston City Hospital revitalized my aspiration to become a clinical psychologist.

My experience at Boston City Hospital also made the prospect of becoming a family therapist more real. White psychiatrist and family therapist Norman Paul (now recognized as among the first generation of family therapists) participated actively in psychiatry department staff meetings. He extended an open invitation to observe his multiple family therapy group at his home office. I spent many nights sitting in the observation room, with its full wall of one-way mirrors that allowed me to see him and his co-therapist working with four of five families sitting together, supporting each other as they explored how their family problems had been shaped by unexamined losses.

The following year, I began a full-time paid psychology internship at the Boston Veterans Administration Hospital. Psychology interns were on the admission rotation with the psychiatric residents. When our turn came, we had full charge of a patient's treatment from admission to discharge. I got to do family and group work in addition to individual therapy. Boston luminaries provided consultation and group supervision. John Pearce, one of the first family therapists to explore ethnicity in family therapy, provided group consultation on family therapy. I had the privilege of being in a self-analytic training group with the legendary psychoanalyst Elvin Semrad.

I was not equally impressed by all the luminaries. The psychologists had group supervision with a widely recognized, psychoanalytically oriented psychologist from Boston University. About halfway through the year, I decided to switch out of his supervision group in order to schedule a block of time to learn from Stanley Slivkin, a staff psychiatrist whose unorthodox, vigorous, and direct approach in the Day Hospital appeared to be particularly effective reaching patients with severe character disorders. I made a fairly bold, unilateral reconfiguration of my training schedule, and it earned me an interview with Ralph Fingar, the chief of the psychology service. He was respectful and curious about my decision, which he did not countermand. At one point, he asked me if I saw myself as an "impatient" person. Although I had been transparent with Guy about my psychiatric history, I had chosen to keep silent about it at the VA, where I did not want the stigma to interfere with my training. All my concerns about being known as a former psychiatric patient got activated when he asked me if I saw myself as an "impatient" person. I misheard him as saying "inpatient" rather than "impatient." I recognized my error after I told him that I saw myself as working with outpatients as well as inpatients.

As it happened, I had no control over the information that I had once been a psychiatric inpatient. After the internship, I learned that my Harvard faculty advisor had informed the chief of psychology before I started at the VA Hospital. This discovery transformed residues of shame into anger. Through most of the next decade, I went out of my way to challenge people in my profession with my ex-mental patient status, securing employment with the Massachusetts Department of Correction, then with the Massachusetts Department of Mental Health, while fully disclosing my psychiatric history. I was fortunate to have had enough to offer my prospective employers for them to overlook the provocative (and defensive) arrogance with which I thrust my history forward.

While interning at the VA, I moonlighted at Depot, a community-sponsored drop-in center for teenagers in a suburb south of Boston. Guy Seymour recruited and supervised me there. He encouraged a colleague (social worker Alice Hyslop) and me to assemble and co-lead a multiple family group for the families of troubled youth at the drop-in center. Under Guy's clinical supervision, Alice and I met with the families in a local church parish hall. I was in awe of the power of the families to support each other through the tumultuous journeys of their children's adolescence. I learned a lot of family therapy, and also learned to be comfortable in the role of therapist working with large groups of people whose lives intersected in complex patterns.

Life became more crowded as we moved near to Cambridge from our home near the VA in Boston. Harvard University sent me a letter presenting me with the choice of either finishing work on my dissertation, which had lain dormant as I engaged with the actual work of being a psychologist, or settling for a terminal master's degree. I got back to work on my dissertation, and we decided to have our second child.

Jessica was born after a frightening pregnancy, as Betty had been hospitalized for pneumonia. We experienced first-hand what is now known by the sanitized name of "health care disparities": the life-threatening neglect and misunderstandings embodied in the institutional racism that complicates the care of people of color. Betty survived the pneumonia and the hospitalization, and I spent several months reading for my dissertation in the waiting room as she got respiratory therapy. Jessica was born full-term and healthy; her brother Ransom, six years older, was caring and protective.

LEARNING TO BECOME A NETWORK THERAPIST

Guy asked Alice and me to present our multiple family group work at a Boston City Hospital psychiatry department meeting. He invited a discussant, Carolyn Attneave, a psychologist and family therapist, to comment on our presentation. Carolyn, who identified with her ancestry as an Oklahoma Lenape or Delaware Indian, was the first Native American PhD psychologist. She was a visiting scholar at the Harvard School of Public Health and consulted with the Massachusetts Department of Mental Health. Guy had enlisted Carolyn to help him design the psychology internship program that was to emerge from the practicum at Boston City Hospital where I had trained.

As it happened, Carolyn was the co-developer with Ross Speck of network therapy (which she insisted should be called "network intervention"), the expansion of the family therapy model that I had actively avoided when I first encountered it in a graduate school seminar. Carolyn helped develop a theoretical model for the full-scale family network assembly, which would gather from forty to a hundred network members for a series of face-to-face meetings. She brought a perspective shaped by her work with rural communities in the West and by her familiarity with Native American cultural practices.

Carolyn was particularly interested in complex structures of mutual obligation and dysfunction in their natural community setting, and in the subtle practices of locating oneself and developing influence in webs of relationships. She helped Guy design the internship program (originally the Minority Training Program, now the Center for Multicultural Training in Psychology) as a network, a web of collaborative relationships between service organizations in the community and the hospital-based internship program. The relatively loose-knit web would be held together and revitalized by regular self-evaluation meetings. They would begin with day-long meetings of staff and interns and conclude with a network assembly that included key staff from the wide web of community agencies where interns got much of their training.

I quickly discerned that Carolyn was a founder of network therapy, which had so put me off when I first learned of it. I was now less constricted than I had been a few years earlier, when I had still been recovering from the depression that had succeeded the psychosis and was still wary of taking on "extreme" ideas for fear of reigniting mania. I had learned that I could be competent learning the craft of therapy and was proud of my work with the multiple family therapy group. And Carolyn was a commanding figure, with the physical style and spiritual presence of a Native matriarchal elder, her powerful intellect tempered by generous humor. Alice and I agreed to present our multiple family group work to a family therapy seminar Carolyn was teaching in her living room. I later found myself accepting without hesitation her invitation to participate in her forthcoming seminar on network intervention. Over the course of her two-year seminar on network intervention, Carolyn became my mentor.

I got my first real job as staff psychologist at MCI Framingham, the state prison for women, during a brief period of progressive correctional policy under then-Governor Michael Dukakis. Furloughs and day releases for work and for study supported community reintegration, as did gender integration at MCI Framingham, which helped prepare both male and female prisoners for normal life following their release. Men and women near the end of their sentences prepared for return to their communities by going out to work or school, while living in a gender-integrated prison. To stabilize a potentially volatile situation with young men and women incarcerated together, correctional officials transferred to Framingham a group of older, mature incarcerated men, many serving life sentences at the MCI Norfolk prison where, years before, Malcolm X had educated himself in the prison library.

Working at the prison, I fashioned myself very much as a radical, both politically as a supporter and fellow traveler with the Black Panther Party, and personally as a "radical therapist" in solidarity with psychiatric patients, among whom I explicitly counted myself. With Carolyn my informal consultant and mentor, I applied my network skills to positioning myself in the webs of relationships among prisoners, correction officers, treatment staff, and administrators. The social and relational processes that emerged as prisoners and staff came to live with gender integration fascinated me. There were plenty of opportunities for me to hone my skills as a systems thinker, and an unexpected convergence of my personal and professional life afforded me the opportunity to locate myself in the informal networks of the prisoners.

"John" was one of the lifers who had been transferred from MCI Norfolk, the men's prison, to MCI Framingham. He was popular and charismatic, a tall and stunningly handsome Black man with a rich, deep voice, a singer, poet and natural leader. As life would have it, he had for several years been a cellmate with Betty Ann's brother Richard at MCI Norfolk. My status as Richard's brother-in-law opened the door for a comradeship between John and me as I began to design programs during what proved to be a very brief period of progressive experimentation in the Massachusetts correctional system. I started the "Reality Group," which met Monday through Friday, and was open to prisoners, correction officers, treatment staff, administrators, and administrative staff. It was designed as a radical, collectivist effort, billed as "a collective effort to create and restore its members' sense of reality. At any time, one, many, or all members will seek to understand what is really going on."

Long before I was to study social constructionism, I understood intuitively that reality is constructed in relationships. I could see the discrepancies between the lived realities of prisoners, correction officers, treatment staff, and administrators, and how crazy-making were the misunderstandings that emerged between the groups. Each group had experiences that afforded important perspectives that could contribute to collective understanding, but no group had enough experience of the whole situation to make sense of what was going on in the institution. I conceived Reality Group as a preventive mental health intervention.

I convened a group leadership team open to all the constituent groups. Several prisoners (including John) and several treatment staff volunteered to join the leadership team.

The Reality Group Constitution included the following statement:

> The Reality Group makes strong demands for personal responsibility from its members. Without constant criticism and change, it will rapidly become dysfunctional (that is, not function to fulfill its expressed purpose of restoring and maintaining its members' sense of reality). A dysfunctional Reality Group is a contradiction in terms. If physical attacks occur, or if the group in other ways becomes dysfunctional, it will cease to exist . . . Any new effort necessarily has to go through changes in order to best serve its purpose. Therefore, we can expect mistakes and other events that will render the group dysfunctional. Specific events will be dealt with as follows: Once the group has been determined to be dysfunctional, it is suspended until the situation that created the dysfunction has been dealt with. The Team will decide on each occasion whether or not to intervene in the situation. The Team has the responsibility to determine whether or not the situation has been effectively dealt with, thus determining when if ever the Reality Group will reconvene.

In the two years that I worked at MCI Framingham, we never had to interrupt the Reality Group. The team was able to address challenges as they emerged and to develop strategies for continuing the Reality Group dialogues. The conversations were often intense and always fascinating, literally cross-cultural conversations among participants in a total institution. The superintendent herself participated occasionally. Working with a team to facilitate dialogues among subsystems of the larger system, I learned skills that I would later develop working with a team to conduct full-scale network assemblies for troubled families in their communities.

Carolyn was still in Boston when I moved on to my next job, working for the Department of Mental Health in Lynn, Massachusetts, an economically stressed former industrial city north of Boston. Half of my state job was located at Lynn Community Health Center, which encouraged my efforts to develop network therapy efforts in the community. In the 1970s there was still enough public financial support for community mental health and local social services that agencies would readily allocate staff time for free professional training. With consultation from Carolyn, I designed a curriculum for the Lynn Network Conference, which trained staff from agencies throughout the community in social network intervention. I planned to draw teams from members of the Lynn Network Conference to conduct full-scale family network assemblies.

I was drawn specifically to Lynn because John Garrison, a psychologist who had developed his own model of small-scale network meetings, was on the staff of the local community mental health center.[36] Lynn at the time had a population of 85,000. I envisioned the public health possibilities afforded by our interventions with networks in the community, their effects reverberating through overlapping linkages with a critical mass of Lynn families, contributing to improvements in community mental health. Lynn could have used the help. In the 1970s, the city was suffering from declining industrial employment, deteriorating housing stock, ineffective public schools, serious pollution of its public water supply, and a growing epidemic of substance abuse.

I came to appreciate the city's spiritual history and atmosphere. Lynn is situated just south of Salem, famous for its seventeenth-century witch trials. On a hill overlooking downtown Lynn is High Rock Tower, which was built as an observatory for astrological purposes by the wealthy "Singing Hutchinson Family," who made their fortune as entertainers throughout the country, particularly in California during the Gold Rush. The Hutchinsons were activists for abolition, feminism, and temperance and strong believers in spiritualism. Dungeon Rock in the Lynn Woods is the site of a local legend about the Hutchinson family. Believing that pirates hid their booty somewhere in the Lynn woods before coming to port in Boston, the Hutchinsons were said to have hired a large company of mediums to communicate with the spirits of the pirates. One could argue that the pirates' spirits were accessible, and their nature unchanged, as they advised the mediums to guide an excavation through hundreds of yards of solid rock that produced no treasure.

There were other signs of concentrated spiritual energy in the local landscape. On Broad Street stood the home where Mary Baker Eddy, the spiritual healer who founded Christian Science, wrote *Science and Health with Key to the Scriptures*. Directly opposite the Christian Science Church in Lynn is a park on the ocean with access to the massive stone outcropping of Red Rock, a place of power whose awesome vibrations can affect the most skeptical of visitors. On my daily commute north from Cambridge to Lynn, before passing through the coastal community of Revere, there was a directional sign, "Revere Lynn." After my spiritual awakening, I came to appreciate the sign's double meaning.

Although I was intrigued by the spiritual elements of Lynn's local culture, I was not in a particularly open state when I began to work there. My relationship with marijuana had become more addictive than spiritual, and Betty was succumbing to her family's vulnerability to alcohol. Our substance abuse and our marriage were spiraling down together, Ransom and Jessica holding each other's hands to support each other as they heard their parents arguing bitterly in an adjoining room in our small Cambridge apartment.

Betty and I held it together to support our struggling family, each of us becoming more engaged with our jobs as our marriage became a source more of strain than of support. Carolyn and I agreed that the training at Lynn Network Conference had reached a stage where we needed to experience the intense complexity of a full-scale network assembly by staging a role-play simulation. The leaders of the Network Conference gathered funds from our participating agencies to fly in Uri Rueveni, a colleague of Carolyn's and Ross Speck's, for a full-day conference in which Uri played the role of a conductor and I, together with selected colleagues, served as his support team. The other participants in the event, members of the Network Conference and other human service workers, played the roles of people engaged in a desperate situation invented for the occasion: a mother struggling with depression, her helpless husband and troubled children, extended family and in-laws, neighbors, friends, coworkers, church members, and human service providers were gathered to mobilize in support of a family overwhelmed by mother's loss of function and hints at suicidal intention.

Even in simulation, I experienced the awesome power of the full-scale network assembly. I did not, however, frame the experience as spiritual, despite Carolyn's insistence that a network assembly conductor assume the role of shaman. That idea was too threatening for me, resonating as it did with my conflict-ridden ancestral legacy. Less than ten years after my psychosis, I was clinging to Western science as a safe alternative to the spiritual adventures that had drawn me so recently into raw chaos. Lynn Network Conference colleagues whom I had trained were prepared to serve as team members for our first real live full-scale network assembly, but I was not prepared spiritually for the conductor role. So it was that I could not conduct the meeting for the real, rather than role-played, first network that I was to assemble.

I was treating a Latin American and Caribbean couple with my colleague, Esperanza Herrera, at the health center. She was both co-therapist and translator, as I do not speak Spanish. Our clients, young parents, had invited the husband's sister to come and care for their small children while they were at work. It had soon emerged that sister was suffering from mental illness, a problem that the couple had been concealing from their local community. Without effective support from the sister, they were rapidly becoming overwhelmed. Esperanza and I concurred that the problem was appropriate for a network assembly, and the couple agreed to assemble network members from the local community and from their homelands, sharing with everyone information they had kept secret out of shame. I could not conduct because of my language limitations and Esperanza demurred. There were no other Spanish-speaking members of the Lynn Network Conference.

The 1970s were the heyday of community mental health, whose ideology included building alliances with natural helpers in the community. We settled on training a young heating and air conditioning repair specialist with the requisite charismatic leadership talents and personal stability to serve in Spanish as conductor and assembled a supportive team including Esperanza, members of the Network Conference, Guy Seymour (who spoke Spanish), and me. Over the course of two assemblies, some of whose participants had travelled for thousands of miles and had crossed multiple borders in order to participate, members of the network found ways to support parents, aunt, and children, resolving the immediate crisis and helping them find a way forward.

RAMÓN

One's life unfolds within a broader design. Opportunities emerge, enabling one to bring forth into the world the spiritual truths for which one is particularly responsible, always free to choose whether to embrace or avoid them. Over the course of conversations with our volunteer conductor, I became intrigued by his description of Ramón Jiménez, a member of the network we had assembled. Ramón was an *espiritista*, a spiritualist practitioner from the Dominican Republic. *Espiritismo* is an amalgam of African, Caribbean, and European spiritism.

Espiritistas work with companion spirits to advise and protect the people who consult with them. Clients consult an espiritista to learn of departed loved ones, make sense of and protect themselves from misfortune, and invite good fortune. I was intrigued by the contrast between the conductor's description of Ramón's practice and my own experience as a practitioner. When clients came to my office, I would ask them why they came to see me. When clients came to Ramón, *he* would tell *them* why they came to see him! This activated a dormant curiosity about spiritual healing that I thought I had forever suppressed in the course of my recovery from my psychosis.

Ramón was happy to meet with me. He was a diminutive, androgynous man about my age. He had little formal education and spoke little English, although his English was far better than the Spanish that I was trying to acquire in a local community college course. In his home where he met his clients there were curtains of glass beads, small altars with candles and incense, and throughout the house an assembly of bric-a-brac, pictures, candles and statuettes, most embodying Christian themes. The predominant colors of his home were red and black. Ramón consulted with clients at a small table, on which he traced the client's hand on paper, then entered an altered state within which he communicated with his companion, the spirit of an indigenous man from the island of Hispaniola (the island shared by the Dominican Republic and Haiti), whom Ramón called Carmélo.

Now, nearly fifty years later, I can relive the intensity of the emotions I felt during my visits with Ramón. I was surprised by a powerful and compelling sense of well-being that struck me on our first encounter and persisted throughout the many times that we spent together. As it became evident that Ramón had chosen me for instruction in the ways of the worlds in which he lived, I struggled with feelings of alarm, as I felt drawn inexorably toward experiences that had already overwhelmed me on at least two occasions—my childhood encounter with God and my psychosis as an adult. Betty Ann was as alarmed as I was about my following this path, particularly as I found myself staying up late at night, struggling to come to terms with the disintegration of the scientific ideology with which I had been keeping conscious experience of my spirituality at bay.

As I reflect on my experiences with Ramón, I see how my path toward our encounter was shaped by my personal values and ancestral legacy. I was working in public service and living by a strong commitment to connect across cultural and ethnic differences. Despite my early reluctance, I had embraced social network intervention, which embodied both my commitment to community organization and my legacy of pastoral ministry. In these ways, my relationship with Ramón was the result of conscious life choices. Yet, there are ways beyond one's awareness by which the design unfolds. In retrospect, I see that profound differences between Ramón and me made my transformation possible.

Throughout my life, I had been relying on complex intellectualization to make sense of my experiences and to defend against becoming devastated by my emotions. This defensive style had substantial limitations and had already in my adult life been overwhelmed by psychosis. The latter experience had been so distressing that I had redoubled my practice of intellectualization, as a desperate strategy to keep myself from unraveling again.

In my conversations with Ramón, however, I could not mobilize intellectualization to distance myself from what he was teaching me. Between us, we had perhaps thirty words, mostly English, with which to communicate. I had to devote my full concentration to understanding what he was telling me. In our conversations, I couldn't intellectualize my way out of taking in at face value what he was teaching me. Ramón told me that he had decided to teach me because he perceived that I had "strong *colonnes*" by which he meant a colonnade, or array of columns. That image would resonate with me years later, when I learned how to channel energy through my body's meridians in practicing Chi Gong, and later still when I experienced the spirit of my younger son Jacob as a column of white light in the hours and days after his death.

Although I couldn't intellectualize in our conversations, I tried desperately to put my experience into an intellectual framework, to find scientific explanations for what Ramón was teaching me. I tried to learn as much as I could from as many sources as I could, hoping that I could somehow construct safe abstractions or generalizations in which to contain and explain away the changes I was experiencing. I began to study Carlos Castañeda's writings, and whatever other esoteric texts I could get my hands on.[37] Lynn is just south of Salem, Massachusetts, site of the Salem Witch Trials. At the time that I was meeting with Ramón, Salem was the home of a group of practitioners of Wicca, whose leader, Lori Cabot, had been designated by the governor of Massachusetts as the official witch of Salem. One of my colleagues from the Lynn Network Conference, Iphigenia (Ginny) Dubuque, was a member of Lori's group. Ginny introduced me to Lori, who taught me some of her theory and practice.

These desperate efforts served only to send me further down the rabbit hole. Instead of providing me with a meta-perspective from which to assert my intellectual mastery, they made me more and more aware of powerful spiritual forces just beyond the reach of my consciousness. As alarming as my experiences were becoming, I could not turn away, and I certainly could not stop meeting with Ramón, whose presence continued to fill me with profound feelings of well-being.

Within our limited shared vocabulary, words served multiple meanings. Ramón taught me that I am accompanied by my "god," by which he meant a guiding companion spirit, an entity beyond the manifest world yet connected with this world by its unique relationship with me. This companion is a source of comfort, protection, and wisdom. Ramón's word for person was "body," and he taught that every body has his or her own god. With great seriousness, Ramón announced, "For some decisions, David, only your god is your friend." These words were to comfort and sustain me for years when faced with difficult decisions for which I alone was accountable.

I trusted Ramón completely, and when he chose to give me directions, I followed them without question, even when doing so made me uncomfortable. One day, Ramón directed me to anoint myself with what he called a *fraco*. He gave me a perfumed potion with which he directed me to cover my body in the evening, and not to wash it off until morning. The fraco would give me wellbeing and protection. With intense seriousness, he warned me not to tell anyone about the fraco. I followed his instructions to the letter, further alarming Betty, as I got into bed smelling of strong perfume and refusing to utter a word about what I was doing. Later, when I told Ramón of Betty's discomfort, he responded with some surprise, saying, "It's okay to tell your wife!"

Now, I am sitting and talking with Ramón in his apartment. It is 1975; I am thirty years old. The conversations between Ramón and me, which began a few months ago, are becoming deeper, as he introduces me into mysteries that I strain to grasp. I now recognize the arrogance of my original intention to meet with him, the cultural insensitivity of the impulse to collect an exotic experience. Despite my ambivalence about the knowledge he is teaching, I am drawn ever closer to him and to the profound feeling of peace that I have in his presence. I am unable to disengage, even as I realize that, if there is any collecting going on, I am not the collector.

As I learn more from Ramón, language has become less important, as when he taught me about the practice of being "open." Without verbal instruction, I understood him intuitively and began to cultivate a stance of relaxing the boundary between everyday waking consciousness and spiritual awareness (a distinction that I can make in words as I write about the experience now but which was entirely nonverbal at the time that I was learning to be open).

Now, as I sit with Ramón in his apartment, he has decided it is time. With intense seriousness, speaking in the language that we have developed together, Ramón says, "Dabey, some bodies are this open." He starts with his palms together and moves the top of his hands apart perhaps twenty-five degrees. "Some bodies," he then says, "are this open." His hands are now at right angles to his wrists, heels of his hands together, describing a half circle. "Some bodies," and his hands now somehow spread to describe a full circle, "are all the way open. "For bodies all the way open, not one body, one body, one body. *All one body.*" As Ramón speaks these words, I feel myself slip completely outside of everyday waking consciousness. As I make the transition, the last words I hear my mind saying are, "So, this is what Spinoza was talking about . . ."

It is a challenge to use language to describe experience that is intrinsically beyond words. I write from a first-person perspective; it is the only way that I know how to describe the experience. Yet, for the most important events in the experience, there is no "I," only pure awareness.

I dissolve into the consciousness of the Unity that is all that is, my ego a vanishingly small fractal of the awesome One that is what it contemplates. The One gazes at vast complexity that is beyond the limits of human imagination and is all simultaneously accessible to awareness. Space and time do not frame experience, but are somehow both separate and inseparable from the Unity, intelligible from outside their limits.

As my ego and intellect regain their grip, sequential time returns. No longer pure awareness beyond all limitation, I am once again "I." I turn to face the West, gazing at the setting sun, somehow seeing it through the solid walls and covered windows of Ramon's home. I extend my arms, and feel and see vivid lines of red, violet, orange, blue, and yellow light coursing through them. At that moment, I hear Ramón giggling.

I am suddenly back in the stream of time, and in the flow of everyday waking consciousness. The entire experience, from the moment that Ramón said, "All one body," to my snapping back at the sound of Ramón's laughter, has lasted at most 35 seconds in conventional time. Within itself, however, the experience has been timeless.

This conversation, in which Ramón opened me to direct experience of the Divine, became the touchstone for my spiritual journey. After this experience with Ramón, my explorations were no longer speculative pursuits. Direct experience of the Unity beyond and within the bewildering diversity of the material world gave me what I needed in order to distinguish efforts at self-cultivation that brought me closer to that experience of Unity, from those did not.

Ramón's laughter, which brought me out of my experience of non-ordinary reality, made its own contribution to my journey. Ramón recognized the greed in my attempt to capture in my body the power of the One that is all. Most spiritual traditions recognize that ego is an obstacle to spiritual awareness. Although the self is a useful vehicle for making one's way through the world with others, it is embedded in the material world. The habit of organizing one's experience through the lens of the self therefore interferes with the search to experience the source from which the material world emerges. Identifying transpersonal experience with the self, or attributing the shift into non-ordinary reality to the actions of the self, are seductive obstructions on the path toward spiritual awareness.

Until I became a Jew, years after my encounter with Ramón, my greed for intense spiritual revelation paradoxically set a firm limit on my spiritual development. As I would cross thresholds into new levels of spiritual practice, the combination of self-congratulation and greed for deeper and more intense experience would slow down my progress.

Although it would be decades before I could successfully cultivate my shamanic capacity to send my consciousness deliberately into non-material worlds, my experience with Ramón gave me what I needed to be able to conduct a full-scale network assembly. I learned to depend on my team to track the course of the meeting as I went in and out of altered states of consciousness, states that gave me access to the intense emotions and competing narratives in the room, finding words that sometimes embodied the deep meanings held in the room and sometimes brought forth new meanings that resonated with and guided network members who felt stuck in a hopeless situation. I could now teach others about the shamanic stance of the conductor, often drawing on a quotation from Black Elk's life story to articulate the challenge of becoming obstructed by ego:

> It was even then only after the *heyoka* ceremony, in which I performed my dog vision, that I had the power to practice as a medicine man, curing sick people; and many I cured with the power that came through me. Of course, it was not I who cured. It was the power from the outer world, and the visions and

> ceremonies had only made me like a hole through which the power could come to the two-leggeds. If I thought that I was doing it myself, the hole would close up and no power could come through. Then everything I could do would be foolish . . .[38]

Now that I had a direct experience of that for which I was searching, I committed my life to the search. I continued and expanded my search of esoteric literature available in English. I studied Idries Shah's essay and collection of Sufi texts for English readers in *The Way of the Sufi* (1968). Returning to my interest in Eastern spirituality, awakened in adolescence by reading Alan Watts and Nikos Kazantzakis and during my psychedelic college days by reading Baba Ram Dass, I explored Buddhism and Taoism. I read descriptions of Native American spirituality and found the *Kybalion*, a closely guarded ("hermetically sealed") esoteric text preserved by acolytes of Hermes Trismegistus. I hung out with the community surrounding Lori Cabot. Ginny would often introduce me to members of that community as a "metaphysician." I got occasional, very interesting referrals to help members of Lori's community manage their complex feelings about their clairvoyant experiences. I remember reading about Kabbalah, a Jewish mystical tradition, but choosing not to pursue studying it, as it seemed to me that one could only understand Kabbalah from within the experience of living a Jewish life.

It was decades before I could see that, despite Ramón having led me into transcendent experience of the Divine, I was still in spiritual exile from a dialogical relationship with the personified God who had abandoned me in childhood. I seldom thought of that terrifying nightmare, but its traumatic effects shaped and constrained my spiritual search. To approach God in an "I-Thou" relationship would be to risk another overwhelming experience of abandonment. Although I could grow spiritually, that growth was restricted to domains of abstraction and sensation, not allowing for a personal relationship with God. God and I would not engage directly with each other for decades—and only after an immeasurably more painful experience of loss.

Although I understood that the ego is an obstacle to enlightenment, it was difficult without religion or God to set ego aside in my search for experience of the Divine. In my mid-thirties, I still harbored extravagant ideas about my capacity to transform the dominant paradigms of psychology. Cultivating my spirit, however, did help me to relax somewhat my grandiose ideas of intellectual mastery.

I remember a moment of deep contemplation at a place of power in Lynn: Red Rock, at the shore of the Atlantic. Red Rock is a promontory of huge, reddish-purple rocks onto which one can climb from a grassy park. The flow of the tide, covering and exposing sections of the rocks in eternal rhythm, is a physical manifestation of the intense, living energy of the place. I would often go to Red Rock to meditate, gazing on the water and letting go of my ambitions. Looking out at the dazzling display of sunlight reflecting off wavelets on the water, the ripples shaped by incalculably complex interactions of wind, tide, currents, reverberations of waves hitting the shore and further vibrating the waters in their return, I deliberately let go of the idea that human understanding could embrace such complexity. At Red Rock, I let go of my ambition to transform the intellectual foundations of my profession and replaced it with the ambition to become a wise old man. A more modest and practical ambition—and one that I could reasonably hope to realize.

3

Family Changes

SUBSTANTIAL PROGRESS IN SPIRITUAL self-cultivation requires more than reading texts and meditating. Although I was no longer using LSD, mushrooms, or other intense psychedelic drugs, I was still smoking marijuana and drinking alcohol. No longer tools for self-exploration, they had become ways to tolerate an increasingly unhappy married life, which had deteriorated further as my use of marijuana and Betty's of alcohol became more addictive. By the time that we finally separated, our children Ransom and Jessica had lived through years of unhappy family life. They faced several years of further tumult through the bitter early stages of our divorce.

All the while, I continued to practice network therapy. My position with Department of Mental Health was reduced to half-time and relocated from the neighborhood health center to the DMH Area Office, which aligned my responsibilities more closely with the department's priority mission to serve patients with severe and persistent mental illness. I continued half-time as an employee of the health center and made it the community base for the Hospital Community Program, a training program where psychology interns could provide network therapy for DMH patients. Interns followed their patients as the course of their illnesses determined whether they would receive their care at the nearby state mental hospital or at the community health center. The Hospital Community Program was integral to a substantial DMH effort to reconnect patients, many of whom had been hospitalized for decades, with networks of family and friends from whom they had become estranged over the course of their illnesses and to strengthen these networks by connecting them with new networks of community support.

These efforts came to a focus in the Family House project, whose mission was to build and strengthen a web of supportive relationships around a group of patients and the inpatient staff who had been their caretakers for years in the back ward of the state hospital, which was soon to close. One of our objectives was to deinstitutionalize both patients and staff. Patients were to be discharged as a group, collectively relocated to Family House, a community residence established to be their home. The plan was for the staff to leave their inpatient positions to work in the community with their long-term patients. We helped patients identify, locate, and engage members of their personal networks and began conducting network assemblies at the hospital. Inpatient staff had some of their time assigned to part-time positions in the community mental health center before the patients' discharge, to prepare them for community work.

Several of the inpatient network assemblies were very small, with just a handful of people. Some patients already had small networks before they were hospitalized; some had estranged network members by their symptomatic behavior; some had lost touch with network members over years of illness; or family members and friends had died over the years that the patients had been institutionalized.

Not all the network assemblies were small, however. Susan, a patient in her early thirties, had been a popular high school student before a psychotic episode and subsequent severe and persistent mental illness led to more than a decade of hospitalization at the state hospital. Her parents had hidden her illness from the community, inventing a fictional life away from home, first college then a nursing career in a distant city. Susan became a candidate for the Family House program. Her parents had remained deeply involved with her and were eager to support the effort for her discharge to the community residence. They made the decision to convene Susan's network for an assembly in the hospital, which meant disclosing the fact of her illness as they extended invitations to members of their network, many of whose members had not known of her illness.

Susan's first network assembly had over forty participants, from young adults to elders, including relatives, friends from high school, a former babysitter and a family for whom Susan herself had been babysitter. It included the inpatient staff who were being recruited to staff Family House. I was supported in my role as conductor by a network intervention team that included colleagues and Hospital Community Program interns. It was an emotionally powerful experience of community, what Carolyn Attneave would call "retribalization" of Susan's network.

The morning of that evening's assembly, the DMH Area Office received word from headquarters that the state legislature had cut the funds for the Family House program. This created a serious crisis for patients, family, and staff. We decided to announce the news to the assembled network. Recognizing the consequences for Susan and her fellow patients, leaders in the group spontaneously emerged to organize advocacy for restoration of funding.

The organizing effort spread rapidly through Susan's suburban hometown. Even people who had not been at the assembly volunteered to stand outside a supermarket soliciting signatures for a petition to the legislature demanding restoration of funds to Family House. The local representative to the state legislature reported that he had never seen a larger nor more determined citizen initiative in his years in office. The state legislature restored the funding. Susan's parents, who had hidden the fact of Susan's illness as a shameful secret, were later to organize a local chapter of a national advocacy group for families of the mentally ill.

The powerful experience of working with Susan's network contrasted with the challenges posed by poignant gatherings of ten or fewer members of other patients' networks. It was clear to us that we needed to find a strategy to build more social support for many Family House patients. We decided to plan for a "network of network assemblies," a full-day gathering in the community of all the networks of all the Family House patients, together with members of the local voluntary association of former state hospital patients who had established a community social club, with staff from community organizations who would be serving the Family House patients in the community after their discharge, and with the state mental hospital staff recruited to work with Family House patients.

We drew team members from among my interns, family therapists in the Boston area interested in network therapy, and Jodie Kliman, a psychologist from New York City whom I had met when we presented together on a panel at an Annual Conference of the American Orthopsychiatric Association. Carolyn Attneave had been my network intervention mentor. Ross Speck (Carolyn's co-developer of the full-scale family network assembly) and Ross's wife Joan Speck had been Jodie's mentors. Jodie and I had already started writing together about network intervention. She worked with me to design and lead the network of network assemblies.

This ingathering of all the patients and their networks built a solid base of social support, not just for the patients but also for members of their networks, many of whom were fatigued by the demands of maintaining relationships with their chronically ill friends or family members. They became supports for each other and built solidarity as advocates for services to Family House members, who were discharged as a group to a fine old house near downtown Lynn.

It proved harder to deinstitutionalize the staff than to deinstitutionalize their patients. The occupational therapist from the hospital ward, a relatively recent hire to her state position, had worked closely with me in conducting group sessions for the Family House members in the hospital and made the transition out with the patients, becoming the director of Family House and an employee of the Lynn Mental Health Association. All the other staff we had tried to recruit decided to keep their state jobs and remain at the hospital.

Meanwhile, in our efforts to revitalize our failing marriage, Betty and I had been planning to move to live near her sister in Southern California. I set a termination date for my jobs with DMH and the health center. As my work began to wind down in Lynn, the marriage finally dissolved into separation and divorce. I lived temporarily with a colleague, then settled into a tiny bachelor apartment in Lynn. I set up a private office practice in Lynn, and a couple of years later found more substantial employment in Boston at the Language and Cognitive Development Center, a school and treatment center for children with autism spectrum disorder. Working at LCDC gave me an opportunity to learn a clinical approach based on Clark University Professor Heinz Werner's comparative developmental theory, which had already had a strong intellectual influence on me as a psychologist, having led me to general systems theory and from there into family therapy.

At this very unhappy time in my life, I was not a particularly appealing person. I was still angry about the degrading institutional treatment I had suffered when psychotic and was still responding to that stigmatization by loudly and defiantly proclaiming my status as an ex-mental patient. I was deeply unhappy not to be living with my children. Absorbed in the metaphysical lessons I was learning after Ramón opened me, I publicly identified myself as a "practicing witch." Despite all my obvious shortcomings, as Jodie and I continued to write together, we fell in love.

Jodie loved her community but moved from New York to the Boston area to join my family, respecting the reality that I needed to live near my children. After six months living together in my crowded downtown Lynn apartment, we moved to Brookline, a suburb next to Boston, a community where we felt biracial children would be safer in public spaces and where Jodie would feel comfortable as a Jew.

WELCOMING JACOB

Jodie, who was childless when we married, was from the beginning a generous and loving stepmother. Ransom and Jessica found it difficult to accept her presence at first, their loyalty conflicts exacerbated by toxic conflict between their parents. Jodie remained patient and emotionally available, allowing everyone time to find their way into this new experience of family. Jodie and I knew that we wanted to have children together as well, recognizing the complexity of cultivating healthy relationships with Ransom and Jessica while dealing with pressures from medical challenges that we knew would compromise fertility for both of us.

At Jewish weddings, the couple make their vows under a canopy, the *chuppah*. With January snow on the ground, our chuppah was formed by our siblings holding pine boughs over our heads. Jodie and I used the metaphor of light to put words to our intuitive spirituality. In my vow, I said, ". . . As you have given your whole heart to my children, so is my heart open to the new life which even now we sense drawing nearer to the light of our love . . ." Jodie's vow responded with ". . . The light that gathered around us that healed and strengthened us both is ever deeper and lingering as we come to share our lives more fully . . . I too sense the new life that we will bring into the world drawing nearer, and I welcome it with more joy than I have words for . . ."

Struck by our vows, one of the guests asked us after the ceremony if we were pregnant. Sadly, we were not. I had had a vasectomy during my first marriage and, while I was to have surgery to reverse it, the surgery failed. We went through the ordeal of artificial insemination, painful alternations of hope and disappointment with each of Jodie's cycles. By the time we abandoned the hope of pregnancy, the fertility drugs had exacerbated Jodie's painful fibroid tumors, leading to a hysterectomy. We decided to seek to adopt a baby. Through it all, we meditated deeply on bringing a new person into the world, accessing the light that we had named in our wedding vows and drawing our baby toward us.

Although she had been raised in a culturally Jewish but very secular household, Jodie wanted to raise the children we hoped to have together in the Jewish religion. I readily agreed. At the time, I was studying Sufi, Buddhist, Hindu, and Native American spiritual traditions, and the syncretic Eastern spiritual texts of Meher Baba. I was open to learning about Judaism, although I did not consider the possibility that I might convert. From my study of Sufism, I saw all religions as forms, and understood that a form is only suitable as a vessel for genuine spiritual experience when it is created for a particular person at a particular time in particular circumstances.

As we got ourselves ready to welcome new children into our marriage, I prepared with some trepidation to attend Jewish religious services, remembering my acute discomfort as a child and adolescent participating in Christian services. We began by attending services in a Jewish Reconstructionist *chavurah* (a Jewish congregation less institutional than a synagogue, with an emphasis on fellowship among its members). I was surprised and pleased by the experience, although there were challenges. Neither Jodie nor I could read or understand Hebrew, though Jodie could chant prayers remembered from childhood *shabbat* candle lighting and Passover *seders*. I was put off by triumphalist martial language in some of the psalms, but I found nothing else in the liturgy that I could not accept.

I was bemused that my Sufi studies, embedded in the religious discourse of Islam, had made Judaism more accessible to me. As a student of Sufism, I understood that one's ascent to higher levels of spiritual awareness requires that one take responsibility for the spiritual elevation of people that surround one. I was fascinated by the idea of Jews as an entire people in a covenant with God, whose collective history is destined for the spiritual elevation of humanity.

Here was a collectivist idea of spiritual responsibility that resonated more with my socialist legacy than did the image of an individual spiritual master. I also appreciated that Judaism, unlike its cousin Abrahamic religions of Christianity and Islam, is not a proselytizing religion. As I learned more of the history of the Jews, I came to understand that this virtue might well be an artifact of centuries under Muslim or Christian rule, when conversion to Judaism was a capital offense for both converter and converted. Whatever the reason for the absence of a Jewish proselytizing mission, I was grateful that, unlike Christianity, Judaism did not assume that the redemption of humanity required universal conversion to the Jewish faith.

Jodie was curious and respectful about my metaphysical practice and did some exploration on her own. Some experiences came to her unbidden. Before it had appeared to either of us that we would become life partners, Jodie was walking on vacation along a line of stalls at Venice Beach in California. She was drawn to a T-shirt for a newborn baby, sky blue with a rainbow and stars painted on it. She heard the words in her mind, "I am a shirt for the baby that you will have with David." She dismissed the thought as absurd and walked away but could not get the shirt out of her mind. She walked back and bought it, thinking that she could give it as a gift to a friend's newborn baby. Several years later, our radiant infant Jacob would be wearing it. Today, worn by Jacob's teddy bear, his first stuffed animal, it reminds us that he called to us before we began calling him.

Jacob came into this world on October 31, 1986. The telephone call from his birth mother's sister, announcing that her sister was going into labor, came just as thirteen-year-old Jessica and her friend came through our door, calling out, "trick or treat!" Three days later, his birth mother put our son into Jodie's arms. He was from the beginning a joyously engaged and radiant person.

Jacob's arrival helped to bring peace between Ransom and Jessica's parental households, as their mother recognized how deeply her children loved their little brother. We learned that Jodie's having a baby of her own relieved Betty Ann's concerns that Jodie would try to take her children away from her. Ransom was 19, living with us as he went to college in Boston, and Jessica lived with us on weekends. Before Jacob's first birthday, I finally put an end to my use of marijuana, allowing me to become more fully available in family relationships and helping prepare me for further ascent on my spiritual journey.

The next year, Ransom transferred to a different college and started living about two hours away in Western Massachusetts. When Jacob was in elementary school, Jessica moved in to live with us half-time. Ransom lived with us again after his sister left for college, using us as his home base as he sought more challenging employment than the bicycle repair work that he had taken up after graduating from college. What was to have been a brief stay for Ransom was extended when our family was shaken by his and Jessica's mother Betty Ann's sudden and unexpected death from a heart attack.

Like many members of her family, Betty Ann had avoided medical care. Avoidance of the medical profession is not uncommon in the context of the structural racism that harms people of color, a pattern that medicine has acknowledged with the sanitized term "health care disparities." Betty Ann did sense that her body was failing and gave her children, Jodie, and me the blessing of letting it be known that she was grateful that Jodie was in her children's life, in case anything happened to her.

RECOGNIZING ADHD

In childhood, I had witnessed my brother Robin's suffering over his learning difficulties and my father's rages when his home tutoring failed to remedy Robin's woeful grades. I had been caught up in the complex emotional and family system problems that can develop around learning disabilities. My sister Sheila did well in school, as did I. I was the only one of the three of us who had no difficulty with spelling. Naively, I considered myself the only sibling with no learning problems.

Obviously very intelligent, and accomplished in other domains of study, Ransom was having difficulty in third grade mastering math. When I tried to help him with his math studies, I was appalled to hear my father's angry voice coming out of my mouth. I backed off quickly. His mother and I advocated for him to get evaluated at his school, which documented his learning disabilities and provided help from a learning specialist. Ransom responded quickly to this support, achieving well academically. We were spared another generation of trauma around learning difficulties.

At the beginning of my professional career, I had avoided dealing with the emotional problems and systemic dynamics that can develop among child, family, and school when children (and, not infrequently, their parents) have learning disabilities. I was not confident that I could manage my own emotional challenges in that domain. As I developed my clinical skills, and as Ransom, his mother, his school, and I dealt with the challenges posed by his learning issues, I became more curious about working with the complexities of multisystem intervention for problems around learning disabilities.

Years later, when Jodie and I moved to Brookline, I developed a community practice that included healing inflamed relationships between schools and families with learning disabled children.[39] Earlier in my career, I had learned from Carolyn Attneave the practice of locating oneself as a practitioner in the community of which one is a member, cultivating a web of relationships on which to draw to help distressed individuals and their families. I often walked to schools in Brookline from my home or office to consult with teachers and administrators about children whom I was treating in individual and family therapy. In Jacob's first year of life, he sometimes accompanied me in a carrier harness, sleeping through a school consultation that would end with my changing his diaper on the guidance counselor's conference table.

When we adopted Jacob, I had imagined raising a child who, spared my genetic vulnerabilities, could be a skilled athlete and would not have to struggle with learning challenges. Jacob did in fact grow up physically strong and athletically graceful. He did, however, have substantial learning challenges, repeating first grade because of his difficulties mastering fundamental reading and mathematical skills. A neuropsychological evaluation revealed a set of issues, including attention deficit hyperactivity disorder (ADHD), with associated executive functioning problems and difficulties with sequencing. The testing confirmed what we knew of his strengths, including strong language-based and visual-spatial learning abilities. Although he always had limited frustration tolerance, before school began Jacob had otherwise always been resilient, cheerful, radiant, kind, and connected, with no signs of mood difficulties. Sadly, once he started school he was often demoralized and felt badly about himself as a learner. Sustained difficulties with learning eroded his emotional resilience, although he remained a good friend and positive emotional influence with his peers, teachers, and other adults through elementary school.

I began to revise my narrative about myself as a learner during a rare extended visit from my father, who lived in Saint Lucia. Having more familiarity with learning disabilities by then because of my clinical practice, I could see some of my father's peculiarities as representing his own difficulties with attention and executive functioning—and his irritable "temper" as a reaction to these cognitive limitations. As it happened, during my father's visit, I was Jacob's soccer team coach. I was collecting money and orders from parents for an after-game pizza party. I barely concealed my anger as I became confused by multiple orders and requests for change from large bills coming in faster than I could process them.

As I recognized that my emotional reaction was out of proportion, I began to imagine the possibility that I might have learning difficulties of my own. Shortly thereafter, Jodie and I attended a workshop at the Ackerman Family Institute in New York, where two colleagues, Gillian Walker and Marcia Stern, were presenting their family work with learning disabilities. After we watched videotapes of families that included adult members with ADHD, Jodie gently suggested to me that ADHD might explain some of my own difficulties navigating my way through life. The evidence was beginning to accumulate.

Shortly before these events, we had made the difficult decision to start Jacob on a course of stimulants for his own ADHD. The benefits, in his academic functioning, in his sense of himself, and in his family relationships, were almost immediately apparent. After our visit to Ackerman, I decided that if I was willing as a parent to take the risk of Jacob taking medicine for his attentional challenges, I should be willing to take that risk for myself. I arranged an appointment with a psychiatrist at my health center. She diagnosed me with ADHD and prescribed Ritalin. I began to change the ways I organized my daily life. Taking into account my neurobiological limitations, I took the load off my inefficient forebrain by strategically reorganizing space and time to scaffold my executive functioning.

The improvements in daily life and in my family were substantial and nearly instantaneous. I felt much calmer, no longer haunted by dread that I would forget details or lose time to disorganization. I had not been much of a scholar before that, as it was not uncommon for me to forget what was on the first page of a journal article by the time that I got to the bottom of the second page. In the first two months after I began taking the stimulant, I did more professional reading than I had done in the previous five years. For a while, my increased efficiency afforded me some leisure, although that disappeared as I took on increased responsibilities, which I was now able to handle with more efficient brain function.

Understanding that both Jacob and I had ADHD helped us to make sense of an unfortunate pattern between father and son. As Jacob became more frustrated with school, he was more irritable at home. He and I would often set each other off, reactivity in one amplifying the reactivity of the other. This phenomenon, known as "kindling," is a common pattern in families in which child and parent share the impulsive reactivity characteristic of ADHD. It was a pattern that I often recognized in families whom I treated, and, once I was diagnosed, I came to recognize at home. Although my self-awareness somewhat mitigated the painful process between Jacob and me, Jodie was still the adult who usually had to calm the emotional storms.

Jacob was always a trickster with a sweetly mischievous sense of humor, sometimes creatively and playfully transforming what we taught him into elaborate jokes. Jodie and I took the idea of "externalizing practices" that we were learning from the work of narrative family therapist Michael White and the idea of insatiability from the literature on ADHD. We invited Jacob to recognize and resist the influence of "Mr. Insatiability," or "Mr. I.," who could trick Jacob into uttering whining demands for toys, privileges, or other treats, getting us upset with him as a result. Jacob took all this in and found a way to play with it.

I came home late from work one day, to find seven-year-old Jacob standing firmly in the front hall. He clearly had something on his mind.

"Daddy, Daddy, I want to get this hundred-dollar Lego set!" At first bemused, I told him that we were not buying the Lego set and invited a warmer welcome for my return home. He was not to be diverted, insisting even more urgently that we get him the Lego set. I urged him not to let Mr. Insatiability take over control. We went through several exchanges, Jacob redoubling his urgency and me struggling to contain my irritation at his intensifying demand. I asked him to notice that I was getting annoyed; he persisted. The exchange devolved into what appeared to be a familiar pattern of kindling. Finally, with a visibly angry face and body, I shouted, "Jacob!" At that moment, Jacob whipped out the camera he had been hiding behind his back and took a picture of his father's enraged face. My anger dissolved into laughter and admiration for Jacob's mischievous creativity.

EXPLORING NONMATERIAL REALITIES

Although I had met them briefly a few years before, Jodie and I did not get to know David and Sylvia Hammerman until the four of us joined the faculty at the New England Center for the Study of the Family, shortly after Jodie and I married. This was the first collegial relationship with colleagues that Jodie and I formed together. That relationship developed into a deep friendship that has sustained us over the ensuing decades. We shared family vacations when our children were young and are still informal uncles and aunts to each other's adult children.

Both David and Sylvia are interested in integrating the modern practice of therapy with the spiritual and shamanic practices from which therapy emerged. At a time when the four of us were studying hypnosis, David in particular was interested in using trance to access experience of the soul's previous incarnations. One evening when the four of us gathered, I agreed to participate in his explorations, allowing him to lead me into a trance. Recalling it as I write, I relive the experience of the trance:

> I feel a cold that penetrates my bones. I am in a building, and I discern walls of stone around us. I am in the presence of a powerful, magisterial figure. I feel his fierce energy, and his deep disapproval. I am banished . . . Now, I am in a rural setting. On my deathbed, I remember that I became a healer after I had been banished from the Master's presence. I was beloved in the many villages in which I carried on my healing practice. A multitude, people from the villages where I have practiced, surround me. I feel their deep love and gratitude, which buoys me upward as I leave my mortal body. As I pass, I am aware of profound sadness that, in the mortal life I was leaving, I had neither wife nor children.

As I reflected on the possible meanings of this experience, it came to me that my soul in this life has taken on the task of continuing my journey as a spiritual seeker without disengaging from everyday responsibilities as a father and husband. This felt like a compelling insight, and has shaped the course of my journey, helping me to resist my tendency toward self-absorption in spiritual exploration. I wonder whether it helped to shape my later conversion to Judaism, a tradition in which the masters of esoteric knowledge were rabbis who were expected, even obligated, to be married and have children and to live deeply in community.

A few years later, when struggling to recover healthy vitality after a serious illness, I explored another past life. David and Sylvia had recommended that I consult their colleague, Ann Drake, a psychologist and shaman. Ann had been a Peace Corps volunteer in Borneo, where she had witnessed a shaman's healing practice. After her return to the United States to get her doctorate in psychology, she made her way back to Borneo to apprentice to the shaman.

I visited Ann in her home office. After I answered her questions about my reason for consulting her, she directed me to lie on a mat on the floor and close my eyes. Ann started a drumbeat on her tape player and passed her hands through the energy field over my body. She then lay on her own mat and entered into trance to travel in the spirit world.

As she later reported to me, after entering the spirit world she was approached by a horse that she recognized was one of my spirit guides. The horse invited her to ride on its back, and she rode on until a very old Chinese man, another of my spirit guides, beckoned to her to stop. He directed her to enter a cave that stretched down into the underworld. She arrived onto a horrific scene, in which fragments of my wife's soul and my own hovered over our violently dismembered remains.

Ann learned that, in that life, I had been a wealthy Chinese scholar whose esoteric studies had aroused the suspicion of local villagers. Believing me to be a witch, a mob of villagers had burst into our home and murdered my wife and me. Ann saw that my wife in that life was a prior incarnation of Jodie and that the mob leader was a prior incarnation of Betty Ann, who in this life had died several years before. Ann retrieved Jodie's and my soul fragments, with the intention of returning them to me, and through me to Jodie.

It came to Ann that Betty Ann's soul had possession of some of my remaining soul fragments. Drawing on her spirit guides to protect her, Ann traveled to the world of the dead to confront Betty Ann's soul. After some initial blustering resistance, that soul shared deep sadness and regret that, in our most recent incarnations, her soul and mine had not found the healing that our souls had sought for that murderous encounter in our previous incarnations. She relinquished the fragments of my soul that she had been holding.

Ann's spirit traveled back to her body in her office, bearing fragments from the scene of the murders and from her engagement with Betty Ann in the world of the dead. On the way back, she encountered my other spirit guides—a moose, a beech tree, and a woman with a musical instrument. Returning to her body, Ann blew the spirit fragments into me, leaving it to me to return to Jodie her soul fragments from that murder by the mob.

As Ann and I discussed her journey in the spirit worlds, it came to me that the scenario she encountered had occurred earlier in my soul's journey than the banishment, in a later incarnation, from the monastery. As I understood it, that later life as a celibate monk embodied an effort to work out the karmic consequences of my soul's greedy search for esoteric wisdom in its earlier life as a wealthy man, which had caused so much harm to my family in that life. Although I would find love in the communities in which I served as healer, my soul in that incarnation would not risk having beloved family members who could again be hurt by my spiritual explorations.

I had previously developed my own sense of shamanic practice from conducting network assemblies, in which I opened myself to intuitive connection with conscious and unconscious process in the room. As conductor, I would allow myself to be a vessel for network members' thoughts and feelings. Relying on my fellow team members to support me and to maintain the coherence of the group process, I would allow myself to become absorbed in altered states of consciousness and to come forth with utterances that moved the assembly in the direction of healing and growth.

After my experience with Ann, I decided to explore more formal study of shamanic practice. I attended a workshop for mental health professionals that Ann offered as an introduction to shamanism. As we lay on the floor listening to recorded drumming, Ann encouraged us to allow ourselves to travel into the spirit worlds:

> I find myself on a flat, treeless tundra, a beautiful expanse of brown and orange vegetation interlaced by clear, cold streams. A moose, my spirit guide, appears and leads me to an opening in the earth. I travel down through the earth and emerge through the high ceiling of an enormous room. There is a woman sitting at a piano at one side of the room. From floor to ceiling, every wall is covered with fully stocked bookshelves. I can barely contain my excitement as I float to the floor and make my way to a bookshelf. Eagerly, I take a book from the shelf, draw a breath, and open the book. All the pages are blank. As I struggle with my confusion and disappointment, the woman at the piano, whom I now recognize as one of my spirit guides, beckons me to sit beside her on the bench in front of the piano. As I sit, she bids me to start practicing scales . . .

Reflecting on the destructive effects of my greed in an earlier incarnation as a Chinese student of esoteric knowledge, I thought of my vulnerability to overreach as a seeker. I remembered the greed that had me trying to capture the energy of the Divine in my body when Ramón opened me (and from which he protected me by giggling at my hubris). I interpreted this visit to the spirit world at Ann's workshop as giving me the message to attend to self-cultivation rather than to try traveling in the spirit world before I was ready. Later, as I experienced growth in the slow and painstaking process of learning the complex movements of Chi Gong, undertaken with humility under the guidance of a master, I wondered if this served as the equivalent of practicing my scales at the piano. Later still, as I endeavor to decipher Hebrew in sacred texts, I speculate about the relevance of this experience in the spirit world. Are my Jewish studies the equivalent of practicing scales in order to gain access to knowledge?

LEARNING CHI GONG

For a while after my visit to the library in the spirit world, my travel on the path of spiritual growth did not have much focus. I continued to read texts in a variety of traditions and would occasionally meditate in an unsystematic fashion. Although I was moved by the spiritual atmosphere of *Shabbat* (Sabbath) services, I had no interest in converting to Judaism. From my study of Sufism, I understood that a form only affords genuine spiritual experience when it is constructed for a certain person at a certain time in certain circumstances. As soon as any of those conditions change, the form becomes empty. For me, any organized religion was by its nature an empty form.

A minor infection in my nose bloomed into a life-threatening medical crisis as I developed what the doctors called a "fulminating infection." I was hospitalized with facial cellulitis and was placed on the critical list for several days. I recovered with massive doses of antibiotics over the course of a month, wearing a pump to deliver the medicine intravenously following my discharge from the hospital. After recovering from the acute infection, with the microscopic companions of my biome destroyed by the antibiotics, I was exhausted and depleted. I asked a colleague for a referral to her acupuncturist. After an initial evaluation, the acupuncturist referred me for *tui na* massage (a form of deep massage grounded in the same principles of Chinese medicine as acupuncture) provided by a colleague who shared his office suite. Out of curiosity I bought a book on the Chinese energy practice of Chi Gong, for sale in the acupuncturist's waiting room.

The *tui na* practitioner was not the kind of person that one might expect in a skillful and effective healer well-grounded in Chinese medicine and its roots in Taoist philosophy. Physically and energetically, Brian Collins is a larger-than-life figure. He grew up as a timid Irish kid in a South Boston housing project. He began his studies in childhood, impressed by his uncle's demonstration of Asian martial arts, which his uncle had learned during a tour of military duty in the Pacific. Brian's studies of martial arts included learning how to treat the injuries that his energetic blows were capable of inflicting. Mastery of martial arts led him into study of its philosophic roots. With the same dedication he had shown in his study of martial arts, Brian mastered the study of healing.

As deeply grounded as he was in Asian esoteric knowledge, Brian never lost his connection with his working-class roots. On occasion, when I would cry out from a particularly painful penetrating move in his massage, he would wisecrack, "You flatterer . . ." He was a perfect foil for my tendency to take myself too seriously in my esoteric studies. Like Ramón before him, Brian discerned my capacity to develop spiritually, and offered to teach me Chi Gong.

The early stages of learning Chi Gong were indeed much like practicing scales. I had always been physically clumsy, and nothing about the deliberate, precise body movements of this practice (related to the graceful *Tai Chi* exercises that one may see Asian elders practicing outdoors in many communities) came easily to me. I cultivated patience and persistence, acquiring mastery of the movements slowly over many months. Perception of the movement of subtle *chi* energy in my body came even more slowly.

As I learned to recognize the flow of chi, I perceived how sensitive it was to what I took into my body. I quit drinking coffee, and a cup of wine at Passover at the beginning of the millennium was my last alcoholic drink. Nearly a year after I began my Chi Gong practice, I faced a decision. I could see how the practice was helping me to regulate my ADHD and could also see how the stimulant medication I was taking for ADHD symptoms was interfering with my emerging energetic practice. I couldn't be sure how I would be able to manage myself should I go off medication and was well aware that I had become easier to live with when the medication controlled my ADHD symptoms. I decided to keep my decision to myself for a several days after I stopped taking the medicine, to demonstrate both to Jodie and to myself that my Chi Gong practice could effectively replace medication for controlling my ADHD symptoms. Jodie was indeed alarmed to learn that I had stopped taking the medicine but was reassured by the evidence that my symptoms had not flared in the time that I had, unbeknownst to her, not been taking it.

A COMPANION ON THE JOURNEY

Changes in American healthcare, beginning with the radial disassembly of the community mental health system under President Ronald Reagan's administration and extending through the industrialization of psychotherapy by managed care, undercut financial support for network therapy. The emergence of neoliberalism, an exaggerated emphasis on individual search for gain in a competitive marketplace, contributed to a model of payment for mental health services restricted to individual face-to-face encounters. Full-scale network assemblies are labor-intensive and costly, requiring a team of professionals working together for hours over the course of several assemblies. The cost of full-scale assemblies is best measured against their value to the community. That value was rendered invisible as corporate health care replaced community mental health.

Jodie, our colleagues, and I did a telephone follow-up study after a series of network assemblies for a young woman caught up in a dangerous repetitive suicidal pattern.[40] The intervention helped end her suicide attempts. A few years later, she was married and a loving mother. We found many lives touched by the intervention, both within and beyond the network.

One relative, who had come to the network assembly to help the family in crisis, experienced a profound shift in his experience of chronic depression. Years before, he had made a bargain with himself to end his life after his children graduated college. He renounced his secret suicidal intention after witnessing the effects of this young woman's suicide attempts on their overlapping networks. A business manager who previously had little interest in the personal lives of his employees, he set the intention to make his workplace supportive of his workers' emotional needs. These kinds of benefits serve communities, not just the individuals at the center of a network assembly.

With few opportunities to practice network therapy in the United States, I kept up with the evolution of this practice by publishing *Netletter*, an informal international newsletter for network therapists in countries with social welfare democracies, such as Sweden, where the long-term social and clinical benefits of the practice were understood to be worth its short-term financial costs. I found ways to adapt Carolyn Attneave's network intervention approach, which was grounded more in community organizing than in gathering assemblies, for my office practice, particularly for my work with the problems that develop around learning disabilities.[41]

With no opportunities to develop my shamanic practice conducting network assemblies, I continued to explore mystical and esoteric ideas in texts from a variety of traditions. Jodie and I began attending the Annual Culture Conference, a gathering of progressive, culturally sensitive family therapists hosted by Monica McGoldrick and Nydia Garcia-Preto of the Multicultural Family Institute in New Jersey (Kenneth Hardy later became the third Conference Co-Chair). Although I did not discuss my esoteric pursuits with many professionals, I found Nydia, the granddaughter of a Puerto Rican espiritista, to be a curious, knowledgeable, and respectful listener. CharlesEtta (Charlee) Sutton, who acknowledges her Native American, African, and Irish ancestors, joined one of Nydia's conversations with me, and we quickly discovered our common interest in engaging with spirit worlds. Charlee and I became spiritual companions, witnesses to each other's journeys, often bringing messages from the spirit world to each other.

DECIDING TO CONVERT TO JUDAISM

As Jodie and I raised Jacob in a Jewish family life, I was comfortable attending occasional services and observing the Jewish holidays. Although I had no intention to adopt a religion, I found nothing in Jewish liturgy to interfere with my own spiritual journey. Unable to keep up with the Hebrew in Reconstructionist religious services, Jodie and I tried a couple of Reform synagogues, settling on Temple Sinai in Brookline, with its warm, welcoming congregation and supportive, informal atmosphere. Jacob found Hebrew school on Tuesday afternoons and Sunday mornings as challenging as he found public school, but he was able to learn, with the goal of becoming a *bar mitzvah* (through a rite of passage into Jewish adulthood) when he reached age thirteen.

There is a moment in Jewish religious services when the Torah (a parchment scroll on which the first five books of the Bible have been written by quill and ink in Hebrew) is removed from the ark in which it resides. In rituals both solemn and joyous, the Torah is acknowledged as embodying God's words. According to a central myth of Judaism, God transmitted those words to Moses when God appeared to the entire assembled multitude of the children of Israel. That transformative event took place at Mount Sinai, after liberation from bondage in Egypt and at the beginning of forty years' journey through the desert to the land pledged to the descendants of Abraham, Isaac, and Jacob. According to Jewish lore, all the children of Israel at that moment at Sinai, together with all the Jews who are now living, all who have ever lived, and all who will be born in the future are simultaneously present from the moment when the Torah is borne out of the ark until the moment it is returned following its reading. During Torah readings, I began to sense the presence of the ancestors in the sanctuary. Over time, experiencing the presence of ancestors and descendants became a constant whenever the Torah came out of the ark. I began to give some thought to converting to Judaism.

As I explored texts on Judaism, I discerned a dynamic relationship between preserving nearly three thousand years of tradition on the one hand and adapting to changing historical circumstances while maintaining coherent cultural identity on the other. I was struck by the dance between evolution and stability in Jewish religious forms.

I encountered three obstacles to making a commitment to conversion. The theological culture at Temple Sinai at the time was traditionally Reform, grounded in the rationalist perspective of the eighteenth-century Haskalah, a Jewish movement influenced by the European Enlightenment. It was hard to see how conversion to Reform Judaism could incorporate my transpersonal and esoteric spiritual journey. At the time, in the first decade of the twenty-first century, conversion to Reform Judaism also required affirmative commitment to the state of Israel. As a veteran of the Civil Rights Movement, I had deep concerns about the Israeli occupation of Palestinian land and the subordinate status of Palestinians within Israel itself. Finally, I also did not want to upstage Jacob, who was a few years away from his bar mitzvah and struggling more and more with his life. I decided to wait until after Jacob's bar mitzvah before exploring conversion further.

JACOB'S STRUGGLES

Throughout his childhood, even after his struggle with learning began in first grade, Jacob had a radiant and generous disposition, with a mischievous sense of humor and the capacity to experience and to share great joy. He did have difficulty regulating himself when frustrated, reacting intensely and requiring help to soothe himself. Given his ADHD impulsivity, and my own, we could get caught up in kindling, reactivity in one setting off reactivity in the other. As Jacob and I would get caught in a downward spiral devolving into my raised voice and his angry tears, Jodie would step in to interrupt, calm things down, and make peace. As difficult as these moments could be, we managed to maintain a generally positive equilibrium, a household of three or four, with Jessica or Ransom (at 19 and 13 years older than Jacob) sometimes visiting and sometimes living with us, making ours their home base as they navigated developmental transitions through high school, college, and young adulthood.

In 1998, a few months before Jacob's twelfth birthday, we opened our home to my brother Robin, who was facing the prospect of homelessness. Diagnosed with bipolar disorder and gradually losing his vision because of glaucoma, Robin was unable to mobilize himself to find new lodging after his rental apartment was converted to a condominium. He was in the process of transitioning from owning and driving a taxi to being supported by Social Security Disability Insurance. Depressive by temperament, Robin was taking eye medication that exacerbated his depression. Jacob got caught up in the dysphoric cloud of Robin's presence in our home and showed more difficulty managing his own moods. He lost it emotionally during his twelfth birthday celebration and for the first time expressed suicidal ideation.

With our sister Sheila's financial help, Robin left a few months later, but Jacob continued to struggle with his moods. Despite strong verbal, artistic, and mechanical intelligence recognized by his teachers, he did more and more poorly in school. We learned to disengage from increasingly toxic family struggles over his resistance to doing homework, hiring tutors to provide what support he could accept. He suffered recurrent episodes of depression. Although we can't reconstruct with precision, it may have been around his thirteenth birthday that he began the secret use of alcohol and marijuana in his struggle to feel better. He nonetheless rose to the considerable demands of training for his bar mitzvah, which we delayed until relatively late in his thirteenth year.

The extended family gathered for joyous celebration of his bar mitzvah. He read a Hebrew passage from the Torah. His *d'var Torah*, the speech to the congregation about his understanding of that passage, beautifully articulated the values of social justice, respect for every human being, and fundamental fairness shared by both sides of his extended family.

Despite this success, Jacob continued to struggle with his schoolwork and with his moods. When not depressed, he more frequently sought excitement in risky behavior, which we attributed to his ADHD. Hope and heartbreak fueled our denial, as we avoided confronting the questions of substance abuse or serious mood disorder. Overdiagnosis of bipolar disorder in children was an unfortunate local fashion among Boston area child psychiatrists, which contributed to our resisting the suggestion by Jodie's father and stepmother (both psychiatrists) that this mood disorder might be implicated in Jacob's struggles.

It was easier to invoke ADHD to explain his difficulties. Jacob failed history in eighth grade because he did not hand in his homework. We took the opportunity while he was at camp that summer to sort through the contents of the backpack that he had kept away from us so jealously during the school year. In the backpack, we found all his history homework assignments, completed but never handed in, a classic example of executive functioning difficulties characteristic of ADHD.

A freak accident at one of Jacob's soccer games added to the complexity of our family dynamic. A little sister of one of Jacob's teammates threw a stick up into the air. It landed on Jodie's head, giving her a concussion. An immediate, fortunately temporary, effect of the injury was disruption of Jodie's emotional self-regulation for several months. Suddenly, she was not available to soothe escalating reactivity between father and son. Instead, as Jodie was even more vulnerable than I was to anger at Jacob's provocations, I was called upon to assume the soothing role between mother and son. Although I rose to the occasion, to the benefit of the relationships among Jacob, his mother, and me, Jacob had to cope with a change in his mother's manner of helping him with self-regulation.

As Jacob moved further into adolescence, the storms got far worse. He was more prone to going into a rage when frustrated, and increasingly insatiable in his need for external means to soothe himself. Although we had become aware of his use of substances for self-soothing, we were still ignorant of its extent. We struggled with his demands for clothing, electronic devices, money, trips to the movies, etc. On the one hand, we did not rush to gratify his material demands, recognizing that too much indulgence was interfering with the maturation of his capacity to regulate himself emotionally. On the other, alarmed by the intensity of his meltdowns, we would sometimes accommodate his demands in order to mitigate emotional and relational harm. The only certainty in these difficult situations was that we would sometimes make mistakes.

Jacob's judgment and impulse control continued to deteriorate. He started getting into legal difficulties from impulsive acts associated with the substance abuse that was becoming glaringly apparent. We began family therapy with David Treadway, a former colleague of Jodie's, who was experienced at working with issues of substance abuse in families. Jacob had been prescribed an antidepressant for his migraines, in addition to stimulant medication for his ADHD. When Jacob was sixteen, we discovered that he was not taking his medication. Knowing that it was dangerous to drink while taking the antidepressant, he would skip his medication in order to drink alcohol.

We started monitoring to assure that he was taking his medicine, unintentionally setting off a rapid cascade of changes. His teachers reported a dramatic improvement in his academic performance. He engaged us in intense conversation about his intelligence, which devolved within a few days into an increasingly manic flow of delusional thinking and speech. The same child who had wailed over feeling stupid when he struggled with homework now claimed with great enthusiasm that he was the smartest and strongest person in the world. When he did not show up at his after-school job and left us a disturbingly disorganized voicemail, we had to call on the police (who already knew him from his scrapes with the law) to locate him. They brought him, psychotic, to a hospital emergency room, where he spent the night while they sought an inpatient psychiatric bed.

Before we arrived to keep him company in the ER, he had punched a cement wall, breaking his hand. Believing that he had superpowers, he thought that he could escape by breaking down the wall. We could not ignore the evidence that Jacob had bipolar disorder, particularly as the antidepressant medication, which he had been taking regularly under our supervision for several weeks, is known to precipitate psychotic symptoms in people with the disorder. Our efforts to make sure that he was taking that medicine now appeared to be a precipitant of his psychosis.

On the inpatient unit, Jacob stayed psychotic for over a week, getting surgery for his hand in the hospital where he was staying. It was clear that he was not ready to return home immediately after recovering from the acute psychosis. He was transferred to an adolescent acute residential psychiatric treatment program, where he made a slow recovery. As network therapists, Jodie and I saw that it was important to integrate the network of Jacob's helpers into his treatment and recovery. David Treadway, our family therapist, agreed to convene a meeting at the residential program, which we attended together with the leader of his high school specialized learning program, his individual therapist, and the police sergeant who had become involved with Jacob during his tangles with the law.

When he returned home, Jacob seemed stronger and somewhat better regulated. School was still a struggle, but his moods were less intense and protracted. We saw fewer signs of substance abuse, although with hindsight we recognize that this was probably because he was better able to conceal it. What we could see that he was more vulnerable to emotional meltdowns in the face of the inevitable challenges of adolescence. Difficult as Jacob could be, he clearly yearned for more family peace and less fraught emotional connection with his parents. All three of us worked hard together with David Treadway in family therapy.

When Jacob was seventeen, we got a letter from his birth mother, Delana. She had respected our privacy as Jacob's parents but had never forgotten the child whom she had entrusted to us when Jacob was a few days old. She wrote to tell us that she had planned to wait until Jacob made the decision to seek her out but that now, if he wanted to see her, it would have to be soon, as she was dying of lung cancer. We called to say that the three of us could be with her in Texas the next day, but she asked that we delay for a week, as she had already made plans for the coming weekend. We made our travel arrangements according to her preference. We asked Jacob if he wanted to speak with her on the phone, but he decided that he wanted to hear her voice for the first time when they would be in each other's physical presence, and he could hug her. Days before our flight to Texas we got the call that she had gone into a coma and died.

We agreed with Delana's family that we would keep our promise to visit. Jacob, Jodie and I landed in Texas hours after his birth mother was buried. It was a complex, emotionally intense visit, as Delana's mother, her siblings and their families both grieved their loss and lovingly welcomed the reappearance of a family member who had gone to a life on the East Coast days after Delana had given birth to him. During the visit, we learned from her family that Delana had been abusing drugs during her pregnancy and that she and other members of her family had been diagnosed with bipolar disorder.

Jacob was grateful for his connection with his birth family but wasn't able to recover from the unexpected loss of his birth mother. He was barely hanging on in a specialized therapeutic program at his high school. At our request, David Treadway convened another network assembly at the therapeutic school. In addition to school faculty, participants included Jacob's individual therapist, his psychiatrist, another psychiatrist on whom we had called for consultation, and the police sergeant (who went to our house to persuade a reluctant Jacob to come with him to join the meeting). Despite these collective efforts, Jacob continued to spiral downward. None of us were taking in how deeply Jacob had fallen into alcohol and substance abuse.

On the first anniversary of Delana's death, at age 18, Jacob was psychiatrically hospitalized again, at which time we learned how much more serious his substance abuse had become. After a shorter hospitalization than the first one, Jacob was discharged with a treatment plan including individual therapy and substance abuse counseling, to complement ongoing family therapy. Jodie and I were in constant dread and despair, as we struggled to provide our beloved and increasingly troubled child with the support, nurturance, and limits that he needed. Even at his worst moments, screaming and cursing at us after punching another hole in the wall, we could see our Jacob's radiant soul, and hear the child within crying out with yearning for his parents to help him handle his pain.

It is not uncommon for adoptive parents to have to come to terms with profound differences in motivation and temperament between their child and themselves. From early in his adolescence, Jacob had complained about the chasm between his expectations for his own life and his parents' advanced academic degrees and intellectually absorbing life. He shared fantasies about how different his life would be if he had grown up in East Texas with his working-class birth family. After the visit to his birth family, Jacob felt powerfully affirmed by his experience of Texas relatives who were living secure and meaningful working-class lives. Jodie and I had a deep conversation with each other about reasonable aspirations for our son's life. We committed ourselves to keeping him alive, supporting him to build a life that would be meaningful to him, and keeping him in relationship with us. We relinquished what might have remained of any dreams of his going to college.

Troubled families are vulnerable to descending spirals of acute stress, narrowing perspectives focused on crisis in the moment, and depleted emotional reserves that distance them from their networks. They may have less available energy to reach out to others, and others may disengage to avoid their own emotional discomfort. We were perhaps less isolated than others might have been in these painful circumstances. Ransom and his wife Kim were available from where they lived a few towns away; Jessica from New York and Jodie's family in California and New York stayed in touch by phone. We were blessed by the constant presence of a multiracial, multicultural group of colleagues with whom Jodie and I had taught family therapy at the Center for Multicultural

Training in Psychology years before—Gonzalo Bacigalupe, Hugo Kamya, Jay King, and Roxana Llerena-Quinn. We knew each other's families and had watched each other's children grow up. No longer teaching together at CMTP, we had formed a collegial group, the Boston Institute for Culturally Affirming Practices (BICAP), meeting regularly in each other's homes. Friends as well as colleagues, our comrades from BICAP were constant supports during Jacob's most turbulent years. So were our longtime friends, David and Sylvia Hammerman, Marsha and Mitch Mirkin, Rachel Dash, and a few parents of Jacob's oldest friends. They were engaged, compassionate witnesses and companions throughout the difficult journey.

After the second hospitalization the extent of Jacob's substance abuse was no longer secret. Exposure of the secret, however, did little to interrupt his descending spiral. Jacob, Jodie, and I had by then lived through several years of toxic stress. Despite compassionate support from friends and wise counsel from experienced experts, we were mired in helplessness, confusion, and dread for Jacob's survival. By now 18 years old, Jacob was more often defiant of our demands and limits. After he dropped out of school and stopped seeing his drug counselor, Jodie and I faced a heartbreaking and terrifying choice. We could provide him with food and shelter while he continued on his destructive path, materially subsidizing his dangerous choices, or we could insist on his making more responsible choices as a condition for his living in our home.

As Jacob was now eighteen, the law did not stand between us and the decision to send him out of our home. On the one hand, we had to do something to break the pattern in which we were powerless onlookers to his self-destruction. On the other hand, we understood that were we to put him out of the house, we would be surrendering any power, no matter how illusory, to protect his life. Although friends and experts counseled that we do so, the decision was ours, as were the consequences. Heartbroken, we sent Jacob from our home, making it clear that he had the choice to return should he meet our fundamental requirements that he attend school or hold a job, and that he resume drug counseling.

As it happened, we expelled Jacob from home twice, accepting him back when he accepted our requirements and sending him away when he did not meet them. He did not return to school but made serious efforts to find employment, not an easy task for a high school dropout. The last time, his third departure from our home, he did not bother to show up to be sent away, as he knew that we had discovered he was arranging a drinking party for his friends after their high school prom.

Although he appeared to respect us more for our taking a firm stance, expelling Jacob brought no relief for any of us. Although we were spared daily confrontations punctuated by his destructive episodes of uncontrolled rage, we went through each day not knowing whether or not he was alive, dreading a call that he was arrested, in a hospital, or dead. It was a difficult time as well for Ransom and Jessica, with their own mixed feelings about us as parents and struggling with their own feelings of fear and helplessness. We did not suffer alone. Extended family, the Hammermans, Marsha, Rachel, BICAP, and caring members of our synagogue congregation all were ready to listen and provide emotional and material support. Nonetheless, our hearts were broken and full of dread.

Years before her death, Jacob's birth mother Delana had been "born again" as a Christian. That experience of personal rebirth gave her the strength that she needed to turn her life around, recovering from substance abuse and finding a relationship with a responsible and loving man who became her husband and the father of the youngest of Jacob's three birth brothers. After Delana's death, Jacob had become interested in the Protestant Christian religion of his birth family, which appeared to have turned his mother away from her life's destructive course. Although we wished for ourselves that Jacob would live as a Jew, we wondered if Jacob might find in his mother's story a path toward his own recovery, and we supported his exploration.

The day that Jacob's classmates graduated from high school, we were at a barbecue celebrating the graduation of one of Jacob's childhood friends. The friendship between our families was strong enough for Jodie and me to tolerate the bitter feelings with the sweet—aware that Jacob should have been graduating that day but proud and happy for his friend Sam. While we were at the celebration, Jacob called me on my cell phone to ask me to take him to the hospital for detox. We met up, and I took him to Saint Elizabeth's hospital, where he had last been hospitalized and where he had been getting substance abuse counseling. We learned later that Jacob had been shaken enough to seek treatment after a drug dealer had put a gun to his neck, demanding money. Jodie and I advocated vigorously with his health insurance provider to cover the cost of a well-respected inpatient substance abuse program to follow his brief stay at Saint Elizabeth's for detox. Jodie's parents were prepared to help cover the costs if insurance did not come through.

Several years before, when Jacob's difficulties had been increasing in severity, Jodie's father Gilbert had recommended that we send him to Heartland Christian Ministries, a life recovery program in rural Missouri. Gil, a secular Jew and a child psychiatrist, had been called as an expert witness to evaluate Heartland, in the context of a controversy over their use of spanking with younger children. Although his critical view of corporal punishment did not change, Gil was nonetheless impressed with the positive effects of Heartland's programs on the lost lives of the children, adolescents, and young adults in their care. When Gil first raised the idea, a few years into Jacob's travails, Jodie and I were not warm to the idea of sending our Jewish child to live in a fundamentalist Christian community. By this time in Jacob's troubled life, however, we were open to anything that offered the promise of saving and redeeming his life. Jacob, who was exploring his birth mother's fundamentalist Christianity, was as well.

On his discharge from Saint Elizabeth's, I drove Jacob to Gosnold, an intensive inpatient treatment program for substance abuse in nearby Cape Cod. He was wearing a plastic cross pendant and made it clear that he wanted to pursue his birth family's religion. After Jacob spent a couple of weeks at Gosnold, Jodie and I came down for a family meeting. In a healing moment for all of us, Jacob acknowledged that he had been trying to blame us for his behavior and misfortunes and took full responsibility for his actions. He asked to go to Heartland after his discharge from Gosnold. He had a couple of hours' leave in our company; we bought him a suitcase for his trip to Heartland and a silver cross pendant to replace the plastic Catholic cross. When he finished at Gosnold, I flew with him to Missouri, where he made a commitment to spend at least a year working and living a Christian life at Heartland.

Heartland was founded by millionaire insurance executive Charlie Sharpe, who had committed his life to fundamentalist Christian ministry. Heartland is an agricultural complex of fields, cattle, and goats, with a hotel and other small enterprises on its sprawling campus in rural Northeast Missouri. Young children and adolescents, orphaned, neglected, abused, addicted, or otherwise broken are sent to Heartland by their families or referred by social welfare organizations. Jacob at eighteen was in a dormitory for young adults. Residents' lives were strictly regimented, with work, prayer, and worship services. Those old enough to work in hotel, farm, or small industries (e.g., cheese-making) receive salaries for their work. It took some advocacy by Jacob's grandfather Gil for Heartland to accept him because he was on medications for ADHD and bipolar disorder. Heartland believes that religious faith is sufficient for their residents to master psychological challenges.

I made a good connection with Jerry Parrish, the man in charge of the young adults at Heartland. He proved to be accessible and kept us informed of how Jacob was faring. We heard that Jacob had a good deal of difficulty settling into some kind of work, and he could not handle the available options for schooling. After a few weeks, Jacob found his place as an apprentice mechanic in the garage where Heartland's trucks and farm equipment were repaired. The work drew on his considerable strengths, and Jacob had always been drawn to mechanics. He began to experience his first success as a learner, taking on more responsibilities as he gained in proficiency as a mechanic. We would get occasional brief letters in response to ours, and he would call us from the office of the garage.

After several weeks knowing that Jacob was safe, alive, and in capable hands, Jodie and I relaxed enough to take in how deeply we had been affected by years of traumatic stress, releasing the tears that had been contained by dread and desperation. We continued to meet with David Treadway, who had helped us to repair and strengthen our marriage, stretched at times to its limits during these painful years.

4

Making the Commitment to Convert

I HAD DELAYED MY decision to convert to Judaism, first to avoid upstaging Jacob's bar mitzvah, then because Jacob's early adolescent turmoil required my full attention. I promised myself to start the conversion process once his turmoil subsided. By the time he was seventeen it was becoming apparent that Jacob's struggles might not subside. Accepting that painful prospect, I made the decision to begin my studies for conversion.

My decision to convert to Judaism emerged from my direct experience of the presence of ancestors during services when the Torah was removed from its ark. Although some people are born with powers of spiritual intuition, my ability to recognize the presence of the ancestors was the fruit of decades of self-cultivation, inspired by rare moments of awe and wonder. From my perspective at the time of my decision to convert, my spiritual journey had begun with the moment of revelation in Ramón's company. The cultivation of my capacities was the fruit of study and meditation in a wide range of human spiritual traditions, which followed that direct experience of divine consciousness in Ramón's home.

I now recognize that the first such moment of awe was the ancestral call in my nine-year-old dream, a call from a God who appeared to me, charged me with seemingly impossible responsibility, and then abandoned me. At the time I made the decision to convert, the traumatic effects of that paradoxical call were still far from healed, and fragments from that shattering experience were hidden in a compartment of my mind far from everyday waking awareness.

I was encouraged that our congregation's new rabbi, Andrew Vogel, was clearly more open to transpersonal spiritual experience than was his predecessor, a classically Reform Jewish rationalist. I offered Andy a brief summary of my spiritual journey when I approached him with my formal request to study for conversion. Hearing my story, he responded enthusiastically, announcing that he would teach me "Reform Judaism and *Chasidut*."

Chasidut is the body of stories, beliefs, practices, and traditions of the Jewish Chasidic movement. The movement originated in eighteenth-century Eastern Europe as an effort to revitalize Judaism, posing a radical challenge to the traditional Judaism of the time. In the succeeding century, Chasidism was to align itself with its conservative prior adversary in unified opposition to the Haskalah. That movement, inspired by the ideology of the European Enlightenment, sought to modernize Judaism by aligning Jewish religion, lifestyle, and values with mainstream European society. Reform Judaism emerged from the Haskalah movement. The early adherents of Reform believed that, beyond simply revitalizing Jewish tradition, their Judaism would replace the old form. Rather than supplanting traditional Judaism, Reform instead became one of several forms of Judaism, including Orthodox, Reform, Reconstructionist, Jewish Renewal, and others. Orthodox Judaism includes a range from Modern Orthodox to more traditional and insular *Haredi* and Chasidic variants.

Accustomed to the bewildering proliferation of denominations within the Christianity of my birth, I developed a different perspective on Judaism's variety of forms. They are in many ways distinct in their theologies and particularly in their demands for observance of the *mitzvot* (God's commandments, as embodied in ancient foundational texts and centuries of commentary on those texts). Some adherents of these various forms claim that theirs is the only true Judaism, echoing the claims of exclusive Christian identity by some adherents of Christian denominations. Outside of Israel, however, where Orthodox Judaism maintains its hegemony, contemporary Jews of different denominations are now more likely to accept each other's existence as religious Jews.

Unlike conversion to Christianity or Islam, which primarily require a declaration of faith in their beliefs, conversion to Judaism requires deep study of the texts and traditions of the Jewish religion and commitment to living a Jewish life. To be recognized as a Jew by other Jews, the convert needs to understand the Jew's particular obligations to serve God and must make a lifetime commitment to meet those obligations.

Judaism is identified with a particular people, not just a particular form of religious faith. To convert to Judaism is to be adopted into a family that claims more than three thousand years of continuous existence. It involves learning, in some fashion and to whatever degree, the ancient language of Hebrew, whether that means reading that language fluently, or knowing how to chant central prayers. The Hebrew words in Torah, Prophets, and Writings of the Jewish Bible are continuously read, studied, and argued over.

After the Torah scroll, a beautifully hand-lettered parchment, is unrolled in services, a reader melodically chants its Hebrew verses. In the Torah, Jews share a rich mythology of direct engagement between God and the patriarchs and matriarchs (Abraham, Sarah, Isaac, Rebecca, Jacob [or Israel], Leah, Rachel), and with Israel's descendants at Sinai, particularly with Moses, bidden by God to liberate the children of Israel from bondage in Egypt. God promised the patriarchs that their descendants would inherit a good and fertile land and guided Moses to lead them through the desert to that promised land. Jews all over the world know the stories in Torah of bondage in Egypt from which God redeemed them in order for them to serve God: God's self-revelation at Sinai, God's instructions to Moses on the terms of their obligation to serve, and their arrival at the Jordan River, at the border of the promised land.

The mythology and imagery continue beyond the words of Torah, into the rest of the Tanach. After Joshua leads the children of Israel into the promised land, the narrative continues to and through the first exile from the promised land. The words and stories of prophets from before, during, and after exile reflect on the travails of the children of Israel. The temple, the central location and devotional instrument of the Israelite religion, was destroyed by the Babylonians who exiled the elites of Israel. It was rebuilt when the Persian ruler Cyrus permitted the exiles to return, as his vassals, to Jerusalem.

The common story continues beyond the pages of the Jewish Bible, from the beginning of the Common Era with Christianity, when the Roman occupiers destroyed the Second Temple and evicted our ancestors from Jerusalem and the surrounding region. By then, we were known as Jews, rather than Israelites, named after the tribe of Judah, one of the last remnants of the original twelve tribes, not assimilated into the societies of their Assyrian and Babylonian conquerors.

Over several centuries, a group of leaders who became known as "rabbis" struggled over how to maintain the continuity of a religion founded on the practice of sacrifice at the temple, when the temple was no more. They declared prayer to be the replacement for sacrificial temple offering and articulated a complex set of laws based on the mitzvot in the Hebrew Bible. Preserved originally as an oral tradition, the record of those rabbinic deliberations was recorded in writing known as the Mishnah. Over the next few centuries, the Mishnah itself became the object of further elaboration, argument, and discussion, recorded in the Gemara. The Gemara and the Mishnah combined to form the text of the Talmud, the cornerstone of rabbinic interpretive application of the Law to everyday Jewish lives.

The Haskalah challenged nineteenth-century Jewish traditions by questioning the authority of rabbinic interpretation of the Talmud to determine observant Jewish life. A sectarian divide emerged when the Orthodox Judaism reacted to the Reform movement's effort to bridge Jewish life and secular society. Before that, Judaism had been for the most part consensual throughout the diaspora (Jews in the lands to which they had been scattered by successive exiles). There were some variations of observance and culture between Sephardic Jews, descendants of the fifteenth-century exile from Spain who had scattered to many countries, and European Ashkenazi Jews of central and eastern Europe. More radical departures from consensual Judaism, e.g., Karaite and Sabbatean movements, eventually faded. A small community of Samaritans (a name that Christians may recognize from their Gospels), remnants of the northern tribes defeated and exiled by Assyrian conquest before the Babylonian exile of the Judaeans, persists in what is now the West Bank, territory under Israeli occupation for more than fifty years.

In its youth and adolescence, Reform Judaism directly challenged Orthodox Judaism. Leaders of the Reform movement expected that their form of the Jewish religion would supplant and succeed its predecessor. The struggle between Reform and Orthodox Judaism traveled from Europe to America. The Reform Statement of the Philadelphia Conference of 1869 was explicit that their religion was now the true Judaism, and that many of the mitzvot were no longer binding obligations for Jews. The arrogance of the Reform position was brought home bluntly to the more religiously observant guests at that Conference, when the banquet menu included shellfish among other forbidden, non-kosher foods. Contemporary Reform Judaism, fortunately, holds a more pluralistic stance about Judaism.

Having left Christianity decades before, I was not willing to commit myself to a religion that demanded conformity. Jodie and I had settled on a Reform congregation in which to raise Jacob. We found the liturgy accessible to worshipers not deeply grounded in Hebrew. Reform's strong social justice values aligned with ours. Although patriarchy is firmly embedded in millennia of Jewish texts and traditions, there is an active conversation about gender and power issues in the Reform movement. Reform's flexibility about observance spared us from struggling with gender-specific mitzvot.

Even as I prepared to convert to Reform Judaism in particular, I found opportunities to engage across the boundaries of the different forms of Judaism. Although there was room in more observant Jewish communities for mystical, esoteric knowledge, I had chosen not to accept the restrictions of a more observant Jewish life. Before witnessing Rabbi Andy's spiritual engagement with religious ritual, I had not found room within Reform Judaism's otherwise relatively open boundaries for the mystical ideas and experiences that I felt at the core of my being. Andy's enthusiastic promise to teach me "Reform Judaism and chasidut" offered the openness and flexibility that I needed. In my sixtieth year, I wanted to integrate my learning as a Jew with what I had learned over the course of my spiritual journey.

Over the course of my journey, before I arrived at Judaism, I had often found multiple convergences among seemingly distinct esoteric traditions. These convergences appeared to me to reflect two phenomena. On the one hand, cultural transmission has been fundamental to human civilization from the beginning, long before the idea of a "global culture" shaped by technological innovation. Traders, diplomats, religious proselytizers, expanding empires were disseminating cultural ideas from the beginning of civilization. On the other hand, as I studied with teachers and read texts from disparate traditions, it appeared to me that some of the convergences I encountered were grounded in convergent personal discoveries by masters of their traditions, whether from prayer, shamanic journeying, or other forms of divine revelation. I expected to have a similar experience studying esoteric knowledge in Judaism. Early in my studies for conversion, I made a personal memorandum of the convergences that I had already integrated into my spiritual understanding.

WHAT I HAD LEARNED BEFORE I BECAME A JEW

By the end of my fifth decade, on a spiritual journey that began in childhood and had already marked the milestones first of madness and then of enlightenment by Ramón Jimenez, what follows here is how I constructed my spiritual understanding:

That which human beings seek, know, and name as God (by whatever name they use for this being) is the eternal, limitless All. There is nothing but God. God gazes into nothingness and imagines creation. Creation is organized as levels upon levels of phenomena that are, from perspectives within these levels, "real." From the ultimate divine perspective, all of Creation is "illusion." Creation is the exercise of Divine imagination. Worlds arise and dissolve in God's imagination, while God remains beyond time, space, and distinctions.

The exercise of divine imagination affords a mechanism for divine self-awareness. The material world in which we live our mortal lives has an important role in this mechanism. At each level of Creation, beings emerge with capacities to discern, with awe and love, the countenance of the Divine. Sentient beings in the material world have evolved with capacity for self-awareness, and thereby capacity to encounter the Divine. For the mechanism of divine self-awareness to operate, these sentient beings must be capable of both ignorance and awareness. They must be able to choose, to be free and able to turn both toward and away from God.

There is a paradox about the material world. On the one hand, spiritual beings at "higher" levels, closer to the divine source, have (compared with mortal human beings) superior abilities to perceive both the material world "below" them and the source "above" them. On the other hand, the decisions and actions of human beings in the material world have powerful consequences reverberating to the highest levels of Creation. Between incarnations, our souls occupy higher, nonmaterial realms in the company of spirit guides and supporters. The more successful our service has been in our mortal lives, the more opportunities we have to choose from as we prepare for our next incarnation. We can see and understand more when we are in higher realms, before and after we are born. It is in our mortal lives, when we are least able to see beyond the immediacy of the space and time that we occupy, that we have the most power to serve God.

I understood that my responsibility as a seeker was to cultivate my capacity to develop and sustain awareness of the Source of all existence. I could "ascend" in this practice by seeking the company and instruction of others at higher levels of spiritual evolution than I. I was also responsible for cultivating my capacity to discern the level of spiritual development of every particular human being that I encountered, and I could not raise myself without drawing others "upwards" with me.

Having lived through disillusionment with contemporary political organizations, I had replaced my earlier Marxist-Leninist worldview with the personal commitment that informs this memoir, my commitment to help build a global culture grounded in spirituality. Thanks to my meditative practice, and to reading about multiple universes, some that are being born as others fade away (an expansive view of the Divine promoted by sages such as Meher Baba), I had learned to persist without personal investment in the outcome of my efforts. I had no assurance as to how things would ultimately turn out, but I knew which side I was on.

Although I expected to find convergences between my existing knowledge and esoteric Judaism, I was to encounter much that I had not learned before. I was to find language for spiritual knowledge speaking more powerfully to my heart than anything I had known before. My determination to persist on my spiritual journey was to be fortified, for example, in the talmudic injunction "You are not expected to finish the work; neither are you permitted to desist."[42]

STUDYING FOR CONVERSION

Learning to be a Jew began in my first serious encounter with Jewish practice, attending services with Jodie as we prepared to raise our yet-to-be-born child as a Jew. Before I attended my first service, I had feared that I would get tangled in an internal argument with the liturgy; that I would feel angry and resentful at the expectation that I utter words with which I could not agree. I had left Christianity to escape from that inner discomfort and fully expected that I would encounter it in Jewish religious services. I also struggled with the notion that the Jewish people were somehow chosen and favored by God, which I interpreted as an elitist perspective that resonated uncomfortably for me with White supremacy.

At my first experience participating in a Jewish service, the only words in the liturgy that stuck in my throat were some phrases in Psalms that thanked God for triumph over enemies. Otherwise, I could interpret the liturgical language about God into deistic ideas that I associated with

Spinoza and with my own personal understanding of spirituality. The experience made me conscious of how much my estrangement from Christianity had been grounded in my rejecting its doctrine that Jesus is God.

Somehow, in that first service, I came to a very different perspective on the idea of "chosen people." My studies of Sufism (a mystical practice grounded in Islam) had already led me to a strong sense of responsibility for supporting the spiritual evolution of others (without proselytizing), particularly those with whom I was in close relationship. As I took in the Jewish idea of collective spiritual influence on the world, I felt my understanding of relational spiritual responsibility transform and elaborate. Jews are not morally superior to others; rather, they have a specific role in history.

The evolving, centuries-old story of the Jewish people stimulates human spiritual evolution. I was captured by the similarities, and the differences, with my own sense of personal spiritual responsibility. As a Jew, whether or not one consciously cultivates one's spiritual capacity as an individual, one participates in collective responsibility for the world. This perspective formed a seed that was to grow into a strong sense of purpose in my spiritual life. At that moment in my first Jewish religious service, I was both intrigued and relieved that the idea of "chosenness" was not a major obstacle to my participating in Jewish life. I was bemused that my understanding the chosenness of the Jewish people was grounded in Sufi ideas, given the uneasy relationship between Jews and Muslims in the Middle East.

When Jacob was old enough to attend Hebrew school, I took some adult introductory Hebrew classes, learning the alphabet and rudimentary grammar and vocabulary, which helped me to decode Hebrew liturgy and read the prayers aloud. With time, I came to understand the meaning of many of the Hebrew words uttered by members of the congregation in a Reform service. Although my knowledge of Judaism was still sparse, I was able to incorporate what little I knew into a personal spiritual frame of reference that I had shaped through decades of personal search. Once I began sensing the presence of ancestors when the Torah came out of the ark, I knew that it was only a matter of time before I began formal study for conversion.

Andy Vogel was true to his word, teaching me Chasidut as well as Reform Judaism. In our first session, he shared a passage in Talmud prescribing that the prospective convert be vigorously dissuaded before being accepted. He also shared an English translation of a passage from

Yosheir Divrei Emet, a book of teachings from the Chasidic Rabbi Meshullam Feivush of Zebriza. It introduced me to the goal of *deveikut,* merging with the Divine. The description of deveikut resonated for me with my experience at Ramón's home and with descriptions of similar experiences in several of the texts and traditions I had encountered in my journey. I was moved by the metaphor of the soul merging with the Divine as a single drop of water merges with the sea.

I studied eagerly. I read Maimonides on the eight levels of *tzedakah* (an untranslatable Hebrew term with connotations of generosity toward those in need and dedication to social justice, particularly in personal relationships). Martin Buber's writing introduced me to myths of the life of the Baal Shem Tov, the rabbi and shamanic healer who inspired the Chasidic movement, and to tales about the early generations of Chasidic rabbis.[43] Texts by contemporary rabbis Arthur Green and Lawrence Kushner resonated powerfully with my experiences of the sacred over the course of my journey. At Andy's recommendation, I registered for two years of study in *Me'ah,* one hundred hours of instruction in Jewish history, thought and practice, taught by the faculty of Hebrew College, a pluralistic Jewish seminary and center for adult learning in Newton, Massachusetts, near our home in Brookline. The four semesters of Me'ah covered the Bible and the early rabbinic, medieval, and modern eras.

In my Me'ah studies, I came to wonder how it was that Jews survived as a distinct people. Biblical legends name peoples contemporaneous with the ancient children of Israel, e.g., Canaanites, Hittites, Hivites, Perizzites, Girgashites, Amorites, etc. How is it that the Jews continue to exist, claiming continuous history from their ancient times as children of Israel, when none of these ancient contemporaries have survived as identifiable groups?

Curiosity about this question shaped my learning of Jewish history. Jews have lived through multiple experiences of exile, from the mythic stories of Egyptian bondage through conquest and exile forced by Assyrian, Babylonian, and Roman Empires. This dispersion of the Jewish population throughout much of the world is known as the diaspora. Everywhere in the world that Jews have lived in exile, they have assimilated elements of local culture while maintaining their identity as a socially coherent people. Even as they assimilated knowledge, language, and technology from the countries where they lived, they organized their lives according to the mitzvot, laws for living rooted in biblical and rabbinic sources. Many of these laws, including dietary laws, injunctions to study sacred texts (which required widespread literacy, even among the poor), and laws against participating in non-Jewish religious practices assured that the Jews would be a people apart in the lands of their exile.

Many groups in human history faced with conquest and/or exile clung to their cultural identity but ultimately dissolved as distinct peoples. For the Jews to survive, they needed not just clear boundaries but also robust adaptive capacities. My understanding of the human immune system came to me as a metaphor for the persistence of the Jews. The immune system protects the body by mustering antibodies, unique physiological responses that defeat antigens invading the body. Because the environment is constantly generating new antigens from new sources, it is impossible for the body to have a "library" of antibodies for every possible antigen. Instead, the body has a library of components that can be combined and assembled in novel configurations, creating novel antibodies to match novel antigens.

So, it seemed to me, Jews over millennia of exile have acquired a vast library of cultural knowledges that can be assembled into unique configurations for unique social circumstances. The Talmud is one source for this library. A record of centuries of rabbinic discussions and arguments about Jewish law, the Talmud retains both winning and losing arguments. Centuries after the discussions were recorded, the multiple points of view in the Talmud afford rabbis responsible for determining points of law a wide range of possible answers to emerging questions as to how to live in gentile society. Just as the immune system draws from a diverse repertoire of possible responses, so have the Jewish people drawn from a repertoire embodied in millennia of diverse cultural experience to develop creative responses in the face of emerging challenges to group survival.

As I prepared to become a Jew, to the best of my ability I observed Shabbat from Friday evening through Saturday evening, abstaining to the best of my ability from everyday activities. I meditated, read, and studied sacred texts. At the close of Shabbat, with sundown approaching, I would go to the sun room upstairs in our home, listen to a CD of kabbalistic klezmer music, and read *Your Word Is Fire*, a collection of teachings about the practice of prayer from early Chasidic masters, assembled and translated by Arthur Green and Barry Holtz (1993). There are relatively few written records of Chasidic instruction on how to pray. These instructions were usually delivered orally in one-on-one conversations between the tzaddik, or master, and his student, the Chasid. Green and Holz found the teachings among the written records that students made of teachings around the master's table, toward the close of the day on Shabbat. As writing is forbidden to observant Jews on Shabbat, the students would wait until sundown to write the teachings down at home. The problem of memory was compounded by the fact that they recorded in Hebrew their recollections of the master's words, which had been delivered in Yiddish.

Despite these limitations, the words in *Your Word Is Fire*, which I read over and over week after week at the close of Shabbat, affected me deeply, activating my spirituality in transformative ways, often evoking tears. When the tears first appeared, I understood them to be tears of happiness. Over time, I recognized a deeper feeling, a feeling of coming home. I sensed that this was not my first incarnation as a Jew. As I came to accept this, I found in my tears profound brokenheartedness that I had been away from Jewish life for so many lifetimes. As I internalized my Jewish identity, I felt my weeping at the close of Shabbat resonate with the powerful theme of exile, repeated over three millennia in the narrative of the Jewish people.

JACOB MAKES HIS WAY HOME

As I was learning to become a Jew, I did what I could to help Jacob realize his intention to become a Christian. I respected his efforts to follow his own spiritual path and recognized that he hoped to find redemption from his addiction in Christianity, as he knew that his birth mother had done. Reports from his Heartland mentor Jerry Parrish, as well as his calls and occasional letters, told us that he was struggling to experience the personal redemption that he saw in so many around him at Heartland. I wrote Jacob heartfelt letters, sharing what I knew from my own spiritual journey about persistence in the face of internal obstacles and drawing wisdom from our common clerical ancestors about living a Christian life. With help from family and from some of the kinder teachers at Heartland, Jacob appeared to find himself in his newly adopted religion.

At times that year, spiritual life in the family looked like a game of metaphysical musical chairs. As Jacob struggled to become a Christian, I was studying to convert to Judaism, and Jessica was studying for her conversion to Tibetan Buddhism. Jodie continued to enjoy claiming Jewish spiritual life after her childhood in a secular household. Ransom remained firm in his atheism, although he was clearly open to his wife Kim's pagan spirituality, grounded in her Scandinavian roots.

We visited Heartland, in the bleak farmlands of northern Missouri, on Jacob's nineteenth birthday, October 31, 2005. Despite some residual rawness from the anger and anguish of the years before he left for Heartland, we shared moments of healing connection. Jacob was enormously proud of his proficiency as an apprentice mechanic at the repair shop that maintained, repaired, and fueled Heartland's vehicles and farm equipment. For the first time in his life, he was experiencing success as a learner. He had taken readily and naturally to the tasks of mechanical repair. The shop manager told us that Jacob had learned more, and more rapidly, than anyone he had trained. Known at Heartland as "Jake," he had a valued role as the driver of the fuel truck that supplied all the equipment scattered throughout Heartland's sprawling agricultural complex. He proudly displayed to his parents his strength and proficiency changing tires on a huge six-wheeled truck. I went for a bone-shattering ride with him in the fuel truck, listening in on the radio as people called out for Jake to come fuel their equipment. I sat quietly observing as he repaired the brakes on a pickup truck at the shop.

Jacob appeared to have settled into his Christian faith. He sat with us in church services, attended by hundreds of Heartland residents, staff, and people from adjoining communities. Charlie Sharpe led the services, which were broadcast to radio markets in Missouri and two adjoining States. Jodie and I did our best not to react visibly to Charlie's harsh, judgmental monologues, calling out sinners and threatening damnation. We contained ourselves when Charlie angrily rejected imagined objections to the claim that the United States is "a Christian Country" and watched the congregation bless an Arab couple, converted to Christianity from Islam, as they departed on a mission to proselytize for Christianity in their Muslim homeland.

Although Jacob appeared to be finding a spiritual home in Christianity, he shared with us his indignation at clear signs of anti-Black racism in Heartland's differential treatment of its relatively small proportion of African American residents. After our birthday visit, he shared increasing discomfort with Heartland's harsh fundamentalist discourse that consigned his parents and relatives as nonbelievers to hell, and doubly condemned (as both Jewish and gay) his uncles, Jodie's brother and his lifetime partner Lars, who were to marry years later, after the Supreme Court made it possible to do so.

Jacob continued to grow stronger. He was sober longer than he had been for years and very proud of his accomplishments as a mechanic. Unfortunately, as he grew stronger and healthier, he chafed at the requirement that he take the medication that cooled the fires of his mood disorder. He appealed directly to Charlie Sharpe to be relieved of that requirement. Charlie, never having seen Jacob in a mood storm and wary of psychiatry, readily agreed, saying, "All you need is Jesus." Jerry Parrish observed worrying changes, as Jacob found it harder to get up in the morning, sometimes missing early morning Bible study, and showed more irritability. He found it harder to tolerate the negative aspects of Heartland culture.

We were worried that things would go sour with Jacob so far away. When he raised the possibility of returning home, we were willing to negotiate. Before his departure, we had established the condition that he spend at least a year working on his recovery at Heartland before we would let him come home. He argued that he had now maintained sobriety for six continuous months, had learned a trade, and had a goal of getting certified as a mechanic. Life at Heartland was becoming more and more difficult. Stronger emotionally, he was more indignant about Heartland's fundamentalist, reactionary social values, so different from the values in which he was raised. Although there were no acute mood storms, without medication he was less well-regulated emotionally. He visited his birth family in Texas on a pass, where he smoked cigarettes, bringing himself under suspicion on his return. As his disaffection with Heartland became more manifest, he was more likely to provoke disciplinary responses.

Once again, we were caught up in dread and uncertainty, struggling with decisions that we understood had life and death implications for our beloved child. Jacob was better grounded and more mature after months of sobriety and with distance from the chaos of his network of dysfunctional peers at home. He had come to know success as a learner and had meaningful life goals. He was negotiating responsibly, rather than picking fights and haranguing us. We arrived at a set of agreements, including sobriety, participation in drug counseling, and serious engagement with school. He was adamant that he wanted his mind to be clear of medication, and we negotiated the following fateful agreement: "Jacob agrees that if his parents really feel he needs to be on medication to be at home, he will be on medication. But, before he goes on medication, he will meet with [his psychiatrist] Dr. Alexakos. Parents have permission to talk with

Dr. Alexakos. No psychologists!" We agreed on a mid-January date for his return. Through the mother of his friend Silvana, we located Vineyard Christian Fellowship, an evangelical congregation in Cambridge with humane and progressive values, hoping that this could become Jacob's spiritual home.

Jacob was treated more and more harshly at Heartland as word of his plans to return home circulated in the Heartland community. Charlie challenged him during Sunday services, telling Jacob and a very large audience that Jacob was going to hell. Supervisors at his residence punished him more harshly for not keeping his room neat and in order. Other young men living in the residence plundered his room of most of his possessions. Finally, a few days before New Year's Day, 2006, over Jerry Parrish's strenuous objections, the residence supervisors expelled Jacob from Heartland.

When we had made plans with Jacob for his mid-January return, we offered to pay for airline tickets. He had insisted on taking full responsibility for his travel and planned to return by bus. Jodie and I were visiting with her family in San Francisco over the holidays when Jacob called to tell us that he had been expelled. Given one day to arrange his travel, he had been taken to the bus station where he bought his tickets. He called again later to tell us that the tickets were missing. Perhaps he lost them; perhaps they were among the last of his possessions stolen by his residence mates. We got on the phone, buying Jacob a new set of bus tickets and arranging for our own air travel to get home before Jacob would arrive by bus. Jacob got on the bus with only a blanket, a gift from his sister Jessica, all of his other possessions stripped away. He believed that the set of tools that he had proudly accumulated in his work as a mechanic was also gone.

We had been in Boston only hours before Jacob arrived at the bus station on New Year's Eve. He had been traveling for more than twenty-four hours without sleeping, afraid of falling asleep and missing his multiple connections. He was distraught and dysregulated, heartbroken about losing his tools and fixated on his determination to go out that night with his friends. This first meeting quickly devolved into an argument. In the time before he left, after his several car crashes, we had allowed him to use only the older of our two cars, which happened at that moment to be in the repair shop. He demanded to use our remaining car, which we refused. He yelled at us, and we held our ground. Despite his sleep deprivation, his anger and grief over his expulsion from Heartland

and the loss of his tools, Jacob accepted the limit we set. Within an hour of his return to our home, he left with his friends in one of their cars. We went to bed stunned and alarmed, as we seemed to be returning to toxic relational struggles within moments of his return.

RECONCILIATION AND LOSS

When we all arose the next morning, the storm had passed. After getting some sleep, Jacob was determined that Jodie and I come to know the person that he had become. Together, we explored new possibilities in our relationships. Living a sober and productive life while he was away had afforded Jacob opportunities to mature into a young man more capable of living the values in which he was raised. He was present, accountable, flexible, determined to pursue his goals, and committed to sobriety. His success at turning his life around had made him an example to his friends. He worked on restoring his relationship with his high school girlfriend Michelle, who had stopped seeing him before he left for Heartland, when she had insisted that he choose between their relationship and his self-destructive behavior.

Days after his return home, we went with him to buy the car for which he had been saving. In addition to his Heartland repair shop earnings, Jacob's down payment included money his grandfather had pledged to him for six consecutive months of sobriety. We assumed the loan for the balance, in an agreement that stipulated sobriety, drug counseling, meeting with the psychiatrist, and commitment to schoolwork. Jacob understood that his continued access to the car was contingent on his keeping the agreement. He was enormously proud of his car, a powerful Pontiac GTO, which for him embodied both his passion for automobile technology and his achievement of personal redemption. We were concerned about the car's power and speed but recognized that it was important to respect Jacob's values, even when they did not necessarily align with ours.

The weeks after Jacob's return home brought deep healing for all of us. Taking full responsibility for his irresponsible and destructive conduct before Heartland, Jacob worked on restoring a trusting relationship with his parents. Open, curious, and respectful, he re-engaged with us in moments of joy, quiet connection, hilarity, and reflection. He did not make a deep connection with Vineyard Fellowship but was clearly quite serious about spirituality and religion. He spoke in an open-hearted way of his sadness at the prospect of my imminent conversion, letting me know how deeply he had been affected by my writing to him about finding his way as a Christian. "Dad," he said, "you have the power of the Word." Yet he also began to express some skepticism about his adopted religion. "Maybe all you need is God," he wondered aloud in a conversation with his mother. We began to wonder if he might return to Judaism. Jacob had always been reticent to share with us his complicated feelings toward us. It was after he died that we learned from Michelle how grateful he was to us for taking him home after he had violated our trust so many times.

Aside from Michelle, Jacob was still socializing with his old group of friends, most of whom now looked up to him for maintaining his sobriety and living a responsible life, his new car a tangible symbol for others of the benefits of his positive life choices. Gregarious and generous-spirited, he was well-known at his high school, well-liked in many circles even in the past when people had kept some distance from him because of his reputation for reckless behavior. Many of his high school peers saw his life story as an inspiration for recovery and self-redemption. He re-enrolled in the automotive repair class he had blown off before dropping out of school. The shop teacher was skeptical of his claims of proficiency until Jacob demonstrated his skills. The day after Jacob showed that he could weld together two sections of exhaust pipe and write his name in cursive with welding tools, the teacher recruited him to be his informal teaching assistant.

Jacob kept the agreement to meet with his psychiatrist, who engaged with him respectfully around the decision whether or not to take medicine. Although Jacob was at the time free of mood disorder symptoms, his doctor warned him that, without mood-stabilizing medicine, he could relapse very suddenly. Jodie reluctantly accommodated my position that we should respect Jacob's autonomy and accept his decision, against the doctor's advice, not to take medicine. She was, nonetheless, very worried.

Grateful as we were for the relational redemption, we could not ignore growing signs of returning heartache. All of Jacob's executive functioning difficulties were quickly re-activated as he returned to high school classes. Despite returning to a specialized program that provided substantial structuring and support, he began falling behind on his assignments. Although he maintained his sobriety, he would at times come home smelling of cigarette smoke, which triggered his mother's asthma. When we insisted that he not smoke, he switched to tobacco snuff. Although he was in some ways a young adult, Jacob could still reason like a teenager. Using snuff to avoid the relational problem caused by cigarette smoke, Jacob developed an obsessive dread that he would develop mouth cancer, ignoring the obvious cancer risks of smoking.

This became the theater in which we enacted the familiar drama of insatiability and failed efforts at soothing. Jacob pleaded that we work out our family issues together with David Treadway, the family therapist who had been so helpful to us in the past. Sadly, David was not available, as he was hospitalized for life-threatening health concerns. Our hearts broke as Jacob asked us to imagine what it was like for him, having no one but Jesus to turn to for comfort. Once again, we found ourselves struggling with feelings of helplessness and uncertainty over how to meet the needs of our beloved son.

We were in that state of mind when Jacob began to revert to an all-too-familiar alienated and evasive stance, thereby reactivating our vigilance. We could see that things were taking a negative turn but could not name specific acts that would justify our taking substantial corrective steps like reclaiming the keys to the car. In a snowstorm, less than a week before he died, Jacob called for help with his car, having skidded into a snowbank by the long driveway to his rented parking space. Although there was nothing in his mental status to suggest that he had been drinking, I insisted on smelling his breath, a ritual that proved as futile as it has been countless times before.

We learned after he died that it was that night, when I detected nothing on his breath, that Jacob had his first drink in eight months. His friends had cried out in distress when he picked up the bottle but Jacob had angrily declared, "I am a 19-year-old man, and I can have a beer." Distressed as his friends may have been, it was only through their tears at his memorial service that they recognized that they should have told us at the time what was happening. One of his friends later shared with us a letter Jacob had written to her from Heartland, in which he had said to her that if he were ever to drink again, he would die.

A few days later, as we struggled to find clear reasons or clues to support taking definitive action, Jacob woke up late for school, after I had left for work. He adamantly denied his mother's angry accusation that he had been drinking when staying out late the night before. In a brief moment of reconciliation as Jacob left for school, Jodie apologized for yelling, which she explained as coming from her fear for him, and he departed with a heartfelt "I love you—have a good day." He called Jodie later, reporting excitedly that he had achieved As in several of his classes that day. In painful retrospect, we saw that sudden shift in academic achievement to have been an indicator that he was becoming manic. In an after-school phone call, after first avoiding her demand, he made an agreement with his mother to be home for supper that evening.

Others have since told us what else happened on his last day. After school, he took his girlfriend Michelle to a park that we had gone to with him many times. Holding his hand over her eyes, he led her to the spot on a hill he had often visited with us, removing his hand to reveal a spectacular view of Boston. He told her of his dream to own his own auto repair shop, where he would train young prospective mechanics. He promised to come to her basketball game that night. After dropping off Michelle, he spent some time working on a car with friends who shared his passion for auto repair. He joined with them in drinking rum. He blew off his promises, both to have dinner with us and to attend Michelle's game. Instead, he called around to find someone willing to go for a drive on a school night. He eventually connected with his friend Ryan. They shared a few beers and set out on Jacob's last drive in his beloved car.

Under the influence of alcohol and mania, Jacob drove around Boston trying to goad other young drivers of fast cars to race. He and Ryan then set out for a major highway, where Jacob wanted to see how fast his car would go. He brought the speed up to 147 miles an hour. Ryan, by his account, was "mesmerized" by the speed and unable to express his desperate wish that Jacob slow down. As they came around a curve, Jacob saw a car moving well below his speed in his lane. He swerved to avoid collision, losing control of the car, which hit a guardrail, pitched onto its side, and flew off the road into woods. His seatbelt broke, and the door flew off. The engine came to rest fifty feet from the rest of the car, which landed on Jacob. Only his feet were visible from below the car. Ryan's seat belt held; he survived with a concussion, some broken ribs, and bruises from the seat belt. Jacob screamed out "Ryan, Ryan!" repeatedly. There was a brief period of silence, then Jacob's feet were still. When Ryan told Jodie and me of Jacob's passing, we prayed that, in that moment of silence, Jacob found comfort in the presence of his God. He had been home with us for just seven weeks.

DEVASTATION, DESOLATION, AND CONNECTION

When Jacob did not come home for supper and did not respond to multiple cell phone calls and texts, we found ourselves again in our powerless parental position. We went to bed once again not knowing where Jacob was, aware that he had broken promises and dreading that his self-destructive impulsiveness would bring him harm. Over the traumatic course of previous years, I had learned to find sleep despite a sickening mix of frustration, dread, helplessness, and anger. We could not let Jacob's betrayal of his promises go unanswered, and we needed sleep for the strength that we would need to respond the next day.

The phone rang around midnight, waking us up. It was Zulima, mother of Ryan's girlfriend Silvana, telling us that Jacob had been in a bad accident south of Boston. Ryan had called Silvana from the site of the accident. Zulima did not have further details. After a few calls, I connected with the state police, who confirmed that Jacob had been in an accident but told me that I had to come to Milton State Police Barracks for information. Half-awake and full of dread, Jodie and I somehow decided that I would drive to the barracks while she stayed at home to monitor the phone in hopes that Jacob would call.

As I walked down the driveway, I felt a wave of rage and pain. Perhaps, I declared to myself silently, this was the end of our torment. At the moment that part of me found its bitter voice, another part arose to recognize that Jacob might indeed have died and that I would have to live in that reality. I let go of the bitterness and found the self-compassion to forgive myself for the wave of toxic emotion.

At that time of night, the drive to the Milton barracks took a half an hour. I remember driving very carefully, in a strange state of calm. Halfway there, I reached out to make contact with Jacob's spirit, knowing without question that was what I was doing, without stopping to wonder if or how I was doing so. I experienced Jacob as in a state of agitated anguish and confusion. Although I could access his emotional state clearly, I could not distinguish whether he was alive or dead; either seemed possible. I was to learn later that, at that moment when I reached out to Jacob's soul, he had been dead for nearly an hour.

Ryan's girlfriend Silvana was standing outside the barracks when I arrived. She told me that Ryan had been taken to the hospital, and that Jacob was under the car. I felt my heart break, even as my mind did not yet fully take in the devastating truth. I walked into the barracks and identified myself. The officer gave me a moment to prepare myself, saying, "This is the hardest job I have to do." After he notified me of Jacob's death, I asked for some privacy and a telephone. Alone, I first gave voice to a wail of grief that was to echo from the depths of my being for many months to come. I called Jodie and told her the news. As she screamed, "NO!" I said through my tears that I was grateful for Jacob's life.

I drove home even more mindful of safety, determined to protect Jodie, Ransom, and Jessica from further loss. I was in a kaleidoscopic mental state, shifting between storms of intense grief, attention to the details of going on (funeral and *shiva*, canceling patient appointments, gathering family from across the continent, etc.), and a profound state of calm, accompanied by a sense that the boundary between material and spiritual worlds was dissolving. In those latter moments, I experienced *knowing*, unquestioning awareness that the knowledge that was coming to me was from a source in worlds beyond my material being. I *knew* that Jacob's soul had chosen us to be his parents before he was born into his mortal body and that he had chosen us because he knew that we had the emotional and spiritual strength not to be destroyed by his early death after his short and incandescent life.

I could not relinquish the mental habits formed over years of intense efforts to care for our beloved and difficult child. When I arrived home, I told Jodie that I wanted us to buy three burial plots, so that the two of us would eventually be buried alongside Jacob. I also told her what came to me about Jacob's soul: that, with foreknowledge of the brevity of his life, he chose us to be his parents. Jodie readily agreed to the burial arrangements and firmly disagreed with the idea that Jacob's early death might have been foreordained. We accepted without challenge or conflict our difference in making sense of his death. This set a pattern of acceptance—each of us would be grieving in our own way, while knowing deeply how much we had to be present for each other through the painful journey of grief. This precious wisdom was rooted in the years we had already traveled parenting our troubled child and in the guidance that David Treadway had provided along that way.

We wept and wailed, clinging to each other, telling each other that we loved each other. We made the calls with the awful news to our children, Jodie's parents, and extended family, including Jacob's aunt from his birth family. It was four in the morning when we went to bed. As I was getting into bed, I found myself again in the state of profound calm that had settled over me during the drive home. With my mind's eye, I saw a shimmering pillar of white light, which I recognized as Jacob's spirit—calm, clear, and present: not in the agitated state that it had appeared shortly after his death.

Life went on, absorbing us in countless decisions and preparations alternating with moments of nearly unbearable pain, holding each other up even as the sight and sound of each other's anguish broke our hearts more profoundly. Walking our dog the next morning, I saw through my tears that Jacob's high school nearby had its flags at half-staff.

Jacob's death was too close to Shabbat for us to bury him as soon as would otherwise be the custom for Jewish funeral ritual. This afforded time for family to gather from New York and the West Coast, for us to negotiate with the medical examiner to release Jacob's remains, to prepare for the Sunday funeral at our synagogue, and to arrange with Vineland for a Christian memorial service later in the week. Rabbi Andy Vogel told us that he would delay his departure for vacation so that he could officiate at the funeral. We assembled pictures of Jacob through his life in displays for shiva, the traditional Jewish practice of daily gatherings at our home for prayer and community solace in the days that would follow burial. Neither Jodie nor I felt a need for sleep as we walked together along our terrible path of grief. I began to write, working on the draft of my statement for the rabbi to read at Jacob's funeral, as Jodie worked on hers. Each of us began writing statements that we would read in our own voices at the Vineland memorial.

It was again nearly 4 AM when we prepared for bed on our second night living in this awful new reality. The calm descended on me again as I saw the pillar of light. At the sound of Jodie's crying, it shook and faded away, returning as she fell silent. Jodie was grateful the next morning when I told her about the pillar, telling me that she yearned to have such an experience herself. As I explored the experience reflectively, I understood it as a profound connection with Jacob's spirit even as I knew that it did not take away any of the raw pain of grief that was to hit me repeatedly for days, weeks, and months to come. From my studies of diverse mystical and esoteric traditions, I understood that Jacob's soul was older and wiser than his 19-year-old embodied self. I knew that my soul was also older and wiser than my mortal being and set the intention to engage with Jacob soul to soul. I was practicing Chi Gong at the time and decided to reach out to Jacob while standing in the open stance of Chi Gong meditation. Each afternoon for the next five days, I would engage with the shining white column of light, the form in which Jacob's soul appeared. I *knew* that he was aware of my awareness of him, even as I felt that his soul was very much on its own journey.

Jodie and I, Jessica, Ransom and his wife Kim, Jodie's parents Gil and Ann with their spouses Harriet and Don, Jodie's brothers Steven and David, sister Becky, Steven's wife Raquel, and my brother Robin gathered in a room at the synagogue before entering the sanctuary for funeral services. The funeral director, David Decter, gave us all black pins with black ribbons attached. We each tore our ribbons halfway through, enacting the biblical ritual of rending one's clothing in grief. Wearing the ribbon for days, even weeks, afterward would afford wordless communication with others that we were in the first month of mourning.

We entered the sanctuary as a family after the others in attendance had already assembled. The synagogue was completely full; more people were in the sanctuary than during most gatherings for the High Holy Days. More than half of those there were young people from Jacob's high school, weeping and stricken by the sudden, unexpected loss of their schoolmate. Jodie and I had prepared our statements with particular attention to the high-risk members of his circle of friends, well-aware that previous sudden deaths in his friendship network, including an overdose and a homicide, had precipitated dangerously self-destructive acting out. Andy read our words in a strong and clear voice that carried our deep pain.

Through Andy's voice, I said:

> From the beginning, Jacob showed amazing abilities to feel and share joy, to be fascinated by the world around him, to love, and to care deeply about respecting other people—abilities that are so familiar to those of you here who remember him. Jacob loved excitement, and he hated to be bored . . . Those of you who remember Jacob from his early years at Pierce School know that he was sunny most of the time, except when schoolwork confronted him with his difficulties with learning. Then, he would struggle against feelings of shame, often using his quick intelligence to find ways to avoid learning challenges. As he entered his teenage years, however, Jacob had more and more difficulty handling his moods and his feelings of shame and anger. He had the ability to rise above these difficulties, as witnessed at his bar mitzvah here in this sanctuary, where he blessed us all with his generosity, his moral passion, and his deep and thoughtful reasoning about his Torah portion . . . Jacob's teenage years were marked by ever deeper and more destructive involvement with substance abuse. Jacob thought that he had found in alcohol and drugs a way to soothe his pain and deal with his moods. His difficulties with school became more and more intolerable to him . . . The road to recovery is not a straight path nor a smooth one.

In the days before his death, Jacob struggled with the realities of life demands that he had avoided for so many years. The voices of peers urging him to join them in substance use proved at moments to be louder and more compelling than the other voices that Jacob was striving to cultivate within himself. He faltered and he stumbled. We have no doubt that, had Jacob lived, he would have overcome this setback, restoring his faith and humility, and continuing to set an example by his determination to make a good life for himself . . . Here, we want to speak especially to those of you who, like Jacob, sometimes feel that the pain and frustrations of life are more than you can bear. We know that, for young people living in the relative comfort and safety of Brookline, just a few miles from areas of Boston where nearly every young person has had to face death, the possibility that you might actually die seems remote. Even if you feel that life is not worth living, it is hard for you to imagine that your life could actually come an end, or to imagine the pain that your passing would bring to those around you. We know that Jacob did not get in his car Thursday night intending to die. We ask that all the young people here help us to extend the blessing of our son's life by making Jacob's life a blessing in your own life. Be inspired by his love of life, of people, and of the world. Treat each other with respect. Have fun and laugh. Thank Jacob for showing you that, no matter how bad your life may seem to you, it is possible to redeem yourself, to turn yourself around, to discover what it is that you are really good at and what you can do to make the world better for people around you. As you make life-shaping decisions in the future, please remember the pain in your heart as you hear these words now. As hard as it is to believe that you are mortal, that your own acts can bring yourself or your loved ones harm, please remember that Jacob did die. Make your lives a blessing by taking the blessing of Jacob's life into your heart the next time that you are confronted with a decision about whether to get into a car with someone who has been drinking, whether to take just one chance on risky sex, whether to let an argument escalate into physical violence, whether to tempt the law to try to make a fast dollar. If you can hold Jacob in your heart, and honor Jacob by accepting that you are mortal and vulnerable to harm at such moments of decision, you will help us continue to make our son's beautiful life a blessing to the world . . .

As tears and cries coursed through the assembled multitude, Andy's voice carried Jodie's words:

Jacob will always be the light of my life. He taught me how to love in a way I never thought possible. He helped me to be less serious and less judgmental. He drove me absolutely crazy and he made me laugh—a lot. I pray that Jacob knows how happy and proud I am to be his mom. I cannot begin to put words to how grateful I am for Jacob's nineteen short years, in which he touched hundreds of hearts, above all those of his entire family. His life was short but precious. His last months, in some ways, have been the most precious, because they brought him back to us, when he had been lost, and helped him and us to heal . . . When Jacob was five, and for years after, he asked, "Mommy, why are we here?" I was astonished that such a tiny person could ask so profound a question—his spiritual quest began early and ran deep. I thank God for that spiritual place in his heart, and for all the forms it took, because his spirituality ultimately brought him back to us after his—and our—years of anguish, and helped make him whole again . . . My family is grateful to all of Jacob's friends for letting us know how he would talk about his love for us, and how he knew how much we love him, and for helping us know that he was excitedly embracing life the day he died. Knowing that gives us some measure of peace . . . I would do anything to cry at his graduation next year, instead of at his funeral, but I will always rejoice in my beautiful boy . . .

At the last of Jodie's words, Andy allowed his own tears to show in his eyes and for his voice to reflect for a moment the brokenheartedness in the room. Then, in a rich, firm and clear voice, he sang the prayer *El Maleh Rachamim* (God of Compassion) connecting us all with the source of the strength to go on with our broken hearts. At the end of the service, Ransom joined Jacob's friends and his teacher, Bill Grady, to carry the coffin out of the sanctuary. The procession to the cemetery extended dozens of blocks behind us. Imagining the frustrations of motorists waiting to cross the road, we remembered Jacob as the provocative trickster, and imagined his enjoyment at this last prank.

On that bitterly cold and windy February day, David Decter made sure that we were wrapped in warm blankets at the graveside. Jodie's cry of Jacob's name as his coffin was lowered into the ground, and the sound of the first shovels of earth hitting the wooden coffin, are to this day sharp pains in my heart that are as much felt as remembered. After everyone who chose to do so had thrown their shovel full of earth into the grave, Jacob's dear friend Olga took the shovel and with fierce determination filled the rest of his grave. Olga was to be one of Jacob's friends who would take our words to heart. She has made Jacob's life a blessing for her own. After a tumultuous adolescence in which she also spent time away from home in institutional care, Olga went through college into a successful professional career that now has her working internationally.

We returned home to shiva, the Jewish tradition of community members gathering at the home of the bereaved to comfort them in their mourning. Our dear friend Rachel Dash took a leave from her job teaching medical residents at West Virginia University, taking charge of logistics and profoundly present for us in our brokenhearted state. For seven days, our home was full of food and flowers, pictures and stories as scores of visitors came to provide emotional and spiritual support, sharing stories, bringing food, and participating in evening prayers, led on the first day by Rabbi Vogel and later by our dear friend Marsha Mirkin, by congregants, and by our student rabbi, Chaim Koritzinsky.

Our BICAP comrades were among the first to come to our side at the news of Jacob's death, arriving even before family could travel to us. Roxana Llerena-Quinn was out of town at a conference when she got the news, which she shared with our New York friends and colleagues, several of whom, including my spiritual sister Charlee Sutton, joined us at shiva following the funeral. Our dear friends the Hammermans were there for us. Sylvia Hammerman took on the role of family spokesperson with the local news media. Among the many who came to shiva were Boston areas colleagues with whom we shared warm relationships and mutual respect. Familiar with Jodie's and my work as network therapists, Kaethe Weingarten told us that she saw our messages at the funeral inviting the transformative experiences and deep witnessing that can occur at a full-scale family network assembly.

We were grateful that others could see how we had drawn on our knowledge of network therapy, determined that our grief provide opportunities for healing and redemption in the circle of Jacob's troubled and reckless friends. Monica McGoldrick from New Jersey had also witnessed this community healing process. Several weeks later, she and her co-editor Kenneth Hardy asked Jodie and me to write, for the next edition of *Re-Visioning Family Therapy* (their text on socially just family therapy), our story of mobilizing our networks in our grief.[44] Kaethe readily agreed to our request that she post our words for funeral and memorial service on *The Witnessing Project*, the website that she had created to advocate for the supportive practice of witnessing others' pain.

At some time during those seven days of shiva, we got a phone call from Jacob's supervisor at the Heartland repair shop. He had carefully assembled all the tools that Jacob acquired as he learned his trade and had called to arrange for us to receive them. We decided to donate the tools to Jacob's high school auto shop. When my brother Robin, a former automobile mechanic, heard our plans, he offered to donate his tools as well as his massive tool chest. Months later, the auto shop teacher worked with us to create a memorial in the auto shop, with Jacob's photo and his cautionary story on the lid of the chest, as a setting for Jacob's tools.

I continued to connect each afternoon in meditation with Jacob's spirit. I began to discern other pillars of light in the distance, beyond the pillar that embodied Jacob's soul. Each day, Jacob's pillar approached more closely to the others. The afternoon before the next day's memorial service at Vineland Christian Ministries, my experience changed. Instead of visual imagery, I felt strong sensations of warmth and light in my throat and in my forehead. I interpreted the sensations as Jacob preparing me to talk before the congregation the following day.

We were warmly welcomed at Vineland the next day. The minister had given us a great deal of latitude as we planned the memorial, at which both Jodie and I were to speak. He was very curious about our torn ribbons and eager to learn about Jewish customs of mourning. He told us his own heartbreaking story of a family vacation in Europe, when he and his family were in an automobile accident that killed one of his children. On his return, in contrast to Jewish customs of gathering to help a family bear their loss, his colleagues, acquaintances, and friends could not even initiate conversation about the wrenching changes he and his family were going through. He expressed fascination and appreciation for our Jewish practices of community support for the bereaved.

The service at Vineland embodied warmth, support, and generosity of spirit, affording healing contrast to the harsh judgmental fundamentalism we had experienced in Heartland church services when we visited Jacob on his birthday. Speaking in our own voices to a smaller assembly, with a greater concentration of Jacob's troubled friends, we exhorted them to draw on the blessings and lessons of Jacob's life to guide their own. Several friends, sobbing with grief and remorse, recalled moments when they had seen Jacob return to his former self-destructive ways and had failed to lead him back on the path to personal redemption themselves or to call on us for help.

In the days after the Vineland service, I witnessed in meditation the further progress of Jacob's soul. The group of pillars of light, which I had earlier discerned in the distance, had grown into a forest. As Jacob's pillar entered the forest, I experienced everything dissolve into intense white light. The experience resonated with my experience more than thirty years before in the home of Ramón Jimenez, and with Rabbi Meshullam Feivush of Zebriza's metaphor of the drop of water dissolving into the sea. After lingering for a moment in the sea of whiteness, I returned to everyday waking awareness, feeling deep calm. Looking back later, I was to interpret those seven days witnessing the journey of Jacob's pillar of light as my accompanying his soul on its return to its source.

Ransom, Kim, Jessica, and Robin were often present at shiva gatherings, including evening prayer services. On the last day of shiva, toward the close of the service, our dear friend Marsha Mirkin invited our family into the center of our living room and then everyone in the room to put their hands on members of the grieving family, directly or by putting their hands on those whose hands were touching us directly. Everyone in the room was connected in a web of encircling hands. As we sang *Oseh Shalom*, the prayer for peace, I was deeply aware of Ransom's presence. Despite his obvious profound sadness, Ransom, whose personal style tends toward the emotional reserve of his maternal Narragansett and Nipmuc ancestors, had not shown his tears before. Drawing deeply from my own spiritual reserves, I sang in a voice rich with peace and love. As I sang, Ransom buried his head in my shoulder, sobbing with grief over his loss.

Although friends and family continued to check in with us, after the last day of shiva, Jodie and I slowly reengaged with life, now irrevocably transformed by Jacob's physical absence. The date of my conversion was rescheduled, as the original date now fell within the period of *sheloshim*. Sheloshim, the first thirty days of Jewish mourning, ease the bereaved's transition back into daily life. The custom involves some restrictions, including abstaining from celebration, and concludes with another gathering in the mourners' home on the thirtieth day.

Having witnessed the return of Jacob's soul to its source, I did not expect further encounters with him. Throughout shiva and for several days afterwards, I had been going to bed around 4 a.m. Recognizing that I could not go on with so little sleep, I resolved to go to bed at a reasonable hour. I fell asleep easily, sleeping soundly until Jodie and I were suddenly awakened at 4 a.m. by the sound of our front doorbell. Not fully awake, I made my way down the stairs feeling a familiar surge of stress hormones, conditioned by several late-night appearances by the police at our door with Jacob. Half-awake, in a fog, I was halfway to the door before I was conscious that Jacob was gone forever. I opened the door to find that no one was there. I slept little the last few hours of that night.

The next night, I somehow got to sleep shortly after retiring, again at a reasonable hour. I came fully awake at 4 a.m., this time without hearing the sound of the doorbell. Lying in bed, aware of my need for sleep, I reflected on the idea that Jacob's soul and mine were older and wiser than our mortal beings. I prayed that both souls work together to help me get back to sleep.

> I am alone in a small rowboat, floating on a perfectly calm, still ocean. Smoothly and silently, a humpback whale rises from the deep, gently lifts my boat on its back, then sets it back onto the water. As the whale swims down silently into the deep, I sink into a deep sleep, my soul at peace.

In the morning, Jodie was comforted when I recounted this dream vision. We thought of the gift that Jacob had given me years before, a brass whale paperweight that I still keep on my desk. Several weeks later, gratefully accepting an offer from our friends to spend a few days alone together at their Cape Cod summer home, we went on a whale watch, holding Jacob in our hearts as a humpback whale swam under the vessel. Months later, as we were going through his personal papers, we found a story fragment that Jacob had written, in which he and his friends were walking down the street when a whale fell out of the sky onto Jacob, crushing him. We saw this story as something that Jacob and his teenage peers might have called "random," were it not for the juxtaposition of images connecting the reality of his death under the crushing weight of his car and my vision of Jacob's soul in the form of a whale, gently leading my soul into sleep. From the moment I awoke the next day, I *knew* that Jacob's soul had engaged with mine in that dream vision. Even as I was comforted by this knowledge, I could not find an explanation. How is it that I could experience the presence of Jacob's soul, after I had witnessed its distinct existence dissolve into the eternal Unity like a drop into the ocean?

The question was tantalizing, as I could not identify the esoteric text I had read previously that described the soul as existing in multiple forms.[45] Perhaps it was one form of Jacob's soul that had been absorbed into the One, while another was still capable of communicating with the material world. I made some efforts to locate the text but soon was more absorbed in preparing for the day of my formal conversion to Judaism.

More important than the persistence of the question was the assurance, grounded in my vision, that Jacob's soul was, in some form, still accessible to me in the material world.

CONVERSION

We rescheduled my conversion to follow the ritual of sheloshim, thirty days after Jacob's death. Our grief was still new and raw. Joy and anguish came to live together in our hearts without supplanting each other. While preparing for my formal transition to become a member of the Jewish people, I was undergoing spiritual transformation through my engagement with Jacob's soul. As the boundary between material and spiritual realms unsealed to afford connection between our souls, my intuitive understanding of how to be open, which I had learned from the espiritista Ramón Jimenez thirty years before, was becoming more explicit. I saw that I was in a liminal state, at the threshold between worlds. It was in this state that I prepared the two documents that I would share on the day of my conversion.

I prepared the first document for review by the *beit din*, a panel of rabbis who were to examine me and, if they found me ready, to welcome me as "a Jew in all respects." This document included a brief narrative of my spiritual journey, including the moment of revelation with Ramón and my subsequent discovery, through determined search, of underlying commonalities among a multitude of spiritual and religious beliefs and practices across cultures. I recounted how, after years of spiritual self-cultivation with no intention to participate in organized religion, I began to attend Jewish services as the prospective parent of a Jewish child, finding meaning in Jewish religion and comfort in the role of a "stranger in the camp," living a Jewish life in many ways without practicing the religion. I alluded to my experience of the presence of the ancestors when the Torah came from the ark.

In my remarks to the congregation that I wrote for services later in the evening in synagogue, I wrote:

> The more Torah and Tanach I read, the more powerful for me became the metaphor of Divine breath. Breath is an organizing practice, and organizing idea, for many religions and spiritual practices. As I followed the narrative of the people Israel, I was struck by the grand repetition of connection with God followed by alienation from God, followed by redemption and reunion with God, followed by alienation, followed by redemption, etc.

Estrangement was the metaphorical exhalation, redemption the inhalation. Neither inhalation nor exhalation is ultimately "better"; both are essential to breathing. It was easy to integrate this with Meher Baba's *Discourses*: The One gazes into Nothing and imagines Creation. The most sentient of the beings in Creation (on this planet, human beings) yearn to find, know, and reunite with the One. This process of yearning and seeking is in fact the mechanism of Divine self-awareness. God knows God's self through the yearning and seeking of God's creatures. For the process to operate, human beings must be capable of turning away from, ignoring, and not knowing God (what some religions construct as "sin"). Human ignorance of God is as critical to Divine self-awareness as human realization of God; exhalation is as necessary for breath as is inhalation. I found the metaphor of breath to fit with what I had learned about travel on the spiritual path, with its progress and reversal, connection and disconnection, moments of ecstasy and of despair.

The day of my conversion began with a visit to Mayyim Hayyim, a beautiful, sun-drenched *mikvah* (a ritual bath with ever-flowing, "living" waters) in a nearby community that welcomes Jews of all denominations and levels of religious observance. The ritual of conversion includes circumcision, examination by a beit din, and then total immersion in the "living waters" of the mikvah. Like most American men of my generation, I had been circumcised medically within days after my birth. In such cases, the *mohel*, who has responsibility for this ritual, makes a small cut to draw blood—the *brit dam*, or covenant of blood. My brit dam was conducted following my interview with and during the deliberations of the rabbis of the beit din—Rabbi Steve Arnold, a progressive Reform rabbi; Rabbi Rim Meirowitz, who had led the Temple Sinai religious school when Jacob was a student there; and Rabbi Toba Spitzer, the rabbi for a local Reconstructionist congregation.

My rabbi, Andy Vogel, introduced me to the beit din and served as my advocate. During the hearing, the rabbis presented me with a challenge: given that I had sojourned among so many spiritual traditions, how could they be assured that my immersion in Judaism might not someday be replaced by another new interest, in a different spiritual practice? I acknowledged that the concern that they expressed was well-grounded, given the story of my spiritual journey. I assured them that I was not taking my commitment to religious conversion lightly and that I saw in Judaism an expanse of beliefs, ideas, and practices, built over thousands of years.

I could explore Judaism with my restless curiosity for the rest of my life. Whatever I could possibly learn in the rest of my lifetime would be at most a drop in the ocean of Jewish lore. I would continue my search within the boundaries of the religion to which I was about to commit myself.

After they concluded their deliberations, I was invited in and was welcomed as a Jew. Rabbi Spitzer firmly offered counsel that I took to heart: she bid me to seek and adopt traditional Jewish ritual practices, to ground me in my adopted faith. So it is that my weekday routines today start with Jewish prayer, beginning with my strapping on head and arm *tefillin*, ritual objects (leather boxes containing Hebrew prayers) whose use in prayer has been required of observant Jewish men for nearly two millennia. For years, until the straps finally wore out, I used the tefillin once worn by Jodie's great-grandfather Israel, in whose *tallit* (prayer shawl) Jacob's body had so recently been shrouded for burial.

After my welcome from the beit din, I showered and meticulously cleaned hair, nails, and teeth to prepare for immersion in the mikvah. Andy Vogel and my dear friend David Hammerman were my formal witnesses as I immersed thoroughly, my eyes and mouth open, fingers and toes spread, with every available surface touched by the living water. After immersing, I stood up in the water and sang the *Shema*, the central prayer of the Jewish people, affirming the fundamental unity of God and Creation. David told me later that, with his capacity as a shaman to see beyond the boundaries of the material world, he saw my Methodist minister ancestors surrounding the mikvah, celebrating.

That Shabbat evening, as the Temple Sinai congregation welcomed me as a Jew, Jacob was very much in Jodie's and my hearts. Jacob had been disappointed that I was planning for formal conversion. Remembering what I had written to him when he was at Heartland, when I had encouraged him to embrace his Christian faith, he said to me, "Dad, you have the power of the Word." He had at first declared that he would not attend the Temple Sinai celebration of my conversion. His girlfriend encouraged him to change his mind. With the original date set for March 17, Saint Patrick's Day, he had declared that he would attend services wearing green! So it was that the remarks that I read to the congregation during services included these words: "Returning home, Jacob recovered the generosity of spirit that shone through the words of his *d'var Torah* at his bar mitzvah here at Temple Sinai. He promised to come here to celebrate my conversion. The original date set was March 17, Saint Patrick's Day, and Jacob pledged that he would appear all dressed in green. Now, I have read esoteric texts describing the prophet Elijah (Eliyahu) manifesting in this world as a green-robed figure. If any of you tonight catch a flash of green light out of the corner of your eye, please welcome Yaakov Eliyahu [Jacob's Hebrew name] to tonight's celebration." David Hammerman later told me that he saw Jacob dancing joyously on the *bima*, the elevated platform from which the Torah is read and the clergy lead services, as I stood there reading my remarks to the congregation.

The process of transformation, which began when I reached out to and connected with Jacob's soul within an hour of his death, accelerated from the moment of my emergence from the mikvah. During a moment of collective silent prayer in synagogue that evening, eyes closed, I became aware that I had a spirit body that hovered just a few inches outside and in front of my physical body. Without hesitating, or wondering how or why, I connected my spirit body with the spirit bodies of my fellow congregants in silent prayer. I heard an airplane engine above us and reached out to connect with the spirit bodies of the people on the plane. Hearing a streetcar passing by outside, I reached out to the spirit bodies of its passengers. Connected in this web of spiritual energy, I reached with intense love and yearning toward the source of all being. After a few moments directing the flow of energy "upwards," I felt an enormous surge of energy returning, into and through my body and through the web of connection with others around me. Later, on reflection, I recognized that my experience resonated with descriptions of Chasidic prayer. At the time, I simply acted as it came to me in the moment. As the period of silent prayer came to a close, I became aware that the visual field behind my closed eyelids was filled with green radiance.

A MOMENT OF CONVERGENCE

Jodie and I recognized from the beginning that our ways of grieving, and our ways of making sense of losing Jacob, would be different. Experience had already taught us that the idea of closure after the death of our child is a fiction. From the beginning, we knew that we would not, nor would we want to, "get over it," that our bereavement would remain a powerful influence shaping the course of our lives. Rather than getting over it, we continue to learn how to go on: together, but each in our own way.

We knew how profoundly we needed each other to make our way forward. Even as we accepted our very different ways of grieving, Jodie and I have found experiences in common. From the beginning of our bereavement, we have cherished shared memories of Jacob. We keep Jacob's memory alive, in stories, pictures, and memories of how he would speak, play, and laugh, often borrowing his words to share between us in intimate exchanges. We remember his turns of phrase, his efforts as a very young child to make sense of the world, his wisdom, his humor, his playfulness. Remembering that he had found beauty in the stark Missouri agricultural landscape ("Out here, we look to the sky"), we connect deeply with Jacob and with each other whenever we gaze at beautiful cloud formations, sunsets, or sunrises.

It was at first difficult for Ransom and Jessica to know how to be with us. They were struggling with their own bereavement and seeing us as less available emotionally in our grief, even as we felt their distance from us as another loss. I imagine that the tumult of their parents' separation and divorce, my self-absorption at that time, and their mother's sudden death had cast a shadow over their experience of their relationships with me and with Jodie. The journey of healing in those relationships continues—and continues to bring us much closer over the years.

Although she had not yet entered direct engagement with Jacob's soul such as I had known in the days after his death, Jodie acknowledged my experience and yearned for her own way to stay in connection with our beloved son. Desperately needing to relinquish her prior agnostic stance about the survival of the soul, she found an experience of connection through the Shema, a prayer that acknowledges the unity of all being. As she prayed the Shema, Jodie came to envision a vast network of silvery spiritual filaments connecting everything in the universe, thereby connecting her soul with Jacob's.

A few months after Jacob's death, at the Annual Meeting of the American Family Therapy Academy (AFTA), we found ourselves in conversation with Judith Landau, a psychiatrist and family therapist whose nearly fatal childhood illness in her native South Africa had opened her door to the spirit world. Judith perceived in Jodie a natural spiritual capacity grounded in a lineage of spiritual masters. Jodie was reluctant to take this in. She found it painful to hear Judith's direct and matter-of-fact statement that Jacob was moving aside to allow for Jodie's spiritual development.

I do think that Jodie, like my daughter Jessica, was born with more natural spiritual gifts than I. She has been wary of cultivating her capacity, remembering her experience of dread as a young adult when she had a visionary dream of Khrushchev's death in the Soviet Union, within hours of the moment in time that it happened, two days before it was revealed to the world. She recalls how as an adolescent, hours before she received word of his unexpected death, an intense wave of deep grief hit her the moment a dear family friend, a "second father" to her, had passed.

A year after our conversation with Judith, Jodie and I for the first time together experienced a direct encounter with Jacob's soul. At the 2007 AFTA Conference, the Just Therapy Team from the Wellington, New Zealand Family Centre received the Award for Distinguished Contribution to Social Justice. A team member celebrated the occasion with a *haka*, a Maori warrior dance. Years before, at his summer camp, I had witnessed Jacob and his cabin mates perform a pre-game haka under the direction of their Maori counselor. With the first stomp of the Maori Just Therapy Team member's foot, Jodie, who had not seen Jacob perform the haka, suddenly felt Jacob's spirit enter and inhabit her entire body, and heard his urgent twelve-year-old voice calling out, "Mom! Mom! Mom! Look at this! Mom, look! This is really cool, Mom!" The conference hall and the haka disappeared from her awareness in that moment of direct awareness of Jacob, present in her body and speaking directly to her. After the moment passed, she turned to see tears streaming down my face, as I came out of my own direct experience of Jacob's presence. Although our experiences were different, each of us knew beyond question that, during the haka, Jacob had connected with each of us.

Recovering from our astonishment at the convergence, we sought out the haka dancer. We caught up with him on the sidewalk outside the hotel, where we told him what had happened to us during his performance. He acknowledged our gratitude, telling us that he had sensed the presence of someone whom he did not know entering the room.

MEETING A GUIDE AND FELLOW SEEKER

Jodie and I continued to find ways to go on, together and in our own professional and social lives. As we built new routines of work and life, I continued to struggle to make sense of how it was that Jacob's spirit, which I had witnessed dissolve into its source within days of his death, nonetheless continued to manifest its presence to me.

As Jacob's soul showed up repeatedly, I kept searching my memory to locate a text in which I had read about multiple manifestations of the soul, a text that might explain how Jacob's soul could have dissolved into its source yet so unmistakably manifest itself afterward. Then, I discovered that an anthology of teachings on Chasidic prayer, which I read regularly on Shabbat, might offer a clue. One of the teachings used two different terms: "spirit" and "soul."[46] Did this offer a Jewish perspective on multiple manifestations of the soul? Was it possible that I might find an answer in Jewish esoteric lore that might explain my experiences with Jacob's soul?

My efforts to find meaning in that Chasidic teaching were to lead me to a meeting with Rabbi Arthur Green, who, with his colleague Barry Holtz, had assembled and translated the teachings in the anthology, *Your Word is Fire*. Through my town library, I borrowed the original Hebrew text from which Green and Holtz had translated an excerpt. I asked my Rabbi, Andy Vogel, to help me find the words for "spirit" and "soul" in the Hebrew. Andy could not find in the Hebrew text the distinctions I had found in its English translation. He offered to arrange for me to meet Rabbi Art Green, the Rector of the pluralistic rabbinic school at Hebrew College in the neighboring community of Newton, Massachusetts. I was a bit star-struck, as I had already read several of Rabbi Green's books, and had been captured by his theology, which envisions God as the embodiment of an evolving universe.

With Andy's introduction, I wrote to Art, sending him my statement for the rabbis of my beit din and my remarks to the congregation on the day of my conversion. Art responded enthusiastically, thanking Andy for the *shiddach* (the Yiddish term for matchmaking), and inviting me to meet with him at Hebrew College. He greeted me warmly, asking many questions about how I had come to be where I was on my spiritual journey. He read through my photocopy of the Hebrew text on prayer and determined that the terms "spirit" and "soul" were in fact translations of the same word in the Hebrew text. Understanding why I had made the inquiry, Art directed me to the section of Tishby's *Wisdom of the Zohar* that articulates three forms of the soul in Kabbalah, each with its own name—*nefesh*, *ruach*, and *neshamah*.[47]

Art's suggestion opened the door for me to begin serious study of Kabbalah. I knew as soon as I opened my local library's copy of *Wisdom of the Zohar* that I needed to acquire my own copy of this three-volume work, an English translation from the Hebrew of a massive scholarly work on the *Zohar*, including exposition of its complex texts, generous excerpts from the original, and exploration of its literary history.

The *Zohar* is a foundational text of Kabbalah, esoteric knowledge grounded in traditional Jewish texts and religious observance. The language of the *Zohar*, like that of its predecessors, *Sefer Yetzirah* and the *Bahir*, is deliberately obscure and allusive. The language embodies deep and awesome truths while cloaking them to make them impenetrable to readers who are uninitiated and unprepared to engage with their deeper meanings. My Shabbats were quickly absorbed in study of Tishby's volumes.

I sought to pursue a relationship with Rabbi Green as my mentor. He responded generously to my inquiries about Kabbalah and Chasidut and read early drafts of my writing about discovering Kabbalah and integrating it with the knowledge that I had already acquired on my spiritual journey. Gently, he let me know that he preferred not to take on the mantle of my mentor, a role that he had with many generations of rabbinic students at the Reconstructionist Rabbinical College in the 1980s and at the non-denominational rabbinic school that he founded at Hebrew College in 2003. Art made it clear that he preferred friendship between us as fellow seekers, a relationship that I treasure.

Nearly two decades after our first meeting, I reflect on how the pattern of one's individual spiritual journey resonates with the invisible design of the universe. Conversations with Art have guided me into ever-deeper learning about the mystical and esoteric domains of my Jewish faith. My relationship with my beloved son, particularly the soul connection that we shared intensely in the years after his death, took me on a path that led me to my friendship with Art, itself an important source for the meanings that inspire the writing of this memoir. My love and yearning for Jacob led me to the meeting with Art. Art opened the door for my study of Kabbalah. That study led me to understand how Jacob's soul and mine were connecting so profoundly in the years after he died.

A GLIMPSE INTO MY UNDERSTANDING OF KABBALAH

When I began to study esoteric Judaism, I encountered ideas from mystical traditions I had already explored; for example, God as the limitless All that creates worlds out of nothingness, worlds populated by conscious beings whose purpose is to recognize their source, a purpose that is met when these conscious beings choose freely to search for this truth. As I studied more deeply, I fell in love with the particulars of Kabbalah. I learned of a hierarchy of worlds above and beyond the limits of our material world. The limitless Unity I had learned of from other traditions is, according to Kabbalah, the world of *Ein Sof* (Hebrew for without limit or ending). I learned of a mysterious radiance that emanates from Ein Sof. Described metaphorically as a flow of light or blessing, it descends from upper to lower worlds of creation, flowing through a pattern of vessels or channels until it both forms and fills our material world.

As I write, late in the seventh decade of my life, I have been immersed in study of Kabbalah for little more than a decade and a half. I cannot expect to attain more than a glimpse of this vast domain of knowledge in the years that remain to me. I can offer you only a glimpse of what I have learned.

You may not want to be distracted from the narrative of my life and spiritual journey by this account of my understanding of Kabbalah. Kabbalah is replete with abstraction, complexity, paradoxes, and outright contradictions. At any point in this section, you may choose to pass over it and go to the next section, "Weaving Strands Together," where the narrative resumes.

Here are some of the challenges that I wrestle with as I study Kabbalah: nearly all my learning is conveyed through language, primarily written language. Though I can sound out Hebrew words, I can read neither Hebrew nor Aramaic, the languages in which most of Kabbalah has been transmitted. Until I began studying Hebrew texts with translation and guidance from a teacher seven years ago, everything I have studied of Kabbalah is in English translations and commentaries. I have also learned much from conversations with Art and with our mutual friend Joel Ziff, those conversations only in English.

The sages of Kabbalah tell us that the phenomena they describe in words ultimately defy verbal description. They use words to point toward ineffable experiences, attained through religious observance, prayer, and meditation. Their writing, whether in the original or in translation, is deliberately obscure and esoteric, to protect the wisdom from the uninitiated, and the uninitiated from the wisdom. Rather than being a logically coherent system of ideas, Kabbalah is a complex web of associations. The same word can have very different referents, depending on its location in associational context.

There are two very different perspectives on the origins of Kabbalah. Scholars agree that the foundational documents were written in the early centuries of the second millennium of the Common Era, emerging from circles of Jewish mystics in Spain and southern France. They point to the flourishing Spanish culture of the time and the interpenetration of

Jewish, Islamic Sufi, and classical Greek (particularly Platonic) ideas. In contrast, kabbalistic sages insist that Kabbalah was transmitted orally from generation to generation, originating in teachings from rabbis in the first centuries of the Common Era. According to the sages, the teachings were preserved as an oral tradition by Jewish academies in Babylon. From the sages' perspective, the teachings of the *Zohar*, a foundational kabbalistic text, were written down solely for teaching in closely limited circles. They claim that the *Zohar* manuscript was sold without permission by the widow of Moses de Leon, the Spanish mystic to whom most scholars attribute its authorship. As I study *Zohar*, I hold in mind both of these irreconcilable narratives of its origins.

I try to integrate what I learn about Kabbalah into my meditative and contemplative practice. Its complex imagery describes both the origin and invisible structure of creation and the origin and redemption of the soul. Although I cannot avoid the use of temporal terms like "before," "after," and "next," and spatial terms like "above," "below," "inside," "outside," etc., I am well aware that the phenomena I describe are beyond the limits of space and time. Descriptive language can at best serve only to suggest metaphors for invisible realities that are inaccessible to ordinary human consciousness. As in my account of my experience of revelation with Ramón, I acknowledge the limits of language to convey experience beyond words.

The mysteries of the world of Ein Sof are inaccessible to ordinary human consciousness. What we do know of this world is from the words of the mystic sages who have achieved the state of *deveikut*, or complete unification with the limitless all. Ein Sof is beyond all time, space, and human comprehension. We learn from the sages that, within this perfect Unity, there emerges the divine will to give pleasure or blessing (metaphorically described as light) to created beings. A vessel to receive that light of blessing begins to emerge.

In the upper worlds, distance is measured not in spatial terms but by degree of similarity. When the vessel starts to form in Ein Sof, it yearns to reunite with its source. The light in Ein Sof is so intense and pervasive that, as the vessel starts to form, its yearning for closeness makes it dissolve into its source. In order to complete the intention of the Divine will, the light must flow down through a descending series of worlds, each coarser than its predecessor, until it arrives at the threshold of what we know as the material world. Through the process of *tzimtzum*, or contraction, the intensity of the light fades enough to allow the formation of a completely empty vessel that is capable of receiving a full measure of divine blessing.

The Ladder. A diagram of the *sephirot*.

- **CROWN** — כתר *Keter* — Will, *Ayin* (Nothingness)
- **UNDERSTANDING** — בינה *Binah* — Palace, Womb
- **WISDOM** — חכמה *Ḥokhmah* — Primordial Point, Beginning
- **POWER** — גבורה *Gevurah* — *Din* (Judgment), Rigor, Red, Fire, Left Arm, Isaac
- **LOVE** — חסד *Ḥesed* — *Gedullah* (Greatness), Grace, White, Water, Right Arm, Abraham
- **BEAUTY** — תפארת *Tif'eret* — *Raḥamim* (Compassion), Blessed Holy One, Heaven, Sun, Harmony, King, Green, Torso, Jacob, Moses
- **SPLENDOR** — הוד *Hod* — Prophecy, Left Leg
- **ENDURANCE** — נצח *Netsaḥ* — Prophecy, Right Leg
- **FOUNDATION** — יסוד *Yesod* — *Tsaddiq* (Righteous One), Covenant, Phallus, Joseph
- **KINGDOM** — מלכות *Malkhut* — *Shekhinah* (Presence), Assembly of Israel, Earth, Moon, Queen, Apple Orchard, King David, Rachel

The structure of giving and receiving through which the light flows is in the form of ten spherical vessels, called the *sephirot* (the plural for *sephirah*). They are arranged in a hierarchical pattern that is sometimes referred to as the ladder or the tree of life.

The ladder first forms in the highest Sephirah, *keter* (Hebrew for "crown"). At the level of keter, the ladder is called *adam kadmon*, which translates as "primordial human." The pattern of the ladder maps onto a hermaphroditic form of the human body. In a fractally replicating, recursive formative process, the ladder repeats itself through and within each of the sephirot, through descending worlds. Each sephirah embodies all ten sephirot, each in turn subtly influenced by its location within the particular sephirah in which it is embedded.

The upper triad of the ten sephirot, sometimes referred to by scholars as the Godhead, is composed of the sephirot keter (crown), chochmah (wisdom), and binah (understanding). The English translations of their names capture only a fraction of the wealth of meanings associated with each sephirah. Chochmah receives light from Ein Sof in the form of *or d'chochmah*, the light of wisdom, and sends it coursing through the sephirot below it. Binah receives *or d'chasidim*, the light of lovingkindness, from Ein Sof. This is the light of pure giving. At the very last stage of its formation, binah also receives the light of or d'chochmah, to nourish the flow of blessing it directs toward the lower sephirot.

Below the upper triad are six sephirot, named collectively *tiferet* (beauty), which is also the name of the central sephirah of the group. They are *chesed* (lovingkindness), *gevurah* (power), tiferet, *netzach* (eternity), *hod* (splendor), and *yesod* (foundation). Again, the English translations of their Hebrew names carry only a fraction of their meanings and associations. Unlike chochmah and binah, who receive light directly from Ein Sof, the sephirot of tiferet serve as channels through which the light from binah (and through binah, chochmah) flows. All the light that radiates through the nine upper sephirot flows into *malchut* (kingdom). Malchut is the empty vessel, whose emptiness affords the capacity to receive the full measure of the light of blessing from its source in Ein Sof. Malchut cannot radiate light; it can only reflect it. Metaphorically, malchut is the moon reflecting the light of Ein Sof as the sun. Malchut is at the boundary between the upper spiritual worlds and our material world and is the source of both blessing and creation that is proximate to our experience. The sephirot are associated with gender: binah is the greater mother and malchut the lesser mother. When the upper worlds are in alignment, malchut aligns with binah to manifest as Shechinah, the feminine manifestation of God. A Jewish myth about exile from our ancestral home of Israel depicts Shechinah as accompanying us in our wanderings.

Our souls exist simultaneously in our material bodies and in the upper worlds. Jewish mysticism challenges Jews to recognize and overcome a dilemma that is built into the structure of Creation: our God uttered our world into being for the purpose of bringing pleasure to us, God's created beings. We were created in the form of empty vessels in order to receive the full measure of God's blessing. That emptiness manifests as a powerful will to receive pleasure. Yet, if we receive for the sake of receiving, we are as different (and therefore as distant) as possible from our God, Hashem, whose nature is to give. The journey of the soul to reunite with its source requires that we transform our desire to receive for the sake of receiving into passion to receive for the sake of giving.

As a family therapist, I already had decades of experience working with complex phenomena when I began to study Kabbalah. I was trained to understand systems of multiple elements forming patterns through their reciprocal influence on each other, at multiple levels of complexity from individual psychology to sibling relationships to generational hierarchies to households to extended families to larger relational networks to larger society. My training in systems theory helped me to navigate my understanding through the patterns of reciprocal influence among the sephirot in the upper worlds. I learned the principle "as above, so below," i.e., the patterns of the ladder in the upper worlds are embodied in the lower worlds, including, in the material world, in the human body.

WEAVING STRANDS TOGETHER

My first couple of years of Kabbalah study were for the most part intellectual, although there were moments as I studied text when I was struck by powerful feelings of awe or bliss. I was still practicing Chi Gong, cultivating my capacity to direct subtle energy through my body using slow and careful physical movements and poses. My practice changed when the cumulative strain on my joints from years as a runner finally took its toll on my aging body. Pains in my feet and knees had become too distracting for me use the postures and movements of Chi Gong to concentrate on energy work. I began to develop a sitting meditation, a practice that I continue to cultivate.

In meditation, I concentrate my attention on a set of Hebrew prayers and Psalms, attending to their multiple esoteric associations, and on visualizations, particularly of the sephirot. Using abilities I acquired in Chi

Gong, I illuminate regions of my body corresponding to the pattern of the sephirot. I concentrate colorless light at the crown of my head for keter, white light on the right side of my head for chochmah, red light on the left side for binah, and so on through the sephirot according to their pattern in the ladder as they map onto the body. I found a commentary in the *Zohar* that associates words of a psalm with the sephirot, singly and in combinations. As I silently utter the words of the psalm, I illuminate my body according to this pattern of the sephirot.

A few years into this practice, an insight came to me as I ended a meditation session. Meditation was cultivating my capacity to project my consciousness into the upper, nonmaterial worlds. I discovered that linear, sequential time is a property of the material world. I saw that, from the perspectives afforded within nonmaterial worlds, time is a tapestry graspable as a whole, rather than a river that carries one from the past through the present into the future. As I went downstairs to share this insight with Jodie, I came to understand how it was that, a few years before, I had apparently required no preparation to engage with Jacob's soul within hours of his death. I realized that my capacity to do so years before was the fruit of a meditation practice cultivated several years later. I wept as I shared this insight with Jodie, saying, "I am still taking care of our son."

AN IMMIGRANT WITH FRESH EYES

As the scion of generations of Protestant ministers who converted to Judaism at the age of sixty-one, after twenty years living in the Jewish community as a "stranger in the camp," I am an immigrant to the Jewish world. Like many immigrants, while I feel deep love for my adopted community, I know that I will always be a stranger in some ways. Although I have acquired more knowledge of Jewish ritual, theology, and history than many in the congregation of my Reform Jewish synagogue, there are aspects to their experiences of Jewish life that are impossible for me to attain. My childhood was not organized by the rhythms of the annual Jewish holidays. Even though some ritual prayers may now flow for me with the ease of acquired habit, they do not carry the rich associations that come from having learned them as a child. I did not have to struggle as a child with parental demands that I go to Hebrew School. I had my bar mitzvah when I was sixty-three, not at the traditional age for a Jewish child of thirteen. I did not grow up with some awareness that I was part of an often hated and imperiled minority group.

I thank Rabbi Lawrence Hoffman for offering, when he was a Temple Sinai visiting scholar, the metaphor of the convert as immigrant. Rabbi Hoffman affirmed what I already learned from my rabbi, i.e., that converts have a positive role in shaping the future of the Jewish religion. Andy's open-minded and open-hearted stance has emboldened me to ask questions out of ignorance, and his aphorism, "'Reform' is a verb," supports me as I shape my own religious perspective, grounded in a lifetime of searching through a variety of spiritual traditions.

I have been moved by their interest in my perspective on Judaism that some learned Jews have shared with me. They tell me that they are eager to learn what I am seeing with my "fresh eyes." So it was that I spent one summer studying in *chavruta* (intimate dialogue in study of sacred texts) with Rabbi Reuven Cohn, of blessed memory. We studied the Mishnah, the written version of Jewish oral law, at the beginning of the Talmud. Reuven guided me to memorize recitations of the texts we were studying together. I developed a deep appreciation for talmudic language, crafted for oral transmission generations before it was written down. As I recited words in Hebrew exploring the particulars of laws regarding liability for carelessness with livestock and fields, I felt a kinship with Jews who had recited, studied, discussed, and argued over the same words of sacred text for two millennia. Reuven had taught the Rabbinics semester when I studied *Me'ah* at Hebrew College, and I later took his adult learning class on the biblical story of Joseph. He sought me out for friendship, offering the opportunity for chavruta study as our way into that friendship. Sadly, before we had enough opportunity to weave the tapestry of that friendship, Reuven died of a sudden heart attack that struck him in synagogue on Yom Kippur.

I am grateful for the blessing of friendship with Art Green, whose writing powerfully shaped my Jewish perspective during my conversion studies and whose work with Barry Holtz assembling Chasidic teachings on prayer for their book *Your Word is Fire* led to my first meeting with Art. That meeting opened the door for me to study Kabbalah. Despite the vast differences in our knowledge, Art has welcomed me as friend, colleague, and fellow spiritual seeker. My friend and colleague Joel Ziff and I occasionally spend a couple of hours in the evening with Art, hanging out and schmoozing in his home.

Joel grew up in an observant family and continues to live as an observant Jew. Art grew up in a secular home, only a few generations removed from Eastern European Chasidic forebears. His grandparents encouraged his interest in Jewish practice and study. Although he was formerly President of the Reconstructionist Rabbinical College, he has not affiliated himself formally with any Jewish movement (e.g., Reform, Conservative, Reconstructionist, Jewish Renewal, Haredi) and led the non-denominational rabbinic school that he founded at Hebrew College. He lives an observant Jewish life. Art and Joel are open-minded, open-hearted, and pluralistic. They welcome engagement with Jews on whatever path they might be following. As the conversation in Art's living room turns to "Jewish geography," discussing the lives of Jews in their local community, in Israel, and throughout the Jewish diaspora, I enjoy the vistas that their conversations open for me as I, the immigrant, learn more about the world I have chosen. They are always open to the questions that I, in my obvious ignorance, might occasionally ask.

THEOLOGY AND PSYCHOLOGY

My pursuit of mystical experience had prepared me well for Art Green's theology. Reading his book, *Seek My Face*, I recognized the experiential truth of the idea that what we call God is the totality of all being. Years before, Ramón had guided me to direct experience of this totality of all being, an experience ultimately beyond human description or understanding. I accepted Maimonides's "negative description" of God, which rejects the use of any adjective to describe God. Any effort to make the distinctions involved in description would diminish God's seamless and unknowable Unity. As I learned Kabbalah, I saw how an ultimately unknowable God makes God's self accessible to human awareness through a process of self-diminishment (*tsimtsum*). Kabbalah describes personifications (*partsufim*) formed through combinations of the sephirot. I, however, had little interest in seeking experiences of God as a personified being. I was far more interested in "ascending" to higher levels in meditation through unification of sephirot.

Art's theology is *panentheistic*, which is to say, grounded in the belief that God, the All that embodies all that exists, is evolving over time. From that perspective, humanity is both a manifestation of and a partner with an evolving divine consciousness that organizes all of Creation. I quickly absorbed and embraced Art's panentheistic perspective, which I found compatible with my lifetime of commitment to progressive activism. It afforded me a way of understanding my Jewish responsibility for *tikkun olam*, the project of repairing our broken world. The panentheistic perspective informed my decision to write this memoir.

When I began studying Art's writing, I was unaware of how my traumatic childhood experience of God was shaping my personal theology. I could not accept a personal relationship with the God who had called my name, abandoned me, then shattered me with a charge of impossible responsibility. Wordless mystical states of mind, abstract ideas of panentheistic theology, and my understanding of Kabbalah protected me from recognizing the consequences of this childhood trauma for my spiritual, intellectual, and emotional life. Jacob's spirit, nearly six years after his death, would finally lead me to that awareness.

5

Restoration

SEPTEMBER 16, 2011. It is five years and seven months after Jacob's death. I am at Friday evening services at Temple Sinai, where Jacob had become bar mitzvah and where I myself became bar mitzvah years later. It is mid-September, the seventeenth of the month of Elul in the Jewish calendar.

Jews are obligated to spend the month of Elul preparing for the Days of Awe—the period starting at Rosh Hashanah and closing with the final moments of Yom Kippur. The Days of Awe call on Jews to examine ourselves, our relationship with God, and our relationships with others as we prepare for these holy days, in which we face an inventory of our actions in the world. We seek forgiveness and reconciliation with the Divine and with each other. Elul has been particularly challenging for me this year. As I examine my relationship with God, I am aware of the distance that has grown between God and me over recent weeks. Months before, I had found a path in my meditative practice toward intense experience of *kavod Adonai*, the majestic spiritual energy embodied in every aspect of creation. Examining myself in preparation for the High Holidays, I realize how seldom in recent weeks I have been able to attain that rung of awareness.

I recognize that my current spiritual crisis began over the previous summer, when I read Rabbi Abraham Joshua Heschel's *The Prophets*.[48] I had been both absorbed and disquieted reading Heschel's passionate and compelling argument that prophetic experience entails empathy with God's passion and intimate awareness of divine yearning for human recognition. I was troubled by the implication that human beings could know God, the ultimately unknowable—Ein Sof, which is without limit or distinction.

Heschel's writing itself had afforded some solace for my discomfort. As I understood it, Heschel considered prophetic empathy with God to be limited to those divine qualities that can be accessible to human awareness. Heschel acknowledged that we cannot know qualities of the One that are beyond our capacity to grasp. Although this satisfied my intellectual theological concerns, I finished Heschel's book with a deep disquiet that persisted just below the threshold of my awareness. As I sit in services, I reflect on how in recent weeks I have become acutely aware of this disquiet, and the challenge that it embodies.

There is a task I cannot escape. I must, once again, attend to healing the terrible wound in my relationship with God. Fragments of my soul have been pressing urgently for reunification. Different parts of me have begun to operate together without my full awareness. I have been experiencing difficulty in my meditative practice, without full consciousness of its implications. In meditation, I strive to hold multiple, sometimes seemingly contradictory ideas simultaneously in my awareness. It has been difficult to hold dual awareness: awareness of God as the Unity of which I am a manifestation together with awareness of God as being in relationship with me. I had corresponded with Art to see if he could recommend biblical text, liturgy, or literature from the sages of Judaism that I could use to focus myself in meditation on this dual awareness. In his response, Art offered helpful ideas about texts. What affected me more than the texts was the emotion with which he responded about his own dialogical relationship with the Divine. I was moved by with his struggles with belief and uncertainty, his challenges to embrace both the acceptance of faith and the critical curiosity of the search for meaning.

There is Chasidic lore about access to knowledge of divine mystery. Once, we had the keys: complex esoteric knowledge that afforded us access to the presence. The keys have been lost. Now, we have but one way to come face-to-face with God: we must smash the lock with tears from our own broken hearts. As my own emotions rise in response to the emotions in Art's letter, I start to become aware of what has been hiding below the surface of my consciousness. The vague discomfort aroused by reading Heschel, and my difficulties accessing experience of kavod Adonai, arise from a common source. This Elul, my work is to wrestle with the challenge of returning to the moment of my first encounter with God—that childhood nightmare of God calling my name, announcing God's impending death, and charging me to carry on God's work.

Despite years of restoration and reintegration of my soul, so shattered by the trauma of the first encounter, I see that there are fragments still trapped within that early trauma—and thus not available for me to draw on to carry on my holy work. As a psychologist, I understand that the wholeness of my being is limited by the traumatic fragmentation that remains and that I cannot retrieve the fragments unless I allow myself to engage with the feelings of terror and loss that shattered my being as a 9-year-old.

It is now the moment in the evening service, after the prayer for peace, when we are invited to pray silently. Years before, during the first service I had attended after becoming a Jew, I had found myself engaging during silent prayer in a practice that I had read about in Chasidic accounts of prayer. I raised my own yearning, and the yearning of the people around me, upwards towards the source of all and then served as a vehicle for the divine response to flow downwards among and into us. Since then, whenever the service calls for silent prayer, I have striven thus to serve God and creation. Today, as soon as I clear myself for the task, I feel my forehead and then my throat suffusing with intense spiritual energy.

I recognize this feeling. I had experienced it once before. It had come to me in the same unbidden and unexpected fashion the evening of the day before Jodie and I were to give our testimony at the Christian memorial service for Jacob. I felt that same illumination of my forehead and throat that I am now feeling as I meditate in services. On that one night, a few nights after his death, I had felt Jacob's soul taking the initiative in our connection between worlds, as he prepared me to deliver the one sermon of my life in a Christian place of worship.

Now, in services more than five years later, I give myself up to the feeling of illumination in throat and forehead. As it has often since his passing, Jacob's spirit serves as my guide. My memories turn to our correspondence when he was living at Heartland Christian Ministries, despairing in his search for religious experience to sustain him in his struggle to build a sober and meaningful life. I remember how I had written to him, drawing on our Christian minister ancestors to lead him:

> God is always ready to enter our hearts, at any time or place. It is up to us to open our hearts to Him. You may find that it doesn't come to you right away. You may need to show God and yourself how strongly you want to feel His presence in your life. Don't be

> surprised to find that, even after you have made up your mind to accept, the joy of feeling his presence may not come to you right away. In every spiritual tradition in the world, the joy of being in the Divine presence comes to those who yearn for it with all their minds, all their hearts, all their souls, and all their beings. You may be on your knees in despair when it finally comes to you. God will know when you are ready, and God will not fail you. I love you deeply, and pray that you are able to find the spiritual connection that can, at long last, give you the peace and calm that you have ached for, and have tried to find in so many dark and destructive places.

I never shrink from the pain and sorrow that I feel over Jacob. I welcome the arrival of these emotions, as they connect with me with my deep love for him and with my gratitude for his life. Feeling the connection with him as I pray in synagogue, I pray that opening my heart to sorrow over Jacob will free my soul to restore its relationship with God.

September 23, 2011. Now, a week later, I sit in services on the evening of the last Shabbat before Rosh Hashanah. In my meditation during the week, I have been able to recapture experience of kavod Adonai. This practice feels a safe distance from intense dialogical relational engagement with a personified God. It is less threatening to experience myself merging into the One, or contemplating divine majesty, than it is to take the risk of engaging in an "I and Thou" relationship with God. As much as I may yearn for this relational intimacy, it still feels inaccessible, a fragment from my soul-shattering initial encounter with God that I have yet to re-assimilate. Safely sequestered away from my conscious awareness are the devastation I suffered in my childhood dream and its aftermath and visceral dread that, if I engage with God again, God will again abandon me. The week has otherwise been stressful, as I have been absorbed in keeping up with my professional obligations and dealing with a physical ailment that has made it difficult for me to carry my weight at home. I am distracted as I enter solitary prayer following the prayer for peace, remembering neither last week's revelation nor the restorative experiences in meditation during the week.

Then, Jacob appears. He seldom manifests in this intense fashion. He is fully and unbearably present. At such moments of intense intimate connection following his death, I am deeply aware of his being aware of me and of his being aware of my awareness of him. I don't see the green light that accompanies his manifestation at other, less intense moments;

I don't hear his voice or feel any other sensation—only the deep and certain experience of our intimate mutual awareness. My tears flow as I feel again the anguish that I felt at the time we lost him. I cling to the connection, even as my heart breaks once again. Jacob then makes it clear why he has appeared. He directs my awareness to the presence of God, not as a Unity beyond all measure or as glorious majesty to contemplate in awe and wonder but as a loving and compassionate companion. Without losing its intensity, the sorrow becomes bearable as Jacob steps aside and I open myself to Divine embrace.

EXPLORING EMERGING POSSIBILITIES

Not long after Jacob's soul mediated that moment of direct engagement between my God and me, my sister-friend Charlee Sutton and I met to continue our conversation about our spiritual journeys. At moments in our conversations, messages for one of us may come from the spirit world through the other's intuition. Charlee listened intently to my story of weeping and divine comfort in synagogue and, just as intently, told me to listen to a message that she was getting: I am not to cry when such intense encounters occur across the boundary between worlds. I should feel joy and recognize that this ability to connect between worlds affords opportunities for Jacob and me to do things in this world that might not otherwise be possible. I took in the message that came to me through Charlee, opening myself to the possibility that I might have a different experience the next time that Jacob's soul would manifest. I wondered if that might happen in my office during a session with a patient.

I was already engaging explicitly with spirituality in conversations with some patients. In 2001, Mark Rivett and Eddy Street published "Connections and Themes of Spirituality in Family Therapy," an article in a major family therapy journal. Rivett and Street challenged therapists to be accountable for the spiritual dimension of their therapeutic practice.[49] They distinguished two ways to integrate spirituality with therapy. Using the "instrumental" approach, the therapist focuses on patients' spiritual experience without reference to the therapist's own spirituality, exploring the influence of religion or spirituality on patients' lives as a source of strength or of conflict and distress. In contrast, the therapist using the "metaphysical" approach participates explicitly as a fully embodied spiritual being, embracing the risks and opportunities of authentic, generative spiritual dialogue.

I had, on occasion, practiced metaphysically as a therapist well before I began to consider conversion to Judaism. Even before reading Rivett and Street's challenge and invitation, I had been drawing on shamanic capacities cultivated since my transformative experience with Ramón Jiménez, and on energetic practice cultivated from studying Chi Gong with Brian Collins. Sitting with patients, I would draw on intuition to discern the state of their soul's evolution. With some patients whose souls were early on their journey, the best that I could do would be to use my therapeutic skills to address obstacles to their spiritual growth. I would help them recognize how habitual responses intended to protect themselves from emotional distress were in fact perpetuating their unhappiness. I would serve as compassionate witness and guide as they learned to accept and manage their feelings. Operating instrumentally, I might explore their participation in religious congregations as a source of either support or conflict. Unless they themselves raised questions about spiritual development, I did not raise such matters directly. I saw them needing to establish healthier emotional lives as a precondition to spiritual awakening.

Other patients with souls further along in their evolutionary journey brought with them complex difficulties that I saw as affecting both emotional health and spiritual growth. With them, I would explore the possibility of our working collaboratively on both spiritual and emotional challenges. Because metaphysical conversation is not common practice in my profession, I was (and am) careful to assure that patients willingly give their informed consent to participate in this alternative approach to standard practice. Being acutely aware that metaphysical conversation is outside the secular tradition of psychotherapy, I was determined not to impose my beliefs about spirituality onto people who came to me vulnerable and in pain. Not every patient whose soul I see as "ready" for metaphysical work is interested in pursuing it. Some might, for example, have developed attitudes shaped by painful childhood entanglements with their families or their faith communities over religion. Taking these considerations into account, I am careful to raise the proposal of spiritual work with sensitivity, so that patients can accept with confidence my assurance that I will still provide them with my services if they should choose not to explore questions of spirituality in therapy.

I had to take a further complication into consideration. Not only is explicit conversation about spirituality outside the mainstream of psychotherapeutic practice, but my spiritual practice is outside the Christianity-informed dominant religious discourse of United States culture. The potential range of spiritually informed psychotherapy is constricted by the silencing power of dominant discourse. Although the United States Constitution permits the free exercise of religion, Christianity is the United States' dominant religious discourse, shaping what is considered to be "true," "real," or "normal." Religious or spiritual ideas that differ too much from the dominant Christian discourse may be marginalized, silenced, or even forbidden.

I count the following precepts among permissible, Christian-informed mainstream beliefs in the United States: Love is a redemptive spiritual force. A soul incorporated in our physical bodies continues to exist after we die. The practice of forgiveness frees us from the pain of resentment and self-absorption. Living a moral life improves the quality of the human soul, with implications for its state of being after this physical life. God responds to our earnest search for God's presence in our lives. Remorse and repentance are redemptive spiritual forces.

The following beliefs are not as mainstream but still permissible within a dominant Christian discourse: To the discerning eye, God's purposes manifest in events in this world. People who have cultivated their relationship with God can achieve abilities to heal illness. Other people are simply born with this gift of healing through faith.

Negotiating informed consent for authentic metaphysical practice necessarily included some disclosure that I might operate outside the dominant, Christian-informed spiritual discourse. By that stage in my own journey, some of my beliefs were more consistent with many non-Christian faiths than with much of Christian-informed dominant discourse. I might, for example, draw on the following beliefs: the soul undergoes a journey through multiple physical incarnations, culminating with direct experience of unity or identity with God. People who have cultivated their spiritual capacities can achieve abilities to project their consciousness through space and time, beyond the limits of their physical bodies. There are worlds beyond, yet interconnected with, the manifest physical world. Such worlds could include, for example, the shamanic worlds (including the animal spirit world and the world of the dead) and worlds of energetic beings (sometimes called angels or spirit guides) that are more evolved than human beings. Spiritual practitioners like shamans can enter states of mind that enable them to travel in these worlds beyond the material world, and to collaborate with companions from these worlds (for example, power animals, spirit guides, divine messengers).

RAYMOND[1]

Several years after we had concluded an earlier course of psychotherapy, eighteen-year-old Raymond returned. He was struggling to finish high school. He showed symptoms of hypomania, grandiosity, and delusional thinking, which I suspected were signs that he was in the early stages of a psychotic episode. I recommended that Raymond meet with a psychiatrist. I wanted another set of eyes on what was happening, from a medical colleague who could consider prescribing medication to interrupt the onset of psychosis. Raymond refused my strong recommendation that he see a psychiatrist and made it clear that he was opposed to taking psychiatric medication. He readily accepted my offer that we include a spiritual perspective in our work. In our conversations, I met him where his mind and self were dissolving into glimpses of universal reality beyond the ordinary world. He was surprised that I seemed to understand his references to spiritual realities that he found too beautiful to abandon. His experience had been that others could not make sense of what he was talking about.

I was not transparent with my patients about my own history of psychosis at that time, although I certainly resonated with Raymond's experience at the intersection of madness and spiritual revelation. Raymond felt profoundly lonely and afraid and was relieved to feel that I understood his experience. Thus soothed, he could listen to me distinguishing spiritual insight from delusional confusion. Reassured by my validating his spiritual experiences, he listened to my concern about the danger he was in and accepted my belief that in time he could develop the capacity to connect with spiritual reality without risking sanity. His mother needed reassurance that my conversations with Raymond were not feeding his delusions but rather were restoring him to relational connection. Raymond let me lead him back from the edge. He restored his sleep and activity routines and later graduated from high school. I followed him for a while, helping him to stay healthy and witnessing his creative efforts to

---

1. As will be the case throughout this book when I talk about my work with patients, I am employing a pseudonym and disguising key identifying information. "Raymond" is not his true name.

capture the spiritual reality he first encountered at the edge of psychosis. Shortly before we concluded this episode of his treatment, we listened together to a CD of his awe-inspiring musical composition, which embodied his experiences of wrestling with the Divine.

It was nearly ten years later that Raymond reached out again for my help. He and his wife, Adriana, had lost their young child to an unexplained sudden death from a previously undiagnosed medical condition. At the time of death, however, there was no explanation. Raymond was himself a medical professional. His trauma from the sudden loss was complicated by the fact that, even as he had recognized that their child was already dead, Adriana had insisted he continue to try to revive their inert child. Raymond's traumatic loss was further complicated by Adriana's announcement, two days after they buried their child, that she no longer wanted to be married to him.

During this brief treatment episode, I worked with Raymond alone and together with Adriana to help them come to terms with their loss. I was transparent about my experiences around my own child's death. Adriana and her family came from Caribbean island culture and were familiar with *espiritismo*. She and her sister were actively exploring their relationship with the spirit world, and with the spirit of Adriana and Raymond's child. Although they remained separated, Adriana and Raymond worked together to make meaning of a message that Raymond was getting from their child, that Raymond needed to bring "his own light into the world."

Four years later, Raymond wrote to share news about the progress of his life. He wrote, "For reasons beyond my understanding, I have been thinking of you lately. I want you to know that my wife [Adriana] and I, although having our ups and downs (presumably like 99% percent of marriages) are still together, raising our new child. He's a great kid and I'm so damn grateful. Life can be hard to navigate. And the suffering that we witness almost daily with our respective professions can at times become a heavy burden. We do our best to fight against the darkness and death that gets placed in front of us. At the ripe old age of 35, I feel like I'm beginning to understand that's what people like us were born to do. I don't want to come off like as self-aggrandizing, I just want you to know I have purpose: purpose which probably wouldn't exist if not for you . . ." As we corresponded, Raymond and I agreed that it was not a coincidence that he felt moved to write to me within a week of my starting to write about him in my memoir.

Our correspondence included the following poignant exchange. Recalling that I began working with Raymond and his family when he was in elementary school, I wrote, "The work that we did, starting when you were in primary school, was actually very healing for me. As a kid in school, all the way from first grade through my sophomore year in high school, I was tormented by bullies. You may remember that, at the time I started working with your family, the school was reporting that you were aggressive with weaker kids, behavior which I understood at the time to be a way that you were dealing with your own pain about your family situation. Please know that opening my heart to you was deeply healing for me. I wonder if you remember that I challenged you about your schoolyard aggression by suggesting that you were attacking weaker kids because you couldn't face your own feelings of vulnerability and sadness. I know that your openheartedness now in the face of the suffering that you face in your professional work is evidence that you have developed profound emotional honesty." He responded, "I actually never knew you were bullied as a kid. It's funny (if you want to call it that) the person who helped me would've been a victim of mine at recess . . ."

DEBORAH

A few years before I began with Raymond and his family, I had been working with Deborah's sons in individual and family therapy. Deborah had set a clear boundary around her own personal psychological issues, declaring them off limits for exploration. She had reacted with some indignation to my suggestion during one family session that she might benefit from treatment for depression. I was therefore surprised when she approached me some time later to request individual therapy for post-traumatic stress resulting from a rape in college.

I had a strong intuitive sense of Deborah as embodying an old soul and had privately wondered about the divine purpose behind such a spiritually advanced person adopting these two brothers in particular, each of whom was extremely bright, quite neuroatypical, and very challenging temperamentally. I worked gently and carefully with Deborah as we began her individual therapy, respecting her vulnerability as a sexually traumatized woman working with a male therapist and mindful of her indignation when I had moved too fast with her earlier during family therapy.

As Deborah described encounters with strangers in public places and exchanges with members of her community, I saw that many people were responding to her spiritual gifts. Even as she described these experiences, she made it clear that she was not interested in discussing her spirituality. In my notes from that initial period, I wrote, "Not open to metaphysical remedy."

Deborah, however, was determined to make progress in therapy. Beginning at a rapid pace, she quickly uncovered a history of severe sexual abuse by Joe, an uncle who had free access to her childhood family home. After a few months Deborah decided that she had done the work that she needed to do and terminated her individual treatment, although I continued with work with one of her sons.

Deborah returned to her individual therapy not long thereafter. Her heart had continued to open following our healing work with her trauma. She had become increasingly aware of difficulties in her relationships with others, particularly with close family members. She set a goal of transforming the way she treated the people she loved. She said she wanted to "go back to work on Joe, in order to treat people better." She described Uncle Joe as an emotionally vulnerable, dependent person. She had learned in childhood to gain some power over this man who was keeping her sexually subjugated by wounding him with her words, as she felt she was now doing to people whom she loved.

A theme that had emerged early in therapy was to evolve over several years of our work together. Deborah felt caught in a state of mind as "the monitor," or observer of her own actions and experiences, rather than as fully and directly present in them. I could see that this state created painful emotional constriction for her.

Deborah explored the complexity of her feelings about Joe courageously. She also struggled with her ambivalence about discussing spirituality. On the one hand, she guarded against direct discussion. On the other, Deborah, who was a practicing Jew, brought in more and more stories of her spiritual experiences. As she continued to heal childhood trauma, I perceived stronger radiant emanations from her old soul. She reported vivid dreams, rich with Jewish mystical symbols. In one such dream, I appeared to her with a "glow of perfection."

Deborah reconstructed transpersonal experiences from adolescence. She recounted how she had astonished her friends with direct knowledge of their private family conversations at which she herself had not been physically present. At the time, she became afraid for her soul and her sanity and therefore renounced her adolescent exploration of her spiritual gifts. She had continued to pursue meaning in Jewish text and ritual, however, and her studies brought her to the attention of distinguished mentors. After being raped by a sadistic boyfriend in college, however, she had angrily rejected God.

Determined to heal by making sense of her traumatic history, Deborah visited the childhood home where her parents still lived. She searched through old childhood drawings, journals, and possessions from childhood for clues. Together, Deborah and I reconstructed her childhood survival strategy. She had protected fragments of herself from destruction by splitting them off and sequestering them from awareness. She had left herself clues and keys to these sequestered fragments in her artwork and other personal artifacts. The artifacts proved to serve as vessels for buried memories, memories retrieved in detail with each discovery. She brought these artifacts to my office where she could recover and reintegrate the fragments that she had so carefully and lovingly stored away. Her strategy resonated for me with the shamanic practice of restoring lost fragments to a soul shattered by trauma and with the kabbalistic image of redeeming divine sparks, scattered from broken vessels at the time of creation.

Deborah continued to make rapid therapeutic progress. As she did so, her distress over her unusual spiritualities abilities grew. Despite her renunciation of God, Deborah could not escape her gifts. Unbidden, strangers would tell her their stories and find relief in her responses to them. She did not understand how she knew what she knew about people or why they found such healing in her. She strove to make sense of her talents, yet she resisted spiritual interpretation. Negotiating the boundary between us about this issue was as critical and delicate as it had been at the beginning when we had begun to explore traumatic history. I was finding it increasingly difficult to be fully, authentically present in our conversation while being silent about the metaphysical dimension of our work. We agreed that I could speak of the spiritual dimension of my *own* experience stimulated during our conversations, with the explicit understanding that I was neither trying to persuade her of my perspective nor demanding that she acknowledge her own spirituality.

Over time, however, my intuition strengthened that Deborah could not find *shleimut*, or wholeness, without accepting all of herself. She herself acknowledged a developing impasse in therapy. So it was that I offered, and she accepted, my suggestion that she read the biblical book of Jonah, whose protagonist struggles against taking responsibility for his relationship with God.

When I prescribe the reading of a sacred text, patients may discover meanings that I don't predict they will find. For Deborah, the crucial words were among the last of Jonah's in the text. Translated into English, the words are "Please, LORD, take my life, for I would rather die than live" (Jonah 4:8). The Hebrew translated as "life" in this biblical passage is *nephesh*, a word for the soul. Deborah told me that she decided to accept herself fully as a spiritual being, as to refuse to do so would be to allow her soul to die. This belief allowed her to accept her spirituality, and our psychotherapy thereafter incorporated explicit spiritual guidance.

Deborah's complex physical health challenges included a seizure disorder. As it happened, Deborah found improvement in this condition to be another reason for her to persist in the difficult process of psychotherapy. I learned that she had dissociative experiences of traveling outside her body. She was understandably ambivalent about these experiences, as they would sometimes lead to a seizure. "I feel there is a monster at the end. I feel so good I would let myself go with it, but it always ends so bad."

She feared that exploring transpersonal experience would take her back to her childhood exploration of her gifts, exploration that she had renounced after a terrifying encounter with an entity she had encountered looking into a mirror. She told me, "To believe in the spirit would be to go back to the time before the mirror. I try not to go out of my body, but do so often in little ways, with little things." I cautioned that dissociation could also be associated with personal disintegration. I told her that if she chose to proceed in this domain, I was willing to do so, but that we would move slowly and carefully. She chose to do so, saying, "I feel like it is the only way." As we continued on this course, she reported a substantial decrease in seizures.

Encouraged by Rivett and Street's description of metaphysical use of spirituality in therapy, and Deborah's decision to embrace the gifts of her spirituality, I worked openly with her from my position as a fully embodied spiritual being. As she learned more deeply about herself as a spiritually gifted woman, I learned to navigate the technical and ethical challenges of a therapeutic conversation with such a strong metaphysical dimension.

Recognizing her need to understand herself spiritually, Deborah moved as rapidly in this domain as she had earlier when uncovering and healing her trauma. As she experienced more personal integration, she felt that her internal "monitor" was not as active. She reported, "I am glad that I am a nice person without trying to be." Having accepted her gifts, she worked on cultivating them. She found classes on kabbalistic meditation. She focused mindfully on what happened when she would "read" people who sought her witnessing or advice. As she was more open and curious about her dreams, she found herself engaged in worlds beyond the material world. She encountered spirit beings who advised her and guided her journeys, at first traveling in the dream world, and, increasingly, providing guidance for her waking life. She found spiritual meanings in synchronistic events, apparent coincidences that she recognized as relevant to her progress on the spiritual path. She gained control over dissociation, using it as a tool to help her retrieve memories of her past and to explore spiritual experience.

As Deborah learned to manage altered states of awareness, her spiritual horizons widened. She wrestled with the quandary of how to fit her emerging abilities into everyday life. She spoke of her struggle to "discern the limit of acceptable experience." At this stage of our work, that limit manifested in her resistance to being curious and open about how other people experienced her. I would occasionally test that limit gently, by telling her something about my experience of her. I was cautious about going too fast, as she was powerfully guarded against feelings of vulnerability that were stimulated.

I found my way to serve Deborah in my expanded roles as both therapist and as guide for her spiritual explorations, specifically affirming that I saw my therapist role as primary. I explored, supported, and encouraged Deborah's spiritual development for its own sake, and because it was clear that her spiritual gifts were integral elements of her personal identity.

At that time, I understood my spirituality to be grounded in studies of esoteric texts from a variety of spiritual traditions, as informed by my experiences with my teachers Ramón and Brian. At that point in my own spiritual journey, I was moved spiritually by the experiences of raising Jacob as a Jew, by synagogue services and by the Jewish holiday cycle. Yet, I still considered myself to be a "stranger in the camp" (a term that describes members of the "mixed multitude" who accompanied the children of Israel in their escape from Egypt and travels in the desert on their way to the promised land). I did not expect that I would later become a Jew.

As a witness and guide for Deborah's unfolding spiritual capacities, I would ground myself using Chi Gong skills I learned from Brian and would "open" myself as Ramón had shown me, dissolving the boundary between my embodied soul and worlds beyond the material. There were moments, particularly when I was responding to Deborah's accounts of her dreams, that I experienced images, ideas, or words that I recognized as coming from the spirit world. I would often share these experiences with Deborah, marking their source. At rare moments, my words would flow forth directly, without mediation, intention, or reflection. With such utterances, I felt like the vehicle rather than the author of the words.

Deborah reported a moving and somewhat mysterious encounter during a public event featuring Manitonquot, or Medicine Story, an elder and storyteller of the Assonet Wampanoag nation (the Wampanoag are one of the major indigenous groups who were present at the first encounter with English colonists who took their land and renamed it "New England"). Deborah and her son approached Manitonquot at the end of the event to thank him. He stood wordless, looking at her intently, without speaking. As she told me the story, I could feel the sacred energy from this encounter.

Deborah came to learn a great deal from Manitonquot, who taught her, "All of us were once tribal people. We return to our places in the 'sacred circle' by reconnecting with the caring and respect that is our tribal legacy." As a Jew familiar with Judaism's foundational texts, Deborah recognized the relevance of Manitonquot's teaching to the stories of the children of Israel, twelve tribes descended from the biblical patriarch Jacob's sons, whom God led out from slavery in Egypt to revelation at Mount Sinai and travels through the desert to a land promised to their ancestors. Deborah identified herself with the Tribe of Dan, who served as the rear guard of the tribes traveling through the desert and who were responsible for retrieving whatever and whomever might have been left behind by the tribes traveling to the fore. She came to understand her own sacred mission to include the retrieval of lost souls. She remembered the decision of the principal of her Hebrew school to change her Hebrew name to *Nechama*, which translates as "comfort." She understood more deeply her extraordinary ability to bring comfort to others, including strangers in apparently chance encounters.

Psychological healing afforded Deborah further spiritual growth and more profound connection with tribal spiritual wisdom embodied in the land. She encountered male and female Indigenous spirits in her dreams and visions, including Red Feather, who served both as her personal spirit guide and as a protector for her sons. She joined in gatherings for Native rights and restitution, including Thanksgiving mourning events in Plymouth, the site of original English colonial settlement in the region.

As she trusted her powers more, she sought to understand her struggle to recognize and accept how she was seen through the eyes of others. With more access to her gifts, Deborah found not only how to see herself through the eyes of the other, but more generally, to have direct access to others' experiences. Once she learned how to control and modulate this ability, she sought a way share her experience of God with others. She discovered an ability to transmit her own experience directly to another person. Her explorations in this domain led to a crisis in the course of treatment.

As Deborah accepted and cultivated her own personal spiritual work as a counselor, teacher, and guide for others, she reflected on my role in our work together. She distinguished her work from that of a therapist by her intention to reach directly to people's souls. She was grateful for my witnessing of her spiritual growth, as it helped her feel that she was not on her journey alone. Yet she also felt that therapy was moving toward an impasse. She wanted me to experience direct transmission of her experience. She recognized that this would require me to set aside my stance as a therapist, as this would involve interdependence beyond the boundaries of my ethical responsibility to serve her. She declared, "I want to change it so that it flows both ways." Given the transformations that she had achieved, she was feeling that therapy was not true to her experience. She felt that this was "the beginning of the end of therapy for me." Yet, even though she did not want therapy anymore, she also did not want to be alone. She asked me to consider relinquishing the therapist role "in the spiritual domain only." If I could not, she would terminate from therapy.

I struggled with this dilemma, drawn toward continuing our conversations about her unfolding spiritual abilities yet recognizing that I could not continue as her therapist if I did as she sought. I understood intuitively, as did she, that opening myself to her emerging practice of direct spiritual influence would make me relationally dependent on her to a degree that would not maintain the primacy of her interests essential to the therapeutic relationship. She had her own ethical concern, saying that in such changed circumstances, she might "use" her "leverage to change the relationship in a way that you would not want."

Deborah had made substantial progress in therapy. One could argue that the progress was sufficient to justify termination. I told her that I needed to take some time to decide about whether or not to agree to terminate and to continue the metaphysical conversation on different terms. I discussed the dilemma with Jodie, as we often consult on each other's work. We agreed that I needed to get consultation from a professional peer other than a family member. We recognized that it would be challenging to find a colleague who would not be put off or alarmed by misunderstanding the metaphysical work that Deborah and I had been doing, which was far outside the bounds of the dominant Christian-informed spiritual discourse of United States society. We agreed that I would approach our mutual colleague, Hugo Kamya. Hugo is a practicing Roman Catholic and is also true to his roots in traditional East African spirituality.[50] He is one of the most radiantly spiritual people I know.

Hugo is respectful, curious, and attentive. He listened deeply to my account of the work that Deborah and I had been doing. He resonated with my feelings of awe about Deborah and could empathize with my impulse to accept her terms in order to witness more of her spiritual journey. From his position as observer and consultant, he pointed out that I was still treating her sons. It therefore would not be ethically permissible to have therapeutic relationships with some members of the family and a more personal, interdependent relationship with another. This was apparent to me as soon as Hugo pointed it out.

Deborah accepted my decision with sadness. She felt that this limitation on my witnessing of her journey was too great an obstacle for her to go further in individual therapy, and we concluded this chapter in the course of her treatment. I continued my important and necessary work with one of her sons. Thanks to the consultation with Hugo, I was very much aware of how my own spiritual yearnings had tempted me to divert from my course as a therapist, absorbed as I had been in feelings of awe as I witnessed Deborah's journey.

Over time, Deborah found her way to resume our therapeutic conversations, as she was encountering new and emerging problems in her life. Even as she struggled with challenges of divorce and parenting, she continued her spiritual journey. She developed intentional strategies to explore the spiritual implications of what others might see as coincidences or random events. She would enter a bookstore with a question in her mind, finding an answer by wandering among the shelves until intuition led her pick out a book and read what was on whatever page her hand opened. The questions she formed often concerned the direction of her journey. Allowing her steps to lead her, she was drawn to heal the land that European settlers had stained with the blood of generations of the peoples indigenous to that land. She set out for a family vacation in Canada, carrying a strong message from the spirit world of her responsibility to heal the land. After her return, I witnessed her stories of profound and awesome encounters, including a night that she experienced cries of anguish from wounded souls in a valley that had been desecrated by colonial exploitation.

DEVELOPING AN INTEGRATED SPIRITUAL AND CLINICAL PRACTICE

The work that Deborah and I did was a milestone in my clinical practice. Thanks to my original professional training in the Boston area (informed by psychodynamic ideas grounded in psychoanalysis), I could attend simultaneously to what my patients were showing and telling me in sessions and to my own internal flow of personal memories, associations, feelings, and ideas. Working with Deborah I refined my capacities to attend to phenomena from worlds beyond the material world and to distinguish them from the flow of my own materially embodied experiences. As I cultivated the skill of tracking and distinguishing these three distinct streams of information (my patients' words and gestures, my internal associations, messages from the spirit world), I could better discern patterns formed by their interactions, resonances, and disjunctions.

I was fortunate that my early training had also included family and network therapy. While psychodynamic training had urged me toward mastery of complex flows of information, my experience working with teams leading scores of people gathered in network assemblies and engaging in my office with multiple family members had taught me important lessons in true collaboration that required humility. I had to let go of the illusion that I could "master," in the sense of having comprehensive understanding and control, the phenomena with which I engaged.

I learned a poised, attentive stance that kept me open to the moment-to-moment emergence of new events and experiences. I learned that I would not lose my way for long in therapeutic conversations if I trusted my fascination with complexity, openness to novelty, appreciation for surprise, and collaborative relationships with my patients. For decades, I taught family therapy at the Center for Multicultural Training in Psychology, to psychology interns in the early stages of developing their clinical skills. As they struggled to make sense of their experiences with patients, they could find it daunting to embrace uncertainty and surprise. I sought to comfort them with the aphorism "Don't try to hold the complexity. Let the complexity hold you."

Working with Deborah taught me that I had to develop ethical standards and boundaries specific to working metaphysically in therapy. While these ideas were taking shape in my work with Deborah, I received an invitation from social psychologist Joseph Trimble. Joseph and I are distant cousins through a common Scottish ancestor from the fourteenth century, William Rule, who rescued Robert the Bruce from a wounded bull and was then dubbed Sir Turnbull. All the Turnbulls and Trimbles are descendants of that common ancestor.

Joseph's address at an Annual Conference of the American Psychological Association (APA) some years earlier had opened the eyes of professional psychologists to the importance of spirituality in psychological practice.[51] He invited me to present on a panel at an APA Conference, in a symposium honoring the memory of the late Carolyn Attneave, his colleague and my mentor. I accepted the invitation with some trepidation, as this would be my first public acknowledgment of my metaphysical practice and also because it was to be my first time leaving home without Jodie since we had lost Jacob. I went because I felt an obligation to honor Carolyn's teaching about working with the person as a "biopsychosocioculturospiritual system."

In my address, I acknowledged my initial resistance to Carolyn's teaching about the spiritual dimension of network intervention.[52] I said:

> I was open to Carolyn Attneave's idea of the person as a biopsychosocioculturospiritual system but closed to her claim that one conducts a network assembly in the role of shaman. Descended from Protestant clergy, I was determinedly secular. The closest I came to religious belief was dialectical materialism.

I spoke of the double challenges of engaging with spirituality from my unconventional position, at a time when the profession of psychology was still resistant to incorporating the metaphysical in scientific practice and in a United States society where the dominant discourse about spirituality was shaped by Christian ideology. After describing my work with Raymond and with Deborah, I offered the following perspective on the dilemmas and ethical challenges of working metaphysically in psychotherapy:

The rules are different for scientifically informed psychotherapy and for metaphysical practice. Scientific claims must be supported by empirical evidence. The methods used to acquire the evidence must be clearly and publicly disclosed, so that other scientists can use those same methods to determine if using the same methods will produce the same evidence. Metaphysical knowledge, however, may be closely held, revealed only to those who are prepared to hold the knowledge. The esoteric can be harmful to the unprepared or uninitiated.

There may be a spiritual-developmental mismatch between clinician and client. The client may be an "older soul" but less well-developed psychologically or less healthy emotionally than the "younger soul" clinician, who may at times be struck with awe at the manifestations of the client's older soul. This situation challenges the clinician to recognize the seductive influence of the experience of awe. The temptation to be absorbed in powerful transcendent experiences can challenge the clinician's ethical imperative to place the client's needs and experiences first.

Consideration of these dilemmas led me to derive the following three ethical principles: first, metaphysical practice requires an additional component to the standard practice of assuring informed consent. All mental health disciplines agree that ethical psychotherapy requires that the client have some understanding of the nature of psychotherapy before consenting to participate in the therapeutic process. If therapists consider proceeding metaphysically, they are also obliged to clarify the distinction between conventional psychotherapy and psychotherapy that is integrated with metaphysical practice. They must provide the client with sufficient information to decide whether to enter into an informed agreement to proceed in that direction.

Second, in a situation where a therapist discerns conflict between metaphysical and psychotherapeutic imperatives, the psychotherapeutic imperative overrides the metaphysical. Using the metaphor of a ladder for the soul's journey toward higher levels of attainment, a client may be on the verge of ascending to a "higher rung" of that ladder. That ascent may be critically important for the client's soul journey. All such ascents, however, involve a degree of risk, either from conventionally understood psychological stress or from hazards specific to expanding consciousness beyond the boundaries of the material world. The spiritual gain must be weighed against potential psychological harm, including disruption of the psychotherapeutic process. As a healing professional, the therapist must always decide such conflicts in favor of psychotherapy.

Third, responsible therapists understand that the complexity and emotional intensity of psychotherapy make them vulnerable to error. They are wise to rely on respected colleagues whom they trust to provide honest and clear-sighted consultation about their work. If they choose to integrate spirituality into their clinical practice, they should establish regular and active consultations with professional peers who can operate comfortably with both psychotherapeutic and metaphysical discourses.

I learned this latter lesson in my work with Deborah. I am grateful that Hugo so generously provided his clear-eyed and respectful consultation. As he and I discussed developing an ongoing conversation about our spiritual practices in psychotherapy, I readily accepted Hugo's suggestion that we include our mutual colleague, Jay King, in our group. For Jay, the murder of Martin Luther King had created a spiritual crisis that he resolved through departing from his parents' Protestant and Catholic faiths to embrace the Taoist spirituality he had first encountered in his martial arts training. The three of us later invited Patricia Romney into our consultation group. Pat draws on her multicultural ancestral legacy and her Christian faith as she works psychotherapeutically with elders in liminal space as they come to terms with their mortality. Dubbing ourselves "The Spiritans," we meet online regularly in regular rich conversations about our work. As fully embodied spiritual beings engaging openheartedly with each other, we often enter together into experiences of sacred space.

EXPLORING THE PATH OF THE SHAMANIC HEALER

As with many heretofore closely held spiritual secrets, the doors have been opening for more to explore the practice of the shaman. Although I chose not to seek shamanic training, I found I could not ignore Carolyn Attneave's challenge that I take on the role of shaman as conductor of a family network assembly. Her words prepared me for the powerful altered states of consciousness I entered when working with a team to guide a large group of people gathered in concern over a family in crisis. Trusting my team members to hold me while they assured the coherence of the group process, I could allow myself to be possessed by powerful emotions and wordless awareness, emerging from those moments to utter words carrying meanings that touched the minds, hearts, and souls of the assembled network members.

Shamanic traditions are probably older than recorded history. I do not venture here to offer definitive description or explanation of the shaman's practice. I have learned from David Hammerman, who has systematically pursued shamanic training, and from his wife Sylvia Hammerman, both psychologists who incorporate their experience and knowledge of the spirit world into their clinical practices. I found personal healing with shaman and psychologist Ann Drake, whose work afforded me some knowledge of my soul's journey in previous mortal lives. Intuitive learning with Ramón Jiménez taught me to open the door to worlds beyond the material world. These and other experiences have afforded me the capacity to recognize and respond to moments when my consciousness ascends beyond the limitations of my physical body. So it was that, in the moments and days after Jacob's death, I accompanied his soul's return to the source of all being, and that, for several years that followed, our souls remained in communication with each other.

I have learned from Charlee how to pause and listen, a helpful contrast to my own intense manner of searching. I bore in mind the message that she had brought me from the spirit world—that Jacob's soul and I could act in concert in the material world, using the opportunity afforded by our ability to connect between worlds. I took this to heart and opened myself to this possibility, without pressing forward to act.

Charlee's words came forcefully to me later, at a moment in my office when a client asked me to help heal an estranged relationship with a family member who had died years before. I found myself shifting suddenly into a powerful state of consciousness. I felt Jacob's presence with every inch of my body's surface, not on the outside but from the inside. Remembering Charlee's words and experiencing Jacob's presence in a way that I never had before, I did my best to help. I gently guided my client into a light trance and invited her to connect with the soul of the departed. I sat silently as she wept deeply, and I simply allowed myself to be present with Jacob's spirit. After a few minutes, each of us returned to fully materialized presence in the room. Although she had few words to describe her experience, she was clear that she had been moved and had found it helpful.

Although I was unable to repeat that experience with such intensity, I was grateful for the moment that my client and I had experienced. I set the intention to cultivate my capacity to work with Jacob's soul to help my patients. I considered seeking training in shamanism, but Charlee brought me the message that this was not to be my path. I was by that time formally a convert but had not yet learned enough to see how to access my Jewish religion as the source for my metaphysical psychotherapeutic practice.

I learned, instead, by doing. I relied on my clinical experience, on my developing capacity for spiritual practice, and on the gift afforded to me by ready connection between Jacob's soul and mine. When it appeared to be appropriate, safe, and useful with certain patients who had given me their informed consent for metaphysical work, I would on occasion ask for their permission to pray for them. With that permission, when alone and meditating, I would ask Jacob's soul to help me ascend beyond the limits of my body to enter the spirit world for the purpose of helping and healing my patient.

As you read these words, I am conscious of the challenge I face in my effort to recount such experiences. Although my recollections of praying for my patients are vivid and clear for me, the experiences themselves were in states beyond the limits of language. Whatever words I choose can at best point toward rather than describe the experiences. Recognizing the limitations of language, I can tell you that once my soul was traveling in immaterial worlds, often with active assistance from Jacob's soul, I would search until I located my patient's soul. Holding my patient's soul in my soul's gaze, I would open my soul fully to the presence of the Source of all being. I would present my request or intention, asking that if it were acceptable, it be granted. Working with this approach, adapted intuitively from shamanic traditions, I was helpful for several of my patients.

Gracia struggled in this mortal life with a legacy of intergenerational trauma and the persistent trauma of living with an abusive spouse. Devoutly religious and deeply spiritual, she embodied a soul far more advanced than mine. Hesitantly at first, she told me of her visions and revelations; she feared that she was losing her sanity. Once reassured, she was more open about her spiritual experience, including her ability in sessions to perceive the aura of my soul's radiance. She would on occasion ask me to pray for her and I would do so. She sometimes reported that she sensed my prayers for her and could see them influencing her situation for her benefit.

At that time, in most situations I would pray for my patients' psychological healing. In the one case that I prayed for physical health for a patient, the successful outcome opened a path for them to return to the religious faith from which they were estranged.

Sadly, learning by doing includes making mistakes, and I made blunders that I continue to regret. The successful outcomes that I had witnessed with other patients had made me overconfident, and I reached for more in a manner that only later, with painful reflection, I realized was impulsive. I did not continue for long on the shamanic path of healing. I was to relearn, in another fashion, the lesson that I had been given traveling in the spirit world during the workshop with Ann Drake.

In that experience of traveling, I had reached greedily for a book on the shelves of an immense library of knowledge, opening it to find the pages were blank. In that vision, my spirit guide had beckoned me to sit beside her on a piano bench, where I was bidden to practice scales on the piano. The lesson for me was that to learn deeper spiritual knowledge I needed to cultivate my capacity to hold that knowledge safely. This was a difficult lesson for me to remember. I was still vulnerable to deception by my ego, which was greedy for the experience of triumphant mastery. In the words of Black Elk, "If I thought that I was doing it myself, the hole would close up and no power could come through. Then everything I could do would be foolish . . ."

On one occasion, I blurted out my intuitive perception that my patient was possessed by a malevolent spirit. That impulsive utterance led, understandably, to premature termination of the treatment. Although I was able to protect myself from harm when I entered the spirit world to disengage the malevolent spirit from my patient's soul, I became acutely aware of my soul's vulnerability during encounters with such dangerous entities in that world. I never again addressed the challenge of soul possession by directly engaging in the spirit world.

My practice, when I sense that a patient's soul is far enough along on its journey, is to open a conversation about the decision to incorporate a metaphysical dimension into our work. I learned, from my mistakes, that observant Jewish patients might see such descriptions of my work in the spirit world on their behalf as challenging the tenets of their faith. I learned from a patient of mine that he had consulted with a prominent Modern Orthodox rabbi, whose perspective draws on Maimonidean rationalist traditions, for a judgment as to whether it was permissible to work with a therapist who speaks thus of working in the spirit world on behalf of his patients.

The rabbi's response was grounded in careful consideration of Judaism's wide range of traditions. He explained that my work, as he understood it from the description, resonated with centuries of Jewish esoteric traditions, including Kabbalah. As the rabbi's approach drew from a different stream of Jewish tradition, he stated that he did not consider himself qualified to make a judgment on what he determined to be the critical question of monotheism. If David Trimble's practices and perspectives were determined to be monotheistic, the rabbi declared, it would be permissible to work with me. The rabbi told my patient that Rabbi Arthur Green is widely acknowledged as a scholar on Jewish esoteric tradition, and that he, the Modern Orthodox rabbi, respects and acknowledges Rabbi Green's work. "If Rabbi Green sees David Trimble as monotheistic," declared the rabbi, it would be acceptable to work with me.

So it was that I came to Art's home with the request that he examine me for monotheism. Years before, he had been careful to welcome me into friendship, even as he discouraged my wish that he become my spiritual master. I am grateful for his grace and generosity as he agreed on this occasion to examine me in his role as rabbi. I answered his questions with the same care that he took in posing them to me, and he concluded that my theology is monotheistic. When I described my praying on behalf of my patients, his response was firm and clear: "Don't pray for your patients."

He also found another area of concern. Acting, at my request, in his role as rabbi responding to questions of Jewish law, he told me he was concerned about my practice of engaging with Jacob's soul in therapy. He noted that the Jewish *mitzvah*, or commandment, that prohibits consulting with spirits is grounded not just in rabbinic elaborations of Jewish law but also in God's commandments in the Bible. He told me that he would consult with a colleague deeply versed in the history of the sixteenth century circle of mystic practitioners assembled around Rabbi Isaac Luria in Safed, Israel. Later, Art shared his colleague's response: the practice of engaging with souls of the departed is permissible "in the service of *yichud*," i.e., the mystic practice of unifying the upper and lower worlds of creation.

As I understand my obligation as a Jew, if I approach a rabbi with an explicit request for a judgment about Jewish law, I am bound not to question the rabbi's response. Since that consultation with Art, I have never traveled in the spirit world to petition on behalf of my patients. Although I was curious about what informed Art's directive, I did not at the time venture to engage him in dialogue about the reasoning behind it. It appeared to me that he was concerned about my accepting fees for my services when my services included petition for divine intercession. A conversation with Art and Joel a few years later gave me further perspective. When I retold the story of my seeking his rabbinic judgment, he teased me about my venturing to pronounce myself a *tzaddik*, a term that means both a pious Jewish master of esoteric practice and the title for leader of a Chasidic community. As I remember Art's comment, I recognize my aspiration to combine the roles of shaman and therapist as the greed of my ego, the same greed for which I received correction in my earlier shamanic vision of opening a book to discover blank pages.

Art's directive converged with other changes in my life to bring my exploration of shamanic healing to a close. The connection between Jacob's soul and mine was changing. I was integrating my religious faith and identity more with my spiritual explorations, and I was soon to find a teacher and mentor to guide me along the path of mystical Judaism.

There is a Sufi aphorism that a form only serves as a vehicle for spiritual experience when created for a particular person at a particular time, in a particular place, and in particular circumstances. When any of these conditions change, the form loses its vitality. Although I had come to appreciate the genius of Judaism in renewing and revitalizing its forms, I still found that repetition tended to drain the energy out of my individual spiritual efforts. I would fill with energy when I mastered a practice to the level of fluency, until it started to become routine. Once the practice became automatic, my attention would easily wander despite my earnest intentions. I could feel this beginning to happen when I would reach out to connect with Jacob's soul, and this troubled me.

As often happens when I begin to have doubts or questions about integrating spirituality with my clinical practice, the occasion arose for Jodie and me to visit with the Hammermans, who are far more experienced than I with metaphysical therapeutic practice. As I described working with Jacob's soul to help patients in my office, Sylvia gently suggested that perhaps Jacob's soul had other things to do. This helped me to let go of seeking to connect with Jacob across the boundary between mortal and immaterial worlds. Now, those moments of connection are increasingly rare. When they do happen, they come not when I seek them but, it seems, at the initiative of Jacob's soul.

This transition took place as I intensified my studies of esoteric Judaism. I was incorporating my explorations of spirituality into living a Jewish religious life. Mindful of the advice of Rabbi Toba Spitzer, the Reconstructionist rabbi of the beit din that had accepted me into the Jewish community, I expanded the range of my observance. I pray regularly each morning, observing the commandment to wear *tefillin* (small leather boxes that hold parchment scrolls of Torah verses, bound to the arms by leather straps during prayer) on the days that it is required. Whenever I can, I devote the seventh day of each week to Shabbat, setting aside the work of weekdays and Sundays to absorb myself in study, meditation, walks with Jodie, and visits with friends and family.

Although my practices and beliefs diverge increasingly from many fellow congregants in my Reform synagogue, I do not expect to change my denominational affiliation. I experience Reform Judaism as a liberal, tolerant, and accepting Jewish community. The Reform movement has softened the aggressively modernist stance shaped by its origins in the Haskalah, or "Jewish Enlightenment" of the nineteenth century. It is now open to a wider range of religious observance, ritual, and belief. Although Andy Vogel, my congregational rabbi, is not as deeply immersed as I am in studying Kabbalah, he is curious, accepting, and affirming about my mystical explorations. His aphorism, "Reform is a *verb*," embodies his affirmation of every Jew's journey in their search to find meaning in the vast and varied traditions of Jewish religion.

6

Adversary and Companion

FROM THE MOMENT OF revelation under Ramón's guidance when I was thirty, I have understood my life to be a spiritual journey. Looking backward through that lens, I see my childhood nightmare as a terrifying initiation into that journey. My adolescent discovery of meditation helped me to start gathering together fragments of my shattered soul, while my later exploration of psychedelic drugs led me to discover spiritual ecstasy. My encounter with psychosis opened doors of revelation and warned me of the dangers of the journey.

My time with Ramón set me on the path of a conscious, self-reflective seeker. I studied spiritual texts and engaged in dialogues with other seekers I encountered along my path. I found Brian Collins, my Chi Gong teacher, who taught me to perceive the invisible energy of the Divine that courses through the universe and to channel it through my body. Later, living through the heartbreak and devastation of Jacob's early death, I found in his immortal soul another teacher, as we connected across the boundary between life and death.

Throughout that journey, I have wrestled with an inner adversary. Every tradition I have explored acknowledges and warns of this challenge. Its names are various in various traditions, including the ego, the self, pride, self-absorption, etc. I am particularly conscious of this adversary's presence as I write this book about my individual journey, with the intention to touch your heart and invite you to free your own soul. As mortal beings seeking the wisdom that emanates from within our immortal souls, we seekers respect the tenacity with which the ego clings to the limits of self and identity. My prayer, as you read this narrative of my life's journey, is that you may enter moments of timeless awareness transcending those limits within yourself.

As a psychologist, I understand that healthy functioning requires that my brain's cerebral cortex organize my being in the world. Although I find my diagnosis of attention deficit disorder useful for understanding myself, as well as some of my patients and their families, the term does not capture the complexity, unpredictability, frustrations, and gifts that can come with this temperament. I must manage the peculiarities of my forebrain, or prefrontal cortex, a specialized region of the cerebral cortex that enables one to discern priorities, set intentions, and track progress as one works to realize plans. Psychologists call these mental operations "executive functions." As I reflect on the problem of ego, I see how much mental bandwidth I must allocate to the challenge of staying on track to manage life's demands, ranging from everyday activities of care for self and others to the larger demands of living a meaningful life. As vital as they may be for my wellbeing, these mental operations also strengthen my attachment to ego.

Meditators learn to deal with the "monkey mind," the tendency to drift away from sustaining open awareness toward the restless chatter of a mind seeking distractions and diversions. I struggle with the convergence of monkey mind and ego as I meditate. I drift away from contemplation of the sacred toward mundane thoughts of what I will prepare for the next meal, what I need to do next in work projects, managing personal funds, getting in touch with people, etc. These activities of the ego are particularly compelling for me. They are driven by the shame, frustration, and confusion of my earlier years living a disorganized life, disappointing others and myself with my scattered ways of being in the world. Relatively early in my adult life, these emotions drove me to train my mind toward more effective executive functioning. As adaptive as my executive skills have become, they are still connected to their roots in painful emotions associated with failure, in my own eyes and those of others.

I have learned a lesson common to most meditation traditions. Meditative practice requires that I loosen the constrictions of executive functioning and monkey mind to access boundless open awareness. Mastery of this practice lies not in the disappearance of distraction, but in my manner of responding to it when it appears. I learn to exercise patience and compassion toward myself, to observe the appearance of distraction with equanimity. Thus freed of emotional reaction to the distraction, I learn to return readily to my contemplative focus. It is this ready return, rather than complete disappearance of distracting thoughts, that allows my consciousness to ascend.

Although cultivating the capacity to meditate helps me relax the limits of my ego, I face another obstacle that is embodied in human psychology. As I learn to live with my monkey mind and my need for executive functioning, I must also learn to live with the narratives that shape and constrain my experience of self. We human beings generate narratives to make sense of our world. Stories are as important for us in organizing and making meaning of information about ourselves and our surroundings as are our theories, explanations, beliefs, or recognition of the familiar. Particularly in Western cultures, we tell stories of a unitary self that changes with experience but nonetheless remains the same entity as it makes its way through life from birth to death. We associate this idea of self with an intuitive sense of continuous experience from moment to moment over time, with memories of our past and expectations for our future. We reinforce our sense of self with the stories we tell ourselves and others about our lives and the stories others tell about us. As we locate ourselves in the stories we hear and we tell about ancestral history, we access powerful feelings of belonging. Should circumstances challenge our narratives, we may experience confusion, emotional turmoil, incoherence, or fragmentation.

I had already encountered Buddhist critiques of the self as a "delusion" before my psychotic episode at age 23. Throughout that intense, kaleidoscopic experience, I felt profound shifts in my experience of self. I later said of the experience that I had never lost my mind. I had, rather, lost my self. Indeed, although I never lost the thread of continuous experience as I made my way through that passage, I often felt more an observer than a participant in the indignities and humiliations to which institutionalized mental patients of that time were subjected. As the fire of psychosis burned out and I resolved to return to the world of the sane, I was intuitively aware of the need to reconstitute my experience of self. So it was that I made peace with my failure to master the spiritual practice described in *The Way of the Pilgrim* by deciding to make my life a ceaseless prayer. Although that decision was soon to disappear below the threshold of conscious awareness, it has since that moment been integral to my sense of self. Seven years after I made that decision, my self was strong enough to remain coherent when, under Ramón's guidance, my soul could briefly shed its mortal garment, ascend beyond the limits of ordinary human understanding, then return safely to everyday consciousness.

Although a coherent sense of self protects me from disintegration, it is also an obstacle to my spiritual development. The metaphor of a vessel is well-suited to this paradox. A vessel can be a container. Rabbi Zalman Schachter-Shalomi said, "Although we cannot improve on the divine that flows into our vessels, we can and must take responsibility for keeping these vessels clean and transparent and not at all as essential as the light they contain."[53] A vessel can also be a ship. Of travel with and without a vessel, said the Sufi sage Niffari, "In the one case, the end is not known, and there is no guidance. In the other case, the means becomes an end, and there is no arriving."[54]

As I became more firmly rooted as a Jew, I was better able to find my balance with this paradox of self as protector and self as obstacle. This opened paths through and beyond the obstacles of ego and self. With that balance, I recognize the power of narratives grounded in events of my own life, in the current historical moment, and in archetypical human myth. My absorption in the powerful narratives of the Hebrew Bible enables me to contemplate the shaping power of narratives, with an awareness that holds them lightly without being constrained by them. With that awareness, I can observe the formation of my mortal being embodied as David Trimble, respecting the uniqueness of this vessel and the opportunities and challenges it affords, without mistaking it for the eternal soul that acts in Creation through this material embodiment.

Looking through that narrative lens, I see myself as a neuroatypical little White boy raised by parents who had left the Trotskyite socialist movement to raise children in a White Christian Republican town. There, I was marginalized for my shy, anxious, awkward temperament by peers who were influenced by how they saw their parents treating mine in the dark postwar period of McCarthyism. Under strict orders from our pediatrician, I missed most of kindergarten in bed with rheumatic fever, losing opportunities for early social learning which would have been difficult enough already given my temperament.

Memories of the small bedroom in which I recovered from illness and in which I awoke a few years later in terror and confusion from that nightmarish encounter with God are deeply engraved in my brain. Desperately lonely, I found companionship in heroic fantasies. I entered school a year behind my peers in opportunities for social learning but quickly established myself as an eager and talented student at the top of my class. I soothed my pain over rejection by peers with an image of myself as special, exceptional, and triumphant, an image reinforced by approval from teachers and other adults. With a child's mind, I shaped a core narrative of the misunderstood genius who would one day triumph over his tormentors, made famous by his brilliant accomplishments.

I have spent much of my adult life deconstructing and relinquishing that narrative. With the advantage of having lived with full conscious awareness through a florid psychotic episode, I could compassionately observe and examine grandiosity, the exaggerated extreme of a triumphalist personal narrative. That experience sensitized me to the triumphal narrative's influence on my stream of consciousness. As I relaxed the constraints of that narrative, I could better repair my capacity to understand and accept my emotions, to balance my head and heart.

The soul navigates its way through its material incarnations using the ego's vessel of the self. As a family therapist, I understand the self to be formed and maintained in relationship. The structure of the self incorporates the stories others tell us about us and the stories we tell about ourselves. The ego weaves these stories together into the complex narratives at the core of our sense of who we are in the world. The spiritual journey challenges seekers to discern the soul and distinguish it from its vessel. Even as we respect our embodied beings, we recognize that our spiritual nature transcends the limitations of our embodiment.

Beyond the boundaries of personal, face-to-face relationships with other individuals and groups are our relationships with our societies and cultures. Cultural discourses, shaped in historical context by human societies, have powerful influence on our sense of who we are. They embody narratives that are woven into our experiences of self, particularly in our experience of identity based on our social location in society's arrangements of power, e.g., gender, race, class, etc. The influence of these discourses is not always apparent to us. They are often not explicit; sometimes they are even disguised to prevent their critical examination.[55]

As my capacity for critical awareness emerged in adolescence, I became aware of the influence of cultural discourses on my understanding of who I was in my world, particularly as a White man. The narrative of whiteness is central to the contemporary discourse of White supremacy in the United States. It centers Europeans and their colonial legacy in the history of humanity. In the whiteness narrative, White people "discovered" regions of the world beyond the boundaries of their previously known world. These were, of course, not discoveries, but rather intrusions into the lives of the people who already lived there. White perpetrators saw their conquest and subjugation of much of the rest of the world as the advance of "civilization" into "backward" lands.

The whiteness narrative identifies White people with humanity itself. In this narrative, people of other races are depicted as lesser, savage, primitive, the Other. Whiteness in United States culture is indelibly stained with the blood of indigenous people massacred and forcibly relocated in colonial expropriation of their lands and with the torture, blood and sweat of kidnapped and enslaved Africans. These atrocities are rendered invisible in the triumphal narrative of whiteness as the normal, natural state of humanity.

My engagement with the civil rights struggle began my education about my unconscious internalization of the whiteness narrative. My lifelong commitment to the anti-racist struggle requires constant self-examination, including my painful recognition of the pain that my internalized whiteness causes to people of color, including people whom I love and without whom I would not be who I am. I am still learning to discern insidious ways that I internalize that discourse, despite my strong intention to resist it. I see how it resonates with residues from my childhood triumphalist fantasies.

However well I may deconstruct internalization of the narrative, it is impossible for me escape it. The dominant cultural discourse of White supremacy assures an inexhaustible flow of attributions that contribute inevitably to a White person's self-formation. I coined the term "microentitlements" to describe the daily affordances of power and affirmation that we White people encounter based on how we are seen in the world.[56]

I am ethically obliged to be critical and vigilant about whiteness's influences on my thought, speech, and action. I know that despite my conscious efforts I have, do, and often will miss the injuries that I inflict on others through my unwitting enactments of the whiteness narrative. My enactments of whiteness are sometimes made visible to me only in trusting personal relationships with People of Color, or with other anti-racist White people, in situations that are painful for all of us. The best that I can do in such situations is take full accountability for my actions and recognize that my moral pain about my actions is less important than the pain and suffering my actions inflict on people whom I care about.

The damage that whiteness does to my soul is more pernicious than the moral pain that comes with my awareness that my actions hurt people of color. The acute discomfort of my remorse has motivated changes in my behavior and made me more accountable relationally. However, given the power of the discourse of White supremacy at social, cultural, and institutional levels and the ubiquity of micro-entitlements at the level of face-to-face relationships, it is impossible for me as a White person in current historical circumstances to step entirely outside of my whiteness. It is therefore a moral necessity that I monitor and track my enactments of whiteness.

The moral necessity of this vigilance is an inevitable constraint on the ascent of my soul. On the one hand, I am ethically obliged to maintain awareness of my self as it is enclothed in whiteness. On the other hand, the search for spiritual wisdom beckons me to shed the garment of my self and cultivate consciousness of worlds and truths beyond the limits of my self in the material world. This dilemma, in addition to the moral corruption that comes from hurting others, contributes to spiritual malaise.

Perhaps more powerful than narratives shaped by individual and historical circumstances are cultural narratives that span generations, ancestral myths that form human archetypes, patterns of meaning embodied within us at the deepest levels of our being. The myth of the hero is pervasive among human cultures across vast spans of space and time. Its core narrative is the story of a person who ventures out beyond the boundaries of native community and culture into a realm of transformational forces rich with opportunities and dangers. Engaging with these forces in the ordeals that come with such journeys, the hero survives and is transformed. The hero's own transformations transform and revitalize community and culture.

After decades of struggle with ego and self as adversaries on my spiritual path, I have learned that it is sometimes better to accept dilemma and paradox than try to solve problems. My adversary is also my companion. In the spiritual warrior narrative, a worthy adversary is an important influence and even teacher on the journey. The same details of my individual life and historical circumstances that constrain me also contain me. They constitute the garment for my soul, the vehicle in which I journey, the vessel which receives the light of the Divine and which I must make clear and transparent enough to radiate that light back into the world. It is with that intention that I address the narrative embodied in the myth of the hero.

Only in retrospect, after I entered through the door of my religious faith, did I come to understand my dance with this myth. I cannot escape the resonance between the story of my life and this powerful archaic narrative. As I dance, I bear in mind Niffari's and Schachter-Shalomi's sage counsel. I must be embodied in the vehicle to dance, but I stumble and lose direction whenever I become attached to the vehicle, mistaking my mortal vessel for the divine light through which it flows.

I do not dance alone as the dance carries me forward. Even as Jodie and I are on our own journeys, we witness and support each other, warning each other of dangers, celebrating successes, and comforting each other when we stumble. My sister Sheila and son Jacob of blessed memory, and daughter Jessica and son Ransom are also companions without whose companionship I could not dance. Nor could I dance without my personal community of friends, colleagues, comrades, fellow seekers, and fellow Jews. Within the formal boundaries of therapeutic intimacy, my patients and I dance as we learn and grow together.

Jodie, my closest companion in life, is both witness and support. We met when I was raw and impulsive, struggling to assimilate what I was learning from my psychotic episode and from the revelation under Ramón's guidance. I was angry and defensive over the stigma of mental illness. As a scion of generations of Protestant ministry, I was also very much aware that my spiritual path was outside the range of what is permitted within dominant Christian discourse. I was not quiet about my disquiet. I dared the world to accept me on my own terms. I am forever grateful that Jodie could see through my defensive bravado and fall in love with me. Over decades sharing life with Jodie, our relationship helps me come to terms with the world. Seekers can get lost on their journey, losing direction or connection, particularly when the adversary becomes an obstacle. At moments when I don't recognize that I am lost in ego or trapped in self-absorption, she makes those moments visible with her clear, firm, non-shaming voice.

To write and reflect on the resonance between the story of my life and the myth of the hero is to accept the dilemma and embrace the paradox. I know that would not have become possible without my religious faith. From that perspective, I can play with the symbols and imagery of the hero myth, observing how it resonates with my life story without succumbing to its gravitational force.

As a network therapist, I know that boundaries open as one moves from the center to the margins of one's group. I see how often I have stood at the margins of the groups I occupy. I make my way through life with a neuroatypical brain. I embrace radical progressive political ideology while living in a conservative society and culture. My spiritual search has taken me beyond the boundaries of the dominant discourse of spirituality in United States. I was White husband and father in an interracial family. I carry the label of an ex-mental patient in a profession still holding prejudices against those of that ilk. I converted to Judaism from the mainstream Protestant Christianity of my ancestors, separating myself from my society's dominant group and becoming an "immigrant" among Jews. These and other aspects of my life locate me at the margins, opening boundaries between groups. Although I have often struggled with feelings of loneliness, I have also enjoyed the freedom that comes at the margins, with the doors open to connect across boundaries between groups.

The hero may be summoned by a vision to sojourn beyond the boundaries of the group. As my father, his father, and their forefathers (and at least one of my mother's forefathers, my namesake David Spinney) were summoned by God in calls to serve as ministers, I had my own encounter with God in early childhood. The vessel of my self was shattered by that experience. It led me away from the path of Christianity my ancestors followed and on which they guided others. Overwhelmed by terror and loss by the experience of divine abandonment and crushed by the weight of impossible responsibility, I was driven to embark on a journey that has taken me far from the path of my ancestors. For many decades, I traveled in a broken vessel, struggling to heal and repair even as I sought to move forward on my spiritual path.

The teachers and texts of my profession, and my patients, have taught me to understand the complicated and uncertain process of recovery from trauma. Damage results from encounters with threat or injury that overwhelm one's capacity to cope with a situation. Shattered, one loses the thread of continuous autobiographical experience. After the traumatic experience, one goes on carrying fragments of sensations, emotions, thoughts, and language in an unstable assembly rather than as integrated in a coherent sense of self. On the one hand, we yearn for the wholeness of healing. On the other, powerful survival instincts impel us to avoid a fully embodied memory of the trauma, or, sometimes, even reminders of it, for fear that the memory itself may trigger the horror of the trauma and overwhelm us again. Relational trauma, in which the threat and injury are perpetrated by a powerful figure on whom one's physical and/or survival depends, is particularly challenging to heal. Healing depends on trusting, loving, and safe relationship. Yearnings for trust, love, and safety battle with vigilant survival impulses to avoid re-experiencing betrayal and devastation.

My childhood encounter with God was such a relational trauma. It took well over half a century for me to heal enough to restore my faith in God. It is from this place of wholeness that I can now see how I had drawn unconsciously on the hero myth to live with my brokenness. I formed a false sense of self that provided continuity but not coherence as my self lost its root in authentic relationship with others. As a child, I absorbed myself in fantasies of heroic acts that would earn respect and appreciation from my peers and affectionate devotion from girls for whose attention I yearned. Absorption in fantasy afforded temporary protection from the pain of loneliness and rejection. I imagined myself as a hero in the prosaic sense rather than mythic sense, seen and admired by the community. I did not understand the archaic narrative's power to reinforce loneliness. That mythical journey renders the mythic hero separate, outside, superior, and alone.

Today, I live in a society I see as suffering from a spiritual disease, whose dominant discourses are rooted in pernicious perversions of the hero myth. These toxic discourses of patriarchy, White Christian supremacy, heteronormativity and gender normativity, capitalism, and individualism combine in the ideology of neoliberalism, a grotesque caricature of the hero myth. Neoliberalism's highest value is the triumph of the individual in and over other individuals in competition for the victory of material "success"—a success that is structurally denied to most.

Shattered by that early call, I spent much of my life disconnected from the spiritual root of my soul. I formed a self and attached myself to an ego that aligned with my location in this spiritually corrupted society. As I now struggle with self and ego, I do not try to destroy them but, rather, to refine them as instruments. When I am grounded in my spirituality, I see them now as tools that my soul requires to realize its purpose in this material incarnation. It takes effort and persistence to make these adversaries visible enough for me to transform them into tools.

Through retrospective lenses, I see the position of spiritual estrangement from which I formed ego and self that aligned with pernicious perversions of the hero myth. I transformed pain and shame from my loneliness and learning disabilities into aggressive academic triumph, with its attendant feelings of superiority. Decades later, Roxana Llerena-Quinn, my BICAP friend and comrade, helped me to see how these childhood classroom feelings of superiority were embodied in my unconscious enactments of whiteness.

My memories of the nightmarish childhood call were clothed invisibly in individualist discourse. Because I had been shattered by trauma, I was not aware of the emotional state of triumphant grandiosity implicit in the idea that I had been chosen by God to replace God. That grandiosity was to wait by the door of awareness until it entered my consciousness in a later firestorm of psychosis. As I recovered from psychosis, I learned to recognize and contain that impulse to transform the pain of loneliness into feelings of superiority.

I found healing in psychotherapy and in loving and healing relationships. Not yet ready to take the risk of trusting in God, I was nonetheless able to reinterpret the divine purpose behind the call. God had opened a path through paradox, a response to a powerful loyalty dilemma. On the one hand, there was the powerful obligation to serve God that had shaped the lives of my paternal ancestors. On the other hand was my father's determination that his sons not follow the path to Christian ministry that he and our ancestors had followed (it had never occurred to him that his daughter herself might get the call). From my perspective as psychotherapist and family therapist, I can understand how it was that I could have experienced the call well before I was told the stories of my father and his ancestors. My studies and my experiences with patients have shown me the power of legacy to shape lives, even without conscious knowledge of the ancestral stories that embody that legacy. The unique form of my experience of the call resulted in a life that has honored both my ancestral legacy of serving God and my father's wishes that I not become a Christian minister.

It took nearly sixty years after my experience of the call to enter through the door of religious faith and nearly five years after that before I could fully experience direct relationship with God. By that time, at nearly seventy, I had gained understanding and cultivated the spiritual capacity that brought me ever closer to accessing the divine consciousness that I had so briefly attained under Ramón's guidance at age 30. As high as I might rise, however, before I attained religious faith, my attachments to ego and self formed a ceiling beyond which I could not rise. I needed relationships with God and with my faith community for my spiritual ascents to have purpose and meaning beyond individual attainment of enlightenment. As I saw how my individual ambition, pride, and self-congratulation had obstructed my journey, I could almost hear Ramón's laughter drawing me back from my reckless greed to grab onto mystical awareness for its own sake.

TIME, TRANSITION, AND TRANSFORMATION

Early winter, 2021, in the last months of my seventy-seventh year, I took a long reflective pause from writing. Thirteen years before, two years after the death of our beloved son Jacob, I had made the decision to write this memoir. For years, I wrote in intense bursts with long intervening interruptions, struggling to find time in my busy and demanding life for the sustained emotional and intellectual effort that such a project requires. As I found my way to sustain that effort, I had to come to terms with the challenge of reflexivity. For more than a decade, I had been living the very life within which I was writing its story. In the pause, I saw that to go forward I needed to acknowledge the process of mutual transformation by which my life and writing about my life continuously shape each other.

The summer before the pause, in the mountains of New Hampshire, Jodie and I were taking our first full three-week vacation. Away from the distractions and demands of our busy working lives, I contemplated our mortality. The year before, Jodie had fallen seriously ill with an unusual kind of heart failure that had been developing slowly, unrecognized for many months. Her cardiologist, Dr. Marshall Katz, was familiar with this rare condition, which many cardiologists had never encountered. Experienced at diagnosing it, he feared that Jodie had AL cardiac amyloidosis, an immune disorder that was understood at the time to be inexorably and rapidly fatal. We went through weeks of medical tests, dreading the possibility that her cardiologist's concerns would be confirmed. The diagnosis was confirmed on Yom Kippur—the Day of Atonement. We clung to each other as we faced the prospect of Jodie's imminent death. Jodie was 68.

Nine days later, we were stunned and blessed with a reprieve. Jodie met with Dr. Katz's colleague, one of the world's three leading specialists on cardiac amyloidosis. With the COVID pandemic disrupting everyday life, Jodie had to meet alone in the specialist's office, keeping me connected to the conversation by cellphone. We learned that the specialist, Dr. Rodney Falke, had very recently developed with his colleagues a treatment, not yet FDA-approved, that had proven effective with nearly seventy percent of cases. The resulting remissions, he said, could last as long as ten years, possibly longer. Treatment required six months of weekly chemotherapy and immunotherapy, followed by another year of monthly immunotherapy. As my prayers joined with prayers from our family, our congregation, and dear friends of several different faiths, Jodie responded remarkably well to treatment. Her medical team was delighted, and we were relieved, when she went into remission a week after her first chemotherapy session. Her remission was faster than that of any of the patients Dr. Falk and his oncology colleague, Dr. Giada Bianchi, had treated before. That summer, although some of her heart damage was and would be irreversible, she had recovered enough for us to take easy hikes through the woods together.

We were already acutely aware of mortality. My sister Sheila had died of lung cancer five and a half years before. During summer vacation two years earlier, we got news that Jodie's younger cousin had died unexpectedly from sepsis. Weeks earlier than that shocking news, we had learned that Jodie's brother and 91-year-old father had survived an accident in an airplane landing, leaving Jodie's father severely injured and her brother traumatized. Medical tests after the crash revealed that her father had previously undetected prostate cancer, his fifth different cancer. He responded well to treatment and was back to his remarkably productive professional life within the better part of a year. Shortly after returning from vacation, still reeling from the dire medical news in Jodie's family, I got an anguished phone call from Ransom. Our daughter-in-law Kim, while waiting in the hospital for toe amputation as lifelong diabetes took its toll on her body, had died of a sudden heart attack. My brother Robin died in hospital several weeks later, his body giving out after a hard life struggling with medical and mental illness. A couple of weeks after we buried Robin, I fell down stairs and got a concussion, narrowly avoiding career-ending injury.

Although I was in good health for my age, in the context of all these reminders I had to confront the implications of my mortality for the memoir project. My mental faculties were relatively sound, with an accumulating store of life experience fortifying a relatively intact left brain. The resulting gains in pattern recognition capacity were compensating for the naturally more rapid decline of my right brain with aging. Nonetheless, I could see that I was slowing down. Each year increased the number of years elapsed from the beginning of this life, while it reduced the number of years remaining toward its end. In the time afforded by the extended vacation, I had to decide how to proceed with the memoir project.

Recognizing the reality of my mortality, I knew that I might die leaving an unfinished, unpublished manuscript. By that moment in my spiritual journey, I could accept that prospect. Without anxious attachment to the outcome, I took steps on that vacation to increase the probability that I would complete the project. Jodie's heart condition and the effects of her ongoing treatment had her sleeping much later in the morning. I began to rise early, long before Jodie awoke, taking time after morning prayers to write. I maintained that discipline after returning from vacation, several days each week going to bed early and rising before dawn after eight hours' sleep to write.

By the end of vacation, I had caught up with drafting a few sections that I had been working on through bursts and interruptions. I contemplated the next steps, aware that my writing had already crossed a chronological border. Almost everything that you, the reader, will encounter in the forthcoming narrative relates events that have occurred since I began writing the memoir. I have experienced that decade and a half as a rich harvest after a lifetime of spiritual self-cultivation. The transformations that they wrought have shaped my being.

The voice with which I began this project, embodied in the Introduction, spoke to you from a moment more than a decade before when I invited you to join me on my journey. My intention is unchanged—I pray that you become absorbed in the narrative and are inspired by that experience to reflect more deeply on your own soul's journey. In the Introduction, I called to you with the voice of a man in his early sixties, still wrestling with issues that appeared at the time to be obstacles to my spiritual development. The voice with which I write to you now is the voice of a man in his late seventies, who understands many of those apparent obstacles to be opportunities for further growth.

My soul continues to clarify and fulfill its purpose in this life as its companion, my ego, transforms from its adversary to its servant. The soul wound of my shattering childhood experience of the call continues to heal. I revere, love, and serve Hashem, God in the form that She, He, They appeared to the Jewish people and Who has accompanied us on our collective journey through human history. Even as I found my way to worship the God of the particularistic religion of Judaism, my own journey assured that I would remain faithful to the ultimate reality beyond the limits of any particular human understanding.

I am the same, and different, and the same as the person in the Introduction who wrote to you then, inviting you on this journey. I borrow that phrase, "the same, and different, and the same," from British family therapists Mark Rivett and Eddy Street, with gratitude for their influence on my clinical practice. Their journal article on spirituality in family therapy gave me permission to explore what they called "metaphysical" practice, in which the therapist engages in the therapeutic relationship as a fully and authentically embodied spiritual being.[57] Over the course of my editing an earlier book on spirituality in therapy, I had occasion to correspond with them, inquiring as how they had come to adopt the phrase.[58] Eddy Street wrote:

> Spirituality and psychotherapeutic practice have differences but are contained within the same universal process of (shall we say) 'becoming.' At times in the psychotherapeutic process, elements will certainly have a difference to spirituality endeavours ... But these differences are also contained and dealt with practically within the process of becoming, a process that has a similarity for both the therapist and client. And it is that similarity that informs the therapist's activity even though occasionally it may be different to what the client is about at that moment. This is the struggle in the therapeutic endeavour for a healing intimacy and this in turn is part of the struggle to abide in true intimacy, with another person, with others, with nature and with the universal. Each of us in some way seeks a resolution to this koan of who we are within our intimate relationships. In this each of us is the same and different and the same. It is the nature of us becoming and the nature of our humanity.

You, the reader, and I, the writer, immersed in this process of becoming, are the same, and different, and the same. As the river of time carries us from beginning to end of our lives, we may at times feel in command of the vessel and at times feel helpless. At moments, we may be blessed with experiences that lift us beyond the limits of materiality. At such moments, we stand outside the river of time, no longer bound by the sequence of past, present, and future. Time becomes a thread in the tapestry of creation. In a metaphor from Jewish mystical tradition, there are moments when "the curtain briefly parts" and we catch a glimpse of the design woven into that tapestry. My prayer is that this story of my own becoming is helping you on your journey—the same, and different, and the same as my own.

This process of becoming has transformed my perspective on the life that I am narrating. I am no longer a seeker struggling through my own efforts to overcome obstacles in my spiritual journey. I no longer seek extraordinary transpersonal experiences for their own sake. Still a seeker, I now seek to serve Hashem. I seek to cultivate qualities of humility, generosity, persistence, patience, faith, and acceptance. When I enter upper worlds solely for the purpose of serving God, no longer seeking mystical experience for its own sake, the limit that ego once imposed on my ascent dissolves. Less vulnerable to self-congratulation, I can more often glimpse the tapestry of creation. I accept all that was, is, and will be as coming from and through Hashem. At moments when grace manifests, I am less likely to mistake my own efforts for their source.

As I write, and you read, we engage with each other in our imaginations. Perhaps, you and I may one day meet face to face as fully embodied persons in this world, engaging with each other in the process of mutual transformation that emerges in open-hearted dialogue. I write to you at this moment in January 2022, a little more than a week into the seventy-eighth year of my lifetime. Although I don't know how long I will live, nor do I know that I will live to finish this memoir, I have discerned the horizon of the memoir project. My story will conclude with the interconnected, interanimating events of family healing surrounding the end of my sister's life, the publication of a book that I edited on spirituality in psychotherapy, and my studies with a teacher of Kabbalah as I become more firmly rooted as a Jew.

ACCOMPANYING MY SISTER ON HER JOURNEY

It is late December, 2015. I am keeping vigil with my sister, Sheila, as she drifts in and out of sleep. She is suspended between the world of the living and worlds beyond. She has already experienced the presence of people who have gone before her, calling out to me excitedly, "David, they all came!" Now, her body is clinging intensely to life, and her mental clarity comes and goes. During one of those rare moments of clarity, as I was lowering her into her bed after a trip to the bathroom, she smiled at me radiantly and said, "Goodbye, David."

For a little more than a year, starting within a month or two of her getting a diagnosis of Stage Four lung cancer, I have accompanied her on her journey, visiting her periodically at her home in Portland, Oregon, across the continent from where I live near Boston. On this, my last visit, I have attended her as she made the transition from walking around with only four hours a day of personal care attendants to lying in her deathbed with round-the-clock care. During earlier visits, she was vigorously engaged with the world of the living, even as she acknowledged that she was engaging from a "liminal" position, standing on the threshold between the worlds of the living and dead. She and I have healed longstanding wounds between us, and she has been actively encouraging me to heal wounds between my older children and me, injuries from before and after a bitter divorce with their mother.

We have had rich conversations about spirituality in which we have worked out our misunderstandings and explored each other's experiences. Ours is the first of many generations in which none of the children entered the Protestant clergy, but our lives have nonetheless been shaped by our legacy, leading us into transpersonal experiences of one kind or another. Sheila for a while was channeling the souls of the dead; I was opened to an experience of divine consciousness by an espiritista from the Dominican Republic. Sheila has found a home in Tergar Tibetan Buddhism, and I am a Jew exploring the esoteric world of Kabbalah, which informs my spiritual practice.

A few months before, Sheila had asked me to arrange my October visit so that the two of us could attend a two-day workshop, led by Andrew Holocek, on the Tibetan Buddhist approach to dying. At her request, before the visit I read Holocek's *Preparing to Die*.[59] I learned wisdom about the journey of the soul acquired by generations of monks through disciplined meditative practice. I learned about the three *bardos* through which the soul passes in the process of dying and rebirth, and about the pure land of Amitabha, where some souls enter after death into a higher, incorporeal existence. In this tradition, all the beings in this pure land are well-advanced along the path toward full enlightenment, and when a soul finishes her existence in this pure land she is freed of the cycle of death and rebirth. Souls in the pure land can see into the mortal world and can in some fashion communicate with the living.

This has not been my first encounter with Buddhism in one of its many forms. It is only one of many traditions my journey has led me to explore. David Hammerman, a dear friend and colleague who practices in the tradition of shamanism, taught me about "thought forms," entities that form in nonmaterial worlds, shaped by human thought and emotion. The more people believe in them, he explained, and the longer belief persists across generations, the more durable these thought forms become. David and Sylvia meet with colleagues who employ esoteric practices that most psychotherapists would marginalize or disqualify. They rely on their consultation group to keep their practices ethically accountable as they explore domains unfamiliar to Western minds.

The group happened to meet on the day of the 2001 attack on the World Trade Center and decided together that each of them would journey beyond materiality to help the souls of people who died in the attack, supporting them on their journey by making their experiences intelligible. David and his colleagues recognized that some souls, experiencing sudden death in fiery inferno, would experience themselves as having arrived in hell. Hell is a robust and enduring thought form, continuously reinforced by text, preaching, and belief. David, as the member of the group who least believes in the literal existence of hell, was assigned the task to visit hell and retrieve the souls of people who had died in the World Trade Center towers and were interpreting their death experience as their damnation. In spirit form, David poled a boat along the river Styx and invited those confused souls onto his boat, on which he bore them out. I asked David if he could have rescued other souls already there, and he said that they believed in hell too strongly to free themselves . . .

Exploring the Buddhist ideas I was encountering, I was moved by the power of the ideas of the bardos, respecting them as perspectives on realities just as real (and, ultimately, just as illusory) as the material reality in which most of us live. I was finding useful ways to reinterpret my own experiences of nonmaterial reality—my escorting our beloved son Jacob's soul to its Source and seeing his soul dissolve into the One, and the unexpected manifestation of his soul a couple of weeks later.

At one point over the weekend workshop, Holocek threw himself with enthusiasm into Buddhist metaphysics, and I was moved by the closeness of fit between his images of materiality emerging from and returning to emptiness and kabbalistic images of the emanation of the material world from Ein Sof, the limitless unknowable that manifests materiality out of nothing.

In a flash of awareness, I saw that the pure lands of Buddhist understanding shared many qualities with the garden in Kabbalah, a place to which the souls of the righteous ascend after shedding their mortal garments and where they delight God with their presence. The same, and different, and the same. It came to me that, although many different spiritual traditions afford the possibility of knowing worlds beyond everyday reality, the "same" worlds are inescapably shaped by the particulars of the spiritual traditions of their mortal observers. Thought forms shaped by spiritual constructivism, as it were.

I saw how my own experiences could be enriched by the wealth of wisdom acquired by generations of Tibetan Buddhist monks. Learning about the pure land helped me, for example, to see how Jacob's soul could at times be so intimately accessible to me. One of my reasons for laboring over a memoir of my spiritual life is my yearning for new understandings to emerge out of dialogic engagement between different spiritual traditions, facilitated by the contemporary breaking of seals on the secret esoteric traditions of so many cultures. Emergent understandings of spirituality afford some hope, I believe, of protecting our planet from destruction by its dominant life form.

As Sheila and I reflected on the workshop, she quickly grasped my idea about the shaping of worlds beyond the material by the beliefs of the mortals who explore them. She talked of her experiences when she channeled souls of the dead, inviting them to speak through her to their loved ones. Each of these souls spoke of being in "heaven," but the heaven experienced by each was dramatically different from heavens experienced by others.

On this, our final visit, the time for that kind of conversation has passed. One thing I have learned from accompanying Sheila through the process of her dying is that none of us can really know how we will handle the experience when it finally arrives. Despite all of Sheila's clear-eyed intentions to allow herself to go with the flow of dying, now in her final days she is hanging on, literally, for dear life. Although in Tibetan Buddhist tradition the state of mind at the moment of dying is important for the destination of the soul, the relationships Sheila formed are nonetheless assuring her passage. Her spiritual advisor, Lyle, a wise and big-hearted man, has promised that, after she dies, he will read her the *Tibetan Book of the Dead*, which will guide her soul safely on its journey.[60] Yongey Mingyur Rinpoche, the leader of her Tergar Meditation Community, recorded a video offering her his support and emailed it to her via Lyle, who hosts the Rinpoche when he visits the Portland area. A week ago, at a moment when she was more connected with this world, Sheila had been moved to learn from Lyle that the Rinpoche had told him that he would personally guide her soul through the bardos. All this support will be there whatever Sheila's state of mind when she finally passes. For now, she is asleep much of the time and emphatically rejects when awake any effort I make to engage her in conversation about dying.

I sit quietly in her bedroom, where she can see me when she opens her eyes. I read and meditate. I brought two books with me for this visit, Nikos Kazantzakis' *Report to Greco*, a memoir, and *The Way of a Pilgrim*, a book by an anonymous nineteenth-century Russian Orthodox Christian pilgrim. As I sit reading while Sheila sleeps, my mind drifts to work I am doing at home on a section of my memoir about the turmoil of my early twenties. I remember bringing *Report to Greco* and *The Way of a Pilgrim* with me when I had admitted myself to the psychiatric hospital. Reading *Report to Greco* and *Way of the Pilgrim* as I keep vigil with Sheila are helping me retrieve memories from that darkness of madness.

After a few weeks in the hospital decades earlier, I had begun to relinquish the ecstatic states of manic psychosis. I had been wrestling with the rigorous demands of the Pilgrim's practice of ceaseless prayer and had accepted that it was beyond me. I vividly remember the evening on the screened porch of the hospital when I made the decision to make the best of it by making my life a ceaseless prayer. Now, sitting at Sheila's bedside, I see how that decision has shaped my life. Conscious awareness of the decision faded as I returned home, but it has continued to operate outside my direct awareness.

As Sheila sleeps, I read *Pilgrim* through lenses shaped by decades of study and meditation. I am transported by the book's narrative and aware that I may now have the capacity to cultivate the practice articulated in the text. A challenge remains: when I first read *Pilgrim*, I was still wrestling with an ancestral voice calling me to Christian ministry. Now, although I may be able to grasp the method of ceaseless prayer, what am I to do with its language? "Lord Jesus Christ, have mercy on me" won't work for me as a Jew. I search for a Jewish prayer that is similarly brief, relational, and petitionary. I decide on a Hebrew prayer from the book of Lamentations that already moves me: *Hashiveinu Adonai eilecha, v'nashuvah* (Turn us toward you, Eternal, and we turn to you).[61] It meets the criteria: it is brief, relational, and petitionary. It adds the paradox that I find so appealing in Chasidic mysticism: if everything is God, who is doing the praying? Here is a practice that embodies my aspiration to generate new possibilities from dialogical engagement between spiritual traditions.

It is late January, 2016. Although none of us expected her to hang on for so long, Sheila was still clinging to life when I flew home to Boston. Months before, she had welcomed my promise to help her soul on its journey after death, as I had done when Jacob died, at that time not knowing what I was doing or how I was doing it. Jacob had died nearly ten years before. I have since learned how to make sense of that ability to accompany the soul of the departed and how to cultivate it.

I have also arranged for a monastery of female Tergar monks to pray for her soul. Her loving friends in the Portland branch of her Buddhist community would of course be praying for her, as would Jessica, her niece and my daughter, also a Tibetan Buddhist. Lyle would be reading the *Tibetan Book of the Dead* to guide her soul through the third bardo. Most efficacious, of course, is the intention of the Rinpoche to accompany her soul on its journey. I didn't expect my efforts to make that much more of a difference, but I have kept the promise.

I began to act on that promise when I learned of Sheila's death. According to the Buddhist teaching, time in the third bardo varies, but it is often about 19 days in mortal time. Several times a day, I released my spirit from its corporeal form and located Sheila's spirit in worlds beyond the material. Jacob's spirit joined me, as it would at other times that I traveled in spirit worlds. Not versed in the particulars of Tergar Buddhist esoteric practice, I simply set the intention to connect with Sheila's spirit and help it to rise "upward."

Each day, as I found and supported Sheila's spirit, I have experienced myself as exerting metaphysical energy to lift her. Today, when I reach out again to lift her, I experience myself as being lifted upward on wings of joy and peace. I check the calendar and see that it has been 19 days since she died. I call Jessica, and she tells me that about the same time I felt the lifting, she felt a blessing from Sheila . . .

HEALING FAMILY WOUNDS

My older sister and I did not start our lives together in the loving relationship that held us when her life ended. We were born into positions shaped by our roles in irreconcilable parental conflicts. All couples must find ways to go on in the face of differences they never fully resolve. My parents did not do well living with their differences. Although in childhood we felt and witnessed their love for each of us and each other, their conflicts carried bitterness that we felt in their harsh and angry voices when they argued with each other or when they were frustrated, angry, or disappointed with us. Periods of peace, love, and calm in our home alternated with disruptions that ran their course from sudden eruptions of intense anger through periods of sullen resentment into grudging truce and eventual restoration of peace. My father could be loving and tender, but he was often irascible. His temper flared in an angry voice that subsided quickly after outbursts. My mother's anger flared less frequently, but her rages had an irrational quality that was terrifying for a child. Her anger did not subside rapidly. She could harbor resentment for days after an argument.

Even as they fought over how each treated their own favored child, they found in that child some solace for their disappointments with each other. Sheila was my father's favorite; I was my mother's. Robin, the youngest, had a difficult road to travel. His health problems and disabilities from early in life evoked parental guilt, pity, or anger. Without the intense devotion that his older siblings felt from one parent or the other, he developed a counterdependent stance that created challenges for all three of us siblings, particularly toward the end of his life.

Years after their deaths, and after decades of working with families more troubled than ours, I came understand how my mother and father brought the unhealed injuries of their pasts into the family they raised together. The shadow of her grandmother Olive's childhood bereavement from losing her father in the Civil War weighed heavily on my mother's childhood. Olive Withington lost her eyesight after her daughters had grown up and started families of their own. The family story was that her blindness was the result of medical neglect by an alcoholic doctor. At the age of five, my mother was moved into her grandparents' home "to be her grandmother's eyes." Although her grandfather doted on her, she suffered from living in close relationship with a harsh and cold grandmother whose frustration over her blindness inflamed lifelong bitterness over her double abandonment in late childhood by her father killed in war and by her mother who retreated into pathological grief.

On the one hand idealized by a grandfather who called her "my little sunshine," on the other obligated to serve as a vital appendage for a harsh and bitter grandmother, my mother's childhood contributed to a confusing sense of self. As an adult, my mother could regress into treating Sheila and me as different appendages of her being. She saw her daughter as embodying negative qualities that she could not accept as her own and harshly and irrationally condemned Sheila for them. She needed me to be the mirror in which she could see the "sunshine" of her grandfather's adoring gaze. As I grew older it became apparent that she needed me to see the world from her perspective. When I resisted accepting her sometimes irrational views, she could turn on me with frightening hatred.

There was an intergenerational family pattern of selecting one child among siblings to be targeted for projections as the bad child. All of us in the household I grew up in were familiar with oft-repeated anecdotes about our Aunt Olive, my mother's sister and Olive Withington's granddaughter. Aunt Olive was described as the "bad" daughter and sibling, who, according to the family stories, disrupted the harmony of the household with her selfishness and assumptions of entitlement. Her adult relationships with my mother and grandmother were fraught with conflict. I speculate that my great-grandmother Olive chose one of her daughters for the bad daughter role, but there is no one among the living with whom I could now explore that possibility. My grandmother chose Robin for the position of bad offspring, skipping a generation to accuse her grandson of stealing money from her. My mother recruited Sheila for the role of the bad daughter. Sheila projected this in turn onto Jessica when she was a small child. By the time Jessica entered adulthood, Sheila's persistent search for spiritual and emotional healing had redeemed their relationship. I am grateful that Sheila's healing spared Jessica the burden of toxic intergenerational projection.

Paternal bereavement also cast its shadow over my father. He grew up in a household shaped by dread of the terminal illness of tuberculosis with which my grandfather struggled. My father remembered his father as exhausted by constant reassignments to revitalize yet another congregation, his only respite a stay in a tuberculosis sanitorium in an ultimately futile effort to hold the disease at bay. My grandfather feared infecting wife or children with the deadly germ. If he discovered a dinner plate with a tiny crack that could harbor the bacterium, he would snatch it from the table and hurl it to floor or wall.

Although my father did not grow up to express his anger by throwing and breaking things, he did grow up with an indelible image of explosive masculine anger. His father's deathbed command to be "the man of the family" crystallized my father's twelve-year-old understanding of what it was to be a man. His feelings of obligation to his mother compelled him to accept the ancestral imperative to become an ordained minister of the Methodist Church, despite, to his dying day, his blaming the Church for his father's death. He was ambivalent about his obligation to his sisters, particularly as one of them acted out her grief in scandalous behavior that proved how little power my father really had.

My father was gentle and physically affectionate with me as child, despite episodes of flaring anger and impatience when he saw me as not living up to his expectations for his older son. I remember his starting to withdraw from me emotionally when I turned twelve. I was unaware at the time of his experience as a twelve-year-old at his father's deathbed. It seems to me now that my reaching the age at which he lost his father activated the loss that my father had never fully grieved, retreating instead into remote emotional constriction, male anger masking his feelings of vulnerability.

As children, Sheila and I had little knowledge of how family unhappiness was shaped by these invisible ancestral ghosts. She and I fought constantly, and she was older and stronger enough to dominate me with her physical aggression. I would hear my father reading her bedtime stories in her bedroom across the hall from mine, something I can't remember his ever having done for me. Sheila was jealous of me as the child favored with the flowing affection from my mother that she was denied and for which she yearned. I took out on my younger brother my anger and helplessness over Sheila's treatment, evoking Sheila's protection for Robin that kept me outside their sibling coalition.

Each of us departed our childhood home to enter adulthood haunted by unfinished business. By her mid-teens, as my mother's harsh treatment increased, Sheila had recognized that getting out from under her mother's roof was imperative for her existential survival. She got a job as an au pair, spending most days and nights in the home of a family in the neighborhood. She persuaded our parents to send her to a residential private school, contributing money from her own earnings toward her tuition. Although she freed herself from direct exposure to our mother's toxic projections, she never stopped yearning for family connection, striving for loving relationship with Robin and me and working to establish and maintain connection with members of our maternal and paternal extended families.

I had different reasons for wanting to leave my parental household, which I did in the orderly way that was the norm for White middle-class families of that time, finishing high school to go off to live at college. I did not have Sheila's childhood experience of the emotionally neglected child yearning for love from family. Although I felt secure about being loved, I sought escape from my mother's dependence on me to ratify her sometimes irrational views of reality. In my struggle to differentiate from her I could be hurtful with my anger. It felt to me like an existential struggle to develop a coherent sense of self, distinct from my role affirming my mother's reality. My early marriage as a college junior to a woman whose race and class could not have been more different from my parents' was emblematic of my struggle to get away from my family of origin.

Our sibling conflicts had continued well into adulthood, their origins in formative childhood experiences of family not always apparent to us as we conducted our separate lives. Each of us responded in our own way to the paradox of heeding the ancestral imperative to serve God on the one hand while honoring my father's determination that his children cast off the burden of obligation to the Methodist Church on the other. Each of us sought vehicles for our spiritual journeys outside of formal religion, although Sheila's husband Earl was, like our father, a sociologist who studied the Protestant Church. My father's professional career as a sociologist involved research that both studied and served Protestant denominations, as director of research first for the Massachusetts Council of Churches and later for the National Council of Churches. Early in his career, Earl wrote one book about organized religion, but from the perspective of observer rather than of participant-observer. The focus of that study was noteworthy, given his wife's legacy of spiritual paradox. His book, *To Comfort and Challenge*, explored the dilemma of the minister's role, embodied in the aphorism, "Comfort the afflicted, and afflict the comfortable."

Ironically, one of the flash points for our sibling conflict involved Sheila's early choice on her own spiritual path. She, Earl, and Robin all became deeply involved in "est training" (Erhard Seminar Training), one of the more influential of the "Human Potential" organizations that emerged in the second half of the twentieth century. Drawing heavily on Eastern spiritual traditions, at its best the est training helped its participants recognize how they could be trapped in their constructions of reality, enabling them to take responsibility for their decisions about their lives. For Sheila, participation in est opened a door to relinquishing much of the bitterness and resentment that she had absorbed from our family legacy. It helped soften her in her relationship with her son Aaron, who developed into a generous and loving man and a good father, with strong personal integrity.

Beset by scandal about its founder, the est program eventually faded into a much smaller remnant. Before its ultimate demise, both Sheila and Robin made repeated futile attempts to recruit me into taking the est training. This issue became a battleground beset with bitterness, rage, and verbal aggression that resonated with our childhood sibling conflicts. In our struggles with each other, Sheila and I embodied the effects of our childhood wounds. Sheila, the exile who yearned for family connection, wanted very much to share a precious experience with me. She experienced my refusal to participate in est training as rejection. She clung to her memory of my saying to her, in one of our bitter arguments, "I will never allow you to give me anything."

I do not remember saying those words, but I can imagine having done so. Neither Sheila nor I had the benefit of healthy "launching" from family of origin and therefore brought our family ghosts into our adult lives. While Sheila as an adult yearned for connection with her family, I sought to leave it behind me. If Sheila's experience was of exile, mine was of escape. By the time I graduated from college, I had become husband and father in a family of my own choosing. Sheila's struggle while still a teenager to have enough control of her life to get away from her mother shaped her need for control in her adult relationships. When she felt her control threatened, she would embody our mother's irrational rage. In my efforts to escape my family, I did all I could to leave it behind, literally to "forget it."

Both Sheila and Robin retained more detailed memories of childhood than I did and carried more bitterness. The vagueness of my global memory of being a victim concealed both my mother's intense and confusing emotional over-involvement with me and my own power to hurt members of my family with harsh and cruel words. We kept our ghosts alive in an intense dance that family therapists call a positive feedback runaway. The more Sheila, driven by her yearning for family connection, pressed me to take the est training, the more firmly I would resist. I in turn was driven by echoes of my mother recruiting me into her irrational beliefs. The more Sheila persisted, the more I resisted. The more I resisted, the more she persisted. Each of us embodied the anger of the parent who had favored the other. Sheila's rage could take on the tone of our mother's hateful words. I would rage in the loud and dominating tones of my angry father.

In those last two years of her life, as Sheila and I deconstructed old family patterns and helped each other let go of them, we built on gains that we had already achieved in our efforts to support our younger brother. Unlike his older siblings, Robin as a child was not able to find an anchor for self-esteem in academic achievement. My parents' futile efforts to help him with school were constrained by the limitations of professional knowledge about learning disabilities in the fifties. The state of the art at the time involved drilling a student on phonics, an arduous and intrinsically boring training that had proven helpful with children who had difficulty learning to read. My father took on that task, regularly and diligently putting Robin through the paces.

The training had little effect on Robin's grades, and his continued failures evoked intense paternal anger. Psychological testing when Robin was in his forties revealed that he tested in the ninety-ninth percentile in phonics. He had in fact responded well to the training, but it proved to be a remedy for the wrong ill. The testing also found evidence of profound attention deficit disorder. His untreated ADHD limited his capacity to learn in school, to retain what he had read moments earlier, and to organize his life, from daily activities to setting goals, planning, and tracking progress.

Robin also suffered from an undiagnosed hearing impairment in his first years of life. Born deaf in one ear, he lost hearing in the functioning ear from a buildup of earwax. This rendered him essentially deaf for months in his second and third year of life, a period critical for laying the foundations of language-based learning. Robin learned to use language primarily from learning intuitively how to read lips, rather than from hearing. His apparent capacity to listen and respond delayed our parents' discovery of his impairment. The family story is that our mother, suspecting that there was a problem, stood behind him where he couldn't see her mouth. She asked him if he wanted ice cream, and he did not respond.

In his own way, Robin was as smart as other members of the family. His gifts were different from ours, in ways that made it hard for him to feel seen. Unlike Sheila or me, Robin was exceptionally gifted in visual-spatial learning skills, as evident in his teaching himself to read lips. He would build complex plastic models from kits without consulting directions and could take apart, repair, and assemble mechanical devices with confidence and skill. Although, like Sheila and me, he was targeted for bullying as a child, Robin had a gregarious temperament different from both of his shy siblings. Despite being difficult in his relationships with family members, particularly with me, he made and kept friends readily through most of his life.

Without academic achievement to buffer the torment of bullying, Robin developed a pattern of fabulizing. Once his hearing was restored, he caught up quickly, learning spoken language, with which he would make up elaborate stories about his life and experiences that he would cling to, sometimes even after they were proven to be untrue. Unlike his siblings, Robin stayed home with our parents for years after most teenagers graduate high school, enrolling and failing in a succession of private schools after dropping out of public school. He became heavily involved in marijuana and alcohol abuse. Always accident-prone, he was involved in several crashes after he learned to drive. To protect themselves from legal liability for his car accidents, my parents persuaded him to establish his legal emancipation.

Always protective of her younger brother, Sheila arranged for Robin leave home and come to live with her and Earl in California. Robin settled into a lifetime pattern of counter-dependence, on the one hand stubbornly insisting on his independence, on the other mismanaging his life dramatically enough to require rescue. He responded with resentment and hostility to the supportive efforts that he would make necessary for his well-being and survival. He did have some success in California, getting training that drew on his visual strengths at a school of photography, where he established lifetime friendships. For a time, he worked as a photographer for Bill Graham at the Fillmore Auditorium. His striking photographs of Janis Joplin, Mick Jagger, and other rock stars still decorate the hallways of Mount Pleasant Home in Boston, where he spent the last years of his life. He built a network of personal relationships in the est community.

Despite these promising beginnings, Robin's substance abuse issues made life in our sister's home untenable. He was dealing drugs, primarily marijuana, in quantities large enough at the time to threaten everyone in the house with potential criminal prosecution. Living on his own, he got deeper into the life of a drug dealer. I will never know which of his dramatic stories of life in the margins were true and which were fabulized. It seems to be true that he learned, some time after her birth, that he had fathered a daughter. He had very few direct contacts with her, and she ultimately cut him off entirely. He never gave Sheila or me enough information to be able to locate her ourselves. As his only surviving sibling at the time of Robin's death, I had no way to let my niece know that her birth father had died.

Eventually, predictably, Robin was arrested and convicted after selling drugs to an undercover police officer. While incarcerated, he was hospitalized for a psychotic episode. Released on parole, he persuaded the California Board of Parole to allow him to leave his criminal life behind him in California and serve out his parole in Massachusetts. Returning to Massachusetts with his very difficult girlfriend, he did in fact succeed at leaving that life, getting a job as an automobile mechanic and later settling into steady work as a taxi driver, ultimately acquiring his own vehicle with the medallion that authorized it to operate as a taxi in the city of Cambridge. He drove his taxi until his vision failed him and he had to support himself on Social Security Disability Income.

My difficult relationship with Robin did not improve on his return from California. His ambivalence toward me, wanting connection but harboring lifelong resentment, manifested in hostility and passive-aggressive dependence. First Betty, then later Jodie, found him to be a very difficult brother-in-law, particularly with his obnoxious girlfriend, whom he met in California and who returned with him to fraught relationships with her own family in Massachusetts. Our parents had retired and moved to Saint Lucia in the Caribbean, and Sheila was living on the West Coast. Before Robin returned to the East Coast to live in a nearby community, I seldom thought about the family that I firmly believed I had left behind.

Although Robin and I could avoid each other for months after arguments, we did not cut off from each other. He was included in family holiday gatherings, but we otherwise seldom visited each other. He built his own personal networks, including people from the est community and the taxi industry. He organized and led an association of Cambridge taxi drivers and owners. Years after returning to Massachusetts, he served as an active board member for his local church.

Our uneasy relationship became more difficult as Robin became increasingly disabled. He lost vision from failed cataract surgery in one eye, and glaucoma gradually but relentlessly robbed him of vision in the other. He was diagnosed with hepatitis C, probably contracted from his drug abuse in California. His hoarding problem intensified after he and his girlfriend separated. He could not throw things away, nor did he put things where he could find them, even if he was able to see clearly. I struggled to suppress shuddering at the chaos when I visited him in his apartment.

Tensions among siblings intensified as Robin became more disabled. By telephone and correspondence, Sheila and Robin maintained their coalition. When it became apparent that Robin could not handle filing his income taxes, working with his taxi as a sole business, Jodie volunteered to help him file. Stubbornly clinging to his independence, he turned down her offer. He probably had not told Sheila of the offer, nor of his refusal, when Sheila called Jodie and me to demand, a week before the filing date, that we drop everything and go to Robin's house to help him prepare his tax return. When we declared that this was impossible, she excoriated us in a vituperative tirade that rivaled my mother's worst hateful and irrational outbursts. All three of us were shaken by this relational rupture. As we struggled for repair, I became more careful to track Robin's situation and to stay in touch with Sheila.

Robin lived in a multi-family building in nearby Somerville, where he paid minimal rent in exchange for building management, including heating system maintenance. When the building owner decided to transform the rental apartments into condominiums, Robin faced losing his home. As his efforts to pack up his cluttered household and find a new home failed repeatedly, we realized that he was facing homelessness. With considerable trepidation, Jodie and I decided to take him in as he continued his search for housing. Ransom and Jessica were long out of the house, but Jacob was almost twelve at the time.

Robin's six-month sojourn at our home created enormous strain. He resented us for his dependence on us and exhausted us with his passive-aggressive stance. We worried about danger to our health from his hepatitis C, particularly given his poor personal hygiene. He did little to take on household domestic responsibilities. On the one occasion when we were truly dependent on him for help, with Jodie, Jacob, and me all laid low by the flu, he disappeared from the house for days. When confronted, he explained that he was avoiding us for fear of catching the virus. He would sit by the television during the day, going out in the evening to bars. He would return after we had all gone to bed, reeking of tobacco smoke that triggered Jodie's asthma, disregarding her repeated entreaties that he consider her vulnerability. He took eye drops for his glaucoma that exacerbated his depression. Jacob found it very difficult to try to watch television in a room where his very tall uncle splayed out on the couch, half-awake and deeply depressed after taking his eye medicine, which was also sedating. His uncle's depression seems to have accelerated the onset of Jacob's mood difficulties. It was during Robin's time in our home that Jacob, on his twelfth birthday, first expressed suicidal feelings.

Connected with the situation through frequent telephone calls, Sheila recognized that the situation was untenable. She told me that she had to act or she "wouldn't have any siblings." With a combination of financial support and firm direction, she mobilized Robin to find lodging. Without ever returning to live in our home again, he went through a couple of tenuous situations, renting as a roommate with strangers before he secured a room in an informal rooming house where he built a supportive personal community. By the time that house was sold, he had made it up the waiting list to settle into a subsidized apartment in the former Jamaica Plain High School in Boston, adjoining the lot of the house where we had lived when he was born.

The ordeal with Robin in our home shifted the relationships among siblings. Sheila saw that Jodie and I would not abandon him to homelessness. I was grateful to her for her consistent and determined efforts, from the other side of the continent, to compensate for Robin's decreasing ability to manage his own life. Although my relationship with Robin remained strained, I was better able to accept my relational obligation to my brother and very grateful for Jodie's respect and support for our fraternal relationship. We made sure to include him in family gatherings with Ransom, Jessica, and Jodie's mother, who had moved to the Boston area from her previous home in New York. I began taking him out occasionally for lunch.

As his vision and his mental health deteriorated further, I was ready to take on the increasing shift of the caretaking load from Sheila to me. Robin was diagnosed with bipolar disorder, and I would try to fill the communication gap between his caretakers at the state Department of Mental Health and the private psychiatric hospitals where he would be taken from hospital emergency rooms. Barely able to see, he walked with a cane, holding my arm for support and guidance as we went to restaurants for lunch. I would accompany him to his apartment when taking him home from lunch or a family meal, where the cluttering and hoarding accelerated with his loss of vision. I would find food that we had sent home with him after a family meeting weeks or months before, spoiling on kitchen counter or in the refrigerator. Several inches above six feet tall, he was falling more frequently, often stumbling over the clutter that he could not see in his apartment.

When Robin was hospitalized medically after one of those falls, it was hard to imagine how he could continue to live alone. Help came forth providentially from Robin's social network. He had been volunteering at the Mount Pleasant Home, a rest home in Jamaica Plain not far from his apartment and about a mile from us. The director, aware of Robin's situation, proposed that he transition from the role of volunteer to that of a resident. Difficult as it was for Robin to surrender his independence, he recognized that he could no longer live alone.

I called on Sheila to come to Boston to help me clear out his cluttered apartment. In the days that we spent sorting out his possessions, we strengthened our relationship as I took on more responsibility for our brother. She transferred modest funds to me that our paternal aunt had left for Sheila to provide for Robin, with the understanding that Sheila would supplement them as necessary. Shortly after Robin moved to Mount Pleasant, he agreed to make me his medical proxy, and to give me power of attorney. I paid the personal organizer Sheila had hired, did my best to coordinate services with mental health and medical caretakers and keep the peace with the caretaking staff at Mount Pleasant, whose patience Robin often tested with resentment over his dependence and with his deteriorating mental health.

In childhood, I had felt little affection for Robin. He and Sheila had kept me the outsider in our home, and I was frustrated and embarrassed by his fabulizing. He had resented me as our mother's favorite and for having such easy success at school, where he suffered shame and failure. As he grudgingly allowed me more into his life as his caretaker, I did feel affection for him. The relationship did not feel reciprocal. Although his friends, including the former pastor of his church, clearly held him in high esteem for his intelligence and generosity of spirit, I did not feel any generosity directed toward me or Jodie or even our children. I once took a chance to share my vulnerability in a story of Jodie and me opening our hearts to bereaved parents not long after Jacob's death. Referring to the years that we lived in dread of losing Jacob, I told the story of the father in this bereaved family who had struggled to save his son from a riptide, grabbing his son's hand then losing his grip as his son was swept to his death. I said to Robin, "Jodie and I had for several years the experience that man had in those few seconds." Robin responded, simply, "I can't find my glasses." I instantly regretted sharing my experience with him. It hurt to discover him so self-absorbed as to ignore my sharing of vulnerability.

Sheila was diagnosed with lung cancer a year or so after that difficult exchange with Robin. During my visits with her, my busy daily routines set aside, she and I absorbed ourselves in long conversations about our own relationships and our relationships with other family members. With wisdom and peace of mind acquired over the course of her spiritual journey, aware of her mortality, Sheila sought healing between the two of us, between her brothers, and between my older children and me. I shared my pain over Robin's self-absorbed response to my story of Jacob slipping away from our efforts to keep him alive. Speaking in a voice full of love for both brothers, Sheila said, "Robin just can't do it." Her words shifted my feelings from frustration to compassion.

That shift held when I returned home and opened my constricted heart to him. I came to enjoy our lunches and expressed my deep compassion for his sorrow that his disabilities made it impossible for him to travel across the continent to visit with his beloved sister. Jessica told me that she could see the shift in my feelings toward Robin at our occasional family gatherings. Already acting as his advocate with his poorly integrated systems of care, I was his fierce and determined protector as his psychiatric and other medical illnesses accelerated over the last month of his life. He was hospitalized in and out of sepsis for weeks in terrible pain. After a sharp decline, when Robin had been unconscious and unresponsive for several days, his doctors informed me that they had discovered an abscess on his spine. A decision had to be made immediately. He would not survive without surgery, and he might well not survive the surgery itself. If he did survive surgery, his slow and painful recovery would ultimately leave him paralyzed for the remainder of his life. With respect and compassion, his doctors told me that, with Robin unresponsive, as his medical proxy the decision was mine. I faced the prospect of living with the decision without certain knowledge of what Robin would have chosen. Broken-hearted, I decided that Robin would not have wanted to go on in such circumstances. Too fragile to leave the hospital, Robin's status was changed to hospice care, under the supervision of a kind and wise palliative care physician.

The very night of the day I made that decision, Robin unexpectedly regained consciousness and telephoned me. I told him of the decision, for which he wholeheartedly thanked me. Jodie and I rushed to his rest home to bring with us the fellow resident who had become his companion to visit him at his hospital bed. Learning of the situation, Jessica called in, and we all listened on speakerphone to her gentle and loving words as she soothed his tormented body and soul. We felt grace fill the room as her voice led him to imagine himself rising and falling with the gentle waves of the sea in Saint Lucia, where our parents retired, and which Robin loved to visit. Robin's last few days were peaceful, as his doctor assured that he was appropriately medicated for effective pain control.

Although Sheila's life passed before Robin's, the peace and love that she nurtured between her brothers assured that Robin would be lovingly cared for through the rest of his life. Sheila was equally determined to nurture healing between the generations of my family. Throughout their lives, Sheila had maintained active relationships with her nephew and niece. When Ransom was a teenager and Jessica still a child, she took them with her to Saint Lucia for a visit with their grandfather. She would visit with family on the East Coast and arrange for Jessica and Ransom, with his wife Kim, to visit with her on the West Coast. She had listened deeply to their accounts of the distance that developed in their relationships with Jodie and me after Jacob's death and encouraged restoration of those relationships. In the conversations between Sheila and me during my visits, I was better able to see the family situation through my children's eyes. I discovered that, as Jodie and I had seen them as distancing from us after Jacob's death, they were seeing us distancing from them. Working from both sides, helping us to shift our perspectives, Sheila helped bring the East Coast generations closer together. By the time that we all gathered for a memorial service in Portland a few months after Sheila's passing, we could feel distance was closing among Jodie and me, Ransom and Kim, and Jessica.

Sheila, who had grown up suffering in the intergenerational role of the "bad daughter," had found herself assigning that role to her niece when Jessica was very young. Determined to leave this legacy behind, Sheila nurtured deep connection with Jessica. This was particularly affirming, and very important, for Jessica. By the time that Jessica was born, her parents' marriage was deteriorating. Ransom had been born six years earlier than Jessica, when his parents were still deeply in love, and the home was not full of the tension that was emerging in Jessica's first years of life. I found it poignant to see Ransom's devotion to Kim resonating with the love he experienced between his parents at the start of his life, so different from the turbulence of parental conflict in Jessica's early years.

By the time that she could speak, Jessica was dreading that her parents would divorce. Like many children in such situations, she imagined that her own actions could somehow keep her parents together and felt that she had failed when her mother and I divorced. Her fear of losing a parent grew more intense when divorce did not ease the bitterness between her parents. Clinging to the idea that she had to be "good" to hold on to each parent, she struggled with how to present herself in two households with two very different parents. Flooded with my own pain over having to live separately from my beloved children, I was not the responsible parent that Jessica needed. Rather than finding the strength to soothe her fears, I was overwhelmed with my distress over her pain and my own broken heart.

Years later, as Jessica and I heal the wounds in our relationship, I feel deep remorse. I learned from her as an adult what she experienced as a child, believing that she had to take care of me well enough not to lose me as a parent. Between my self-absorption and marijuana abuse, and her mother's alcoholism, Jessica's childhood was marked by an existential struggle to hold on to the parents whom she needed to survive. This burden of fear and helplessness distorted the development of a healthy self. As a very young adult after her mother's premature and sudden death, she struggled with the challenge of becoming her own person while still in relationship with me. We went through a couple of decades of strain, with periods of estrangement, before the profound reconciliation that we are building together. The restoration of our relationship is grounded in the work that each of us has done with maturation, psychological healing, and spiritual development. We both acknowledge and feel great gratitude for the vital role that Sheila played in that reconciliation.

Much of that healing began on a road trip that Sheila and Jessica took from Oregon through San Francisco on the way to explore the awesome natural beauty of Death Valley Natural Park. Jessica talked of her emotional struggles with her father. Even as she yearned for connection, she chafed at what she believed were conditions that she be, act, and feel in certain ways to be in relationship with me. She would try to solve the conflict by avoiding engagement, which intensified the pain of her (and my) yearning for connection. The more she kept her distance, the more powerful were the images she built in her mind of the father who caused her so much suffering. On the road trip, she didn't want to hear her aunt's wise words of counsel, yet she remembered them. Her memory of those words, which she shared with me six years after her aunt's death and more than a decade after that trip, matches word for word with the memory that Sheila shared with me on one of my visits with her. She said to Jessica, "Has it ever occurred to you that, besides being your father, he is also a human being? Yes, he's your father, but he's also a person, just like you are a person."

During those long conversations on the road, they talked about Jessica's finding her spiritual home in Tibetan Buddhism. Sheila, having been awakened to her spirituality by her experiences with est training, was still searching for a spiritual home. After a difficult divorce, she had explored another spiritual practice grounded in Eastern body movement that she found helpful. Sensitized by her experiences with the est training, she disengaged from the organization promoting that practice when she recognized signs of cult-like leadership. Sheila's genuine curiosity brought forth Jessica's heartfelt love for her Buddhist practice, her spiritual teacher, and her community. Inspired, Sheila joined the Tergar Meditation Community *sangha* in Portland. This was to open later, rich conversations among Sheila, Jessica, and me about our spiritual journeys. A conversation between Jessica and me about the journey of Sheila's soul after her death and the resonance between Jessica's Buddhist and my kabbalistic perspective inspired me with an idea that became the central theme of a book that I was editing at the time.[62]

The redemption of loving relationship has been transformative both for Jessica and for me. There had been a time when Jessica could only imagine having her own life if she could live as far away as possible from me, to protect herself from the intense storms of her ambivalent emotions. We now engage with each other fully as our own persons, neither needing the other to compensate for old losses. After living in California and New York, and a couple of years as a travel nurse working in hospitals in several different states, Jessica settled in Nantucket, where she helped establish an elder care service on the island. During the COVID pandemic, she, Jodie, and I adopted a routine of weekend visits by video. In contrast to her determination earlier in her life to keep us at a distance, Jessica eagerly collaborated with us on a plan for our future retirement in Nantucket, where Jodie and I could be sure to receive the support we would need toward the end of our lives. Sadly, we had to relinquish that plan when it became clear that Jodie's medical vulnerability made it essential that we live nearby Boston's outstanding medical facilities.

As painful as the distance from Ransom and Jessica could be for Jodie and me, their parents' divorce and their struggles with me as their father never produced complete cutoffs. Ransom lived in Jodie's and my home for periods before and after he was in college, and Jessica lived partly in our and in partly in her mother's homes during her last years at high school. Sharing a home with Jacob in those years strengthened their already warm relationships with their brother. They were, like Jodie and me, troubled and confused by Jacob's struggles in the last few years of his life. Ransom and Kim disapproved of our handling of the situation, which created some distance between us. Parents and siblings alike struggled with fear and helplessness as we tried and failed to hold Jacob back from his self-destructive course. As Jodie and I grieved at the distance between us and our remaining children after Jacob died, Ransom and Jessica perceived us as so absorbed in our grief over Jacob as to be less available for them. As we gathered in Portland for Sheila's memorial, the restoration of our relationships was a fitting tribute to Sheila's loving concern for our family.

Sadly, Kim's early death after a lifelong struggle with diabetes helped Ransom, Jodie, and me draw further closer with each other. His voice choking with grief, Ransom called me from the hospital where Kim died and opened his broken heart to me as I guided and supported him through the acute stages of raw grief. Jodie and I accompanied him as he made the preparations for her funeral. Jodie and I are witnesses and supports as he finds his way to build a new life without the partner whom he loved so deeply and so well.

ASSEMBLING A GATHERING IN SACRED SPACE

Six years after I made my decision to write this memoir, I was making relatively little progress on that project. Although I remained firm in my intention to contribute to cultural change and I had done some writing, the memoir project was at that time more in my imagination than on the page. Then, Carmen Knudson-Martin, the American Family Therapy Academy's director of publications, invited AFTA members to submit manuscripts for the AFTA Springer Briefs book series. I was inspired by this opportunity to publish my writing on integrating spirituality with psychotherapy. It felt like a way for me to move the memoir project forward. By editing a book with chapters by multiple authors, each grounded in their different faith traditions, I hoped that I could develop and share ideas about a common human spiritual discourse, an idea at the core of my inspiration to write the memoir. The time felt right to take on that Springer book opportunity. It was several months after I had begun traveling west to visit Sheila. I was learning so much from the process of deep and intimate spiritual dialogue with my sister and with my daughter, both of them as deeply grounded in their adopted Tibetan Buddhism as I was in my adopted Judaism.

I hoped that a book intended to bring spirituality to the foreground might stimulate a change of perspective in therapists who experience faith and spirituality as either irrelevant or irreconcilable with the therapeutic enterprise. The field of family therapy was for me a congenial context in which to first publish my writing about this topic. Challenging "common knowledge" is embedded in the culture of family therapy, which emerged from the margins of the field of psychotherapy to challenge the dominant discourse of individual psychotherapy. I felt that I had grown up professionally together with family therapy, which was still relatively early in its development when I began my professional education.

Family therapy's systemic approach expands the therapeutic lens beyond the boundaries of the individual to focus on the relational processes of family, network, community, society, and culture—and on the well-being of our planet. I had been blessed at the beginning of my career by the mentorship of Carolyn Attneave, who shared generously from her integration of bio-psycho-socio-cultural-spiritual system theory with family therapy and with her own spirituality, which was deeply grounded in Native and European spiritual traditions.

Most family therapists, like most psychotherapists, tend not to think about spiritual aspects of their clients' experiences. Yet, family therapists' attention to context is consistent with spiritual perspectives that see the Divine as the ultimate context encompassing all. The fluidity and inclusivity of systems theory encourages thinking from a "both-and" rather than an "either-or" perspective. The "both-and" stance easily embraces the spiritual paradox of God as simultaneously transcendent and immanent, both beyond and within the world. The relatively recent emergence in family therapy of postmodern, collaborative discourse affords respect for the unique knowledge of both patient and therapist as partners in a collaborative therapeutic process. This perspective resonates with the humble and collaborative stance of the network therapist, which I had learned from Carolyn's teaching and from my experiences working with teams in network assemblies.

Colleagues in Nordic countries have integrated emerging postmodern discourse into their network therapy practice. Network therapy teams in Sweden, Norway, and Finland now engage in transparently reflective conversations with each other directly in the presence of network members who gather to help a family in distress, creatively generating new possibilities for understanding and action. I have been particularly inspired by the emergent practice of "Open Dialogue," an approach that Jaakko Seikkula and other Finnish network therapists developed, drawing on the linguistic and literary ideas of Mikhail Bakhtin.[63] When I read Bakhtin's work, I found it resonating with me as much spiritually as it did intellectually.

Bakhtin's idea of dialogue presents a radical challenge to the idea that communication is a matter of speakers holding, shaping, and transmitting meanings to listeners. For Bakhtin, meaning does not exist "inside" either speaker or listener. Meaning, rather, emerges in the space between them. He argued that, as speakers, we can't grasp the meanings of our utterances without hearing the responses that our utterances evoke. Because responses are themselves utterances, which therefore require response for their meanings to emerge in turn, a dialogue is intrinsically "unfinalizable." These ideas of meaning arising in the present moment struck a deep chord in me, resonating with the spiritual practice of mindfulness and the idea that all we can truly know is the now of the present. I was not surprised to learn that Bakhtin, who lived and worked in the Soviet Union, had been punished by the government for practicing his religious faith in an ideologically atheist society.

Bakhtin distinguished dialogue from monologue. Dialogue is integral to the emergence of meaning in the Space Between. Language in dialogue seeks new possibilities for understanding to emerge. Language in monologue seeks definite conclusions. Monologue is centripetal: its energy draws toward a definitive center. Dialogue, in contrast, is centrifugal: its energy expands outward toward new possibilities. Monologue is determinative and conclusive; dialogue is generative and creative. It is in dialogue that the Space Between emerges.

As I contemplated gathering a group of colleagues to contribute to the book that I would edit, I reflected on earlier work with my friend and colleague Hugo Kamya, who shares my enthusiasms for Bakhtin and for the transparent integration of spirituality with psychotherapy. Hugo would be among the colleagues whom I would assemble for the book. I drew from Hugo's teaching about "sacred space." This expression appears in several locations in the Jewish and Christian Bible, including God's instruction for Moses to take off his sandals when he encountered a bush in the desert that burned without being consumed. I set the intention to engage the book's chapter authors in a dialogical process throughout the process of convening, writing, and editing. I hoped that, in a spiritually grounded dialogical conversation, the Space Between would become sacred space.

I assembled a multicultural group of eight authors, my colleagues and friends. Each is each grounded in their distinct and different faith and/or belief traditions. These co-authors worked with me over the course of four years to produce the book, *Engaging with Spirituality in Family Therapy: Meeting in Sacred Space*, which was published in 2018. We represented Taoist, Sufi Muslim, Sunni Muslim, East African, Zulu, Native American, Sikh, Jewish, and Christian traditions. I invited my co-authors to collaborate on a project that would draw on our diverse experiences of faith and spirituality and on our perspectives as family therapists. Each chapter would locate its author as a cultural and spiritual being and illustrate the influence of their faith and spirituality on their professional practice.

I asked my fellow authors to imagine how a discourse of human spirituality might supplant the dominant global discourse of individualism, and to wrestle with the dilemma of tension between religious particularism and universal human values. I asked them to read Rivett and Street's foundational article on spirituality in family therapy so we could draw on a common language distinguishing instrumental from metaphysical use of spirituality in the therapeutic enterprise. Over the course of the project, we would also come to appreciate the subtle beauty of Rivett and Street's koan-like phrase, "the same and different and the same."[64]

It was important for me as editor to stimulate and facilitate a conversation among the authors that would embody the postmodern collaborative values that resonate with human spirituality. Throughout the process of several years of writing, we maintained an active group conversation by email and occasional video conference. That conversation embodied the values and intentions of the book.

As we began the conversation, I wrote to my co-authors about a family therapy seminar meeting that Hugo and I had shared at the Center for Multicultural Training in Psychology. Over the course of that meeting, Hugo and I had witnessed how Bakhtin's space between speaker and listener became imbued with a shared feeling of the sacred. I wrote to the group of co-authors, "In class this year, Hugo helped me to see how the 'space between' speakers in which Bakhtin believes meaning emerges, is itself sacred space."

Through the process of writing and editing the book, our flowing dialogue embodied what we were learning together: when people engage each other with open hearts and minds, in dialogues grounded in the firmly held particulars of their different spiritual traditions, sacred space can emerge. The universe is experienced not in the language of a meta-religion but in what I called a "'nameless but achingly familiar' feeling."[1] As editor, I actively challenged ideas that either suggested language for a new meta-religion, or that reduced faith and spirituality to wordless experience. Any attempt to reach for a meta-religion embodying all religions would, I feared, inevitably include an implicit claim of universality and

1. Trimble, *Engaging with Spirituality*, 127.

thereby lead into competitive struggle for dominance with other religions that hold their own claims of universality. Although human spirituality may at its heights reach beyond the limits of language, human beings require the language of their faiths, which can serve as ladders to reach those heights.

I wrote to my fellow authors, "I am sometimes moved to tears reading the words of my fellow authors, as I see the realization of a dream. We are engaged in deep conversation about our spirituality, activating Spirit in the space between our utterances, without being tempted to shape yet another religion. What I hope that we are shaping is a culture of respectful conversation between people deeply grounded in their own specific beliefs and practices. In so doing, we are contributing to the creation of a human culture that can someday replace the current soulless individualist global culture that is destroying humanity and the life of our planet."

In the last chapter, I relaxed the conventional boundaries of space and time for an imagined conversation among the co-authors. I assembled from four years of email conversation the voices of all the co-authors as we had written to each other about a range of spiritual matters. The last chapter, embodying all of our voices in dialogical process, invited readers into an experience of sacred space akin to the experiences shared among the co-authors.

Writing and editing *Engaging with Spirituality in Family Therapy* did indeed help me to move forward with the memoir project. It activated my intuitive sense of the power of text to engage writer and reader in dialogical relationship. I write the memoir that you are now reading, with the prayer that it may move you to enter the sacred domains of your own spiritual experience. I have aspired to write this memoir openheartedly, from deeply within the particulars of my own life. My hope is that you read openheartedly, with active curiosity about the particulars of your own life, and that this gives you gain deeper access to your own spirituality. As you do so, may you and I enter together into a common sacred space that is the same, and different, and the same for each of us.

7

The Tapestry of Wisdom

I AM GRATEFUL FOR the blessings of a life lived long enough to afford some reflective understanding of its pattern and purpose. As I contemplate my eternal soul's temporary sojourn enclothed in the garment of the life, name, and identity of David Trimble, I discern patterns in that mortal tapestry. During one of my visits with Sheila, I read neuropsychologist Elkhonon Goldberg's book *The Wisdom Paradox* on emerging neurobiological understanding of the aging brain.[65] As we age, our brain's left side is less vulnerable to the natural decline of acuity that affects the functions of the right side. Although it may be more challenging for us to learn new skills, we elders continue to accumulate a library of patterns in the robust left side of our brains. We are familiar with more patterns and are better able to use the brain's capacity to recognize, integrate, and make use of that accumulating wisdom.

I started to integrate the ideas and imagery of Kabbalah into my meditative practice at the age of sixty-two, a year and a half after we lost Jacob. I planted the seed for this memoir when I shared an essay documenting this evolving meditative practice with a couple of trusted readers. The following year, as my practice continued to evolve, I revised that essay. I made the decision to write this memoir while working on the revision. In the ensuing years, a decade and a half of living up to the threshold of my eighties, living my life and writing about it have resonated with each other in a recursive process that illuminates its themes and patterns. The four years spent collaborating on *Engaging with Spirituality in Family Therapy*, in which we co-authors shared our stories, further enriched the reflective process. As family therapists looking at our process through the lenses of system theory and postmodern thinking, we appreciated our reflexive, recursive processes of mutual understanding as we shared those processes in the present moment.

Once again, I find myself wrestling with the challenges of writing the memoir in linear narrative form. You have already read about some of the events that transpired while I was working on *Engaging with Spirituality in Family Therapy*. My conversation with Art Green about praying for my patients, and the resulting decision to end my exploration of shamanic healing in my psychotherapeutic practice, took place in the first year of work on that book. Much of what you have read of my transformative experiences during visits with my dying sister comes from an email letter I wrote to my fellow authors of *Engaging*. As I write, I contemplate my continuously evolving relationships with my wife, my children, and my God, my study with a teacher of Kabbalah and my metaphysical work as a therapist for observant Jews.

I find myself again turning to a metaphor that transcends linear time. Intuition guides me to unspoken awareness of patterns as I struggle to discern a complex unity, feeling it resonate with the Unity of all being at the core of my soul. Learning to live with aging body and brain, I experience the events of my life as constituting a complex tapestry. Distinct threads of time, persons, relationships, health, illness, aging, and historical events—at personal, family, network, regional, national, and planetary levels—all derive their unique meanings from the patterns that they form and from the patterns of relationship among those patterns, which together constitute the whole.

DANCING WITH GOD

David danced with all his might before the LORD.
2 SAM 6:14[66]

In chapter one, I began the story of my life with a childhood dream that was the same, and different, and the same as the call my ancestors received, commanding them to commit their lives to the service of their Christian God. With my child's mind, I could not grasp the complexity of divine appearance and disappearance. Tormented by powerful emotions of love, loss, yearning, and fear, I struggled intensely in fruitless prayer to revive and engage with a God who had told me that he was dying. As I prayed, I could not fully admit that message from God into consciousness, nor could I contemplate the terrifying message that I had to carry on God's work without Him. I resisted the potential opportunity for a personal relationship with Jesus that sustains many devout Christians, perhaps out of unspoken dread of being abandoned once again. Discovering meditation in high school and psychedelic drugs in college, I could carry on my quest without needing even to imagine a God in a personal relationship with me.

Earlier in the linear sequence of my writing and your reading, in the section "Weaving Strands Together" in chapter four, I invited you to witness the story of my soul moving beyond the linear constraints of time when I acquired the capacity, years after Jacob's death, to accompany his soul in the moment immediately after his passing. Now, I invite you to join me as we look together through the lens shaped by lessons learned in my late seventies, as we witness my life's journey from childhood nightmare on its way to my current relationship with Hashem, the Is-Was-Will Be of the Jewish people.

Living as mortals in the material world, much of what we are granted to know of the mystery of the Eternal is beyond the limits of language. Constrained by our mortal natures, we use language as we struggle to describe and explain the phenomena of our mystical experiences. We may attain these mystical experiences in our own meditative practice, or adept teachers like Ramón Jiménez may grant them in direct, wordless transmission. They may come in visits by spiritual entities from worlds beyond our material world. Through the language of texts and oral teaching, the diverse traditions of human wisdom that flows from wordless revelation are passed from generation to generation.

Jewish lore acknowledges both written and oral transmission in the myth of the written and oral Torah, dictated to Moses by God on Mount Sinai. Moses, we are taught, wrote down the former and disclosed the latter orally to sages who passed it along to their successors, who passed it along in turn to their successors over the course of more than two millennia. Although some of the oral Torah was ultimately recorded in the written text of the Talmud, Jewish mystical tradition insists that there is still much knowledge that can only be granted by master to disciple.

Much of that knowledge is alluded to, without being fully revealed, in *Sefer Yetsirah* from early in the Common Era, and in writings from early centuries of the second millennium, e.g., the *Bahir* and the *Zohar*.

Early in the twentieth century, the kabbalist rabbi Yehuda Leib Ashlag, in whose name Yedidah Cohen teaches me, announced that he had been granted divine authority to reveal more of this secret wisdom in writing.[67]

As I share what I have learned from texts, from conversations with fellow Jewish seekers, and from my teachers' lessons, I encounter again the limits both of my understanding and of language itself to capture the meanings alluded to in sacred esoteric texts. The sages were careful to caution their readers, acknowledging that their words were at most metaphors for phenomena ultimately beyond description or explanation. Please take these limitations in mind as you read what follows. Please know that I alone am responsible for the words I have chosen to communicate my understanding.

The Unity of all being exists beyond all time and space. Time and space emerge from that One. The apparent separation of time and space from their source is an artifact of our material mortal perspective. Source and emanation are both aspects of the inseparable One. The Unity is, was, and will be the ultimate, unchanging reality. In the grandest of all paradoxes, the One (whether we call the One God, Hashem, or any of the multitude of sacred names invented by humanity) is beyond, surrounding, and within all that exists. God is in the world. The world is in God.

The One exists in three states: *echad*, *yachid*, and *meyuchad*. From our mortal perspective, bound in the materiality of space and time, we understand echad to be the state of the One "before" the creation of the material world. In the state of yachid, the One emanates Creation. Creation includes human beings, who embody vessels to receive the intense flow of divine blessing from the One. In the state of meyuchad, the ultimate design of Creation is actualized, materiality dissolves back into its Source, and all souls are fully reunited with the One from which they were never truly separated. Beyond the limits of space and time, all three states are eternal, although we may imagine them from within our limited mortal perspective by using the temporal metaphors of beginning, middle, and end, or past, present, and future. Although we experience the soul as on a journey toward the ultimate unification of meyuchad, meyuchad has, like the other two states, "already" and "always" (using the temporal metaphors) existed.

God emanated Creation for God's creatures to experience God's flow of blessing. In the upper worlds, beyond time and space, separation is not measured by the spatial dimension of distance. It is measured by degrees of similarity and difference. As it is God's nature to give, God forms Creation in order for it to receive. As receiving is different from giving, so is Creation separated from God.

In the Jewish Tanach, Christian Bible, Muslim Qur'an, and the sacred texts of other human faiths, the metaphor for that flow of blessing is light. In Kabbalah, human beings are the vessels that receive that light. Our souls are the light of blessing that our bodies receive. Our bodies are the garments for our souls. When writing about the "body," Ashlag refers not just to the physical body itself but, rather, to the soul's desire to receive the light for itself alone. We have to be able to receive in order for God to give. Yet by receiving, we manifest our difference, and therefore our distance, from the God with whom we yearn to reunite. As the soul awakens to this dilemma, it seeks to overcome the impulse to receive for itself alone. With effort sustained by divine intention, the soul transforms the will to receive for itself alone into the will to receive for the sake of giving. Rather than holding the light, the soul emanates it forth. It can direct its flow either back to its ultimate Source or, by aligning itself in affinity of form with God's desire to bestow blessing on Creation, onto the material world, particularly its living forms including other people and the natural world.

How is it possible for human beings to have learned this wisdom? If the ultimate source of all being is beyond the limits of human comprehension, how can we have any awareness of its existence? How can the complex tapestry of abstraction that constitutes kabbalistic cosmology explain profound and unmistakable human experiences of dialogue with the presence of God? What of the prophets' accounts and the authentic lived experiences of devoutly religious, pious individuals who speak to us of experiencing God's passions of love, indignation, compassion, or sorrow? Answers for these questions may be found in the idea of *tsimtsum*, a Hebrew word meaning contraction or divine self-concealment.

In kabbalistic cosmology, tsimtsum affords an answer to another challenging question: if God is all and everything, how is it possible for God to create anything? A creation is, after all, by its nature different and therefore separate from its creator. In the Kabbalah of Yitzhak Luria (the *Ari*, or Lion, a sixteenth-century kabbalist in Tsfat, Israel), tsimtsum is the process by which God produced Creation. In order to create, God contracted Godself, thus producing a "space" of emptiness. In the Lurianic creation myth, God fashioned vessels within that emptiness to receive the light of blessing. The first time that God emanated the light, it was more than the vessels could bear and they shattered. We live in a later version of Creation; our vessels are less vulnerable to shattering. It is our obligation to practice tikkun olam, to repair the brokenness of our world, to find the shattered remnants of the original vessels, which contain remnants of the original light of Creation, and to return the light to its Source.

Why are our vessels less vulnerable to shattering? This is not merely a matter of sturdier vessels. Drawing on another sense of tsimtsum, we may find answers to the question of how it is possible for human beings to experience God's presence. Knowing our fragility as vessels, God recognizes that we would shatter if we were to receive the full intensity of the light of blessing. God therefore diminishes Godself, reducing the intensity of the light as it descends through a series of worlds, flowing through the channels of the Sephirot of each world. Tsimtsum makes it possible for us to engage openheartedly in intimate dialogue with our God without dissolving or shattering.

The rich, complex language of Kabbalah thus forms the lens through which I invite you to witness the journey of my soul in this lifetime. Two years after I began working on *Engaging with Spirituality in Family Therapy*, I started to correspond with Yedidah Cohen, a Kabbalah teacher who lives in Tsfat. I sent her an extract from my memoir that documented my journey from the childhood dream that sparked my spiritual yearning to the moment in synagogue, five years after Jacob's death, when I experienced his soul reuniting me with the compassionate Presence of God. Yedidah responded warmly, telling me that, of course, God did not die when I was a child but that the light had been too intense for my vessel to contain it, thus shattering the vessel that was my young self. The more I have since learned Kabbalah, the more this explanation resonates with my understanding of my soul's journey.

In the years through childhood, adolescence, and early adulthood, I was unconsciously building a sturdier vessel to receive the light of blessing. In high school, I learned a meditation practice that did not require belief in God. I also found, in Nikos Kazantzakis's sequel to the *Odyssey*, a map for a spiritual journey that reaches beyond the limit of a personified God. In college, my experiences with the psychedelic drug LSD afforded me direct encounter with the Unity of all being without my needing to recognize that Unity as the author of Itself. I studied the writing of Jewish philosopher Baruch Spinoza, whose pantheist theology I could live with, as it did not threaten me with the idea of a God who could be in relationship with me—and therefore abandon me.

Almost on a different track, I developed as a social activist, thus honoring the legacy of my father's and his ancestors' embrace of action for social justice embodied in Jesus' "social gospel," a gospel whose roots, years later, I would come to recognize in the Jewish prophets' calls to repair our broken world.

I found myself drawn to the company of the occasional freelance minister or priest who would visit our campus to awaken the souls of its students. I was not tempted to adopt their religion, but I was curious about my ancestral pastoral legacy and moved by their faith and spiritual presence.

Throughout those formative years of early life I had little intuitive awareness and no reflective understanding of the deep inner conflict between my love and fear of God, nor of my struggle over being called to serve. There was a part of me that knew with unshakable certainty that God had called me by my own name, and that felt with the same certainty that I was loved by a being whose love was wider and deeper than the ocean. There was another part of me that felt utterly and eternally abandoned by God's stunning announcement of God's impending death. For a child's mind, the prospect of abandonment evokes existential dread: how can I survive if there is no one to take care of me? As this part of me felt existential dread of abandonment, another part dreaded being crushed by the impossible responsibility of carrying on God's work without God's loving Presence. These parts, fragments of the shattered vessel for my childhood soul, remained hidden from full conscious awareness much of my early life, until the crisis in my early twenties in graduate school, precipitated by the assassination of Dr. Martin Luther King.

How is it possible for human beings to hide such strong emotions and states of mind from themselves, particularly when these mental and emotional states have such determinative effects on the course of their lives? That question has inspired the development of my chosen profession, from the work of Sigmund Freud to the contemporary Internal Family Systems (IFS) approach of Richard Schwartz. From the IFS perspective, I survived the childhood trauma by sending troubled parts of my fragmented self into exile, making them inaccessible to awareness in order to protect the rest of my developing self from being overwhelmed by intolerable emotional states. Doing so enabled me to go on but at the cost of self-constriction that restricted my access to the exiles' gifts of childlike wonder, awe, and curiosity.

Jewish mythical lore offers another metaphor for this process of sequestering yet retaining our brokenness. In the Bible, Moses came down from his first direct encounter with God to discover the children of Israel practicing idolatry, thus violating the first commandment that God's thunderous voice had uttered only days before when God had appeared to the assembled multitude. Moses threw to the ground the tablets on which were inscribed the covenant between God and the Israelites, breaking the tablets and nullifying the contract. According to a Jewish myth, after Moses and God had revived the covenant, inscribing it on new tablets, and Moses had placed the tablets in the ark, God told Moses to gather the broken pieces of the first tablets and place them together with the whole tablets in the ark. So it was that the Israelites carried both whole tablets and fragments of the shattered tablets with them on their journey.

Like the story of the whole and the shattered held within the ark, the story of the Jewish people contains evidence of deep love, faith, commitment, and connection between God and human beings, together with evidence of misunderstanding, estrangement, abandonment, rejection, and isolation. Together, these elements of love and fear combine in biblical tales of loyalty, faith, failure, exile, reconciliation, restoration, and redemption. As far as we may flee from the awesome responsibilities that Hashem assigned to our ancestors or stray from the path laid out for us when Hashem liberated us from Egypt, our sacred stories show us that there is always a path of return, *teshuvah*, restoration of our relationship with the God who calls to us.

Fragments of my shattered soul cried out to me from their exile when I listened to broadcast recordings of Dr. King's prophetic voice from the night before his assassination. Drawing on the story of the intimate relationship between God and Moses, Dr. King told us that God had shown him that his life was drawing to its close and had granted him a vision of the ultimate redemption of the world. Although I did not consciously retrieve the memory of my childhood shattering, I could no longer suppress the belief that God can and does appear to God's mortal servants. Love overcame fear, and I threw myself into service. With desperate recklessness I cast my graduate studies aside, embarking on an impossible individual effort to organize the Boston Center for the Liberation of Revolutionary Consciousness, adopting the conceit that I would somehow in the process become ordained as a "lay minister." The vessel of my being could not contain the contradictions in my life, and the vessel shattered again, this time plunging me into madness.

I recounted that experience with psychosis in chapter two. I invite you to revisit that story with me now, written through the lens shaped by fifty years of life since that ordeal. Remember that I told others after I had recovered from psychosis that I never lost my mind but rather my self. Although that language at the time captured a vital truth about the experience, I now use different words to grasp the same clear memories of my journey through madness. I would still say that I lost my self, in that the adversary and companion of ego dissolved in the process. What I called my "mind" then I now recognize as my soul, which danced for a time in a clear flow of vivid conscious awareness. My soul reclaimed fragments that had been in exile since the childhood spiritual trauma and guided me in forming a sturdier vessel of self with which to continue the journey.

My soul selected the texts that I brought with me to the hospital, shaping an adventure in which I discarded the vessel of a self that was too constricted to continue my spiritual journey, and found my way to go on. In my interview with the admitting psychiatrist, I drew out my copy of Kazantzakis's memoir and declaimed from its epigraph, "I am a bow in your hands, Lord . . . Overdraw me, Lord, and who cares if I break!" I tried to master the method of prayer in *The Way of the Pilgrim*, but I could not. My mind was racing and soaring as my soul embraced its exiled fragments, and I could not concentrate on the text. Looking back with wisdom acquired over the succeeding decades, I understand that at the time I was not strong enough to maintain regular openhearted dialogue with my God. As I made the decision to make my life itself a ceaseless prayer, my soul set the course of my life toward a future time when I could safely engage in the dance with Hashem.

Re-entry into the world of the sane was painful. My life appeared to be ruined. I was unaware at the time of the hospital social worker's warning to Betty Ann that her husband had schizophrenia and that she faced a future with a husband vulnerable to repeated, unpredictable psychotic episodes. I was only to learn this from her years later, as our marriage was coming to an end. With the estrangement between us palpable but unspoken as I returned home from the hospital, I withdrew into self-absorption, terrified at the possibility of again losing my sanity. My self constricted as I set the modest goals of simply becoming a psychologist and earning a living to support my family. My ego strove to protect me from another experience of psychosis as I struggled to find my way back onto the path of professional training. My soul had set its course, however. As opportunities emerged for further spiritual growth, I chose to embrace them. My soul, strengthened by shedding some of its brokenness in the journey through psychosis, could speak with a stronger and clearer voice through my self's everyday conscious awareness.

Not long after my return to graduate school, my soul let me know that it could not survive the invisible whiteness of the culture of Harvard University. Harvard was so White that it did not know that it was White. I could not deny my ancestors' legacy of activism for social justice, my own lived experience in the Mississippi freedom struggle, nor my life in a multiracial marriage with multiracial children in a multiracial extended family of in-laws. I could see how the institution training me for my profession sustained the dominant discourse of White supremacy. Silenced by the power of a dominant discourse that rendered itself invisible and unnamable to protect the comfort of its privileged beneficiaries, my voice unheard in the Harvard setting, I felt my soul dying.

Life organizes itself around the seeker, affording possibilities and dangers on the path. Choices emerge; one is free to choose whether to embrace or avoid opportunities to bring forth into the world the spiritual truths for which one is particularly responsible. When I returned to graduate school after my psychiatric and spiritual crisis, two opportunities presented themselves in a clinical training seminar. One I chose to avoid. In a seminar discussion of the then-emerging field of family therapy, we heard a description of network therapy. My ego pulled me away from contemplating the practice, which for me embodied the shattered dream of moving my family to Africa to study tribal healing and which was uncomfortably similar to the pastoral work of my minister ancestors. The idea of network therapy threatened my ego's self-protective, safe, modest goals of acquiring a profession and supporting my family.

I seized on the other opportunity that appeared in that seminar. Guy Seymour, a young Black psychologist from a prominent Guyanese family, was invited as a guest to describe a pilot project he was developing in collaboration with Mike Rossi, the director of psychology at Boston City Hospital. I gratefully accepted Guy's invitation to participate in a program specifically designed to train psychologists for work with urban working-class people of color. I trained under Guy's supervision in a practicum at Boston City Hospital for several hours a week for a year, then volunteered for another year there in a part-time unpaid internship before starting a year of full-time formal internship at the Veterans Administration Hospital in Boston. This began my affiliation with the Center for Multicultural Training in Psychology (CMTP, originally named the Minority Training

Program, or MTP), which has persisted throughout my entire professional career.

As it happened, my decision to train with Guy led me to Carolyn Attneave and thereby to the very same practice of network therapy that my ego had resisted on first encounter. That decision, in turn, led me to my relationship with Ramón Jiménez and the moment when my ego dissolved into an experience of divine consciousness. When I returned from that moment to full mortal awareness, my intoxicated ego had reached greedily to absorb all the intense light into my body, a reckless move that could have led to another shattering. The laughter of my gentle mentor Ramón saved me from my impulsivity. With full sober awareness, I then set out to learn the steps of the dance with the Divine, to find safe ways to cultivate states of transpersonal awareness. The texts that I studied from a wide range of practical spiritual traditions, particularly Sufi texts, helped me to learn the dance. Through the lens that I have offered us, we can see that I was refining and strengthening the vessel to receive the light.

I learned much from practicing network therapy, both as conductor of the full-scale network assemblies developed by Carolyn and her colleague Ross Speck and by doing the community organizing of "community network intervention" that Carolyn had developed before she worked with Ross. You may remember that I could not serve as conductor for the first network that I assembled as I do not speak Spanish. Ramón was a member of that network. After Ramón had opened my spiritual awareness, I was able to step into the role of network assembly conductor, which indeed can be understood as akin to the role of a shaman. Relying on members of my team to guide me, when necessary I could as conductor allow my ego to dissolve into the intense field of physical, emotional, and spiritual energy in an assembly. In that altered state, I could allow my words to be shaped by that experience of resonance with the collective unconscious mind of the assembled group. Those words offered new possibilities for hope and healing.

Working with a network perspective to organize communities in Lynn, I came to recognize patterns of synchronicity, apparent coincidences that cohere in a design around people's lives on their souls' spiritual journeys. Later, in my community network practice with troubled networks of parents and educators centered on children having school difficulties, I learned to cultivate a detached awareness of the influence of my person on the people with whom I engaged. Facilitating conversations in the highly polarized sectors of the networks of troubled children,

I could hold people in states of loving awareness as I witnessed and retold redeeming stories of love and caring, carrying them in my person from one polarized group to another.

Later still, as a volunteer helping my friend David Hammerman develop his skills in hypnosis to help people access their souls' memories of past lives, I experienced moments of a previous incarnation. I encountered images of being expelled from a monastery, of becoming recognized as a healer in my community, and of deep regret on my deathbed, when I was surrounded by that loving community yet yearning for spouse and children I never had known in that life. As a client of psychologist and trained shaman Ann Drake, David's colleague, I learned of a still earlier life in which my ego's greed to acquire secret knowledge had provoked frightened villagers to kill and dismember both my wife and me.

These experiences of my soul's earlier journeys tell a story of struggling to fashion a vessel strong and safe enough to contain the awesome light of the sacred and of dangerous impulses to reach for more than it could hold. That heedlessness was apparent in my melodramatic citation of Kazantzakis's memoir on my admission to the psychiatric hospital, inviting God to overdraw me as a bow in God's hands. God's mercy spared me then, and it was more than fifty years later, at my sister's deathbed with a stronger vessel tempered by loss and shaped by mindful self-cultivation, that I could access the secret of direct engagement with God in the pages of *The Way of a Pilgrim*.

My journey through psychosis was my last solo wandering as a seeker. On the next major occasion, Ramón was there to laugh and gently protect me from my greed after that moment of dissolving into divine consciousness. Later, Brian Collins recruited me to become a serious student of Chi Gong. I acquired the skill of accessing and directing subtle energy and cultivated a stance of obedience to my master's guidance. When I went on a spiritual journey in a shamanic training workshop led by Ann Drake, my spirit guides led me to the enormous library of secret knowledge, letting me discover for myself that the pages were blank in the books that I grabbed so greedily. One of my guides had then guided me to sit at the piano and practice scales. For a time, I thought that my Chi Gong study embodied the metaphorical task of practicing scales. It did provide me with a stable root for my shamanic abilities. Those abilities allowed me to perceive the multitudes from past, present and future who emerged in the synagogue when the Torah was taken out of the ark. This inspired the decision to convert and to study with my Rabbi. I found many opportunities to "practice scales," as I learned enough Hebrew to study and to learn more deeply.

Although my heart broke when Jacob died, my soul's vessel did not shatter. My soul found its way to connect with Jacob's and accompany it on its path of return to the Source. My soul received the light needed for the task, for the sole purpose of caring for my beloved son. The vessel became stronger and more capacious as I developed the capacity to receive for the purpose of giving. Emerging from the ritual bath of the mikveh as a Jew, I began my transition from seeker to servant of God. The childhood trauma of separation had not yet healed. I kept my experience of God at a safe theological distance from a genuine dialogue in which I might yet again be devastated by abandonment. Jacob's soul was my primary teacher in the five years between his death and the moment in synagogue when his soul healed the terrible breach enough for me to experience God's comforting compassion for my grief.

Even then, after that brief encounter with Hashem, I could not fully open myself to the flow of a dialogical dance with my God, the flowing intimacy so exquisitely embodied in the words of the Song of Solomon in the Bible. It was, nonetheless, for me the beginning of the end of a solo dance. The David who danced in the passage from 2 Samuel, the words from the Bible that began this section, danced alone. Ecstatic with his faith in the presence of God, he nonetheless kept a safe distance from the ark whose lethal power he feared.

It is through the words of the Psalms that we know the mythical David who balanced that fear with deep love and opened his heart to the risk and reward of intimacy with his God. It took six more years after Jacob opened my heart to divine comfort for me to receive the assurance that I can rely on the presence of God whenever I choose to accept it. In those intervening six years, the changes in my life accelerated as more and more threads made themselves apparent and wove themselves into a larger, more intricate tapestry.

FINDING GOD IN TEXT

At the end of chapter five, in the section "Time, Transition, and Transformation," I described taking a reflective pause in early winter, 2021, to contemplate the challenge of writing about events that had transpired since I began writing this memoir. Life for Jodie and me at that moment was in a process of profound transformation, as Jodie was undergoing the arduous treatment that saved her life, and I was responding to the challenges the situation demanded of me. In that pause, I reviewed my correspondence with Art Green, with the co-authors of *Engaging*, and with Yedidah Cohen. As I revisit and relive those moments, I reflect on the dance between text and direct experience, between words and wordless Knowing. It takes me to a moment studying *Zohar* with Yedidah Cohen when I shuddered with deep intuitive awareness of the Sephirah Binah (understanding) as it emerged from the Sephirah Chochmah (wisdom). As I review the correspondence with Art, I see how he and I, both of us seekers and intellectuals, find our way along the path between words and intuition.

During that pause, I came upon correspondence that Art and I had exchanged in the days leading up to Rosh Hashanah in 2011, five and a half years after Jacob's death. I uncovered a forgotten prelude to the moment that Jacob's soul had led me to the comfort and intimacy of God's compassionate presence.

The correspondence reveals that I had been preparing myself—intellectually, emotionally, and spiritually—for that moment of relational restoration with God. Using the vessel metaphor, I see that I was strengthening and clarifying the vessel of my being for a direct encounter with the God who had appeared to me in childhood. I needed to be open to the flow of intense emanation from the source, to allow it to flow through me without shattering me.

I had written to Art about my struggle in reading Heschel's *The Prophets*, with its unmistakable claim that the biblical prophets had engaged in genuine dialogue with Hashem, resonating with their own emotions to divine pathos. I described my struggle to achieve simultaneous awareness of God Outside and God Within, to hold in a single experience both relationship and identity with the Divine. I asked him to suggest texts on which to meditate on divine immanence and transcendence, on God embodying and surrounding creation. Art's response was deeply thoughtful and transparently emotional. He wrote of his own struggle with the paradox of engaging with a God who is present in all of creation including ourselves, yet with whom we can, somehow, engage in the dynamic relationship between self and other.

Moved by the spiritual passion in Art's reply, I wrote to Art about my traumatic childhood experience of direct relationship with God and about peculiarities of my temperament that shape the relationship between my intellect and my emotions. I shared these thoughts:

> ... My first experience was deeply relational—Joy and wonder at hearing God call my name; overwhelming grief and loss at God's announcement that God was dying; enormous loneliness and fear over my inability to take on the responsibility with which I was charged ... As I reflect on my first encounter, and its effects on shaping my life, I turn to the metaphor of a stern Master in esoteric traditions (Zen or martial arts master; Castaneda's Don Juan)—challenging me with a lesson that feels beyond my capacity to learn, but refusing to withdraw the demand that I do so.
>
> I have a complicated relationship with theology. I don't want theology to obstruct my efforts to experience the Divine directly. Yet, theology provides scaffolding in two ways—both to hold myself in an experience, and also to lead myself into new experience. This is a particular instance of a more general issue that I have with intellectual activity. People who don't know me well often misread me when I talk intellectually about a matter concerning which I have powerful feelings—they either don't read the feelings, or don't believe that I could be feeling so strongly when I am speaking so intellectually.
>
> This is a matter of my temperament ... I still rely on some degree of internal conversation to make my way in the world, and I often use fairly abstract language to embody my passions. Yet, I am sensitive to how words and ideas can occlude important experiences, and strive for moments of wordless wonder. Theology sometimes can lead me to those moments, and it is also hard for me to sustain them unless they make sense to me theologically ... I know that I need to reopen my heart to the experience of being in a living relationship with God, even as I maintain a panentheistic perspective on the One of Whom I am a manifestation. I have some ideas, theology that could lead me to that opening of my heart. But, I must acknowledge the pain that makes this difficult. I was touched by the pain that you shared, stimulated by my request for guidance. As I reflect on the pain in my request and in your response, my thoughts go to Heschel's work on the Prophets, and the Prophets' resonation with Divine pathos. How can a human being presume to know Divine distress, and how can the All beyond all space, time, and human comprehension, feel pain? Heschel boldly asserts that the human heart can know the Divine's yearning for human recognition and loyalty, but stipulates that we can only know those

> elements of the Divine that are accessible to human capacities to know God—that what we know of God's experience of us is all that can be accessible to our awareness. I can feel myself, even as I write, resisting this idea. My work is to distinguish my intellectual/theoretical reservations from fear of the pain that I experienced as a child.

Reading those words that I wrote days before Jacob's soul opened me to that moment of dialogical engagement with the Divine, I see the dance between text and wordless experience, the effort to form a vessel strong enough and sufficiently transparent to receive the light. Rediscovering the text of the correspondence, I recognize that what I remembered after that experience of God's presence in synagogue was the experience itself, not the careful scaffolding that I built to prepare myself for the event. Yet, with the text to remind me, I see that the scaffolding prepared me for that wordless experience of allowing Jacob's soul to guide me in synagogue.

Writing to Art had afforded me a vehicle for healing, as I put my fear of the childhood pain into words. It cleared my mind to exercise theological imagination, using the idea of tsimtsum to speculate about the possibility of relationship with Oneness of whom I am but a manifestation. I wrote:

> I will share some of the theory/theology that I hope will provide me a scaffold for an experience of relationship with God, and a vessel in which I can in the future continue to experience that relationship... The ideas start with the premise that we are formed *b'tselem Elohim* [in the image of God]. Although God is beyond our knowing, we know that our qualities as human beings are manifestations of the Divine... As a psychologist, I do know a few things about human qualities. Human beings are intrinsically relational. The capitalistic fantasy that human beings are by nature self-seeking individuals is scientifically indefensible. If you take a human being who is twenty minutes old, hold her up to your face, open your mouth, and stick out your tongue she will, if she has been looking at your face, open her mouth and stick out her tongue in return.[68] We are born with a map of our own body and a map of another person's body and the capacity to translate from one map to another. Our relationality is embodied from the beginning. The infant's brain cannot develop normally outside of relationship with a caretaker, whose mature brain creates the scaffolding for the development of the less mature brain...

It's easy enough for me to understand theoretically that God as caring, loving, jealous, yearning, etc., human experience of God within the limits of human capacity, is God as experienced from a lower rung. One of the many ways that Zeitlin appeals to me is this idea that one experiences distinction from a lower rung, and unity at the highest of rungs.[69] Yet, as I reflect on Zeitlin's writing, and the wisdom from which it draws, there is more to the story. God chooses to emanate, and God relates to Creation with love and concern. Perhaps this idea is more than human projection. If we are indeed created *b'tselem Elohim*, then our capacities for love and concern mirror the nature of the One who created the world... I think that the gate for me is *tsimtsum* ... As I write, I feel the tears come, as I finally face what has been gnawing at the edge of awareness for several days now. What was God's telling me that God was dying, just after calling my name and manifesting to me, if not withdrawing God's Presence from me? What have I been doing since then, if not trying to repair that awful breach, by struggling to carry out God's impossible mandate?... Even before this awareness, your letters have had me thinking about how it is that one can seek relationship with a Being that one knows one is a part of. Flipping the idea of the Maggid of Mezritch, why can't a human being, formed *b'tselem Elohim,* exercise *tsimtsum,* withdrawing oneself from awareness of one's identity with the Divine to experience relationship with the Divine?... I can feel myself teasing the knot apart, but there is work yet to do. I suspect that there will be moments more like the severing of the Gordian knot, or the *Chasidic* idea of how to break the lock when one has lost the key...

That Chasidic idea of breaking the lock when one has lost the key is to "smash it with a broken heart," as I was to do days after I wrote those words to Art, when I wept for the dead son whose living soul was so profoundly present in my heart. After that event, when I remembered that wordless experience, and not all the words I wrote to Art, I was living the truth of Rabbi Zalman's aphorism, one of the epigraphs to this memoir.[70] I had prepared the vessel of my understanding. I had not treated that vessel as if it were as essential as the light it contained.

The Sufi sage Niffari's aphorism about travel with and without a vehicle, the other epigraph, captures the interdependence of words and wordless spiritual experience.[71] If we become attached to words, no matter how much we need them as our guide, we lose our access to the experiences to which words can guide us.

Six years later, after the correspondence with Art written only days before Jacob's soul reconciled my relationship with the God whom I had lost in childhood, I would write to my fellow *Engaging in Spirituality in Family Therapy* authors of another turning point in that relationship. By that time, the writing that we authors were doing together was illuminating a deeper truth about the dance between language and experience in human spirituality.

Turning the kaleidoscope of memory, contemplating the course of my spiritual journey, I observe experiences leading me to texts and texts leading me to experiences. Lessons from Christian Sunday School texts prepared me to recognize that the words in my childhood dream were uttered by God, as I had understood God at the time. In adolescence, a text on Buddhist meditation rescued me from the torments of rumination over fruitless words of prayer. An adolescent absorbed in the poetry of Kazantzakis's *Modern Sequel to the Odyssey*, I internalized the journey metaphor as I traveled with Odysseus on his quest for spiritual wisdom. In college, I ingested the mind-altering discourses of Timothy Leary and Ram Dass (Richard Alpert), along with the psychedelic chemicals that transformed their experiences—and mine. My social justice activism and my marriage to a Black woman with two sisters in the Black Panther Party led me to regular weekly reading of *The Black Panther* newspaper. Dread at the prospect of racist genocide shaped our plan for safety in a career that would take us to West Africa, where I would study African spiritual approaches to healing mental illness. In the throes of the psychosis that disrupted those plans, I entered the hospital challenging the admitting psychiatrist by reading the reckless prayer with which Kazantzakis opened his memoir. In the hospital, I struggled to master the text of *The Way of a Pilgrim*, to which I would return, older, wiser, and deeply grounded in my adopted Jewish faith, many years later as I kept company with my dying sister.

As I learned the practice of network therapy, I resisted Carolyn Attneave's words, reinforced by texts she and her colleague Ross Speck had authored, enjoining me to conduct network assemblies in the role of a shaman. So it was that, because I couldn't speak Spanish, I could not conduct the meetings of the first network that I assembled. I was thirty years old and already clearly on the journey of a seeker, but I was not prepared for the shamanic role of network assembly conductor.

The course of my spiritual journey was increasingly directed by the synchronistic patterning of the opportunities I encountered and the choices I made. When I learned about Ramón, who had attended the network assemblies, I chose to visit with him and to accept with some trepidation his esoteric teachings. It was no accident that we had so little spoken language in common. The balance between words and wordless experience needed to be shifted dramatically toward the latter to circumvent my powerful intellectual defenses against a way of knowing that so profoundly subverted the rational, scientific world view to which I was tightly clinging, still terrified by the risk of another psychosis.

Paradoxically, it was the dread of losing my mind that started me on the course of reading as widely as I could across a range of esoteric writings, beginning to build the bookshelf that I described in the introduction to this book. My conscious intention was self-protection; in my youthful arrogant pride I fancied that by immersing myself in a wide range of mystical traditions I could extract the common meanings shared at their cores and subject those claims to scientific examination. The momentum of my spiritual journey overcame this effort to protect my sanity by relying on the constrictions of intellectual speculation. Reading works by Castañeda and other mystical writers opened my vistas, activated my curiosity, and amplified my spiritual yearning. It did not, however, provide a safe refuge from my fear. I found that safety and refuge in the transcendent moment when Ramón opened me to divine consciousness. It provided me with a touchstone for further reading and exploration, secure in the knowledge that I knew what I was seeking and determined to cultivate my capacity to enter into that state of awareness freely, safely, and intentionally. Thanks to Ramón, I could thenceforth freely and confidently step into the role of network assembly conductor.

As I refined the intentionality of my search, the universe offered more opportunities for further ascent. As I broadened the scope of my reading, I was curious when I read about Kabbalah but felt that one needed to be a practicing Jew to enter that domain. I could not have predicted the profound and disruptive changes that were to set the stage for my conversion to Judaism thirty years after my visits with Ramón. Brian Collins was to be my next guide and teacher. His wisecracking, working-class Boston Irish style was a useful corrective to my cerebral self-importance. With the gift of intuitive perception that he had refined with his own spiritual practice, he recognized my spiritual striving. He relied on instruction, demonstration, and correction of my practice more than lengthy verbal explanation as he guided me to learn the body movements of Chi Gong and to master the flow of subtle energy through my body. I knew that his work was informed by Taoist philosophy, but he left it to me to struggle alone with the ambiguity and allusiveness of the *Tao Te Ching*.[72]

Physical health issues had led me on the path to find Brian, to whom I had been referred by an acupuncturist. When another health issue emerged later, our friends the Hammermans recommended that I consult with their colleague, the shaman Ann Drake. This led to the experience I described earlier of journeying in the spirit world to enter a vast library of texts—the pages of which were blank. In that same journey, my spirit guide's beckoning me to sit next to her on the piano bench and practice scales embodied the lesson that, at that stage of my journey, I needed to cultivate myself further before I would have the capacity to ascend higher solely by engaging with text.

In the decade before I seriously contemplated conversion, I learned to live a Jewish life, with the conscious intention to honor my agreement with Jodie to raise our child as a Jew. I got basic instruction in biblical and liturgical Hebrew, participated in synagogue worship, and explored English translations of sacred texts, unaware that I was laying the foundation for the Jewish education I would later need for conversion. I was still averse to accepting any formal religion and grateful for the role of a "stranger in the camp," living in Jewish community without considering myself a Jew. The more I learned, the more I resonated with the opportunities for spiritual nourishment in Judaism, until the moment I recognized that it was time to decide to become a Jew. That moment arrived in synagogue services when the Torah was brought out of the ark.

Jewish religious texts are rich with myth, metaphor, and allusive symbols, keys to doors into mystical experience. In the centuries that we lived in the Middle East and Spain under Muslim rule, Jews and Christians were known as "people of the book." This title, based on our relationships with our sacred texts, afforded us protective status in Muslim societies. Our attachments to our texts resonated with Muslim devotion to their sacred books: *Qur'an*, *Hadith*, and *Sunna*.

The most sacred Jewish text is the Torah, which consists of the books of Moses, the first five books in both Jewish and Christian Bibles. In Jewish religious services, the Torah is treated with deep reverence and awe. It is inscribed by hand with quill and ink on parchment scrolls that are housed in the ark, often in the form of a cabinet behind a curtain, at the front or center of the synagogue. The scrolls are clothed in decorated garments, with breastplate and crowns made of precious metal.

When it is time for a reader to chant the text of the portion for the week (the same portion, or parsha, read on the same week by Jews all over the world), the Torah is removed from the ark with singing and great ceremony before its decorations and garment are removed and it is unrolled on the lectern for reading. According to Jewish myth, when the Torah is removed from the ark all the Jews who have ever lived, who are currently alive, and who are yet to be born assemble together for the reading, in a mystical reenactment of the moment at Mount Sinai when God spoke in a thunderous voice to the children of Israel.

In the years preparing for Jacob's bar mitzvah, we attended weekly services fairly regularly. By that time in my journey, with the intuitive capacity I had cultivated through my exploration of shamanism, I could sometimes sense the presence of immaterial spirits. At the moment in services when the Torah was taken from the ark, I could feel the ancestors joining the congregation, gathering for that awesome moment of revelation at Sinai.

Knowing how vulnerable one can be to mistaking the operations of imagination for the subtle phenomena of mystical awareness, I simply allowed myself the experience without drawing any conclusions. After the experience recurred reliably through multiple worship services over time, I made the decision to become a Jew. As we had once decided to adopt a child whom we chose to raise as a Jew, so would I decide to adopt the children of Israel as my people. In the words of Ruth, the ancient convert and an ancestor of King David, "Where you go, I will go, and where you stay, I will stay. Your people will be my people and your God my God."[73]

As I lay the kaleidoscope of memory down for a moment, I contemplate how decades of spiritual journey have led me to the path of Judaism. My deepest passions are often clothed in abstract theological and intellectual language. They have driven me to the project of writing this memoir, text that serves as a vehicle for me to serve my God and honor the legacies of my ancestral and adopted ancestors. My prayer is that, as you read my words in the text of this memoir, your heart opens to fuller awareness of the beauty of your own soul and the boundless love and glory of its Source.

As I write, I feel the presence of generations of my birth ancestors—Protestant ministers sitting in their studies writing their sermons in moments of timeless inspiration, struggling to capture in the manuscript before them the words flowing through them, transported to the moment when their voice will fill the house of worship, resonating with the emotions of congregants moved by the words in the manuscript that will lie before them on the lectern.

I feel the presence of my adopted ancestor Abraham, the ancestor of several religions, of whom God in Torah says, "In you shall all the families of earth be blessed."[74] I hear the voice of Moses bringing forth the words of Hashem, teaching the Israelites how to live in the world as a people treasured by God and responsible for bringing God's light to the world. I resonate with the passions of the biblical prophets, sharing God's pain at Israel's estrangement and calling for repentance and restoration.

Picking up the kaleidoscope again, I discern with humility and gratitude the patterns of beauty, meaning, and grace with which my life has been blessed and see how my relationship with text has been enriched and transformed over the decades of my life. I first encountered the Niffari quote in the epigraph when I was struggling with my fear of disruption by Ramón's loving instruction. Niffari's quote helped me to let go of my youthful grandiose ambition to generate texts that I dreamed would transform the field of psychology. At the time, I did not see how that impulse for domination and mastery was cloaked in relatively invisible privilege from entitlements including my whiteness, my gender, and my birth affiliation with the dominant religious discourse of my society. As I submitted to Ramón, I began to relinquish the colonizing mentality of Western scientific intellectual hegemony and learn to hold multiple perspectives without needing them to coalesce into singular unifying ideas. I would go on to explore texts from a range of spiritual traditions, not all of them Western or colonizing, although many of them insisted on their exclusive claims to the truth.

In my professional life, I sought to work with people and situations whose challenges would stretch me beyond the limits of my intellectual horizon. Teaching culturally sensitive family therapy to racially and culturally diverse cohorts of psychology interns, all well-trained in work with individuals, I came up with an aphorism to inspire openness, humility, and awe as they learned to work with challenging, complicated, and heartrending family situations. "Don't try to hold the complexity," I would urge them. "Let the complexity hold you."

When I first encountered family therapy, I was vulnerable to its exclusive truth claims, as it was still in its brash and arrogant youth as a disruptive movement within the field of psychotherapy. Experience quickly taught me that I could not be helpful to families if I clung with certainty to texts on theory or method as I sat with families struggling with their pain and helplessness.

So I learned to stay open and curious. Although I was passionate about my ideas, including the ideas and methods of family therapy in which I had been schooled, I learned to discard them instantly if they were not working. Long before I was to encounter postmodern ideas as they emerged in family therapy, I learned from my mentor Carolyn Attneave a stance of humility, openness, and curiosity. Carolyn, and the families I served, taught me deep appreciation that progress working with families and their networks is grounded in profound interdependence and respectful collaboration between therapists and those whom they serve.

When I did encounter postmodern ideas in the texts of constructivist, social constructionist, and collaborative language systems family therapists, I felt both intellectual excitement and increased confidence about my stance as a therapist. For years, I had been engaging with my patients as partners in a joint healing enterprise in which our success depended on respectful collaboration, rather than on my treating them as subjects of my expert interventions. I preferred this stance of open-hearted curiosity about what my patients and I would discover together, rather than a reserved professional stance interviewing patients to discern how would they fit within my explanatory models.

Meeting Jaakko Seikkula and learning the Bakhtinian ideas behind Jaakko's Open Dialogue approach resonated with what I had been teaching for years about engaging with complexity. Bakhtin borrowed the word "polyphony" from musical theory to capture the unpredictability and richness of meanings that emerge in the spaces between multiple speakers and listeners. The idea of meaning emerging from dialogical engagement among multiple speakers and listeners, rather than from speakers (or writers) alone, came to inform the rich conversations that emerged on pages of the text in *Engaging with Spirituality in Family Therapy*.

Jaakko's idea of shift from monologue to dialogue offered me language to understand the process in a full-scale network assembly, an early form of network therapy quite different from Jaakko's smaller-scale network meetings in Open Dialogue. Excited by the promise of Jaakko's approach to network therapy, I set out on an intellectual search. I wanted to understand how it was that the collective expression of sorrow and loss in a network assembly that Jodie, our colleagues, and I had witnessed creates the same shift out of monologue into dialogue that marks the healing process in Jaakko's much smaller network meetings.

I started reading widely and voraciously, exploring the works of Bakhtin[75] and his collaborator Volosinov,[76] and texts in developmental psychology, neuropsychology, and interpersonal neurobiology. At the culmination of my ten-year search, Jaakko generously agreed that I could co-author with him a paper he was working on, about the healing elements of therapeutic conversation.[77] My contribution to that article incorporated what I had discovered in that search.

In that same decade, I was preparing myself for conversion. As I began serious study of Jewish texts, I found Bakhtin's idea of polyphony resonating with what I was learning about scholarly study of the Hebrew Bible. The current scholarly consensus is that the text of our Bible (which Christians adopted as their "Old Testament") was skillfully assembled by redactors from at least four different manuscripts during the exile of the Judaean elite to Babylon in the sixth century BCE. Despite considerable overlap in their narratives, there were substantial differences between the manuscripts. Treating all the manuscripts as sacred, the redactors included substantially all of them in the canonical text of the Bible. They did not reconcile all the differences between them. One obvious example is in the book of *Bereishit*, Genesis, which includes two very different versions of the creation story.

The polyphonic structure of the text of our Bible compels Jewish readers to find meaning in the spaces between the disparate voices of the authors of its multiple source manuscripts. For centuries, all Jewish readers approached the text with uncritical belief in the sacred myth that the entire Torah had been dictated to Moses by God on Mount Sinai. Much of the Talmud, the foundational text of the religion of Judaism that emerged after the destruction of the Second Temple by the Romans, is devoted to reconciling apparent contradictions in biblical text. The Talmud itself is more transparently an assembly of multiple voices, a text that preserves the voices of *all* the parties to centuries of arguments over how to interpret text. Preservation of multiple voices in the text has for two millennia made the Talmud a flexible, generative source of ideas for generations of rabbis to consult for guidance as they interpret Jewish law in changing social, geographical, and historical circumstances—and for generations of Jews to argue over.

When I assured the rabbis of my beit din (the panel of rabbis who questioned me and determined my readiness to convert) that I would pursue my spiritual journey for the rest of my life as a Jew, I was but dimly aware of the vast landscape of text that has accumulated in Judaism over millennia. Even the proportion of Jewish texts that is available to me in English translation is more than I can hope to study in the remaining decades of my life. As I explore texts in Jewish history, in Kabbalah, Chasidut (the ideology of the Chasidic movement), the emerging literature of neo-Chasidism, and a range of other classic and contemporary Jewish writers, I feel the recursive generative flow between what I read and what I write.

Rabbi Andy Vogel introduced me to Rabbi Arthur Green, whose writing I had studied in my preparation for conversion and who was to become my friend. By way of introducing us, Andy sent Art the manuscript of my remarks to the congregation on the day of my conversion. That introduction to Art was occasioned by my urgent need to understand the text of his translation of a Chasidic master's instruction. Art's recommendation of a text at our first meeting opened the door to my study of Kabbalah. The friendship Art and I share includes exchanging our writing with each other.

At this late stage of my life, I often find deep spiritual meaning in loving exchanges with others as we engage over text. I cherish the community that assembled in sacred space as we co-authored *Engaging with Spirituality in Family Therapy*. Grounded in our different faiths, my daughter Jessica and I can be transported in our conversations about spirituality. In a conversation with Jessica, each of us informed by the texts of our respective traditions, we talked about the soul journey of Jessica's aunt and my sister Sheila. It was in that conversation that I first discerned that the idea of sacred space offered an answer to the question I posed to my fellow authors at the beginning of the *Engaging* project: how can a global culture affirming human spirituality avoid the perils of murderous religious particularism?

My friend Rockey Robbins and I share deep, loving conversation in sacred space in a video link between Oklahoma and Massachusetts. Deeply curious about Jewish texts, beliefs, and practices, Rockey shares lore from his Cherokee and Choctaw ancestors and from his wide reading in European philosophy, theology, and literature. As we share our reflections on the texts and stories that hold meaning for each of us, we savor sharing the nameless but achingly familiar feelings of sacred space and celebrate our conviction that Rockey and I are embodiments of the same soul, a belief that is grounded in the words and stories of each of our faith traditions.

It has been nearly five decades since my experiences with Ramón led me to abandon my grandiose ambition to master and then transform the literature of psychotherapy. My career followed paths of practicing and teaching the craft, producing occasional contributions to the professional literature along the way. I did not seek a career in academia, recognizing the limitations of my temperament, which resisted the disciplined practice required for comprehensive grasp of a body of literature. I am grateful for friendship with Art, as I often draw on his scholarly mastery of Jewish literature for guidance as I explore the vast domain of Jewish texts. In a recursive process of ascent to higher levels of spiritual experience, approaching that timeless, spaceless moment of awareness under Ramón's guidance, I find in Jewish texts transcendent experiences and guidance on how to walk in the world as a Jew. I engage dialogically with text, seeking inspiration rather than mastery. Words are important as vessels, but most important and primary for me is the light of wordless experience that they can, at moments, contain.

As I was writing this section, I encountered an unexpected posting from Valley Beit Midrash (A Jewish "house of study" based in Arizona) in my email inbox. The posting included a link to a video of a wide-ranging conversation between Art Green and Rabbi Shmuly Yanklowitz, the leader of Valley Beit Midrash.[78] Art's own words in that conversation, on how to engage with text ("Torah" in the inclusive sense of the texts of Jewish learning) capture my experience of finding God in text. Responding to Rabbi Yanklowitz's question about engaging with Torah, Art said,

> Number one: It's not about information. It's not about how much you know. It's about what the learning does to you. How the learning opens your heart. Think of learning as a devotional act, not as a something to make you smarter, not as something to make you be able to be to have an interesting cocktail conversation, think of learning as an act of worship. *Hatorah l'shma* [Torah for itself] doesn't really mean, according to the Chasidic masters, Torah for its own sake, but Torah for the sake of the *Shechina* [the lowest *Sephirah*, and the feminine Presence of God in the world], and that means for the sake of the Divine Presence that's in us and all around us. So use your learning in order to awaken something in yourselves, in order to awaken some kind of inner stirring. And if Torah isn't doing that for you, then either you're not studying the right books, you're not

studying with the right people, you're not studying the right way. Torah should be awakening and inspiring and exciting. And make sure it is those things.

There have been times for me when engagement with Jewish texts has stimulated extremely complex stirrings. Turbulent, confusing states of painful emotional disquiet entangled with spiritual inspiration have sometimes marked turning points on my journey. Such was the case in my reading Rabbi Joshua Abraham Heschel's *The Prophets*. So it was when I read Rabbi Yehuda Leib Ashlag's *In the Shadow of the Ladder*, which was to lead me to my newest teacher, Yedidah Cohen.[79]

PATTERNS IN THE TAPESTRY OF LIFE

In 2014, at the age of 69, I began assembling fellow authors for the *Engaging with Spirituality in Family Therapy* project, which I undertook for the same reason that I write this memoir: to seek a path toward cultural transformation of a world enslaved by the lethal illusion of individualism. That same year, a few months after my birthday, I got news of my sister Sheila's cancer. Brushes with my own skin cancer and heart arrhythmia that year further sharpened my awareness of mortality. My soul, when it left the company of wise mentors and companions in the spirit world to don the garment of this material embodiment as David Trimble, had chosen this particular life for particular purposes, purposes aligned with the divine plan of redemption. In the time remaining for this life, how clearly would I discern my soul's purpose?

As I write these words, approaching age 80, the patterns that emerge in the tapestry of my life affirm my soul's determination to weave the particulars of my birth, circumstances, and actions into a life of service to God and to the world of God's creation. Since childhood, when I needed to use words to make sense of other people and their mysterious ability to understand each other without explanation, my soul has been weaving the tapestry of my life with words. I draw forth the words of the memoir from memories, from reading, from writing, and from rich conversations with fellow seekers, multicolored threads that form patterns in the tapestry.

In my early seventies, having earlier made my way through Aryeh Kaplan's English translations of the foundational Jewish mystical texts of *The Bahir* (Radiance) and *Sefer Yetsirah* (Book of Formation), I started the project of reading through Daniel Matt's English translation of *The Zohar*. Living in the decade about which I now write, my writing draws from words in my correspondence with Art, with Yedidah, and with my fellow *Engaging* authors. Time loses its linearity as I feel the flow of recursive formation among words in my conversations with teachers, words in conversations with fellow seekers, words exchanged with my wife and first editor Jodie, words exchanged with our son Ransom and daughter Jessica, words in the memoir, and words in my correspondence. I see patterns emerge as words flow between settings.

God willing, and with God's help, the memoir's narrative will draw to a close with the manuscript prepared for publication within the last remaining year of my seventies. The seventh decade of my life has marked the sacred time that Sheila and I shared in the last years of her life, including the Andrew Holocek workshop on the Tibetan Buddhist vision of dying. Over four years of conversation and correspondence among the authors of *Engaging* culminated in that book's 2018 publication, three years into the decade.

Conversations with Jessica as we reflected on Sheila's soul journey crystallized for me the idea of sacred space, inspired originally in conversations with my friend and colleague Hugo Kamya about Bakhtin and spirituality and stimulated further in conversations among the *Engaging* authors. It was in this decade that a conversation with Art led me to change direction in my metaphysical practice of psychotherapy. As I find ways to engage and awaken my patients' souls, firmly rooted in my identity as a Jew and openheartedly engaging with them however they construct their religion or spirituality, I see how my stance as a therapist is shaped by what I learned in relationships with mentors, colleagues, and fellow seekers, particularly with Jessica, Hugo and the Spiritans, with Rockey and other *Engaging* authors.

The decade of my seventies was marked by many reminders of mortality, starting with my sister Sheila's death from cancer. Midway through my seventies, in 2019, Jodie's father and her cousin nearly died in an accident, quickly followed by Jodie losing her cousin, our losing Ransom's wife and our daughter-in-law Kim, and my losing my brother Robin. In the midst of these losses, Jodie's father was diagnosed with life-threatening cancer. One year later, in 2020, Jodie's diagnosis of cardiac amyloidosis was confirmed the day before Yom Kippur. The reality of mortality, particularly in the nine days before we learned of the life-preserving treatment that would give us the blessing of Jodie's remission, was amplified in a world just starting to come to terms with the awful reality of the COVID pandemic.

The year before I turned seventy, I picked up a book on Kabbalah that I had acquired at a conference book table a few years before. My experience with that book opened the path for me to seek out my next teacher and guide, Yedidah Cohen.

LEARNING WITH YEDIDAH

As I looked over books on the table at a conference on intersections among psychology, philosophy, and theology, one book, *In the Shadow of the Ladder: Introductions to Kabbalah*, caught my eye.[80] I was curious about what I might learn about Kabbalah from this text, a set of English translations and commentary by Mark and Yedidah Cohen on the *Introduction to the Zohar* and *Introduction to the Ten Sephirot* by Rabbi Yehudah Leib Ashlag. At a different conference at a later time, I picked up *A Tapestry for the Soul: The Introduction to the Zohar* by Rabbi Yehudah Leib Ashlag.[81] I bought each because it caught my eye. I did not notice at the time that both were about the same twentieth-century kabbalistic sage, nor that the two books shared the same translator and commentator.

I spend most Shabbats studying Jewish texts. I acquire texts faster than I can read them. I was seventy, at least a year after I acquired *In the Shadow of the Ladder*, when I started to read it. I was astonished by the accessibility of the text. Even in English translation, the language of most texts on esoteric Judaism is intentionally obscure, allusive, and ambiguous. The texts embody the hidden or secret. Many are transcriptions of oral teaching or were written with the intention that they be read only under the tutelage of an adept teacher. In contrast, Rabbi Ashlag articulated straightforward and clear kabbalistic explanations of Torah. I entered the text greedily, my ego pressing me to ascend from rung to rung speedily and to great heights. The language was straightforward; I thought that the way was clear.

I soon found that obscurity in the language of a text was not the only obstacle to my ascent. Even without its disguises, I found the language of Kabbalah to be abstract and complex. When I study sacred text, I seek for fully embodied experience of the meanings carried by the words. When I encounter what are for me new meanings, it takes time for me to assimilate them into my being. My eagerness to learn pressed me forward through the pages of *In the Shadow of the Ladder*, but I soon discovered my limitations. Striving to read as fast as I could grasp the ideas intellectually, my intellect raced ahead of my body. I frequently fell into deep sleep as I was reading. Waking, I would force myself into full awareness and struggle to figure out where I had been in the text before I began to drift off. By the end of the summer, I had finished the book, but I was well aware that I had not studied it with the full concentration it required and that I had absorbed little of what it had to teach. I put it aside with some humility about my aspirations and attainments, setting the intention to read it again when I had acquired more spiritual maturity. This was yet another form of the lesson that I took from my earlier shamanic journey in which I had greedily grasped for a volume from the library to which I had traveled, only to find that the pages were blank.

A year later, I picked up *A Tapestry for the Soul*, Yedidah Cohen's assembly of her commentaries and translations of Rabbi Ashlag's writings. Approaching this text with the humility gained from my encounter with *In the Shadow of the Ladder*, I was filled with wonder and gratitude as I felt led by a patient teacher to clearer and deeper understanding of Ashlag's work. I learned from reading the pages of *Tapestry* that Yedidah was a very active teacher, leading study groups "from all parts of the Jewish spectrum" in Hebrew and English, broadcasting and podcasting lessons on Rabbi Ashlag's Kabbalah, and maintaining a "constantly evolving" website. I set the intention to study with Yedidah and sent her a message through her website.

Although I had not yet fully articulated my ideas about access to sacred space through dialogue, I was beginning to develop an intuitive awareness of that process through my experience corresponding with the *Engaging with Spirituality in Family Therapy* authors. I hoped to invite a similar experience in correspondence with Yedidah. I decided to send her two manuscripts, an extract from my memoir draft and a meditation I had written on the Jewish *Kedushah* prayer. As I could not send attachments in a message through her website, in my first communication to her I presumed to ask her for an email address to send her the manuscripts. I told her that I was seeking a teacher of Kabbalah and gave a brief account of my experience escorting Jacob's soul to its source in the days after his death.

Yedidah's prompt response was warm and inviting. She gave me an email address to send the attachments and shared her reflection on my experience with Jacob and his soul. Reading her words now as I write, five years after I received them, I am struck by her teacher's voice in this, her first email to me. Embedded in simple language, the depth of whose meanings I could not at the time fully grasp, was wisdom that I have since come to appreciate more as I have learned so much from her teaching and writing. Responding to my account of accompanying Jacob's soul, she wrote:

> You were permitted to experience so much and go so high, because your motive was such a pure one. You were not looking for Divine revelation for the sake of achieving ecstasy or anything like that, but out of a very clean motive, of helping your son's soul ascend on his journey... Rabbi Yehudah Leib Ashlag teaches very clearly that only for the sake of giving may we receive. Even God's revelation, can only be received for the sake of giving... all suffering, especially if offered to HaShem, helps all of Mankind purify.

I sent the attachments to Yedidah at the personal email address she provided. The extract provided a condensed account of my memoir-in-progress. It recounted the journey from my childhood experience of God's manifestation and abandonment, through my adolescent discovery of texts that led me onto a self-conscious spiritual journey, my exploration of psychedelics, my learning from Ramón and from Brian, losing Jacob and connecting with his soul, and Jacob's soul leading me into the embrace of a loving God. Her response led me deeper into lessons that I am still learning from studying with her. She wrote,

> It appears to me that the experience you had when you were nine was of having a vessel for God's light which was pure, but limited in that you experienced His love. But you also needed to allow it to grow and change. It was the vessel that broke and died, not God's light broke or He Himself died. For that is impossible. Simply, the vessel needed to be let go of to allow the new vessel to emerge, which actually it did eventually... Similarly with Yaakov's [Jacob's] soul... It depends with which vessel you are using to perceive it, and you probably don't have conscious choice in this. Sometimes you experience his soul with a vessel which is filled when you see his soul merged with the One, sometimes you experience his soul when you are using a vessel which is filled when you experience his own personal being. Actually Rabbi Ashlag teaches that although we feel we choose the vessel, the ultimate truth is that HaShem also chooses the vessels for us.

As I write, it is hard for me to remember that I have known Yedidah for only five and a half years. We have yet to meet in person; our plan to meet where she lives in Tsfat was interrupted by the Covid pandemic. We know each other through our email correspondence and from studying together on Skype. We met sporadically at first; eight times over the first four years after I met her. I attended a few of her group lessons, often organized around the kabbalistic meanings embedded in the calendar of Jewish annual holidays, and we arranged some individual lessons. In the fifth year after our initial email exchange, I began studying more regularly with her in individual lessons, at least once a month.

In the time that I have known Yedidah, a clearer picture of my soul's purpose has emerged from the threads in the tapestry woven over the course of this mortal life. Embodied in the threads is the story of my soul's journey, its achievements and its remaining tasks. As the picture takes shape, it becomes more difficult to separate out the threads that constitute the whole or to adhere to the linear temporal sequence of narrative. The correspondence among the authors of *Engaging with Spirituality in Family Therapy* developed in a Bakhtinian process of "interanimating voices" that brought forth the sacred in the "space between" helped to shape my experience of dialogue with Yedidah. I found myself sharing my correspondence with the authors with Yedidah, and my correspondence with Yedidah with the authors.

Early in our correspondence, Yedidah told me that she was having significant health issues, and I asked permission to pray for her. My capacity to engage beyond the limits of materiality had been shaped by lessons I had learned from Ramón and from Brian. My practice of requesting permission before I pray for someone comes from my exploration of shamanic practice, as I have seen that my projection of consciousness into immaterial worlds sometimes can have effects in the material world. My spiritual healing practice emerges from the tapestry of my life, which transforms itself as my soul continues along its journey.

A year and a half before I began corresponding with Yedidah, as Rockey and I were corresponding about the draft of his chapter in *Engaging with Spirituality in Family Therapy*, he shared that he and his wife Sharla were facing a serious emerging health crisis. I told him that I was praying for Sharla's health, writing, "Jacob and I have been praying together for Sharla, you, and the family." As he and Sharla worked with Western medical and with Indian healers, Rockey wrote, "Jacob has been around." I wrote, "The prayers continue. Jacob is teaching me to work with him—he works in the world when I give him a root in my mortal body. Everyone rises together—Sharla, you, me, Jacob."

By the time that I began praying for Yedidah, I had begun to let go of relying on Jacob's soul to guide me on my way through worlds beyond the limits of materiality. Aware that I was praying for the healing of an observant Jew, I set my intention carefully. I relinquished any belief that I would be the agent of healing, humbly submitting myself to the will of Hashem. I learned to enter the upper worlds without the accompaniment of Jacob's or Sheila's souls.

As I write, I am reminded of the biblical story of Joseph, whose life experience taught him to let go of the ego of his youth, with which he brashly boasted of his prophetic dreams to his father and brothers. As a man chastened by painful life experience, he was careful when he used his gift with Pharoah's servants to say, "Surely God can interpret" and to say to Pharoah, "Not I! God will see." As I prayed for Yedidah, accepting that the outcome was beyond my control, I projected my consciousness beyond the material world. Rather than asking Jacob's soul to channel the healing energy, I drew on Jewish ancestral imagery. Without reifying the images, I aligned myself with pious Jewish forebears whose power of imagination had generated experiences of approaching God on the throne of glory. I petitioned Hashem to heal, accepting that the outcome was beyond my power. As I prayed, humbly relinquishing control to Hashem, I experienced powerful energetic sensations in my body. I recognized that my material body was merely serving as a vehicle through which Hashem's healing light was flowing.

As I share below some lessons that I learned from my journey with Yedidah, please know that I have learned much more than is embodied in the anecdotes that follow. Much of what you have already read in this memoir has been shaped by my learning with her and by my encounters with other texts and teachers in the time since I first read *In the Shadow of the Ladder* and *Tapestry of the Soul*. What wisdom I have gained from those five years of learning shaped my words in some sections in chapters five and six, and all of this chapter.

I learned an important lesson about suffering from Yedidah after a couple of years struggling with Torah portions early in the book of Exodus, which describe the plagues in Egypt and the drowning of Pharoah's army. My synagogue invites its members to present occasional d'varim Torah, commentaries on the parsha (weekly reading of a portion of Torah) to the congregation on Shabbat. On one occasion, I chose at random a particular parsha from one of dates offered, and discovered to my discomfort that the portion I had chosen recounted the story of Hashem drowning Pharoah's army in the sea. Every year that I read the parsha, I am troubled by its account of God's deliberate "stiffening of Pharoah's heart," for the purpose of setting Pharoah in pursuit of the Israelites only to drown together with his army as the sea closed behind the fleeing Israelites.

Interpreters of this parsha can adhere closely to the words of the text, including God's explanation that God acts thus in order for the Israelites and the world to know of Hashem's great power and glory. As I prepared my d'var, this explanation did not suffice for me. Why would God intervene directly in the world to create more suffering, so soon after causing so much devastation with the plagues in Egypt? Were the plagues not enough? I chose to quote an interpretation by the rabbis of the Talmud that challenged the triumphalism in the text: "When the angels sought to sing a song to God while the Egyptians were drowning, God rebuked them, saying: 'While my creatures are drowning in the sea, you would sing a hymn?!'" When I delivered my d'var, I said, "according to the rabbis, God does not rejoice in the death of the wicked."

At the time I delivered that d'var, I had already begun working on *Engaging with Spirituality in Family Therapy*. I spoke in the d'var of my hope that the book would contribute toward the evolution of a global culture that could celebrate the universality of human spirituality beyond the limits of religious particularism. I suggested that one aspect of a future universalist global culture could be the cultivation of human hearts that are equally moved by the suffering of the Israelites and the suffering of the Egyptians.

Two years later, I volunteered to provide another d'var, for a date a month later than the month I had provided a d'var on the drowning of Pharoah's army. I hoped to avoid thereby my struggle with the apparent cruelty of God's punishments of the Egyptians. I had allowed myself to forget how the lunar calendar of the Jewish year often misaligns with the solar year of the secular calendar. My unconscious mind had led me to select the very parsha describing the plagues that caused so much suffering in Egypt. The struggle with the text that year was even more painful. In this parsha, God tells Moses repeatedly that he will "harden Pharoah's heart" in order for Pharoah to persist in refusing to release the Israelites from bondage. By hardening Pharoah's heart, God assures that more plagues will follow, each worse than the one before, culminating in God slaying the firstborn of the Egyptians.

So it was that ten days before the eleventh *yahrzeit* (death anniversary) of my own beloved son, I found myself preparing a d'var on a passage that describes God creating a situation in which the first-born of all Egypt, human and animal, are deliberately slaughtered by God's command. The passage ends with the commandment that the children of Israel conduct the annual ritual of Passover to commemorate the suffering and slaughter together with the resulting liberation. Every year that I read this parsha, my heart breaks when I come to the "loud cry in Egypt" when God strikes the firstborn of every Egyptian household.

"Not a coincidence!" was the subject line of Yedidah's email to me, two weeks after my first message to her and less than a week after her first reply. Yedidah told me that she had just learned from Mary, a Christian woman who had approached Yedidah to learn Kabbalah, that Mary's grandson Michael had died of a drug overdose. Mary had been getting Yedidah's help with her anguish over Michael's struggles with addiction. Like Jacob, Michael had struggled with self-destructive behavior. And, like Jacob, Michael had a radiant soul. He had served some time incarcerated for his addiction-related actions and was in an addiction rehabilitation facility when he died. Yedidah did not see it as coincidental that she had just heard of Michael's death days after learning about Jacob's life and death. She asked permission to put Mary and me in touch with each other. Mary and I corresponded by email. We were to meet in person sometime later when I attended a conference in Austin, Texas. Yedidah offered to meet online with Mary and me for a *shiur*, or a gathering to study text together.

Mary, Yedidah, and I met online in the shiur, which Yedidah dedicated to the memories of Michael and Jacob. During that meeting, days before I was to give my d'var, I brought my concerns about the parsha to Yedidah. Yedidah offered me a perspective on the text from her study of *Zohar*. From that perspective, one understands the Torah as embodying allusions to the journey of the reader's soul. As in the Gestalt psychologist's interpretation of dreams, in which each actor in the dream is actually a part of oneself, the narrative about the plagues is a coded message about divine intention for the progress of the soul.

Throughout the Torah narrative of the wanderings in the desert, God and Moses often speak of the Israelites as a stubborn, "stiff-necked" people. In Jewish mysticism, the letters of the sacred language of Hebrew embody wisdom deep below their surface. The letters of the Hebrew name of Pharoah appear in reversed order as the final letters of the Hebrew phrase for stiff-necked, *k'sheh oref*. From this is drawn the lesson that the Pharoah of the plague narrative is our own stiff neck! The neck is the connection between the head and the heart. To be whole, our heads must be connected with our hearts. Hashem stiffens our necks. Only Hashem has to power to open the blocked connection in our neck between our head and heart.

We can only be whole if we surrender to Hashem, crying out to our God to help us reach spiritual wholeness. We need God's help to do what is right to act for the redemption of the world. God stiffens our necks to show us that we cannot act on our intentions alone. We must cry out for God's help to open the connection between head and heart. In the words of the Torah narrative, "The Israelites were groaning under the bondage and cried out; and their cry for help from the bondage rose up to God. God heard their moaning . . . God looked upon the Israelites, and God took notice of them."[82] In Moses' first encounter with Hashem, at the burning bush, God sets in motion the liberation of the Israelites from Egypt with the words "I have marked well the plight of my people in Egypt and have heeded their outcry because of their taskmasters; yes, I am mindful of their sufferings."[83]

In the d'var I offered to the congregation, I shared my understanding of Yedidah's teaching. I concluded the d'var with these words:

> In Kabbalah is a story of an eternal, unknowable, infinite, limitless One, from which emerges a will to create. The purpose of Creation is to know the blessings of the Source of Creation, and the journey to that knowledge is often with a broken heart. In my morning prayers, I recite in Hebrew from Psalm 51 the words, *A broken spirit is an offering to God. God will not spurn a broken and crushed heart*,[84] and from Psalm 34, *God comes close to the brokenhearted, and rescues the crushed in spirit.*[85] As I reflect on the role of suffering in the engagement between God and material creation, I am reminded of what struck me when I first encountered kabbalistic imagery of the process of creation. The will to create is often described in kabbalistic lore as accompanied by a powerful emotion of compassion. God suffers as God joins us in our suffering.

Yedidah's lesson stimulated healing in my relationship with Hashem. Five years before, in the same synagogue sanctuary where I delivered my d'var, Jacob's soul had led me into a direct experience of God's comfort. On that day five years before, I had experienced momentary restoration of my personal relationship with God. I had felt deeply comforted by Hashem's unmistakable presence and by the unshakable certainty that God had appeared to me in the form of a deeply loving healer. As important as that moment was to my healing, I had not found the way to maintain the intimate relationship. When I would strive with full intention to restore connection, I could see that I was still wounded by traumatic stress from the childhood vision. I would see my heart beginning to open, then observe myself fleeing from the encounter, unable to trust that God would not abandon me again. These residues of childhood trauma served the function of a "stiff neck." My ego, aroused by the emotions associated with trauma, rushed in to protect me before I could abandon myself in full surrender to Hashem.

One night as I prepared for sleep, without conscious awareness of the relationship of that moment to Yedidah's lesson, I spoke aloud to my God, "Why did you do that to me?" I did not expect an answer but felt the need to hear my words protesting that terrifying childhood vision. Months later, when I described this event to Yedidah, she explained that I was engaging with God through my childhood vessel. I wonder if that direct utterance to my God, in my child's voice, helped in the healing of that shattered vessel.

As I struggled with the challenge of sustaining an open-hearted relationship with God, I got another important lesson. Here is how I wrote about it to my fellow authors of *Engaging With Spirituality* at the time. After explaining Yedidah's teaching on the stiff neck, I wrote:

> In my meditative practice, I work to cultivate my capacity to experience the Divine Presence, strengthening myself as a vessel to hold the emanations of the Light from *Hashem*. The seeker in Jewish esoteric tradition ascends through climbing the invisible "rungs" of the ladder that Jacob saw in his vision as he was escaping his brother Esau's vengeance, on his way to meet the women who would become the mothers of the Children of Israel. Studying Chasidic masters' words on the practice of prayer, I have learned that one starts on a next higher rung with one's body trembling freely. As one becomes more firmly established on a rung, the trembling subsides. One's body, completely still, becomes a clear vessel holding the Divine Light.
>
> I have a tendency to reach beyond the limits of my ability, a tendency that I am still working to understand. In recent weeks, I developed a very intense energetic move in my meditation, going beyond my previous limits. When I became suffused with

the light, instead of trembling as my body needed to at that early stage, I willed myself to be still.

This meditative practice reached a peak last Shabbat when, not coincidentally, I studied the lesson in *Tapestry of the Soul* that Yedidah had been teaching orally during the Skype session with Mary. Once again, I struggled with the challenge to accept that Hashem was keeping me from wholehearted experience of divine presence, in order for me to accept that I could only do so with Hashem's help. When I meditated that day, I remember tensing my body to force it into the stillness that I was seeking for full experience of the divine light.

Some of you may have already figured out what happened next in this story of hubris. I woke up Monday morning crying out with pain from a spasm in my neck, clearly a consequence of my tensing my body before it could naturally still as part of the process of its strengthening as a vessel. There was no way that I could escape from a direct confrontation with my resistance to accepting God's will. Humbly beseeching *Hashem*, accepting the working of *Hashem's* will in the world, I pray for God to remove the obstacle that God has placed in my way in order for me to recognize that I can do nothing without God's help.

Jewish lore is rich with the imagery of God hiding from us and yearning to be found. The hard and terrifying childhood experience of God dying and leaving me alone to find my way was softening within me into the imagery of God withdrawing in order to be sought. As the spiritual trauma from my childhood healed, I could observe my ego's struggle to achieve enlightenment solely by my own individual efforts. Learning to accept Hashem's will, I was better able to receive Hashem's presence.

The healing process continued, and my spiritual exile came at last to an end, three months after I met Yedidah. I was seventy-two years old. Work on *Engaging with Spirituality in Family Therapy* was going very well. My fellow authors' chapters were on their way to completion, affording them the bandwidth to engage more wholeheartedly in the email conversation among inter-animating voices in generative dialogue. We were starting to have occasional gatherings for conversation on Zoom. In one of those gatherings, the experience of the Presence was particularly powerful. As we spoke openheartedly of our experiences and understandings of spirituality, we were all moved by the emergence of sacred space within, between, and around us.

That Zoom meeting was a little over a week before Passover, 2017. In preparation for the holiday, that Friday's Shabbat evening services were devoted to singing verses from the Song of Songs, led by our rabbi, assistant rabbi, and cantorial soloist. All of them had strong and clear singing voices. The assistant rabbi's voice was particularly beautiful, and the cantorial soloist's voice was exquisite. As they led the singing, the three of them were transported by the beauty of the Hebrew texts and music, together creating sacred space for all of us assembled in the congregation. The rabbi advised us to attend carefully to our spiritual experiences in the moment, telling us that what happens during the silences is perhaps even more important than our experiences during the singing.

In the silence, I felt Hashem's presence. I knew with unmistakable certainty that God was engaging with me directly. I was aware of God's awareness of me. I had felt the same sense of the Presence when God appeared to me as a child and when Jacob's soul led me to God's healing comfort six years before. This time, unlike my experience of the Presence through the vessel of my childhood, the message that came to me through my soul's adult vessel was not in words. God's meaning, however, was clear: My long exile had come to an end. I had shown to God that I could carry out the mission with which Hashem had charged me as a child. My God would not forsake me. I could relinquish my fear of abandonment; I could lay down the burdens of trauma, grief and loneliness.

Since that moment, I have known with certainty that Hashem is always present. I know that God can appear to me in forms intelligible to my human awareness as a dialogical partner in intimate personal relationship with me. When my vessel that is capable of experiencing God's personal presence is not available to me at the moment, I have faith that Hashem will bless me by making that vessel available when God wills it to be so. I am no longer gripped by the fear that God's face will disappear from my world. I no longer dread reaching out for fear that I will discover I am eternally alone.

I wrote to Yedidah about that experience of revelation in synagogue:

> We had a special *Kabbalat Shabbat* [Friday services on *Shabbat* evening] service, in which most of our activity was collective singing of verses from *Shir HaShirim* [Song of Songs, or Song of Solomon]. There were lots of silences between singing; it was a very meditative experience. The afternoon before services, I had convened a video conference of authors for a book that I am editing, *Engaging with Spirituality in Family Therapy*. My

vision for the book is that it will contribute to changes in global human culture, transforming a dominant discourse of selfish individualism into collective appreciation for the universal nature of human spirituality. Such a global culture would make war and destruction of our living environment impermissible. You can see how this project is consistent with my Jewish value of *tikkun olam* [healing the world].

During one of the silences in services that evening after the video conference, an understanding came to me with complete clarity: the divine decree that came to me in the only way I could understand it as a nine-year-old boy, that I had to carry out God's work in exile from God's presence, was rescinded because Hashem saw that I was fulfilling the requirement to carry out the work, even without a direct experience of Hashem.

As you may remember from my essay [that I had previously sent her] I have had moments of direct experience of God, but they have been brief, because before now the unresolved trauma of the childhood encounter would make me flee for fear of being abandoned yet again. In the meditative silence between songs, Hashem let me know that God will never abandon me.

Today, I was reading a translation of a passage from *Me'or Eynayim* [The Light of the Eyes, by Rabbi Menachem Nahum], in *Speaking Torah*, an assembly of early Chasidic commentaries on the *parshiot* [weekly Torah portions] by Arthur Green and his younger colleagues.[86] As I read about the Light of Creation, I felt myself transported into a direct experience of that Light. I have had such experiences before; this time was distinguished by a powerful sensation of the musculature of my body being suffused with the Light. I remembered how my *Chi Gong* master had taught me that certain subtle energies can be channeled through one's muscles. Filled with energy, I reached out for *Hashem*, and could not access *Hashem*. Remembering the lesson you taught, I cried out to *Hashem* to open my heart/open my stiff neck. *Hashem* responded instantly, and I disappeared into the flow of love between my mortal being and the Almighty.

These transformations facilitated the change in my spiritual healing practice as I prayed for Hashem to heal Yedidah's medical ailment. Relinquishing the shamanic metaphor, I no longer acted as a soul navigating on its own in invisible worlds to find and direct healing energy to the soul of the person I was seeking to heal. Instead, in prayerful meditation, I concentrated on the person in need of healing, drew on the imagery of my adopted ancestors to approach Hashem, and humbly petitioned for healing, feeling the healing energy of Hashem's presence coursing through the energy channels of my body as it manifested in the material world. Every time I petitioned Hashem for healing, it further restored my direct relationship with God. I had to heal myself spiritually to pray for Hashem to heal others as Hashem used my body as a vessel to convey the healing light.

Yedidah would correct me on occasion as she guided me on my spiritual journey. When our correspondence began, I had sent her the abstract from my memoir-in-progress and an essay that I had written about the *Kedusha* (Holiness) prayer, an important prayer in Jewish synagogue services. She had read the memoir abstract but was not at the time feeling well enough to read the essay. As she recovered and regained her strength, I asked her to read the essay, a description of my efforts to unify the upper and lower worlds using imagery from the Tanach (Jewish Bible) and from Aryeh Kaplan's translation and commentary on *Sefer Yetsirah* (The Book of Formation).

I had also drawn on what I had learned from David Hammerman about "thought forms," phenomena in invisible worlds constructed by human imagination. The language of the Kedusha draws on the dramatic visions of the biblical prophets Isaiah and Ezekiel. Kaplan's work identified specific angels with particular worlds, each world succeeding the next in ascent toward the source of all Creation. Drawing on my reading of Kaplan's work, I could identify the angels in the prophetic visions. Using the utterances of the angels that Isaiah and Ezekiel heard in their visions, I constructed a multi-voiced dialogue between my own and the angels' consciousnesses, first distinguishing then uniting the manifestations of Hashem's presence in upper and lower worlds.

When Yedidah read the essay, she expressed concern about my "materializing," that is, reifying ideas as though ideas exist on the same plane as material reality. She expressed some concern about the risk of idolatry. After she did some further study and learning on the question, she firmly instructed me not to materialize. Referencing the prohibition against idolatry, she wrote:

> There is such a huge prohibition on making mental images of God that no matter what the words say people simply don't make these images... The word is a vessel for the light of understanding. It is interpretative, rather than a one-to-one relationship.

This sage counsel has since guided my meditative practice away from the seductions of materialization. A few years later, I encountered this quote from Rabbi Adin Steinsaltz: "The evil inclination of idolatry is the outcome of a conflict between the deep need for religion, faith, and serving God, and the human difficulty of creating a relationship with an abstraction."[1] Steinsaltz's quote captures the tension and complexity embodied in Yedidah's teaching.

On another occasion, I sent Yedidah an enthusiastic report on my ascent to a higher rung in my meditative practice, describing the experience as filling my body with intense light from the source. She responded with a strong reminder of the fundamental message from Rabbi Ashlag's Kabbalah:

> Say rather 'I give to You as much as I can,'" don't worry about receiving the light. That isn't our concern. The light is always there. *Hashiveinu, Adonai Eloheinu, v'nashuvah* [Turn us toward you, LORD our God, and we will turn toward you] is more turn us toward you, in that help me be in affinity of form with you. Which is giving for the sake of giving. That is unconditionally in affinity of form. Our problem is learning how to give. Not how to receive.

As I internalize this lesson, I find it resonating with what I learned years ago when I served as a conductor for network assemblies. I learned to open my body to the intense emotional and spiritual energies of the participants, as a vehicle to manifest their healing love. For the sake of their own health and well-being, network conductors learn that they cannot hold on to those intense energies within their own bodies but rather must radiate them back into the assembled group.

Teaching the practice of conducting a network assembly, I drew on two distinct meanings for the English word "conductor." A conductor can be the leader of a group of musicians making music together or it can be a material, e.g., copper, through which heat or electricity can flow. Similarly, as I cultivated my spiritual practice in service to Hashem, I worked to make myself a vessel through which the divine light that I receive radiates outward toward creation or upward toward the source from which I am receiving it. Where once I sought to open the channels of my being to become filled with the light, now I seek to clear the channels to conduct in both directions. When the light flows, I feel the flow in

---

1. Steinsaltz, *We Jews*, 136.

both directions, upward and downward as in the biblical Jacob's vision of angels descending and ascending.

Studying with Yedidah has drawn me deeper into the wordless mysteries of Jewish mystical wisdom. Its paradoxes propel my consciousness beyond the boundaries of materiality yet root me in the particularity of my mortal being. As I learn more of the legends, myths, and aphorisms of Kabbalah and chasidut, I am struck by the particular importance of letters, words, and language. Contemplating mystical wisdom about words can take me into altered states of consciousness, with kaleidoscopic shifts from the concrete to the abstract to the ineffable, from one state to the other in a recursive, playful flow.

Studying with Yedidah, I discover new and deeper meanings to the words, aphorisms, and images I have encountered over the years reading sacred Jewish texts and listening to Jewish teachers. Before I met Yedidah, I had learned of the "Upper Torah," which has been present from the beginning of creation, and sometimes described as the blueprint or guide that Hashem consulted in creating the worlds. The Upper Torah is sometimes identified with Hashem Godself.

Through the process of tsimtsum (shrinking or contraction), this source of all being from beyond the limits of space, time, and words shapes itself into the twenty-two letters of the Hebrew alphabet, which, as they descend from world to world, come to constitute the fundamental substance of all materiality. This deep meaning can be discerned in the initial verses of Genesis, in which God's utterances, starting with "Let there be light," bring the world into being. I learned that Torah manifests in the upper worlds as "black fire written on white fire."

I learned about the "five parts of speech," the shaping of the human mouth to make the sounds of spoken Hebrew, and the importance of this activity in the material world for the unification of the lower world with the upper worlds, thereby restoring the Unity of all being. When I have the honor of chanting Torah before the congregation in synagogue, I enter a transpersonal state as I trace the words written by hand on the parchment. As I utter the words, I strive for the sound of my voice to unite the Torah scroll in front of me with the Upper Torah.

When our rabbi directs us to pray, he invites us to find our connection to God in the prayer book in front of us, either through the words printed on its pages, or in the white spaces between the words. That night before Passover in 2017, when the congregation sang verses from the

Song of Songs, our rabbi told us that the silences between the singing were as important as the singing.

Yedidah's teaching brought me into deeper understanding of the wisdom to be found in contemplating written and spoken words. When one studies sacred text, one's soul may become inspired to ascend to the Upper Torah, the "black fire written on white fire." The ink of the letters on the page of the text in the material world can become the black fire written on the white fire of the Upper Torah.

The white page becomes the undifferentiated light of Chochmah (wisdom). Chochmah is the Sephirah (sphere or vessel for the light of Creation) that emerges from the limitless and utterly unknowable Sephirah of Keter (the crown), also called Ein Sof (without limit). All of Creation yearns for the limitless and unknowable Unity that is its source. We cannot grasp Keter with our awareness or understanding. When Chochmah emerges from Keter, we can, when blessed with moments of clarity, be aware of the limitless light filling and surrounding us, but we cannot grasp it with our understanding. We can only say that it is beyond any possible distinction or description.

At those moments when I am blessed with awareness of the light of Chochmah, I recognize it as the light I experienced at that moment when I witnessed Jacob's soul dissolve into the source of all being and the light of Creation that illuminated my experience of timeless, spaceless consciousness into which Ramón had guided me. The black ink on the page in such moments of inspiration becomes the black fire written on the white fire of the Upper *Torah*. The black embodies my human limitations, the operations of my ego that separate me from God's presence. My very yearning to connect with Hashem makes my experience of the black letters a vessel for the light of God, as my awareness of Hashem's absence brings forth Hashem's presence.

Hashem begins to manifest in Creation through Keter, the first Sephirah. Keter is unknowable to all but the most advanced of human souls. The sages who tell us of Keter's world of Ein Sof are careful to warn us that this original Sephirah is beyond anything accessible to understanding or language. Although Keter is beyond the grasp of our experience, words, or understanding, we may at moments have some experience of the pure, undifferentiated light that is in Chochmah, the second Sephirah. All that will emerge in upper and lower worlds of creation is embodied in the pure white light of Chochman. As the light flows into Binah, manifesting as the color red in that Sephirah, distinctions appear.

In Binah, the pure white light is transformed into a fully differentiated pattern for everything that will ultimately emerge as the light continues its descent through the remaining seven Sephirot. The shape of Creation emerges as differentiation, for example, between light and darkness, day and night, self and other, good and evil. With distinctions come the possibility of choice between alternatives. From Binah emerge the remaining Sephirot, culminating in the tenth, *Malchut* (kingdom), also known as *Shechinah*, the Presence of God. This tenth Sephirah is the final stage of God's manifestation in the upper worlds, closest to our material world. Our world emerges from Shechinah, the feminine aspect of God. According to Jewish myth, Shechinah enters the material world to join us in our suffering.

As intricate, grand, complex, and beautiful as the intellectual architecture of Kabbalah may be, it is not the truth to which it alludes. The awesome spiritual truth of Kabbalah is the life within the dwelling, the seed within the shell, Creation at levels far above and beyond the letters and words that emerge at the level of human understanding.

Years before, I had written to Art, "Theology provides scaffolding in two ways—both to hold myself in an experience and also to lead myself into new experience." As valuable as this need to understand may have been over the course of my journey, it has also been a means by which my ego has sought to protect me. I was able to learn deep spiritual wisdom from Ramón because our situation made it impossible for me to rely on my intellect. In the very different situation of learning from Yedidah, there have also been times I have had to suspend my need to understand in order to be present in the moment.

Yedidah and I study sacred text together on the Skype video platform. As she shares her screen, she on her computer in Tsfat and I on my computer in Boston are looking together at a white page densely packed with black Hebrew letters. At the top of the page is a section of *Zohar*, written in its distinct style of Aramaic. Below the words of *Zohar* on the page are the words of Rabbi Ashlag's Hebrew translation of the *Zohar* passage and his Hebrew commentary on the *Zohar* passage. Tracing the words on the page with her cursor, Yedidah reads the Aramaic, reads and translates the Hebrew, and teaches from the text.

My capacity to read and understand Hebrew is quite limited. When I encounter text with which I am not familiar, I need vowel markings added to the Hebrew letters to be able to sound out the words. Through patient and persistent study of familiar prayers and liturgy, I have become familiar with those Hebrew words on the page and learned their meanings. Without the text in front of me, I can recite many of the prayers that I utter daily in the morning. I memorized some psalms and even some brief sections of the Mishnah (the foundational Hebrew text for the Talmud, the assembly of rabbinic commentaries and arguments from the first centuries of the Common Era) that I studied with Reuven Cohn before his early and unexpected death. I spend hours practicing the musical sound of the Hebrew verses that I chant when I read Torah before the congregation.

When Yedidah reads the text, I am in an altered state of mind, concentrating intensely on an experience for which I often do not have words. As I study with her, I track the words as she utters them, with the help of her moving cursor. At times when I am struck by a word, I ask her to help me understand it. Most of my experience of her reading, however, is beyond the limits of my intellectual understanding, until she translates what she has read.

Teaching in the name of Rabbi Ashlag, Yedidah revealed more of the meaning of the phrase "black fire written on white fire." The white fire is the pure, undifferentiated light of Chochmah, at times accessible to our awareness but beyond our understanding. The black fire is the withdrawal of that white light, which activates our yearning to grasp that which is otherwise beyond our reach. The black ink of the Hebrew letters and words reveals Hashem's presence through the process of tsimtsum, God retracting Godself so as to be accessible to us. God withdraws light for us to be able to discern the Presence with our limited understanding.

Several years before I met Yedidah, I had begun studying *Zohar* alone by reading Daniel Matt's English translation.[87] Studying together with Yedidah and studying alone by reading Matt's translation are very different experiences. Each writer approaches the *Zohar* text differently, and my contemplative study of reading text on my own is very different from engaging actively with a teacher in openhearted conversation.

Studying text alone, I enter into a deep contemplative state. I open the web of associations embodying my spiritual ideas and images, allowing that web to resonate with the meanings that I take from the words of text that I am reading. When I am moved by the text, its words and meetings weave into my web of associations, affording glimpses of patterns embedded in the tapestry of my journey.

In contrast, when I study with Yedidah, I enter into the openness and unpredictability of dialogue with a skilled teacher. I surrender to a state of not knowing or understanding and allow myself to be guided. Like all good teachers, Yedidah is always ready to learn from her students, and our study sessions bring forth new understandings for each of us.

Matt, the English translator, is a scholar who is deeply grounded in the traditions of scholarly study of *Zohar*. The annotations to his translation offer important guidance to understanding *Zohar* in the context of other scholarly and sacred texts. Yedidah, although clearly very familiar with a wide range of Jewish texts, sees herself as a teacher, specifically a teacher of the wisdom of Rabbi Yehuda Leib Ashlag.

Rabbi Ashlag was both a scholar and a *gaon*, a master of all aspects of Torah, the revealed and the hidden. He was also a great tzaddik, a sage whose study, prayer, and pious life afforded him levels of consciousness beyond the limitations of scholarly understanding. Through these levels of consciousness he attained access to the specific meanings concealed within the words of the *Zohar*, wisdom that had, according to Rabbi Ashlag, been hidden away by the sages of the Babylonian talmudic academies in the first centuries of the Common Era. Studying Rabbi Ashlag's work with Yedidah, or reading her translations of his writings, take me deeply into the experience of connection with Hashem.

My meditation practice draws from the different practices of espiritismo, Chi Gong, Sufism, Kabbalah, shamanism, and other traditions that have shaped my spiritual journey. I draw particularly on the rich symbolism and imagery of Kabbalah to focus my attention as I meditate.

Two years before I started studying with Yedidah, I encountered an early section in Matt's translation of *Zohar* that deepened my mystical understanding of the *Shema* ("listen" in Hebrew), a foundational Jewish prayer.[88] The Shema calls on Jews to recognize and accept the oneness of God with all Creation: "Listen, Oh Israel, Hashem is our God; Hashem is One."

The instruction that I found in the *Zohar* passage for praying the *Shema* resonated for me with my Chi Gong energy practice and with the six directions (east, west, north, south, above, below) that are invoked in many Native American and other global spiritual traditions. I learned to incorporate these traditions into the instructions embedded in the *Zohar* section.

Drawing on those multiple traditions, aligning them with the *Zohar* instructions, here is how I pray the Shema: I contemplate the six Sephirot that are midway on the ladder between the three upper Sephirot (Keter, Chochmah, and Binah) and the tenth and lowest Sephirah (Malchut or

Shechinah). The *Zohar* associates each of the six Hebrew words of the *Shema* with each of those six middle sephirot. As I utter or meditate on the six words of the prayer, I concentrate my attention on the six directions with which the *Zohar* associates each word of the prayer and with its respective Sephirah. Using capacities acquired through my Chi Gong practice, I illuminate six regions of my body with the colors of each of the six midway Sephirot. I map them onto my body in the specific directions (right, left, in front, above, below, behind) corresponding to the mystical six directions when my body faces east.

Two years after I first drew on Matt's translation of the *Zohar* passage to incorporate it into my praying the *Shema*, I asked Yedidah to teach me about that passage from Rabbi Ashlag's Hebrew translation and commentary. At the end of our session studying that passage, Yedidah recommended that we study the proper context for the passage.

This is the context in which that *Zohar* passage on the Shema is embedded: in Jewish biblical interpretation, there is a sacred myth that the world was created by God's first ten "utterances" in Genesis. The first utterance is composed from the opening words of Gen 1:1 ("In the beginning, God created . . ."). The remaining nine utterances include the words "God said," e.g. 1:3, "God said, 'Let there be light . . .'" These ten utterances are sometimes understood to be the first set of ten commandments in the Bible.

In the narrative of the *Zohar*, the companions (the mystical sage Rabbi Shimon bar Yocchai and his disciples) engage in discussion of the spiritual meanings to be derived from each of those utterances (or commandments) in Genesis. The passage that I had incorporated into my meditation was from the companions' discussion of the third in that original set of divine utterances, Gen 1:9: "God said, "Let the water below the sky be gathered into one area, and the dry land may appear." Yedidah proposed that we study the *Zohar* passages recounting the discussions of each of those utterances, starting with the first, Gen 1:1: "In the beginning God created . . ."

I hope that I can once again stimulate your curiosity and appeal to your patience as I invite you a bit deeper into the rich, seemingly limitless web of associations of Kabbalah, the "garment" of words and ideas that clothes its otherwise inexpressible wisdom. There is a kabbalistic aphorism: "As above, so below." The complex ladder of ascent and descent between higher and lower Sephirot manifests at the uppermost levels of Creation and also within human souls. As students of Kabbalah learn about phenomena in the upper worlds, they are aware that those phenomena resonate within their own innermost beings.

Rabbi Shimon and his disciples understood the first commandment, *yirat Hashem* (fear or awe of God), to be embodied in the first word of Gen 1:1, *Bereishit* (Beginning). They associated "beginning" with Ps 111:10: "The beginning of wisdom is the fear of God" and Prov 1:7: "Fear of God is the beginning of knowledge."

At upper levels of the kabbalistic ladder, Chochmah (wisdom) emerges from Keter (crown), Binah (understanding) emerges from Chochmah, and *Da'at* (knowledge) emerges from Binah. From Prov 2:6: "God grants Wisdom, Knowledge and Understanding from God's mouth." Chochmah embodies the pure, undifferentiated light that flows from Keter, the highest Sephirah. Binah receives the light, from which it generates distinctions, discriminating all the forms that ultimately manifest in the material world. Da'at is the knowledge that emerges from this process of formation through discrimination.

On the morning Yedidah taught from the text on yirat Hashem, at one level my mind took in the teaching at the level of its manifest language. This lesson distinguishes the "lower fear," i.e., fear of punishment either in this life or in the afterlife from the "higher fear," i.e., awe and reverence before Hashem's immensity and sovereignty. At another level, listening to Yedidah's voice while my eyes tracked black Hebrew letters on the white page, experiencing but not fully grasping the words in Hebrew, I entered into an altered state of consciousness.

I lost my awareness of self as my consciousness merged with the brilliant, fathomless white light of Chochmah. As the light of Chochmah flowed toward and into Binah, I felt enormous loss and sadness as the light diminished itself in order for Binah, the great mother of all Creation, to receive the light and direct its flow into the Sephirot below, the vessels through which Creation ultimately manifests in the material world. With those deep feelings of sorrow, the companion of my self reappeared. As my consciousness entered Da'at (knowledge), I found words for the knowledge that had come to me originally through wordless experience: There can be no creation without loss. Creation is formed through distinctions. Distinctions involve choices, and every choice leads to gain of what it chosen, but loss of that which is not.

I continue to reflect on this experience of studying the first commandment, fear of God, with Yedidah. In the deep sorrow that I had felt as the light flowed out of Chochmah into Binah, before my ego reemerged,

I tasted the divine emotion of God's compassion, which the sages report accompanies the emergence of Creation. I recognize in my experience of the pure white light of Chochmah the white light that came to me in the days after Jacob died. Jacob's soul had manifested as a column of white light that I accompanied as it encountered other columns of light, which increased in number until they all dissolved into an undifferentiated, limitless sea of whiteness.

That lesson with Yedidah enabled me to understand more deeply a much earlier moment of revelation with Ramón, when I had experienced time and space emerging through the distinction and articulation of limitless energy into form. I remember how Ramón's laughter brought me back into full conscious awareness, when the vessel of my soul was not yet strong enough to hold on to that experience.

In these last chapters of my soul's journey in this mortal life, I recapture the awe and wonder I felt as a nine-year-old child, when my consciousness was awakened by my God's soundless call of my name and my deep sorrow at the prospect of losing God. I remember how it shattered the childhood vessel of my being, which was not yet ready for such a loss.

I feel enormous gratitude for the journey that began with that moment of shattering, as the journey has carried me through times of wonder, sadness, joy, and revelation to that moment in the study of sacred text with Yedidah. As the pattern of my soul's journey in this life emerges from the tapestry, I reflect on the next *Zohar* lesson I learned with Yedidah, on the second divine utterance or commandment in Genesis, *ahavat Hashem* (love of God). That lesson afforded a deep understanding of the spiritual practice of acceptance.

Life has taught me that everything I encounter, whether moments of heartbreak, joy, peace, or even despair, are all gifts from Hashem, lessons for my soul on its journey back toward its source. As I continue to heal and grow, the walls of the vessel that holds my soul get stronger, and the channels within the vessel clear and expand. My soul, like all souls, is the divine breath that blows through the mortal body. My mortal body is the flute from which the music of Hashem emanates. That flute, my body, will wear out and be discarded. Yet my soul will continue on its journey, always seeking to bring forth the music of creation.

MOVING ON

In the Akan tribe of Ghana, the *sankofa* is embodied in the image of a bird looking back as it moves forward. It symbolizes drawing from the wisdom of the past to prepare for the future. As I work to prepare this manuscript with the hope that you may someday hold it in your hand or read it on your screen, I pray that these stories of a life spanning the middle of one century into the beginning of the next will inspire you to examine your own journey. I pray that the stories will move you to engage with the difficulties and possibilities facing humanity and the world that we share with other beings. From the first words I have written here, I have challenged you to recognize your own spiritual nature and to engage spiritually with others, particularly with those whose beliefs, practices, and allegiances may be very different from your own. I have done my best to speak to you from my heart about my own spirituality. If my words move you to respond from your own heart, then we can enter sacred space together.

In early pages of this book, I wrote to you in the voice of a sixty-three-year-old man with the hopeful vision of a universal culture of human spirituality that could displace current materialist individualist global culture. I suggested that the emergent technology of instantaneous global electronic communication could be a powerful tool to realize that purpose. Writing these final pages in the voice of a seventy-eight-year-old man, I wonder if humanity will achieve that cultural transformation before the climate transformation that we have wrought will bring forth the end of this technological age.

The planet is warming even more rapidly than was predicted when I began to write this book. The sea may inundate coastal ports faster than we can prepare for, bringing an end to the age of global trade vital to industrial and technological civilization. We are living now in what seemed, only fifteen years ago, to be a more distant future. The COVID pandemic's effects on global supply chains has revealed the vulnerability of our material civilization. War and climate change have already triggered growing waves of migration that are radically transforming our world. In the early years of the 2020s, these early signs of massive population shift are triggering the resurgence of tribalism and nationalism.

As these challenges mount, the imperative for cultural transformation becomes ever more urgent. We must find our way to recognize our fundamental nature as spiritual beings embodied in this material world for the purpose of recognizing the Source of all being in the universe. We must recognize that nature within each other, including within those whom we see as our enemies, in every living being, in the ground on which we stand, and in the air we breathe. We must overcome the tribal antagonism to the other with which we are endowed by our evolutionary history. When we can recognize the face of the Divine in each other's faces, we cannot deal with each other as obstacles or as means to our own individual goals. We see how our own selves are formed in webs of relationships. As in the Zulu philosophy of *Ubuntu*, "I am because we are."

I believe that, whether or not we are aware of it, we are each and all on our own individual spiritual journey. That journey of discovery may follow the path laid out by our families and communities within our ancestral religions, or we may find ourselves on journeys down unexplored paths that lead us, as mine did, to a religious home far from ancestral roots. We may, for reasons grounded in the particular circumstance and histories of our lives, renounce or feel no interest in our spiritual nature. From my perspective, such moments of disconnection from spirituality can themselves be moments on our souls' spiritual journeys.

My experience from working with the authors of *Engaging with Spirituality in Family Therapy*, from conversations with other seekers, and from conversations with my daughter, spouse, and son, has taught me important lessons. I have learned that spirituality is strengthened, transformed, and enriched when we are grounded in the faith traditions of our chosen faith communities, while also engaged in openhearted dialogue with others grounded in their own different communities of faith. As we experience the mystery of Rivett and Street's koan, "the same, and different, and the same," our souls blaze with the light that shines through the limitations of language and belief.

One such conversation between my daughter Jessica, the Tibetan Buddhist, and me, the Jew, eight years into the writing of this memoir, inspired me to write to my fellow *Engaging with Spirituality in Family Therapy* authors. I wrote:

> An idea emerged that I found exciting as a possible contribution to global spiritual culture. It was an idea of an ethics of dialogue among spiritual traditions, ethics marked by curiosity, mutual respect, and an assumption that the individuals engaged in dialogue across differences are deeply grounded in the particulars of their specific traditions. The ethics specifically exclude efforts to reduce the dialogue to a common set of ideas, principles, or

practices. Many religions, particularly the Abrahamic religions, have embedded in their ideology a claim to universal truth, with the claims of Christianity, Islam, and Baha'i that they are superior successors to their historical predecessors, and Jewish discourse particularistic about the covenantal relationship between God and Israel. An ethical dialogue across differences would be mindful of these claims, which would be understood specifically as limitations.

I hope that I may have inspired you to search for your own spiritual roots, which may be at home with your ancestors or deep in the soil of unexplored traditions. Firmly grounded in those roots, reach out to others, particularly others with different roots. Open your hearts to each other, taste the awesome beauty of the human soul, and together look toward our world in such desperate need of healing. Do not give in to despair. With hearts full of compassion, and prayerful intention, let us find the paths to redeem our broken world.

When a man [sic] moves from strength to strength and ever upward and upward until he comes to the root of all teaching and all command, to the I of God, the simple unity and boundlessness—when he stands there, then all the wings of command and law sink down and are as if destroyed. For the evil impulse is destroyed since he stands above it... In ecstasy all that is past and that is future draws near to the present. Time shrinks, the line between the eternities disappears, only the moment lives, and the moment is eternity. In its undivided light appears all that was and all that will be, simple and composed. It is there as a heartbeat is there and becomes manifest like it.

—Buber, *The Legend of the Baal-Shem*

Endnotes

1. Armstrong, *Battle for God.*
2. Trausan-Matu et al., "Dialogism," 219.
3. Furey, *Joy of Kindness*, 138.
4. Seikkula & Trimble, "Healing Elements of Therapeutic Conversation."
5. Trimble, *Engaging with Spirituality.*
6. Trausan-Matau et. al, "Dialogism, 219.
7. Three Initiates, *Kybalion.*
8. Neihardt, *Black Elk Speaks.*
9. Sams, *Earth Medicine.*
10. Duran, *Buddha in Redface.*
11. Magpie Earling, *Lost Journals of Sacajawea.*
12. Kimmerer, *Braiding Sweetgrass.*
13. Treuer, *Heartbeat of Wounded Knee.*
14. Morgan, *Mutant Message Down Under.*
15. Watts, *Way of Zen.*
16. Yogananda, *Autobiography of a Yogi.*
17. Shah, *Way of the Sufi; Sufis.*
18. Baba, *Discourses.*
19. Legendary stories about the life of the Baal Shem Tov are in Buber, *Legend of the Baal Shem*, and Buber, *Tales of the Hasidim.*
20. Kaplan, *Sefer Yetsirah; Bahir.*
21. Matt, *Zohar.*
22. Kushner, e.g., *God Was in This Place*, and *Honey From the Rock.*
23. E.g., Green, *Ehyeh*, and Green and Holtz, *Your Word is Fire.*
24. Anonymous, *Way of a Pilgrim.*
25. Fishbane, *Sacred Attunement.*
26. Hoffman, Lecture at Temple Sinai, Brookline, MA, 2013.
27. Trimble, "Making Sense in Conversations About Learning Disabilities."

28. Watts, *Way of Zen*.
29. Kazantzakis, *Odyssey*, 150–51.
30. The term was coined by Pierce, "Stress Analogs of Racism and Sexism" and further developed by Sue et al., "Microaggressions in Everyday Life."
31. Kazantzakis, *Report to Greco*, 1.
32. Seikkula et al., "Five-Year Experience of First-Episode Nonaffective Psychosis in Open-Dialogue Approach."
33. Eysenck, "Effects of Psychotherapy."
34. Von Bertalanffy, *General Systems Theory*.
35. Speck and Attneave, *Family Networks*.
36. Garrison, "Network Techniques," 337–53.
37. E.g., Castaneda, *Journey to Ixtlan*.
38. Neihardt, *Black Elk Speaks*, 163.
39. I described this work in Trimble, "Making Sense in Conversations About Learning Disabilities."
40. Trimble et al., "Followup of a Full-Scale Network Assembly."
41. Trimble, "Making Sense in Conversations About Learning Disabilities."
42. Stern, *Pirké Avot*, 74.
43. Buber, *Legend of the Baal-Shem*; *Tales of the Hasidim*.
44. Kliman and Trimble, "Grieving in Community."
45. Months later, after I had met Rabbi Arthur Green in search of an answer to this question about forms of the soul, I remembered encountering the idea in Hawaiian *kahuna* spirituality, as articulated in Wesselman, *Spiritwalker*.
46. Green and Holtz, *Your Word is Fire*, 57.
47. Tishby, *Wisdom of the Zohar*, 681–82.
48. Heschel, *Prophets*.
49. Rivett and Street, "Connections and Themes of Spirituality in Family Therapy."
50. Kamya, "Harnessing Spirituality Within Traditional Healing Systems."
51. Trimble, "Spiritual Affinity."
52. Trimble, "Treating the Person as a Biopsychosociocultural System."
53. Schachter-Shalomi, *Paradigm Shift*, 37.
54. Shah, *Way of the Sufi*, 205.
55. Trimble, "Whiteness as a Disease of the Soul," 52–53.
56. Trimble, "Whiteness as a Disease of the Soul," 58–59.

57. Rivett and Street, "Connections and Themes of Spirituality."
58. Trimble, *Engaging with Spirituality in Family Therapy*.
59. Holocek, *Preparing to Die*.
60. Evans-Wenz, *Tibetan Book of the Dead*.
61. Lam 5:21.
62. Trimble, *Engaging with Spirituality*.
63. Trausan-Matu et al., "Dialogism."
64. Rivett and Street, "Connections and Themes of Spirituality."
65. Goldberg, *Wisdom Paradox*.
66. 2 Sam 6:14.
67. Gottlieb, *Master of the Ladder*, 131.
68. Meltzoff and Moore, "Newborn Infants Imitate Adult Facial Gestures."
69. Green, *Hasidic Spirituality for a New Era*.
70. Schachter-Shalomi, *Paradigm Shift*, 37.
71. Shah, *Way of the Sufi*, 205.
72. Lao Tzu, *Tao Te Ching*.
73. Ruth 1:16.
74. Gen 12:3.
75. Bakhtin, *Dialogic Imagination*.
76. Volosinov, *Marxism and the Philosophy of Language*.
77. Seikkula and Trimble, "Healing Elements of Human Conversation."
78. https://www.youtube.com/watch?v=HegqF6jhoMQ.
79. Cohen and Cohen, *In the Shadow of the Ladder*.
80. Cohen and Cohen, *In the Shadow of the Ladder*.
81. Cohen, *Tapestry for the Soul*.
82. Exod 2: 23 –25.
83. Exod 3: 7.
84. Ps 51:19.
85. Ps 34:19.
86. Green et. al., *Speaking Torah*, Vol. 1, 258–261.
87. Matt, *Zohar*.
88. Matt, *Zohar*, 82–84.

Bibliography

Anonymous. *The Way of a Pilgrim*. Translated by Reginald M. French. Pasadena, CA: Hope, 1993.
Armstrong, Karen. *The Battle for God*. New York: Ballantine, 2001.
Baba, Meher. *Discourses*. Myrtle Beach, SC: Sheriar, 1987.
Bakhtin, Mikhail M. *The Dialogic Imagination: Four Essays*. Edited by Michael Holquist. Translated by Michael Holquist and Caryl Emerson. Austin: University of Texas Press, 1982.
Buber, Martin. (1955). *The Legend of the Baal-Shem*. Translated by Maurice Friedman. Princeton, NJ: Princeton University Press, 1955.
———. *Tales of the Hasidim (The Early Masters/The Later Masters)*. Translated by Olga Marx. New York: Knopf Doubleday, 1991.
Carson, Clayborne, and Kris Shepard, eds. *A Call to Conscience: The Landmark Speeches of Dr. Martin Luther King, Jr.* New York: Grand Central, 2002.
Casteneda, Carl. *Journey to Ixtlan: The Lessons of Don Juan*. Reissue Edition. New York: Washington Square, 1991.
Cohen, Mark, and Cohen, Yedidah. *In the Shadow of the Ladder: Introductions to Kabbalah by Rabbi Yehuda Lev Ashlag*. Safed, Israel: Nehora, 2003.
Cohen, Yedidah. *A Tapestry for the Soul: The Introduction to the Zohar by Rabbi Yehuda Lev Ashlag*. Safed, Israel: Nehora, 2010.
Duran, Eduardo. *Buddha in Redface*. Third Edition. Bloomington, IN: iUniverse, 2003.
Evans-Wentz, Walter Y. *The Tibetan Book of the Dead*. Calabasas, CA: Ixia, 2020.
Eysenck, Hans. J. "The Effects of Psychotherapy: An Evaluation." *Journal of Consulting Psychology* 16 (1952) 319–24.
Fishbane, Michael. *Sacred Attunement: A Jewish Theology*. Chicago: University of Chicago Press, 2007.
Furey, Robert J. *The Joy of Kindness*. Chestnut Ridge, NJ: Crossroad, 1993.
Garrison, John. "Network Techniques: Case Studies in the Screening-Linking-Planning Conference Method." *Family Process* 13 (1974) 337–53.
Goffman, Erving. *The Presentation of Self in Everyday Life*. Garden City, NY: Doubleday, 1959.
Goldberg, Elkhonon. *The Wisdom Paradox: How Your Mind Can Grow Stronger as Your Brain Grows Older*. New York: Penguin, 2006.
Gottlieb, Avraham M. *The Master of the Ladder: The Life and Teachings of Rabbi Yehudah Leib Ashlag*. Translated by Yedidah Cohen. Safed, Israel: Nehora, 2019.
Green, Arthur. *Ehyeh: A Kabbalah for Tomorrow*. Nashville: Jewish Lights, 2004.
———. *A Guide to the Zohar*. Stanford, CA: Stanford University Press, 2004.

———. *Hasidic Spirituality for a New Era: The Religious Writings of Hillel Zeitlin.* Mahwah, NJ: Paulist, 2012.

———. "Interview with Rabbi Shmuly Yanklowitz." https://www.youtube.com/watch?v=HegqF6jhoMQ.

———., et al., *Speaking Torah: Spiritual Teachings from around the Maggid's Table.* Nashville, TN: Jewish Lights, 2013

Green, Arthur, and Holtz, Barry W. *Your Word is Fire: The Hasidic Masters on Contemplative Prayer.* Woodstock, VT: Jewish Lights, 1993.

Heschel, Abraham Joshua. *The Prophets.* New York: Harper Perennial, 1962.

Holocek, Andrew. *Preparing to Die: Practical Advice and Spiritual Wisdom from the Tibetan Buddhist Tradition.* Ithaca, NY: Snow Lion, 2013.

Joyce, James. *A Portrait of the Artist as a Young Man.* New York: B.W. Huebsch, 1916.

Kamya, Hugo. "Harnessing Spirituality within Traditional Healing Systems: A Personal Journey." In *Engaging With Spirituality in Family Therapy: Meeting in Sacred Space,* edited by David Trimble, 67–82. New York: Springer, 2018.

Kamya, Hugo, and Trimble, David. "Response to Injury: Toward Ethical Construction of the Other." *Journal of Systemic Therapies* 21 (2002) 19–29.

Kaplan, Aryeh. *The Bahir.* Newburyport, MA: Weiser, 1997.

———. *Sefer Yetzirah: The Book of Creation in Theory and Practice.* Newburyport, MA: Weiser, 1979.

Kazantzakis, Nikos. *The Odyssey: A Modern Sequel.* Translated by Kimon Friar. New York: Simon & Schuster, 1958.

———. *Report to Greco.* Translated by Kimon Friar. New York: Simon & Schuster, 1965.

Kliman, Jodie, and Trimble, David. "Grieving in Network and Community: Bearing Witness to the Loss of Our Son." In *Re-Visioning Family Therapy: Race, Culture, and Gender in Clinical Practice,* edited by Monica McGoldrick and Kenneth V. Hardy, 164–71. New York: Guilford, 2008.

Kushner, Lawrence. *God Was in This Place, and I, I Did Not Know: Finding Self, Spirituality, and Ultimate Meaning.* Nashville: Jewish Lights, 1993.

———. *Honey From the Rock: Visions of Jewish Mystical Renewal.* Nashville: Jewish Lights, 1977.

Kimmerer, Robin W. *Braiding Sweetgrass: Indigenous Wisdom, Scientific Knowledge, and the Teachings of Plants.* Minneapolis: Milkweed, 2015.

Lao Tzu. *Tao Te Ching.* Translated by Gia-Fu Feng et. al. Visalia, CA: Vintage, 2011.

Magpie Earling, Deborah. *The Lost Journals of Sacajawea: A Novel.* Minneapolis: Milkweed, 2023.

Matt, Daniel C. *The Zohar: Pritzker Edition.* Twelve Volumes. Stanford, CA: Stanford University Press, 2014–17.

Meltzoff, Andrew N., and Moore, M. Keith. "Newborn Infants Imitate Adult Facial Gestures." *Child Development* 54 (1983) 702–9.

Morgan, Marlo. *Mutant Message Down Under.* New York: Harper Perennial, 2004.

Neihardt, John G. *Black Elk Speaks.* New York: Fine, 1997.

Pierce, Chester. "Stress Analogs of Racism and Sexism: Terrorism, Torture, and Disaster." In *Mental Health, Racism, and Sexism,* edited by Charles V. Willie, et al., 277–93. Pittsburgh, PA: University of Pittsburgh Press, 1995.

Ram Dass. *Be Here Now.* Chatsworth, CA: Harmony, 1978.

Rivett, Mark, and Street, Eddy. "Connections and Themes of Spirituality in Family Therapy." *Family Process* 40 (2001) 459–67.

Sams, Jamie. *Earth Medicine: Ancestors' Way of Harmony for Many Moons*. San Fransciso: HarperOne, 1994.
Schachter-Shalomi, Zalman M. *Paradigm Shift*. New York: Jason Aronson, 1993.
Schwartz, Richard. *Internal Family Systems Therapy*. New York: Guilford, 1997.
Seikkula, Jaakko, et. al. "Five-Year Experience of First-Episode Nonaffective Psychosis in Open-Dialogue Approach: Treatment Principles, Follow-Up Outcomes, and Two Case Studies." *Psychotherapy Research* 16 (2006) 214–28.
Seikkula, Jaakko, and Trimble, David. "Healing Elements of Human Conversation: Dialogue as an Embodiment of Love." *Family Process* 44 (2005) 461–75.
Shah, Idries. *The Sufis*. 7th ed. Hicksville, NY: ISF, 2018.
———. *The Way of the Sufi*. New York: Penguin Compass, 1968.
Speck, Ross, & Attneave, Carolyn L. *Family Networks: A Way Toward Retribalization and Healing in Family Crises*. New York: Pantheon, 1973.
Stern, Chaim. *Pirké Avot: Wisdom of the Jewish Sages*. Hoboken, NJ: Ktav, 1997.
Steinsaltz, Adin. *We Jews: Who Are We and What Should We Do?* Translated by Yehuda Hanegbi and Rebecca Toueg. San Francisco: Jossey-Bass, 2005.
Sue, Derald Wing, et al. "Racial Microaggressions in Everyday Life: Implications for Clinical Practice." *American Psychologist* 62 (2007) 271–86.
The Three Initiates. *The Kybalion: A Study of the Hermetic Philosophy of Ancient Egypt and Greece*. Chicago: Yogi Publication Society, 1912.
Tishby, Isaiah. *The Wisdom of the Zohar: An Anthology of Texts*. Translated by David Goldstein. Portland, OR: Littman Library of Jewish Civilization, 1989.
Trausan-Matu, Stefan, et al. "Dialogism." In *International Handbook of Computer-Supported Collaborative Learning*, edited by Ulrike Cress, et al., 219–39. New York: Springer Nature, 2021.
Treuer, David. *The Heartbeat of Wounded Knee: Native America from 1890 to the Present*. New York: Riverhead, 2019.
Trimble, David, ed. *Engaging with Spirituality in Family Therapy: Meeting in Sacred Space*. New York: Springer, 2018.
———., et al. "Followup of a Full-Scale Network Assembly." *International Journal of Family Therapy* 6 (1984) 102–13.
———. "Making Sense in Conversations About Learning Disabilities." *Journal of Marital and Family Therapy* 27 (2001) 473–86.
———. "Treating the Person as a Biopsychosociocultural System." Paper presented at the 114th Annual Convention of the American Psychological Association, New Orleans, Louisiana, August, 2006.
———. "Whiteness as a Disease of the Soul." In *The Enduring, Invisible, and Ubiquitous Centrality of Whiteness*, edited by Kenneth V. Hardy, 49–73. New York: Norton, 2022.
Trimble, Joseph E. "Spiritual Affinity and Its Influence on Acculturation and Ethnic Identification." Presidential address, presented at the 108th Annual Convention of the American Psychological Association, Washington, DC, August, 2000.
Volosinov, Valentin N. *Marxism and the Philosophy of Language*. Translated by Ladislav Matejka and Irwin R. Titunik. Cambridge, MA: Harvard University Press, 1986.
Von Bertalanffy, Ludwig. *General System Theory: Foundations, Development, Applications*. New York: George Braziller, 1968.
Watts, Alan. *The Way of Zen*. New York: Pantheon, 1957.
Wesselman, Hank. *Spiritwalker: Messages from the Future*. New York: Bantam, 1996.

Yogananda, Paramahansa. *Autobiography of a Yogi*. Commerce, CA: Crystal Clarity, 1946.

Index

Abbie Hoffman, 40, 47
Abraham, 6, 104, 116, 248
Abrahamic, 6, 91, 279
Abraham Joshua Heschel, 159, 253, 286
Acupuncture, 100, 246
Adam Kadmon, 153
Adin Steinsaltz, 268
Adonai, 14–15, 159–60, 162, 205, 268
Africa, 54, 56, 67, 146, 175, 236, 244
African, 24–25, 32, 45, 69, 78, 103, 191, 224, 244
African American, 4, 24–25, 32, 39, 41–45, 47, 49–50, 53–54, 56, 69–70, 125
Afrocentric, 54
AFTA Springer Briefs, 222
ahavat Hashem, 276
Alan Watts, 6, 9, 35, 84
alcohol, alcoholic, 27, 38, 40–41, 50, 67, 77, 86, 101, 105, 107, 109, 131,135, 207, 212, 220
Alexander Leighton, 59–60
Alice Hyslop, 71
Allman, Larry *See* Larry Allman
Alvin Poussaint, 58
Ancestors, vii, 4, 7, 9,11, 22, 24–25, 29, 38, 41, 45, 47, 57, 103–4, 114, 116, 121, 124, 140, 142, 144, 161, 173, 194, 196, 228, 233–35, 236, 247, 251, 266, 279, 287
American Family Therapy Academy (AFTA), 146–47, 122, 222
American Orthopsychiatric Association, 88
Andrew Holocek, 202–3, 254, 283, 286

Andy Vogel xi, 115, 121, 134, 138, 143–44, 148, 185, 251
Animal, 11, 16, 165–66, 261
Ankh, 58, 62
Ann Drake, 97, 180, 182, 238, 246
Antidepressant, 107
Ari, Yitzhak Luria, 183, 231
Ark, 103–4, 121, 142, 234, 238–39, 246–47
Arnold, Rabbi Steve *See* Steve Arnold
Arthur Green, iv, xi, 8, 122–23, 148–50, 156–58, 160, 183–84, 228, 240, 242–44, 251–52, 254, 266, 271,282, 285–86
Aryeh Kaplan, 8
Ashkenazi Jews, 117
Ashlag, Rabbi Yehuda Leib *See* Yehuda Leib Ashlag
Attention Deficit Disorder, ADHD, 93,30, 50, 55, 93–96, 101, 104–7, 187, 212
Attneave, Carolyn *See* Carolyn Attneave
atypical psychosis, unspecified psychosis, 65
authentic engagement, 65
Autism Spectrum Disorder, 30, 32, 89

Baal Shem Tov, 7, 122, 281
Baba Ram Dass, 84
Bacigalupe, Gonzalo *See* Gonzalo Bacigalupe
Baba, Meher *See* Meher Baba
Bahir, 7–8, 149, 229, 253, 281, 286
Bakhtin, Mikhael. *See* Mikhail Bakthtin.

Bar Mitzvah, 103–5, 114, 135, 144, 155, 159, 247
Baruch Spinoza, 232
Behaviorism, 68
Beit Din, 142–44, 148, 185, 250
Betty, 4, 25, 49–54, 56, 64, 66–67, 72, 74, 77, 79, 81, 86, 89, 92–93, 98, 214, 235
BICAP, Boston Institute for Culturally Affirming Practices x, 110–11, 138, 195
Biculturation, 49
Bill Graham, 213
Bima, 145
Binah, 153, 155, 240, 270–71, 273, 275
Biome, 100
Bipolar Disorder, 65, 105–8, 113, 216
birth mother, 10, 92, 108, 111–12, 124
Black, 32, 34, 42–43, 45, 51, 53–54, 57–59, 62–63, 67, 74, 79, 83, 125, 236, 244, 286
Black Elk, 6, 83, 182, 281–82, 286
Black Panther Party, 54, 74, 244
Body, 18, 22, 80–83
Book of *Jonah,* 21, 171
"born again", 111
Borneo, 97
Boston Center for the Liberation of Revolutionary Consciousness, 57–58, 234
Boston City Hospital, 69–70, 72, 236
Boston State Hospital, 61, 66
Breeden, Canon James. *See* Canon James Breeden.
Brit Dam, 143
Brookline, MA, 90, 93–94, 103, 122, 136, 281
Buddhism, Buddhist, ix, xi, 5–6, 9, 35, 84, 91, 124, 188, 202–6, 220–22, 244, 254, 278, 286

Caesural events, 13
Call to ministry, 17, 21, 41, 56–58, 60, 114, 158, 161, 194–96, 199, 205
Canon James Breeden, 59
Carlos Castanéda, 80
Carolyn Attneave, ix, 72–75, 77, 88, 94, 102, 177, 179, 223, 237, 244, 249, 287, 228, 233, 241, 243, 276
Castanéda, Carlos *See* Carlos Castanéda
Center for Multicultural Training in Psychology (CMTP), x, 24, 73, 176, 225, 236
Chi Gong vii, x, 13, 22, 65, 80, 100–104, 134, 154, 164, 172, 186, 238, 245, 266, 273–74
Chuppah, 90
Civil Rights Movement, ix, 4, 40, 42, 45–46, 49, 52, 57, 104, 191
Circumcision, 142
Comparative Developmental Theory, 89
Cabot, Lori. *See* Lori Cabo.t
Cardiac Amyloidosis, 197, 254
Carmelo, 79
Carmen Knudson-Martin, 222
catchment area, 61, 63
Center for Multicultural Training in Psychology, CMTP x, 24,73, 109–10, 176, 225, 236
cerebral cortex, 16, 187
Chabad, 8
Chaim Koritzinsky, 138
character disorder, 71
Charlee Sutton xi., 103, 138, 163, 180–81
Chasidic movement, *Chasidism, Chasidut,Chasid,* 7–8, 115, 118, 121–23, 145, 148–49., 156–57, 160–61, 184, 205, 243, 251–52, 263, 266, 269
Chavurah, 91
Chi Gong vii, x, 13, 22, 65, 800, 100–101, 134, 154, 164, 172, 186, 238, 245, 266, 2734
Chochmah, 153, 155, 240, 270, 272–73, 275–76
Children of Israel, 14, 45, 103–4, 116, 122, 172–73, 234, 247, 261, 263
Chinese Medicine, 100
chosen people, 121
ceaseless prayer, 62
Charlie Sharpe, 112, 125–26
chavruta, 156
chemotherapy, 197–98

Christian, Christianity, 6, 8–10, 14, 19,
    21–23, 25, 28–29, 31, 37–38, 41,
    45, 58, 62, 76, 79, 91, 111–12,
    115–18, 120–21, 124–25, 127,
    129, 134, 139, 144, 161, 165,
    175, 177, 179, 193–96, 204–5,
    224, 228–29, 231, 244, 246, 250,
    261, 279
Christian Science, 31, 76
code switching, 49
Cohen, Yedidah. *See* Yedidah Cohen.
Cohn, Reuven. *See* Reuven Cohn.
consciousness, 11, 13, 19–20, 23, 48, 52,
    55, 57–58, 64, 81–83, 99, 114,
    151, 155, 157, 160, 165, 178–80,
    188–90, 192, 196, 202, 218, 229,
    234, 237–38, 245, 258–59, 267,
    269–70, 273, 275–76
community health center, 75, 86
community mental health, 75–76, 78,
    87,102
community network intervention, 237
community meeting, 64, 66
the companions, 274
Comparative Developmental Theory, 89
Comparative International Studies,
    54, 60
complexity, 2, 17, 48, 55, 68, 77, 82, 85,
    90, 106, 150, 154, 169, 176–77,
    179, 187, 228, 248–49, 250, 268
conductor (of a full-scale family
    network assembly), 77–79, 83,
    87, 99, 179, 237, 244–45, 268
Congregational Church, 31, 35
convert, conversion, viii, 8, 13, 23, 91,
    100, 103–4, 114–16, 118, 121,
    124–25, 155–56, 181, 194, 238,
    247, 250
CORE, Congress for Racial Equality,
    42, 49
covenant, 32, 34, 91, 143, 234, 279
Creation, 11, 12, 22, 119, 143–44, 150–
    55, 154,157, 159, 161, 170, 183,
    189, 200–201,226, 230–32, 240,
    243, 262, 266–71, 273–76, 286

Dan, ancestral Israelite tribe, 173
Daniel Matt, 8, 273, 281, 283, 286

Dash, Rachel. *See* Rachel Dash.
David Decter, 135, 137
David McClelland, 60–61
David Treadway, 106–8, 113, 130, 133
day release, 73
day room, 63–64
Days of Awe, 159
Decter, David. *See* David Decter.
deinstitutionalize,
    deinstitutionalization, 87, 89
Delana108–9, 111
Delusion, 61, 63–66, 107, 166, 188
Department of Mental Health, DMH,
    61, 71–72, 75, 86, 216
depression, depressed, 38, 64, 66–67,
    73, 77, 102, 105, 107, 168, 215
detox, 111
deveikut, 122, 151
Diabetes, 198, 222
diagnostic nomenclature, 65
Diaspora, 78, 117, 122, 157
diethyl tryptamine, DET, 65
dimethyl tryptamine, DMT, 65
discharge summary, 64, 66
Depot, 71
Dialogue, 4–5, 9, 31, 65, 75, 156, 164,
    184, 186, 201, 222–25, 231–32,
    235, 239–40, 249–50, 256, 258,
    264, 267, 272, 278–79, 282, 287
Dissertation, 72
Divine, vi, 10–12, 14–17, 19, 21–22,
    35, 38, 41, 46, 56, 59, 63, 82, 84,
    99, 114, 118–20, 122, 142–43,
    151, 157, 159–63, 166–68, 170,
    184, 186, 189, 192–94, 196, 202,
    223, 228, 230–31, 237–43, 245,
    252–53, 257, 261, 263–64, 266,
    268, 274, 276, 278
Divorce, 4, 86, 89, 146, 175, 202, 219–21
DMH Area Office, 86, 88
Dominican Republic, 46, 78–79, 202
Don McNamee, 60
Drake, Ann. *See* Ann Drake.
Dubuque, Iphigenia (Ginny). *See* Ginny
    Dubuque.
Dungeon Rock, 76
Dukakis, Governor Michael, 73
D'var Torah, 105, 144, 259–62

292 INDEX

Eddy, Mary Baker. *See* Mary Baker Eddy.
Ego, 82–84, 182, 184, 186–90, 192–93, 195–96, 199, 201, 220, 235–38, 255, 259, 263–64, 270–71, 275
Ein Sof, 150–51, 153, 160, 203, 270
El, 14, 137
Elder, 55, 73, 87, 101, 173179, 221, 227
Elohim, 14, 242–43
Elul, 159–60
Elvin Semrad, 71
Engaging With Spirituality in Family Therapy, x, xi, 224, 226–28, 232, 249, 251, 253, 256, 258, 260, 264–65, 278, 283, 286–87
esoteric, esoteric literature, 3, 6–8, 19, 22, 80, 84, 97–99, 101, 103–4, 118, 120, 134, 131, 145, 148–50, 154, 160, 172, 178, 183–85, 202, 204, 206, 230, 241, 255, 263
Erving Goffman, 62, 285
Esperanza Herrera, 77, 78
esperitisa, experismo, ix, 46, 78,103, 142, 167, 202,273
est (Erhard Seminar Training), 210–11, 213–14, 220
El Maleh Rachamim (God of Compassion), 137
executive functioning, 94–95, 106, 129, 187–88
exile, 7, 65, 84, 116–17, 122–24, 153, 210–11, 233–35, 250, 264–66
existential dread, 1, 233
externalizing practices, 96
Eysenck, Hans. *See* Hans Eysenck.

Fabulizing, 212, 217
facial cellulitis, 100
Falke, Dr. Rodney. *See* Rodney Falke.
Family House, 87–89
family therapy, x, xi, 69–70, 72–73, 89, 94, 106, 108–9, 146, 163, 168, 176, 199, 222–28, 232, 236, 244, 248–49, 251, 253, 256, 258, 260, 264–65, 278, 282–83, 286–87
fibroid tumors, 90
Fillmore Auditorium, 213
Fingar, Ralph. *See* Ralph Fingar.

Fishbane, Michael. *See* Michael Fishbane.
Forebrain, 16, 95, 187
form, as a vessel for spiritual tradition, 91, 100, 115–17, 134, 184
fraco, 81
Freedom Summer, ix, 42–44, 56–57
full-scale family network assembly, 72, 88, 138
fulminating infection, 100
furlough, 73

Gillian Walker, 95
Gonzalo Bacigalupe, x, 110
Gaon, 273
"garment", 189, 192, 227, 247, 253, 274
Garrison, John. *See* John Garrison.
Gemara, 117
General System Theory, 69, 89, 287
Gevurah, 153
Gestalt psychology, 261
Ginny Dubuque, 80
"god," a guide and companion from the spirit world, from the teaching of Ramón Jiménez, 81
God, viii, 4, 10, 12, 14–15, 17–22, 31, 35, 38, 41, 56, 59–62, 79, 84, 91, 103, 114–16, 119–21, 129, 131, 137, 142–44, 148–49, 153–54, 157–63, 165, 170–71, 173–74, 189, 194–96, 199, 201, 203, 205, 210, 223, 228–35, 238–44, 247–48, 250, 252–54, 257, 259–76, 279–81, 285–86
Godhead, 153
Godself, 22, 231–32, 269, 272
Goffmann, Erving. *See* Erving Goffman.
Gonzalo Bacigalupe, x, 110
Gosnold, 112
Graham, Bill. *See* Bill Graham.
grandiose, grandiosity, 50, 60–61, 64, 67, 69, 84, 166, 190, 196,248, 252
greed, 83, 98–99, 182, 184, 196, 237–38, 255–56
Green, Rabbi Arthur *See* Arthur Green
Guy Seymour, x, 69, 71, 78, 236
Guyana, Guyanese, 70, 236

Haiti, 79
Haka, 147
Hammerman, David and Sylvia, 96,
    110–11, 138, 144–45, 180, 184,
    202, 238, 246, 267
Hans Eysenck, 68, 282, 285
Hardy, Kenneth. *See* Kenneth Hardy.
Haredi, 115, 157
Harvard School of Public Health,
    59–60, 72
Harvard University, 54–56, 58, 60–61,
    69, 71, 236, 287
Haskalah, 8, 104, 115, 117, 185
Hashem, 14, 154, 199–201, 229–30,
    234–35, 239–40, 248, 257, 259–
    62, 262–70, 272–73, 275–76
health care disparities, 72, 93
Heartland Christian Ministries, 112–
    13, 124–28, 130, 139, 144, 161
Hebrew College, 122, 148–49, 156–57
Heichalot, 7
Heinz Werner, 89
Hermes Trismegistus, 6, 84
Herrera, Esperanza. *See* Esperanza
    Herrera.
Heschel, Abraham Joshua. *See*
    Abraham Joshua Heschel.
Hispaniola, 79
High Rock Tower, 76
Hindu, 7, 91
Hillel Zeitlin, 8, 243, 286
hippy, hippies, 40, 41, 58
Hod, 153
Hoffman, Abbie. *See* Abbie Hoffman.
Hoffman, Lawrence. *See* Lawrence
    Hoffman.
Holocek, Andrew. *See* Andrew Holocek.
Hospital Community Program, 86–87
Hubris, 99, 264
Hugo Kamya, x, 110, 175, 224, 254
Hutchinson Family, 76
hypnosis, trance, 97, 98, 180, 238
Hyslop, Alice. *See* Alice Hyslop.
Hysterectomy, 90

Idolatry, 234, 267–68
IFS (Internal Family Systems Therapy),
    233, 287

"I – Thou", 84, 162
"Immigrant" status of Jewish converts,
    viii, 5, 13, 155–57, 194
immune system, 123
immunotherapy, 197
incarnation, reincarnation, 98–99, 119,
    124, 195, 238
insatiability, 96, 106,130
intellectualize, intellectualization, 80
Internal Family Systems Therapy (IFS),
    233, 287
Interns, 24, 70, 73, 86, 88, 176, 248
Internship, 70–73
Isaac, 104, 116, 183
isolation room, 63

Jaakko Seikkula, 65, 223, 249
Jacob, v, vi, viii, 10, 15, 80, 90, 92,
    95–96, 103–13, 116, 118, 121,
    124–37, 139, 141, 143–47, 149,
    159, 161–1663, 172, 177, 184,
    193, 197, 205, 215, 217, 221,
    227, 239, 256–59, 261, 263,
    276
Janis Joplin, 213
Jay King, x, 110, 179
Jehovah, 14
Jerry Parrish, 113, 124, 126–27
Jessica, v, ix, xi, 4–5, 9–10, 72, 77, 86, 90,
    92, 105, 109, 111, 124, 127, 133,
    135, 140, 146, 193, 206, 208,
    215–16, 218–21, 251, 254, 278
Jewish Reconstructionism, 91, 103, 115,
    143, 149, 157, 185
Jewish Renewal, 8, 115, 157
Jiménez, Ramón. *See* Ramón Jiménez.
"John", 74
John Pearce, 70
Jodie Kliman, v, ix, x, 4, 9, 88–93, 95–
    96, 98, 101–3, 105–13, 118, 120,
    124–35, 138–42, 145–48, 155,
    161, 175, 177, 184–85, 193,197,
    199, 214–19, 221–22, 239–40,
    246, 249, 254, 286
John Garrison, 76
Joseph, biblical story, 156, 259
Joseph Trimble, 177, 282, 287

294 INDEX

Journey, vii, viii, ix, xi, 3, 6, 9–10, 12–13, 15, 38, 41, 55, 82–83, 92, 97–98, 102–4, 110, 114–15, 118–20, 122, 124, 133–34, 140, 142–43, 146, 148–50, 154, 164–65, 172, 174–78, 180, 182, 185–87, 190, 192–96, 198–206, 217, 221, 229–30, 232, 234–36, 238, 244–47, 251, 253–54, 256–59, 261–62, 267, 271–73, 276–78, 282, 285–86
Judaism, vii, xi, 4–5, 7–9, 13, 19, 22, 91, 97, 100, 103–4, 114–18, 120–21, 124, 129, 141, 143–44, 149, 155–56, 160, 164, 184–85, 194, 199, 222, 245–47, 250–251, 255
Just Therapy, 147
Judith Landau, 1446

Kabbalah, viii, x, xi, 4–5, 7–8, 21, 23, 84, 148–51, 154, 156–58, 170, 172, 183, 185, 201–3, 221, 227–28, 230–32, 245, 251, 255–56, 258, 261–62, 261, 268–69, 271, 273–75, 285
Kaethe Weingarten, 138
Kamya, Hugo. *See* Hugo Kamya.
Kaplan, Aryeh. *See* Aryeh Kaplan.
Karaite, 117
karma, karmic, 98
Katz, Dr. Marshall. *See* Marshall Katz.
kavod Adonai, 159–60, 162
Kazantzakis, Nikos. *See* Nikos Kazantzakis.
Kedushah prayer, 267
Kenneth Hardy, 103, 138
Keter, 153, 155, 270, 273, 275
Kim Trimble, 109, 135, 140, 198, 219, 221–22, 254
Kindling, 95–96, 104
King, Jay. *See* Jay King.
King, Dr. Martin Luther. *See* Martin Luther King.
Kliman, Jodie. *See* Jodie Kliman.
Knowing, 133
Knudson-Martin, Carmen. *See* Carmen Knudson-Martin.

Koritzinsky, Chaim. *See* Chaim Koritzinsky.
Kotelchuck, Milton. *See* Milton Kotelchuck.
k'sheh oref, 262
Kushner, Lawrence. *See* Lawrence Kushner.
Kybalion, 6, 84, 201, 287

Ladder, 152–55, 178, 253, 255–56, 259, 263, 273–75, 283, 285
Laing, R.D. *See* R.D. Laing.
Lambo, Thomas. *See* Thomas Lambo.
Landau, Judith. *See* Judith Landau.
language-based learning, 212
Language and Cognitive Development Center, 89
Larry Allman, 63
Lawrence Hoffman, 13, 156, 281
Lawrence Kushner, 122
lay minister, 58, 234
Leah, 116
learning disabilities, 30, 35, 93–95, 102, 195, 211, 281–82, 287
left brain, 198
Leighton, Alexander. *See* Alexander Leighton.
Light, vi, 80, 82, 90–91, 133, 139–40, 145, 150–55, 162, 167, 189, 192–93, 231–32, 237–39, 242–43, 248, 252, 257, 259, 263–64, 266–72, 274–76, 278, 280
Liminal, 142, 179, 201
Liturgy, 9, 13, 19, 91, 103, 118, 120–21, 160, 271
Llerena-Quinn, Roxana. *See* Roxana Llerena-Quinn.
Lori Cabot, 80, 84
The LORD, 14, 56, 62, 171, 205, 228, 235, 268
love and fear, 21, 233–34
LSD, 40, 50, 86, 232
Luria, Yitzhak, the Ari. *See* Ari, Yitzhak Luria.
Lyle, Sheila's spiritual advisor, 204, 206
Lynn Community Health Center, 75
Lynn, Massachusetts, 75–76, 78, 80, 85, 89, 90, 237

INDEX 295

Lynn Mental Health Association, 89
Lynn Network Conference, 75–78, 80

Maimonides, 122, 157
Mary Baker Eddy, 31, 76
Matt, Daniel. C. *See* Daniel Matt.
Merkavah, 7
Malchut, 153, 271, 273
Malcolm X, 54, 56, 74
Māori, 147
mania, manic, manic psychosis, 58, 59, 65, 73, 107, 131, 205
Manitonquot, Medicine Story, 173
marijuana, weed, 38, 40–41, 51, 65, 67, 77, 86, 92, 105, 212–13, 219
Marcia Stern, 95
Marsha and Mitch Mirkin, 110, 138, 140
Martin Luther King, 55, 179, 233, 285
Dr. Marshall Katz, 197
martial arts, 101, 241, 179, 241
Massachusetts Council of Churches, 27, 31, 59, 210
Massachusetts Department of Correction, 71
Massachusetts Department of Mental Health, DMH, 61, 71–72, 86, 88, 89
Massachusetts Mental Health Center, 60
Matriarchs, 116
Mattapan, 61–62
May Unit, 61, 64, 69
Mayyim Hayyim, 143
McCarran Act, 59
MCI Framingham, 73–75
McClelland, David. *See* David McClelland.
McGoldrick, Monica. *See* Monica McGoldrick.
McNamee, Don. *See* Don McNamee.
Me'ah, 122, 156
Medical Examiner, 134
Meher Baba, 7, 91, 120, 143
Meirowitz, Rabbi Rim, 143
Mellaril, 64
Me'Or Eynayim, 266
metaphysical therapeutic stance, xi, 13, 89, 92, 124, 163–65, 169–71, 175, 177–79, 181–82, 184, 189, 206, 225, 228, 254
Michael Fishbane, 71
Michael White, 96
Michelle, Jacob's friend, 128–29, 131
Mick Jagger, 213
Mike Rossi, 236
Mikhail Bakthtin, 5, 223–25, 249–50, 254, 258, 283, 285
Mikvah, 143–45
Milton Kotelchuck, 60
Mirkin Marsha and Mitch. *See* Marsha and Mitch Mirkin.
Minority Training Program, MTP, 73
misattunement, 66
Mississippi, vii,ix, 33, 41–53, 55–57, 70, 236
Mishnah, 117, 156, 272
mitzvah, mitzvot, 103–5, 114, 135, 144, 155, 159, 183, 247
mixed multitude, 172
Modern Orthodox Judaism, 115, 182–83
Modern Sequel to the Odyssey, 41, 62, 244
Monica McGoldrick, 103, 138, 286
monkey mind, 187–88
monologue, 35, 224, 249–50
mood, mood disorder, 38, 31, 50, 65, 67, 94, 106,126, 129, 215
Mount Pleasant Home, 213, 216
Mount Sinai, 103–4, 116, 173, 229, 247, 250
multiple family therapy group, 70, 73
Muslim, 7, 25, 91, 125, 224, 231, 246

"nameless but achingly familiar feeling", 225
Narrative, 4, 9, 12–13, 17, 22–23, 25, 94, 116, 124, 142, 150, 187, 189–93, 199, 205, 228, 254, 258, 261, 262, 274
narrative family therapy, 96
National Council of Churches, 33, 43, 57, 210
Native American, 4, 6, 25, 72–73, 84, 91, 103, 224, 273
Nechama, 173

Nefesh, 148
Neo-*Chasidism*, 251
Neoliberalism, 102, 195
Neshamah, 148
network assembly, 72–73, 77–78, 83, 87–88, 102, 108, 138, 177, 179, 237, 244–49, 268, 282, 287
network of network assemblies, 88–89
neurobiological, 32, 44, 95, 227
neurobiology, 250
Netletter, 102
network intervention, network therapy, 69, 72, 73, 75, 79, 86, 88, 102, 138, 176, 223, 236–37, 244, 249
Netzach, 153
neuropsychological evaluation, 94
New England Center for the Study of the Family, 96
Niffari, vi, 189, 248
Nikos Kazantzakis, iv, 9, 84, 204
nonmaterial, vii, 11, 96, 119, 155, 202–3
Norman Paul, 70

objectification, objectify, 60, 62
Olga, Jacob's friend, 137–38
Olive Withington, my maternal great-grandmother, 26, 207
the One, 82–83, 141, 143, 160, 162, 203, 230, 241, 243, 257
one-way mirror, 58
"Open", 81–82, 142, 173
Open Dialogue, 65, 223, 249, 282, 287
Oral *Torah*, 229
Orthodox Judaism, 8, 115, 117

panentheistic, 157–58, 241
pantheist, 232
paradoxical reaction, 63
paranoid, paranoia, 59, 61
Parrish, Jerry. *See* Jerry Parrish.
Parsha, 247, 259–61
Partsufim, 157
Passover, 91, 101, 261, 265, 269
pastoral ministry, 79
pathos, divine, 240–41
Patriarchs, 116
pattern recognition, 198
Paul, Norman. *See* Norman Paul.

Peace Corps, 97
people of color, 55, 72, 93, 191, 236
phonics, 30, 211–12
Physicians' Desk Reference, PDR, 63
positive feedback runaway, 211
possession, 45–46, 98, 182
Poussaint, Alvin. *See* Alvin Poussaint.
prefrontal cortex, 187
The Presence, 12, 18, 22, 38, 63, 131, 160, 163, 181, 231, 239, 257, 264–65, 271
The Presentation of Self in Everyday Life, 62, 285
proselytize, proselytizing, 91, 118, 121, 125
Profit, Wesley. *See* Wesley Profit.
prophet, 21, 116, 231, 233, 240–241, 248, 267
The Prophets, 159, 240–241, 253, 282, 286
Psalms, 91, 120, 154–55, 239, 262, 272
psychedelic, 4, 8, 38, 40, 50–51, 61, 65, 67, 84, 86, 186, 229, 232, 244
psychologist, clinical psychologist, x, 13, 16, 20, 50, 63–64, 67–68, 70–72, 76, 88–89, 97, 127, 161, 177, 180, 187, 227, 235, 238, 242, 262, 287
psychology, x, 13, 24, 51, 55, 60, 66, 70–73, 84, 86, 97, 110, 154, 157, 176–76, 188, 225, 235, 248, 250, 255
Peace Corps, 97
Pearce, John. *See* John Pearce.
Platonic, 7, 151
Psychoanalysis, 68–71, 176
Psychosis, 59, 61–67, 73, 77, 79–80, 87, 89, 107, 166–67, 186, 188, 190, 193, 196, 205, 213, 235–36, 238, 244–45, 282, 287

Rabbinics, 156
Ralph Fingar, 71
Rachel Dash, 110, 138
racism, racist, 4, 32, 42–43, 59, 72, 93, 125, 191, 244, 282, 286
Ram Dass, Baba. *See* Baba Ram Dass.
Ransom, v, 4, 9, 23, 30, 51–55, 64, 66–67, 72, 77, 86, 90, 92–93,

105, 109, 111, 124, 133, 135,
    137, 140, 146, 193, 198, 215–16,
    218–19, 221–22, 254
resilience, 94
R.D. Laing, 63
The Radical Therapist, 68
Rachel, 116
Ramón Jiménez, vii, ix, 9, 78–84, 89,
    99, 101, 119, 140, 142, 151, 157,
    164, 172–73, 180, 186, 229,
    237–38, 245, 248, 252, 257–58,
    270–71, 276
Reagan, Ronald. *See* Ronald Reagan.
Reality Group, 74–75
Rebecca, 116
Red Rock, 76, 85
Redemption, 5, 22, 69, 92, 124, 128–29,
    138–39, 142–43, 151221, 234,
    253, 262
reflexivity, 197
Reform Judaism, 8, 103–4, 115, 117–18,
    121, 143, 155–57, 185
reincarnation, incarnation, 98–99, 119,
    124, 195, 238
Report to Greco, 62, 204–5, 282, 286
Reuven Cohn, xi, 156, 272
Revelation, 4, 7, 41, 83, 114, 116, 118,
    142, 151, 162, 166, 173, 181, 186,
    193, 229, 247, 257, 265, 276
Richard Schwartz, 233
right brain, 198
Rim Meirowitz, 143
Ritalin, 95
Retribalization, 88, 287
Re-Visioning Family Therapy, 138, 286
Robert Tufo, 66
Robin, 28, 30, 3335, 93, 105, 135, 139–
    40, 198, 207–18, 254
Robbins, Rockey. *See* Rockey Robbins.
Rockey Robbins, x, xi, 251, 254, 258
Ronald Reagan, 102
Rodney Falke, 197
Rosh Hashanah, 159, 162, 240
Ross Speck, 72, 77, 78, 237, 244
Rossi, A. Michael. *See* Mike Rossi.
Roxana Llerena-Quinn, x, 110, 138, 195
Roxbury, 63
Ruach, 148

Rueveni, Uri. *See* Uri Rueveni.
Ryan, Jacob's friend, 131–32

Sabbatean, 117
Sacred Space, viii, ix, x, 4–5, 179, 222,
    224–26, 251, 254, 256, 264–65,
    286–87
Sacred Time, 254
Salem, Massachusetts, 76, 80
Samaritan, 117
the same, and different, and the same,
    ix, 199–200, 203, 226, 228, 278
sangha, 220
Sankofa, 277
Sarah, 116
Scaffolding, 241–42, 271
Schacter-Shalomi, Zalman. *See* Zalman
    Schacter-Shalomi.
schizophrenia, schizophrenic, 59, 63,
    65, 235
Schwartz, Richard. *See* Richard
    Schwartz.
*Science and Health with Key to the
    Scriptures*, 76
Seder, 91
Seeker, i, iii, iv, viii, ix, 2, 4, 9, 11, 38,
    41, 97, 99, 119, 147, 149, 156,
    186, 190, 193, 200, 230, 236,
    238–40, 233, 253–54, 263, 278
self, 11–12, 19, 21, 60, 62, 134, 143,
    157, 166, 186–90, 192, 194–96,
    207, 209, 228, 232–33, 235–36,
    240, 271, 275, 285, 286
self-cultivation, 4, 83, 114, 142, 199, 238
Semrad, Elvin. *See* Elvin Semrad.
Seymour, Guy. *See* Guy Seymour.
Sefer Yetsirah, 7–8, 229, 253, 267, 281
Seikkula, Jaakko. *See* Jaakko Seikkula.
Sephardic Jews, 117
Sephirah, Sephirot, iv, 152–55, 157, 232,
    240, 252, 255, 270–71, 273–75
Sequencing, 94
Shaman, viii, ix, 7, 11, 19, 54, 77, 83, 97,
    99, 103, 118, 122, 144, 164–65,
    170, 177, 179–82, 184, 202, 228,
    237–38, 244, 246–47, 256, 258,
    266, 273

INDEX

Shabbat, 91, 100, 123–24, 134, 144, 148–49, 162, 185, 255, 259, 264–65
Shaddai, 14
Shah, Idries, vi, 2, 84, 256, 281–83, 287
Shaman, shamanism, viii, ix, 7, 11, 19, 54, 77, 83, 97, 99, 103, 118, 122, 144, 164–65, 170, 177, 179–82, 184, 202, 228, 237–38, 244, 246–47, 256, 258, 266, 273
Sharpe, Charlie *See* Charlie Sharpe
shattering of the vessel, 19, 232
Sheila Babbie (my sister) ix, 9, 22, 27, 93, 105, 193198, 201–2, 204–22, 227, 251, 253–54, 259
Shir HaShirim, 265
Shiva, 133–34, 138–40
Shema, 15, 133, 146, 273–744
Shiddach, 148
Simeon bar Yochai, 7
Shleimut, 170
Shmuly Yanklowitz, iv, 252, 286
Shogunai, 9
Silvana, Jacob's friend, 127, 132
Sinai, Mount Sinai, 103–4, 173, 229, 247, 250
SNCC, Student Nonviolent Coordinating Committee, 41–43, 49
social constructionism, 74
social gospel, 23, 233
social welfare democracies, 102
social worker, 64, 66–67, 71, 235
socialism, ix, 2, 23–24, 26–27, 69–70, 91, 189
soul, v, xi, 4, 10–13, 15, 19–20, 38, 62, 64, 97–99, 109, 119, 122, 132–34, 139–42, 145–49, 151, 154–55, 160–65, 168–71, 173–74, 176, 178, 180–84, 186, 188–92, 195, 199, 202–6, 218, 221, 226–40, 242–44, 247–59, 261–62, 264–70, 274, 276, 278–79, 282–83, 285, 287
soul fragment, 98
Source, Source of all Being, 13, 19–21, 83, 119, 113, 137, 140, 145, 147, 149, 151, 153–54, 161, 180–81, 203, 230–32, 239–40, 247, 256, 262, 267–70, 276–78
South Boston, 63, 101
Southern Christian Leadership Conference, 41, 58
"Space Between", 224–26, 258
Speaking Torah, 266, 283, 286
Speck, Ross. *See* Ross Speck.
Spinoza, Baruch. *See* Baruch Spinoza.
spirit guide, 98–99, 119, 165–66, 173, 182, 238, 246
spirit world, 9, 98–103, 103–46, 163–65, 167, 173,176, 180–84, 206, 246, 253
spiritual journey, vii, ix, xi, 3, 9, 15, 41, 55, 82, 92, 103–4, 114–15, 118–20., 124, 142–43, 148–50, 163, 172, 175, 186, 190, 198, 200, 210, 217, 221, 232, 235, 237–38, 244–45, 247, 251, 257, 267, 273, 278
spirituality, x, xi, 5, 9–10, 12–14, 28, 35, 46, 51, 54, 67, 79, 84, 90, 120–21, 124–25, 128, 137, 163–65, 169–75, 177, 179, 184–85, 194–95, 199–202, 204, 220, 222–28, 232, 244, 249, 251, 253–54, 256, 258, 260, 263–66, 277–78, 281–83, 286–87
Spitzer, Rabbi Toba. *See* Toba Spitzer.
Stern, Marcia. *See* Marcia Stern.
Staff Psychologist, 73
Stanley Slivkin, 71
Stranger in the Camp, 142, 155, 172, 246
state(s) of mind, 57, 130, 169, 204, 272
Steinsaltz, Rabbi Adin. *See* Adin Steinsaltz.
Steve Arnold, 143
stiff-necked, 261–62
stigma, stigmatizing, 65, 71, 89, 193
"strong *colonnes*," 80
structural racism, 93
Sufi, Sufism, vi, 6–7, 13, 84, 91, 100, 121, 151, 184, 189, 224, 237, 243, 273, 281–83, 287
suicide, suicidal, 67, 77, 102, 105, 215
Sunny Yando, 59–60
Sutton, Charlee. *See* Charlee Sutton.

INDEX   299

synagogue, 91, 103, 11, 134–35, 142, 145, 155–56, 162–63, 172, 185, 232, 238–39, 242, 246, 259, 262, 265, 267, 269
synchronicity, 237
system, systemic, systems theory, 60, 69, 74–75, 89, 93, 154, 177, 218, 223, 228, 233, 249, 282, 286–87

Tai Chi, 101
Tao Te Ching, 246, 283, 286
Talmud, 7, 117, 120–21, 123, 156, 229, 250, 260, 272–73
The Establishment, 61
Tao, Taoism, 22, 84, 100, 179, 224, 246, 283, 286
Tanach, iv, 7, 14, 22, 116, 142, 231, 267
Tapestry, vii, 13, 15, 17, 155–56, 200–201, 227–28, 231–39, 253, 255–56, 258–59, 264, 272, 276–78, 283, 285
teaching conference, 65–66
tefillin, 144, 185
Teilhard de Chardin, 3
Temple Sinai, 103–4, 116, 143–44, 156, 159, 281, 116, 142, 231, 267
Tergar Buddhism, 202, 204–6, 220
Teshuvah, 234
Tetragrammaton, 14
The Way of a Pilgrim, 9, 62, 64, 204–5, 238, 244, 285
The Way of the Sufi, vi, 84, 287
Thomas Lambo, 59
Thorazine, 63
thought forms, 202–3, 267
Tibetan Buddhism, xi, 5, 9, 124, 202, 220, 222
Tiferet, 153
Tikkun Olam, 158, 232, 266
Toba Spitzer, 143, 185
Torah, 7, 14, 103–5, 114, 116, 121, 135, 142, 144–45, 185, 229, 238, 246–48, 250, 252–53, 255, 259, 262, 266, 269–70, 272–73, 283, 286
Trance, hypnosis, 97, 98, 180, 238
Transpersonal, 83, 104, 115, 169, 171, 200, 202, 237, 269

trauma, traumatic, 19–20, 48, 50, 64, 84, 93, 113–14, 132, 158, 161, 167–71, 181, 194–96, 198, 233, 235, 239–40, 263–66
treatment alliance, 70
Tree of Life, 152
Trimble, Betty Ann Roberson. *See* Betty.
Trimble, Jessica. *See* Jessica.
Trimble, Ransom. *See* Ransom.
Trimble, Robin. *See* Robin.
Trismegistus, Hermes. *See* Hermes Trismegistus.
Tsfat, Israel, 231–32, 258, 271
Tufo, Robert. *See* Robert Tufo.
tui na massage, 100
tzedakah, 122
tzimtzum, 157, 231–32, 242–43, 269, 272

Ubuntu, 2789
Uri Rueveni, 77
United Church of Christ, 35
Unity, Unity of all Being, 10–11, 15, 23, 35, 40, 82–83, 141, 144, 146, 149, 151, 157, 160, 163, 165, 228, 230, 232, 243, 269–27, 280

Vasectomy, 190
Vessel, vi, 19, 150–54, 170, 189–90, 192–94, 200, 230–35, 237–40, 242–43, 252, 257, 263–65, 267–68, 270, 275–76
Veterans Administration, 70, 236
Vineland Christian Ministries, 139
visual-spatial learning, 94
vocation, vocational, 21, 60, 67
Vogel, Rabbi Andrew. *See* Andy Vogel.
von Bertalanffy, 69, 282, 287

Walker, Gillian. *See* Gillian Walker.
Wampanoag, 173
WASP, 22, 24, 51
Watts. Alan. *See* Alan Watts.
The Way of a Pilgrim, 9, 62, 64, 204–5, 238, 244, 285
Weingarten, Kaethe. *See* Kaethe Weingarten.
Werner, Heinz. *See* Heinz Werner.

Wesley Profit, 58
Western science, 77, 248
White, Whiteness, ix, 3, 6, 22, 25, 32, 39–40, 42–45, 48–51, 53–60, 62–63, 67, 69–70, 120, 189–92, 194–95, 209, 236, 248, 282, 287
White, Michael. *See* Michael White.
White Power Structure, 56
White supremacy, 44, 120, 190–92, 236
Wisdom of the Zohar, 148, 282, 287
witch, 76, 80, 89, 98
Worcester Student Movement, 40, 49
World of the Dead, 11, 98, 165
Written *Torah*, 229

Ya, 14
Yahrzeit, 261
Yehuda Leib Ashlag, 230–31, 253, 255–57, 268, 271–74, 285
Yedidah Cohen, viii, xi, 230, 232, 240, 253–59, 261–76, 285

Yesod, 153
Yando, Regina. Sunny *See* Sunny Yando.
Yanklowitz, Rabbi Shmuly. *See* Shmuly Yanklowtz.
Yankee, 24, 29, 40, 42
YHVH, 14–15
Yichud, 183
Yisrael, 7, 15
Yom Kippur, 14, 156, 159

Zalman Schacter-Shalomi, vi, 8, 189, 197, 254
Zeitlin, Hillel. *See* Hillel Zeitlin.
Zen, 6, 9, 241, 281–82, 87
Zohar, iv, 7–8, 148–49, 151, 155, 229, 240, 254–55, 261, 271–74, 276, 281–83, 285–87
Zulima, Jacob's friend Silvana's mother, 132
Zulu, 224, 278

www.ingramcontent.com/pod-product-compliance
Lightning Source LLC
Chambersburg PA
CBHW071957220426
43662CB00009B/1172